RESISTANCE AND POWER IN ORGANIZATIONS

This state of the art collection develops the theme of resistance from below in everyday organizational life. Building on a body of theory dealing with power, control and domination in the labour process, international contributors expand the analysis by focusing on material circumstances and subjective states that lead to subtle forms of subversion and sabotage as well as to more overt forms of defiance and protest.

Throughout the volume discussion is supported by case studies, interviews, surveys and ethnographic data drawn from around the world to reveal resistance practices which range from those hidden in the 'crawl-spaces' of organizations to those that are more public and demonstrative. Recent developments in critical social theory are used to provoke thinking about resistance both as a *response* to power and a *form* of power. Uniquely, the contributions show that oppressive practices at work can be met with powerful counter-forces, and that resistance need not only take the form of 'quiet resilience'.

Presenting an empowering view of insubordination, this volume will be of interest to those in the fields of organizational sociology, organizational behaviour, industrial and labour relations and women's studies.

John M. Jermier is Professor of Organizational Behaviour at the College of Business Administration, University of South Florida. **David Knights** is Professor in Organizational Analysis at the Manchester School of Management, UMIST. **Walter R. Nord** is also Professor of Organizational Behaviour at the College of Business Administration,

D1145791

CRITICAL PERSPECTIVES ON WORK AND ORGANIZATION

General Editors: David Knights, Chris Smith, Paul Thompson and Hugh Willmott

Since the appearance of Braverman's *Labour and Monopoly Capital*, the impact of labour process analysis has been experienced in the fields of industrial sociology, organization theory, industrial relations, labour economics, politics and business studies. This series examines diverse aspects of the employment relationship across the range of productive and service industries. Some volumes explore further the established terrain of management control, the intensification of work, the deskilling of labour. Others are attentive to associated topics such as gender relations at work, new technology, workplace democracy and the international dimensions of the labour process.

LABOUR IN TRANSITION
The Labour Process in East Europe and China
Edited by Chris Smith and Paul Thompson

SKILL AND CONSENT
Contemporary Studies in the Labour Process
Edited by Andrew Sturdy, David Knights and Hugh Willmott

GLOBAL JAPANIZATION?
The Transnational Transformation of the Labour Process
Edited by Tony Elger and Chris Smith

RESISTANCE AND POWER IN ORGANIZATIONS

Edited by
John M. Jermier, David Knights
and Walter R. Nord

London and New York

First published 1994
by Routledge
11 New Fetter Lane, London EC4P 4EE

Simultaneously published in the USA and Canada
by Routledge
29 West 35th Street, New York, NY 10001

Typeset in Garamond by LaserScript, Mitcham, Surrey
Printed and bound in Great Britain by
Biddles Ltd, Guildford and King's Lynn

British Library Cataloguing in Publication Data
A catalogue record for this book is available from the British Library

Library of Congress Cataloging in Publication Data has been applied for

ISBN 0–415–08588–8
IBSN 0–415–11794–1 (pbk)

CONTENTS

ILLUSTRATIONS

FIGURES

TABLE

CONTRIBUTORS

Terry Austrin teaches in the Department of Sociology at the University of Canterbury, New Zealand. He has written articles on the organization of the labour process in the construction, mining and finance industries and is co-author of a forthcoming book on mining, *Masters and Servants: Class and Patronage in the Making of a Labour Organization* (with Huw Beynon). He has worked in Britain, the United States and New Zealand.

Stewart Clegg researches and teaches at the University of Western Sydney Macarthur, where he is Foundation Professor of Management. Previously he has been Professor at the Universities of New England and St Andrews. He is the author of many articles and books on the sociology of organizations, class and power. Among his better-known volumes are *Power, Rule and Domination*; *Organization, Class and Control* (with David Dunkerley); *Modern Organizations* and *Frameworks of Power*. He recently researched 'embryonic industries' for an Australian Federal Government Task Force into Leadership and Management Skills for the Twenty-First Century.

David Collinson is lecturer in Industrial Relations and Organizational Behaviour in the School of Industrial and Business Studies at the University of Warwick. He completed his doctorate at the University of Manchester Institute of Science and Technology, and taught at the Universities of South Florida and St Andrews before taking up his post at Warwick in 1992. He has conducted research and published papers on recruitment, shopfloor culture and humour, management control, sex discrimination, sexuality and sexual harassment, men and masculinity in the workplace and the power and status of human resource managers. Currently, he is researching performance evaluation and safety practices on North Sea oil installations and co-editing a text on *Managements and Men*.

Carolyn P. Egri teaches in the Faculty of Business Administration at Simon Fraser University, Burnaby, British Columbia. She has written articles on the innovation process, organizational power and politics, leadership, and organizational change and development. One of her current research interests is on environmental issues in society and organizations.

Heidi Gottfried teaches in the Department of Sociology and Anthropology, Purdue University. She has written extensively on gender and work issues, and is editor of *Feminism and Social Change: Bridging Theory and Practice*. Her current research concerns post-Fordist regimes in comparative perspective.

John M. Jermier is Professor of Organizational Behaviour in the College of Business at the University of South Florida. He earned his Ph.D in Administrative Science from the Ohio State University. Much of his work has been focused on the development of a critical science of organizations, with a particular interest in research philosophy and methodology. Currently, he is a member of the editorial review boards of *Administrative Science Quarterly* and *Organization Science* and is consulting editor of *Leadership Quarterly*

David Knights is Professor of Organizational Analysis in the Manchester School of Management at the University of Manchester Institute of Science and Technology. He has conducted research and published in the following areas: industrial relations, equal opportunity, labour process, management strategy, the management of information technology and regulation in financial services. His current research is on Financial Services in the Single European Market and on inter-organizational relations and the use and development of IT. He is co-author of *Managing the Multi-Racial Workforce* and *Managing to Discriminate* and co-editor of a number of books on the labour process.

Danny LaNuez is a Ph.D candidate at the University of South Florida and is currently conducting research for his dissertation on Executive Conflict. He presented a paper (co-authored with John Jermier) entitled 'Sabotage by Managers and Technocrats: The Quiet

Revolution' at the 8th Annual Aston/UMIST Conference on Organizational and Control of the Labour Process. His interests are focused on organizational politics and qualitative research methodologies.

Terance D. Miethe is Associate Professor and Chair of the Department of Criminal Justice at the University of Nevada, Las Vegas. He has received grant support from the National Science Foundation and the National Institutes for Justice and published numerous articles on victimization and violent crime. His current research with Dr Rothschild on whistleblowers extends his interest in corporate crime and its detection.

Walter R. Nord is currently Professor of Management at the University of South Florida. Previously he was at Washington University-St Louis (1967–1989). His current interests centre on developing a critical political economics perspective of organizations, organizational innovation and organizational conflict. He has published widely in scholarly journals and edited/authored a number of books. His recent books include *The Meanings of Occupational Work* (with A. Brief), *Implementing Routine and Radical Innovations* (with S. Tucker) and *Organizational Reality; Reports from the Firing Line* (with P. Frost and V. Mitchell). He is currently co-editor of *Employee Responsibilities and Rights Journal.*

Julia O'Connell Davidson is Lecturer in Sociology at the University of Leicester. As a researcher at Bristol University she was involved in extensive research on restructuring in the public utilities. She is the author of a book on the impact of privatization on workers in the water industry and numerous articles on employment relations and work organization in privatized companies.

Joyce Rothschild is Professor of Sociology at Virginia Polytechnic Institute and State University in Blacksburg, Virginia. She has written extensively on organizational democracy, worker ownership and control issues, including *The Cooperative Workplace: Potentials and Dilemmas of Organizational Democracy and Participation.* Her research on whistleblowers, as reported in this volume, extends her scholarship on how participants' values and convictions may shape organizational practices and lead to organizational change.

Theo Vurdubakis is an ESCR Teaching Fellow at the Manchester School of Management at the University of Manchester Institute of

Science and Technology. He has written on the role of financial practices in liberal forms of government and on the sociology of information systems.

PREFACE

This project arose out of a common concern to develop a critical analysis of subjectivity (see Nord, 1974, 1977a, 1977b, 1978; Jermier, 1981, 1985, 1991; Knights and Willmott, 1983, 1985, 1989; Knights, 1990). Our concerns coalesced in this specific project during the 1990 UMIST/ASTON Labour Process Conference held at Aston University in Birmingham, England. Three years later, the project came to fruition and this volume on resistance and power represents the tenth edited book in what is now the Routledge series on labour process theory. While the time-gap between the conception of the volume and its publication was very long (in part due to the fact that the contributors to the volume reside on three different continents), the chapters begin to fill a knowledge-gap that has not been substantially altered since 1990 as they address the nature and meanings of resistance practices in the labour process.

The majority of the chapters are based on previously un-published data about resistance. While recognizing the complexity of the subject matter, we have sought to provoke the authors into generating readable as well as stimulating texts. Consequently, in evaluating and editing the papers, there has been an attempt to remove the dry and technical material so typical of refereed journal papers. Most of the chapters therefore do not include a detailed description of the study's methodology. Aware of the difficulties involved in conducting empirical field work on resistance, we have encouraged the authors to present and interpret their data modestly, blending in or contrasting findings and arguments with what is known about resistance in organizations. Where the data are more suggestive than conclusive, we asked the authors to downplay the nature of the empirical contribution in favour of sharpening understanding through key concepts they developed which were only illustrated by the data.

The philosophical and theoretical underpinnings of the book are closely aligned with labour process theory, but you will not notice a heavy-handed attempt on our part to edit the papers towards a common perspective. Nor was space within the papers devoted to explicating the philosophical and theoretical underpinnings from which the authors wrote. This seemed unnecessary for two reasons. First, the perspectives of many of the authors can be discerned from the text, but second, we did not set out to publish a state-of-the-art social theory of power and resistance that would attend to all the nuances of the most sophisticated debates in the philosophy of the social sciences.

What we did set out to accomplish can be summarized in the following purposes. We intended to (1) call attention to the importance of everyday forms of resistance at work – those aspects of employment relations and organizational life that are widespread but under-appreciated; (2) illustrate what specific forms of resistance might look like in and around different organizational settings (i.e. not limit depictions to conflict in conventional factories); (3) explore the underlying subjectivities of resisters that both condition their acts and give them meaning and significance; (4) develop a preliminary focus on the nature of power and domination in the contemporary workplace that goes both beyond Marxist views of exploitation and the generation of surplus value and Bravermanian views of deskilling and control; and (5) underscore the need expressed by labour process theorists (e.g. Thompson, 1990; Knights, 1990; Willmott, 1990; Collinson, 1992; Sturdy, Knights and Willmott, 1992) for more work that develops a theoretical understanding of identity and subjectivity in the labour process.

In using the metaphor of resistance to power, we link this work, at least implicitly, to theory and research appearing in the fields of political and social theory, cultural and human science, philosophical anthropology, feminism and gender studies, critical social psychology, labour history, organizational sociology, industrial and labour relations, and organizational behaviour. The book's appearance coincides with a number of other new social science works that present a view of resistance as a mode of empowerment within super–subordinate relations. While differing from studies that show the steely resilience of those who experience the harsh realities of slavery, concentration camps, prisons and totalitarian political regimes, the chapters in this book make it clear that both oppressive and subtly dominating practices at work can be met with powerful countervailing powers. As ways of understanding the power of resistance, these studies collectively point to the necessity of examining both subtle and subterranean forms of subversion and sabotage as well as the more overt forms of defiance and protest. They also make it clear that the interpretations provided by theorists and researchers of resistance are more informed when they take account of the meanings that those who resist give to their own practices.

John Jermier
David Knights
Walter Nord

Note Please see References section (pp. 22–4) for full details of works cited above.

INTRODUCTION

Resistance and power in organizations: agency, subjectivity and the labour process

John M. Jermier, David Knights and Walter R. Nord

Whatever our personal frailties may be, the nobility of our calling will always be rooted in two commitments difficult to observe: refusal to lie about what we know and resistance to oppression. (Albert Camus, Nobel Prize Address, Stockholm, Sweden, 10 December 1957)

From the existentialist humanist position of Camus (1956), resistance against the absurdity of existence takes the form of embracing the universe's meaninglessness and irrationality and abandoning the oppressive and inane conformities surrounding the routines of everyday life. So, for example, Meursault in *L'Etranger* (Camus, 1960), shocks the moral sensibilities of conventional citizens by swimming naked and making love on the day of his mother's funeral.

While perhaps parallelling current approaches to the shifting, proliferating and discontinuous nature of meaning in postmodern society, Camus' conception of resistance may seem far removed from that examined previously by students of the labour process and by many of the papers in this volume. Yet, while the content of this book may be very different, the spirit of refusal underlying Camus' existentialism is an inspiration for anyone engaged in resistance, even when it is in the vicarious style of merely writing about it.

In contrast to existentialism, labour process studies have been comparatively silent about a theory of resistance if not about the phenomenon itself. Since the chapters that follow are primarily drawn from, or concerned to debate with, labour process theory, let us trace a brief history of its analysis of resistance. Then, we will make some general remarks about the ways contributors to this volume have answered the calls by labour process theorists for

1

work which begins to develop a critical theory of the missing subject, but without reducing subjectivity to resistance (see Knights, 1990; Thompson, 1990; Wardell, 1990). Finally, we will provide a detailed synopsis of each chapter).

RESISTANCE, SUBJECTIVITY, AND LABOUR PROCESS THEORY

Beginning with Marx (1867/1972), 'real' resistance in and around capitalist work organizations could take many forms, but would derive from only one source: revolutionary class-consciousness. Thus, the meaning of resistance was straightforward and was to be interpreted as struggle against the fundamental defining feature of the capitalist mode of production, exploitation of labour through the generation and extraction of surplus value. Importantly, Marx recognized that one source of surplus value was hidden in co-operative labour. He understood exploitation primarily at the supra-individual level: 'What the capitalist pays is the value of the separate labour powers of a hundred individuals, not the value of their combined labour power' (p. 349). In his view, the severity of the problem of exploitation was complicated and compounded by its collective nature.

Consistent with the labour theory of value, exploitation of labour is considered unavoidable within capitalist production relations because although all value is added to the product by labourers, they receive only a fraction of the proceeds from the sale of the products. There is much debate surrounding Marx's labour theory of value (e.g. Weeks, 1981; Ollman, 1971) especially in discussions comparing his early and later work. But, it seems he assumed, even in *Capital*, that all human beings were degraded from a higher plane of existence as a result of their participation in the capitalist labour process:

> In its blind, unbridled passion, its werewolf hunger for surplus labour, capital is not content to overstep the moral restrictions upon the length of the working day. It oversteps the purely physical limitations as well. It usurps the time needed for the growth, the development, and the healthy maintenance of the body. . . . It causes the premature exhaustion and death of labour power.
>
> (Marx 1867/1972, p. 269)

2

Marx's essentialist view of human nature led him to postulate a natural and 'inevitable antagonism between the exploiter and the living raw material he [sic] exploits' (p. 348). Alienated labourers, separated from ownership of the means and ends of their production, dominated by their output, experience themselves (and all human beings) as inhumane. To overcome alienation, they must abolish private ownership of production which involves building labour solidarity and engaging in class-based resistance.

However, according to Marx, class-conscious radicalism is not predetermined. There is merely a *tendency* for this to occur. Because of 'all the mystifications of the capitalist method of production [and] all its illusions of freedom . . .' (p. 589), the fundamental source of alienation might be obscured, leaving labourers and owners of capital unable to engage in 'real resistance'.

Both the stability and instability of the capitalist method of production undermine the likelihood of class-based resistance. Despite the continuous demand for revolutionary change in the means of production and the intensification of labour to meet competitive pressures, the continuity of the form of the relations of production have a tendency (when supported by legitimating ideologies) to make capitalism appear as normal and inevitable as the laws of nature. And, the longer the capitalist process of production remains in operation, the more difficult it is for participants to see it as a socially constructed reality. In short, its social construction and development by agents (including often indifferent managerial and labour forces) is hidden or forgotten. This is, of course, where some understanding of subjectivity and identity becomes important. Perceptions that it is better to tolerate 'the devil you know' may readily weaken strategies of resistance especially when, partly because of the divisive and individualizing effects of capitalism, identities are precarious and vulnerable. This may be what Marx had in mind when he argued that: 'The organization of the fully developed capitalist process of production breaks down all resistance' (p. 817).

But this is surely too pessimistic, as many of the chapters in this volume suggest. It may be that universal and totalizing oppositions to capitalism are unlikely, at least now that the communist alternative has truly been challenged and abandoned by many. Yet this all or nothing conception of resistance was probably wide of the mark, even at the point of large-scale revolutions. Relations of power and resistance operate in more complex ways than can be depicted in simple all or nothing polarities. What might be seen, from one perspective, as resistance, might just as easily be viewed as conformity, compliance or indifference, from another.

In several sections of *Capital*, Marx indicated an awareness of resistance practices, but he did not connect these incidents to class-conscious revolutionary action, nor did he use them to develop a theory of everyday resistance to capitalist domination. Thus, Marx's theory of the inner workings of the capitalist labour process carefully explained why workers might engage in class struggle and class-conscious revolutionary action, but he did not elaborate on the meaning of resistance by alienated ('falsely conscious') subjects.

Braverman (1974), in his foundational work, which was the inspiration for the labour process conferences to which this book owes its existence, made several simplifying assumptions about subjectivity, primarily to distance his position on class-consciousness from the 'superficial, remote, and mechanistic' (p. 29) approaches of empirical social scientists studying job satisfaction and class identification. He was not specifically opposed to accepting premises about human nature or to conducting studies into the meaning of worker subjectivities. What he did oppose was managerialist social research that reduced the subjectivity of workers to statements of job satisfaction or dissatisfaction, or that took at face value questionnaire reports of class identifications.

Braverman's strategy provoked much criticism and discussion among labour process theorists (and particularly from authors writing in this series), but it can be argued that he was working with a sophisticated, critical understanding of subjectivity. When he chose to write beyond his simplifying assumptions, Braverman displayed penetrating insight. For example, his conceptualization of class-consciousness probed critically into the realm of the subjective as he wrote about the way 'changes in mood draw upon and give expression to the underlying reservoir of class attitudes . . . [existing] deep below the surface' (p. 30).

His focus on deskilling, the intensification of labour and management control was not so much wrong as one-sided. And his criticism of subjectivist managerial sociology was well overdue. Moreover, his neglect of resistance was not as great as some critics have claimed.

For example, the conclusion to the chapter on the habituation of the worker to the capitalist mode of production is highly relevant to the themes of this volume. In particular, there is a passage that must have been overlooked by critics who contend that Braverman was unaware of worker resistance. It can be seen here that he would have recommended that researchers check the crawl-spaces of work settings to highlight specific examples of resistance.

> But, beneath this apparent habituation, the hostility of workers to the degenerated forms of work which are forced upon them continues as a subterranean stream that makes its way to the surface when employment conditions permit, or when the capitalist drive for a greater intensity of labor oversteps the bounds of physical and mental capacity.
>
> (p. 151)

The philosophical anthropology underlying Marx's and Braverman's views on the capitalist labour process has been discussed frequently. It entails labour attempting to develop itself in ways that fulfil the (latent) destiny of a fixed, universal human nature. These assumptions can easily lead to a theorizing of subjectivity that relies on concepts of false consciousness or reification. A result is that sharp distinctions between 'real' or 'genuine' (class-conscious) resistance and everyday forms of resistance are drawn that are not only epistemologically problematic but also undermine subjects by representing them as 'judgemental dopes' (Garfinkel, 1967).

It is possible that when workers consent to (Burawoy, 1979) or accommodate (Knights and Collinson, 1985) the management controls to which they are subject, their actions have effects which further reinforce labour subordination and possibly degradation. Certainly co-operation on the office and shopfloor has not prevented large-scale redundancies and heavy unemployment as capitalist corporations have struggled with the recent severe recessionary downturns in western economies. The worst off clearly continue to bear the brunt of the contradictions of 'free market' capitalism. As long as they remain in the minority and divided from one another, they are hardly likely to constitute a significant threat to the system. The growth in crime, of course, may be such a threat, but that is outside the remit of this book.

Critical studies require close examination of what may appear to be co-operation at work. This is because co-operation often conceals aspects of resistance that, while not a direct threat to capitalism, can change working practices in significant ways and possibly expand the space through which labour affects the conditions of its own reproduction. Knowledge about these matters does not come directly from metaphysical assumptions about human nature. It is derived from an analysis of the workings of specific, historical production systems and of the subjective worlds of actors in the systems. Importantly, this includes their views on the experience of domination they encounter and the meanings they attach to the behaviour we are prone to call resistance.

Marx and Braverman were aware of the importance of subjective consciousness and the part it plays in resistance to capitalist labour processes. Neither could escape these issues, even when their work consciously attempted to limit the scope of analysis to a more 'objectivist' realm. However, neither chose to theorize subjectivity and resistance, leaving scope for detailed analyses of the kind represented by this volume.

Post-Braverman labour process debates have been far-reaching, but consistently they have included calls to redress the relative neglect of resistance (Aronowitz, 1978; Elger, 1979; Gartman, 1978; Nichols, 1980; Littler, 1982; Jermier, 1983; Knights and Collinson, 1985). Although some historical studies of class struggle and the labour process have taken resistance seriously (e.g., Friedman, 1977; Edwards, 1979), they seem to have stimulated more theory about managerial control strategies than about specific resistance practices or the connections between organizational control and resistance (see Gordon, Edwards and Reich, 1982; Littler, 1982; Burawoy, 1985). Other studies have emphasized everyday forms of resistance (e.g., Jermier, 1988; Hodson, 1991; Collinson, 1992; Tucker, 1992; Nord and Jermier, 1994) or have documented union struggles and conflict over wages and/or responses to work intensification (Nichols and Beynon, 1977; Elger, 1979; Littler and Salaman, 1982; Knights and Collinson, 1985, 1987; Thompson, 1986), but development of a theory of workplace resistance is, apparently, still some distance away.

Since it is now widely recognized that resistance is intertwined with subjectivity, it may be that new directions for resistance studies will result from debates among labour process theorists about the constitution of the subject in capitalist production systems. Let us now turn briefly to the growing concern among labour process analysts in developing a critical theory of subjectivity (see Knights, 1990; Thompson, 1990; Willmott, 1990; Collinson, 1992; Sturdy, Knights and Willmott, 1992).

Concepts of social identity have been at the centre of labour

6

process theorists' descriptions of the subject. For example, Burawoy (1979) focused on aspects of the development of consent among shopfloor factory workers engaged in the 'game' of 'making out' (maximizing bonus pay in piece-rate work). He was able to explore, through participant observation on the shopfloor, the way playing the game of 'making out' constituted workers in the labour process as competing and conflicting *individuals*, masking their 'common membership in a class of agents of production who sell their labour power for a wage' (p. 81). Thus, from the realm of subjective experience and social identity, Burawoy (1979) provided an interpretation of traditional Marxist processes of securing and obscuring surplus value.

Burawoy (1979) did not draw out the implications for understanding shopfloor resistance from this analysis, but it is clear that to the extent playing the game becomes an arena for self-esteem testing, factory workers can become locked, unwittingly, into practices that reproduce conditions of exploitation and subordination. That is, absorption in the game at a level where workers' self-images and dignities are affected can have profound negative implications for resistance practices.

Burawoy's (1979) account of worker subjectivity has been critiqued in considerable detail by labour process theorists (e.g., Knights, 1990; Thompson, 1990; Willmott, 1990; Collinson, 1992). As one of the earliest attempts to re-insert subjectivity into the labour process, his work has been praised. The consensus of opinion, however, seems to be that Burawoy did not investigate workplace subjectivity completely enough, leaving out some crucial dimensions of subjective experience. For example, several critics have pointed out his failure to explain exactly how individualizing tendencies in capitalist labour processes lead to fragmented and atomized subjects. Others have noted how his neglect of gender and sexual identity led to a somewhat superficial analysis of the way self is constituted in the labour process. As will be apparent from this short review of interpretations of Burawoy's (1979) analysis of worker subjectivity, labour process theorists have made considerable progress not only in appreciating the significance of subjective phenomena, but in developing a critical understanding of subjectivity.

Foucault's (1980; 1982) work on the close relationship between the subject and power has been particularly influential in stimulating a deeper analysis of subjectivity, especially to the extent that it has diverted attention away from the grand narratives of class conflict and revolutionary struggle in favour of a focus upon more localized forms of resistance and subjectivity. For Foucault, subjectivity is analysed as a 'truth effect' of the exercise of power. Subjectivity in these terms has to be seen not as a synonym for the concept of the individual subject but as a way of desecribing a complex composite of such subjects as a category of persons. Although power is exercised upon the *actions* of others (Foucault, 1980), its effect in defining groups or categories of persons (e.g., prisoners, the mentally ill, schoolchildren, labour) as particular kinds of subjects is what generates what we term subjectivity. Foucault's enterprise can be seen as one that has recorded the ways in which human subjects have been objectified as particular kinds of subjects through science (e.g. economics, biology), stigmatic stereotyping (e.g., the mad, the poor) and subjective self-formation (e.g., ethics, commitment).

In the absence of totalizing, collective consciousness (e.g., class, ethnicity, religion, gender), it is the formation and reformation of self that is the aspect of subjectivity most important for understanding contemporary strategies of resistance. Self-formation is ordinarily a complex outcome of subjection or subjugation, and resistance to it. Although subjectivities are effects of power, subjectification and self-identities are always in process. Power, then, does not directly determine identity but merely provides the conditions of possibility for its self-formation – a process involving perpetual tension between power and resistance or subjectivity and identity.

This is only one amongst many contemporary perspectives on subjectivity that has been adopted by labour process theorists, but it is compatible with certain postmodern views of the subject in a world of proliferating and transitory meanings. It attempts to describe subjects in societies, who experience great anxiety about the pressure their cultures place upon them to construct and maintain stable identities, despite the fact that traditional categories of self no longer are compelling.

In summary, from Marx to the present, labour process analysts have indicated an interest in resistance at work, but only within the past few years has concerted attention been paid to theorizing resistance. As discussed above this coincides with an emerging, broader interest in developing a critical theory of workplace subjectivity. Thus, this book is a timely addition to current debates on the labour process which include widespread recognition that most employees in advanced capitalist societies are neither class-consciousness revolutionaries nor passive, docile automatons.

ADVANCING LABOUR PROCESS THEORY THROUGH RESISTANCE STUDIES

Despite diversity, the most prevalent way of analysing resistance is to see it as a reactive process where agents embedded in power relations actively oppose initiatives by other agents. As such, resistance is theorized to be shaped (but not completely determined) by a particular context and the content of what is being resisted. Therefore, we should expect that the nature of resistance will vary across space and time.

Early uses of 'resistance' in research on organizations focused on how employees (usually in factories) responded to specific changes introduced by management. Given this historically specific starting point and the absence of reflection concerning the special circumstances of its genesis, much of the previous empirical literature on resistance at work has described and attempted to explain the actions of a seemingly homogeneous group of male blue-collar factory workers fighting an assumed, common identifiable cause.

In this book, we contend that this tradition has produced a view of resistance that is both theoretically and practically limited and perhaps even misguided. Specifically, it is associated with an overly simplistic view of who resists and how and why they do so. It fails to examine local and historically specific conditions and the various exercises of power that are both conditions and consequences of resistance.

While this volume should not be seen as a project to solve the numerous theoretical problems surrounding the analysis of human resistance, subjectivity and power in work and society, each author has sought to develop a highly readable and concise contribution without oversimplifying the main theoretical issues.

This means *first*, that the contributors avoid mechanistic and dualistic models of control and resistance, primarily by identifying modes of subjective consciousness that mediate interpretations of, and responses to, situations of domination. They also resist the attractions of reductionist psychology as a way of conceptualizing the subjective worlds of actors. They do not focus on individual personality, cognitive style or attitudes (see Henriques *et al.*, 1984).

9

In analysing the chapters, Clegg (Chapter 9) uses an abstraction 'subjectivities of resistance' to describe how the contributors related power, subjectivity and resistance in their studies. This term is helpful because it highlights the three major ways subjectivity is developed in the book: (1) as a general philosophical term used to differentiate highly voluntaristic conceptions of self and agency from those where self and agency are seen as constituted at least partially through the exercise of power in discursive and other practices; (2) as a non-essentialist concept but one which leaves space for *all* role-bearers to exert wilfulness; and (3) as an orientation towards studying the intentionality of moments or longer periods of resistant consciousness thereby creating a space for a grounded method of assessing the meaning and significance of specific resistance practices.

A *second* way contributers avoided oversimplifying their conceptualizations of resistance is related to the structure–action nexus. In adopting a view of employees as active, willful agents negotiating social realities only partially of their own making (Marx, 1867/1972; Giddens, 1978–1979), they indicate appreciation of the contradictions that shape the production and reproduction of capitalist employment structures. At the same time, the authors break with Marxist orthodoxy in refusing to theorize resistance as simply a reflection of the deep-rooted structural contradictions of capitalism between, for example, productive capacity and private appropriation of surplus value or use and exchange value. Nor is resistance glorified or romanticized as the ultimate refusal of alienated beings denied other forms of creative self-expression. Rather, an attempt is made to avoid both extremes of the structure–action, determinist–voluntarist antinomies while recognizing that analyses can still be informed by insights drawn from such theorizing. Clearly, then, a broad range of critical thinking and research provides inspiration for the chapters in this volume.

Given the present lack of understanding of specific forms of workplace resistance among labour process theorists and other analysts, one of the arguments advanced in a number of papers in this volume is that an expectation for a general theory of resistance is premature, or alternatively, misconceived once traditional grand theory narratives (e.g., class, gender) are abandoned. A strong case can be made for the claim that the lack of understanding of resistance stems partly from the tendency of researchers to *impose*, rather than *investigate*, the meaning that subjects themselves attribute to their actions or behaviour. In this volume, every attempt is made to correct this weakness, especially in those contributions that report on detailed empirical fieldwork. This approach to studying resistance involves avoiding judging, using metaphysical critiera or emancipatory goals derived from macro-politics, the meaningfulness of local struggles. Instead, contributors begin by *taking the word of the participants* in assessing the significance of local resistance practices.

Consistent with the radical intent underlying labour process theory (Thompson, 1990), these challenges to traditional discourse are not purely of an epistemological or methodological nature. While remaining attuned to the potential costs of immodest definitions of emancipation, these studies may be seen both to reflect upon as well as perhaps to stimulate social change.

In summary, the work reported in this volume expands our view of who resists, why they do so, and how they do so, particularly in non-factory settings which have traditionally been a neglected focus for studies of resistance. Consequently, we learn that individuals and groups may exercise their power to resist in certain circumstances and not others and how the nature of such resistance relates to specific managerial controls and their effects upon subjectivity. Taken together, the chapters yield a rich perspective on resistance, increasing our awareness of the diversity and discontinuity of its production and development as well as its conditions and consequences. They reveal certain limitations of traditional perspectives especially those that abstract universal views of resistance from a limited set of historically specific socio-political settings.

By reorientating our attention to specific instances in the field and narrower foci of debate, the authors in this volume make a contribution to theory and research that circumnavigates the worst excesses of universal theorizing and grand narrative designs evident in earlier labour process accounts.

In Chapter 1, 'Strategies of Resistance: Power, Knowledge and Subjectivity in the Workplace', *David Collinson* provides an exemplar of the comparative approach that is needed to come to terms with resistance in organizations. Collinson reports research he conducted in two different work settings in the United Kingdom: a factory and a white-collar setting in the insurance industry. Collinson describes two quite different courses of resistance, each related to a particular mode of worker subjectivity. The dominant pattern of resistance within the factory is what Collinson terms 'resistance through distance' where because they were being treated like commodities, the workers distanced themselves mentally from their work and from management's efforts to make them part of the 'team'. But, as commodities, they completely refused to take any responsibility for production other than complying minimally with the demands made of them by a management to whom they conceded a full prerogative but for whom they had no respect.

In contrast, in the second study of an insurance company, Collinson reports the actions of a woman who was denied promotion, apparently because she was pregnant. Resistance here took the form of deploying formal procedures of protest including drawing upon the assistance of her national union. Since the procedure evolved through a prolonged series of meetings, hearings and negotiations, the label 'resistance through persistence' is particularly apt. Collinson emphasizes the contribution of the employee's beliefs (particularly about the legitimacy of her grievance) to enabling her to pursue this arduous course. While on the one hand, the cases seem to reflect totally different processes, Collinson calls our attention to the fact that understanding each scenario demands careful attention to the subjectivities of the people involved and to how the omission of subjectivity in much of the previous literature on resistance has led to a misunderstanding of the processes involved.

This theme is highly consistent with the findings reported in other chapters as well as with the teachings of Foucault, that play such an important role in the theoretical work of David Knights and Theo Vurdubakis in Chapter 5. Moreover, it provides a useful point of departure for understanding the variety in the forms of processes of resistance reported in the other chapters.

Chapter 2, 'The Sources and Limits of Resistance in a Privatized Utility', by *Julia O'Connell-Davidson*, resembles some of the traditional studies in that it focuses on resistance to a management initiated change – the restructuring of work. It meshes nicely with the portion of Collinson's chapter on the insurance company in that it centres on white collar workers in a British setting (in this case, a privatized utility). The restructuring which sought to reduce staff levels and labour costs, features computerization of previously manual clerical work, increased use of part-time staff, and the introduction of multi-function teams which required the breakdown of functional work patterns and entailed that the clerks undertake an expanded range of tasks.

Although many of the reasons for discontent with the

restructured system appeared to stem from glitches in the system and inadequate training and preparation, changes in employee subjectivity concerning the importance of their work were also highly significant. As the system was introduced, the clerks came to realize that their knowledge and abilities to deal with non-routine aspects of the work were far more crucial than they had assumed previously. Consequently they became more aware of the limits to standardization and deskilling in their work and of contradictions among elements of the company's ideology (e.g., commitment to customer service and to profits). While resistance took many traditional forms (e.g., sabotage) and stemmed from traditional concerns (e.g., work intensification without increased compensation), O'Connell-Davidson's data indicate that much more is involved than simply resistance to management control. An equally important source of discontent here was the workers' view that their work was socially important. Thus we are once again able to see the importance of worker subjectivity in resistance and that different types of subjectivity are apt to be linked to different types of resistance. These distinctions are of both empirical and theoretical importance.

Heidi Gottfried begins Chapter 3, 'Learning the Score: The Duality of Control and Everyday Resistance in the Temporary Help Service Industry', by criticizing labour process theorists for continuing to focus almost exclusively on work settings of the prototypical male worker. Her participant observation study helps to fill the void. Of special value is the grounding of her inquiry in cultural studies and socialist-feminist theory and the reporting of data relating to temporary clerical workers, most of whom were females. From the feminist literature Gottfried expected to find a qualitative difference between the experiences of men and women believing that women would engage in less visible forms of resistance. Informed by this view, she conducted a participant observation study of temporary help workers.

Among other things, she found that the spatial and temporal nature of the work worlds of temporary workers is fundamentally different from that of traditional workers. Whereas the latter work together under one roof, temporary workers are more likely to be separated from each other because they work in a variety of work sites and organizations. Moreover, temporary workers perform on intermittent rather than fixed time schedules. These special space and time conditions make it necessary for the firms that employ the temps, to exercise forms of control that differ from those in more traditional arrangements. Also, the employees are subjected to a second set of control mechanisms – those used by the organizations who are the temporary firm's clients. Gottfried reports that among other things, the employing firm tries to have the temps define temporary work subjectively, as women's work, by emphasizing the importance of emotional labour that such a definition entails. In this context, dress codes and 'proper feminine appearance' are emphasized. Thus, resistance might involve little more than a subtle change in appearance.

It should come as no surprise that temporary work contexts constrain the possibilities for collective awareness and solidarity thereby altering the nature or resistance. As a result, resistance takes the form of individual and creative moves in everyday activities that reflect withdrawal of co-operation without challenge to the basic structures. In short, Gottfried helps us see a new frontier of control and the nature of resistance associated with it. As in the previous chapters and most of those that follow we see the importance of an in-depth understanding of the local work settings and the subjective experiences they spawn for recognizing and comprehending resistance. In our view, this fact does not deny the possibility of theorizing resistance, it does move us towards grounded inquiry that informs us of the dialectical relationships among experiences and the subjectivities and modes of expression they permit.

In Chapter 4, 'Working with Nature: Organic Farming and other Forms of Resistance to Industrialized Agriculture', *Carolyn Egri* shifts our focus to a quite different locale – farmers in British Columbia. She notes that the growth of industrialized agriculture and the associated growing dominance in agriculture of large agribusiness has placed many family farmers in adverse economic states and notes that family farmers have engaged in some, but very limited, collective opposition to the ideology and institutional structure of industrialized agriculture. However, everyday resistance informed by a vision of a 'post-industrial' ecologically sustainable system of family farming, emphasizing the agrarian craft, is present.

Egri bases her analysis on data that contrast organic and conventional farmers and points to the importance of understanding the twin processes of consent and resistance for comprehending the experiences, motives and actions of the farmers she studied. The ideologies of both groups played important roles in their responses to industrialized agriculture. The ideology of the organic group features a commitment to sustainable agriculture and is less concerned with technical efficiency than the conventional position. Also, the ideology of the organic group reflects a more spiritual emphasis and a greater concern with the long term relationship between human beings and nature than does that of the conventional approach.

These different perspectives are associated with quite different views about the nature of agricultural work and Egri draws intriguing parallels between struggle over craft in agriculture and the struggles that centred around the nineteenth-century factory. Further, she theorizes the political correlates of these differences. She shows that the two groups of farmers draw upon different views of agriculture in constructing their responses and that these different constructions are associated with contrasting dynamics of resistance to industrialized agriculture. Whereas the conventional farmers focus on economic aspects, the organic farmers emphasize environmental issues. Importantly, these different values are associated with variations in the operation of farming organizations. This latter point is an especially important insight from her paper – differing ideologies may be associated with different views of the appropriateness of different forms of organizations and hence, the type of collective resistance that might appear.

Egri concludes that the environmentalist agenda has great potential for generating both ideological and practical challenges to exploitative systems of production. Because the organic view is associated with a subjectivity that is inconsistent with the major assumption of the dominant system, it has far greater revolutionary potential than does the conventional view that accepts so many of the fundamental premises of the capitalist order. In short, Egri helps us to see the complex dynamics of resistance and thereby helps us better to understand why some forms of resistance are doomed to reproduce the status quo whereas others, even those responding to the same set of conditions, have greater transformative potential.

Reading across the first four chapters, the local and situationally specific character of resistance becomes clear. We arrived at this conclusion inductively rather than from some previously held theoretical position which might have determined the selection of papers for the volume. Yet, as we shall see in the succeeding chapters the localized and context specific approach to studying resistance continues as a central theme. This is particularly interesting given that all of the papers represent work derived from independent investigators simply using the notion of resistance to examine social events in a wide variety of settings.

In this context, the complementarity of Chapter 5, 'Foucault, Power, Resistance and All That', by *David Knights* and *Theo Vurdubakis*, is particularly noteworthy. Without any intention to do so, it could be seen as providing some conceptual support for the approach taken in many of the other papers. The conceptual concerns of Knights and Vurdubakis stem partly from the implicit and occasionally explicit critiques of labour process theorists and Marxists who believe Foucault's analysis of power and discipline leaves no room for resistance. The authors argue that this misinterpretation of Foucault derives from a projection on to him of their own dualistic conceptions of power and resistance.

The critics first take Foucault's argument that power is everywhere to imply that there is no space for resistance. Second, they argue that if power constitutes subjectivity then no one is uncontaminated and able to become agents of resistance. Third, it is claimed that if power is inescapable there can be no justification for resistance since it will only generate another form of power. From a dualistic position that sees resistance as a polar opposite and outside of power, these criticisms are unanswerable. Knights and Vurdubakis, however, dismiss each of them by arguing that the ubiquitous nature of power does not deny space for resistance since power is neither exhaustive of social relations nor totalizing with respect to subjectivity. There are discontinuities, and gaps that leave considerable space for resistance. At the same time, there are multiple powers that conflict with one another and exercising power, as everyone does to varying degrees, cannot preclude one from also acting as an agent of resistance in relation to some other power. Once the view that power is possessed by one group who then controls the powerless is abandoned, all talk of resistance being eliminated by the omniscience of power can simply be countered by resorting to a recognition that power and resistance are not necessarily exercised by different subjects. What is more important given that power is not omnipotent, Knights and Vurdubakis argue, is how and in what specific circumstances power or resistance is attributed to persons and groups. Finally, the authors seek to defend the more complex and interesting argument regarding the justification of resistance when this can only lead to the displacement of one power by another. It is here that the authors admit no ultimate justification, if by this is expected an endorsement of a universal struggle for an ideal society. Resistance cannot therefore be justified on the basis of reform of society for reforms are no less dangerous than the powers they seek to sweep away. Similarly, support for human rights cannot be a justification for resistance in general – each case would need to be examined on its merits relating to its specific circumstances. Human rights may be all that subjects can mobilize in resisting certain powers and, for this reason, they should be supported but not at the expense of ignoring and being immune to the ways in which rights also subjugate populations. The rights of autonomy, dignity and social mobility can be as debilitating as they are empowering.

The conclusion from all this is that power and resistance are best understood when they are examined in specific sites with definite socio-historical conditions and means of operation. The authors note that ethnographies in the labour process and critical studies traditions are excellent means for exploring resistance, because it is always local and specific. Thus, the theoretical effort of Knights and Vurdubakis indicates the importance of the type of grounded studies reported in the other chapters of this volume even though Foucault has not explicitly been the theoretical stimulus in a majority of them.

In Chapter 6, however, *Terry Austrin* draws explicitly upon Foucault's work as it has impacted on the labour process debate. In particular, his 'Positioning Resistance and Resisting Position: Human Resource Management and the Politics of Appraisal and Grievance Hearings' begins by evaluating critically an earlier study by Knights and Sturdy (1989) which suggested that the introduction of computerized technology in an insurance company generated enormous backlogs of processing that, through self-discipline, staff quickly sought to 'shift'. This stimulation to self-discipline Austrin questions in the light of his own grounded study of performance appraisals and grievances in the finance industry. Austrin finds that the new performance appraisal systems used in connection with technological changes in the development of human resource management produce 'new contexts of "talk"' that are associated with a new form of control. Simultaneously, however, this new form creates new space for workers to resist. The essence of resistance in this context requires being skilled in the operative discourse that the new systems advance. In an intriguing turn, Austrin reports that even though this discourse centres on accounts of *individual* behaviour, the process provides the basis for collective resistance and a new role for unions. He envisions unions as agencies that provide place from which to speak and listen. In the context of the contemporary finance industry, he suggests that unions can best serve workers by offering training for participating effectively in the new discourse. Austrin's position is novel and complex, and we have not captured it adequately in what we have said about it here. However, hopefully, enough has been said to indicate salient similarities with the other chapters, concerning the importance of understanding the mutual evolution of control and resistance as it takes place in a specific social context.

In Chapter 7, *Danny LaNuez* and *John Jermier* shift our attention to another context of resistance, which has received very little previous attention – the worlds of managers and technocrats. To establish a basis for their work, LaNuez and Jermier begin by making the case that in today's world, many managers and technocrats have incentives to resist, because they are subjected to capitalist control strategies that resemble those applied to labour in the past. Although they do not present any primary data, the examples they offer serve as sufficient evidence that managerial/technocratic resistance exists.

Having established the importance of considering resistance of managers and technocrats, they turn their attention to its forms. Somewhat surprisingly, they suggest that one form is sabotage, defined as deliberate action or inaction that is intended to damage, destroy or disrupt some aspect of the workplace environment, including the organization's property, product, processes or reputation. Consequently, the usual assumption that sabotage is confined to blue collar workers, is misleading. This assumption is derived from events of an earlier era, where that particular group was subject to the conditions that would induce almost any group to sabotage. LaNuez and Jermier argue that sabotage is a result of the experience of low levels of control in today's organizations and that many managerial and technocratic employees have this experience. They postulate five macro-level forces that have contributed to this state of affairs: mergers and organizational restructuring; increased use of monitoring and other control techniques; technological changes that have replaced highly skilled with less skilled labour; deskilling and deprofessionalization; and displacement due to technological obsolescence. As a result, there is the potential for sabotage because the interests of many managers and technocrats may be in direct opposition to capitalist imperatives.

Importantly, the types of actions that take place in response to this potential are a function of the social orientations and identities of the managerial and technocratic workers. LaNuez and Jermier advance an informative framework for conceptualizing these identities and the potential for sabotage associated with each. Also, the modes of expression of these various identities are affected by local and historical contexts.

Recognizing that there are a multiplicity of forms of sabotage, the authors offer a typology of managerial/technocratic sabotage. Major forms include: sabotage by circumvention; and sabotage by direct action. Their analysis and the frameworks they propose should be helpful in stimulating and guiding additional inquiry concerning sabotage beyond the shopfloor. Importantly, the nature of the process is such that study of the specific local context must be explored to understand what a particular action or inaction represents. The frameworks they provide offer dimensions for guiding research and theory concerning these important matters of context.

In Chapter 8, 'Whistleblowing in Modern Work Organizations: the Politics of Revealing Organizational Deception and Abuse', *Joyce Rothschild* and *Terance Miethe* develop a fascinating linkage between whistleblowing and resistance. They present evidence of a neglected aspect of the subjectivity of resisters: depending on how managers treat an employee's concerns, a process of transformation can be triggered through which the individual becomes more politicized. The authors assume that from the start, whistleblowing is political behaviour in that it is intended to change something about the way work gets done. However, as a whistleblowing episode runs its course, the political implications turn out to be far greater than initially intended. Among other things they find a remarkable transformation of the whistleblowers themselves. Rothschild and Miethe suggest that prior to blowing the whistle, whistleblowers often have a quite special subjective position. Most notably, they tend to be highly competent and respected employees who have stronger than normal allegiance to extra-organizational principles than to strictly organizational norms. Moreover, they tend to be 'naive' in assuming that the organization is actually devoted to its stated mission and wants to know about and rectify wrong and illegal activity. As the whistleblowing process runs its course, a key aspect of the transformation of these people is awareness that these beliefs are far less true than they had assumed.

In addition, whistleblowing is the product of sociological as well as individual developments. Particularly important in the authors' account is the growth of the information economy and expertise positions staffed by employees who are likely to have developed professional norms and other bases for judgement that may conflict with organizational norms and practices. Likewise, organizations may have become increasingly hidden from public view and require greater internal monitoring, some of which is conducted by a set of occupations whose explicit role is monitoring the actions of others and the organization's systems.

Rothschild and Miethe report considerable congruence between the results of their qualitative field studies and those of other researchers. Typically, whistleblowers set out expecting constructive responses from the organization, in part because they believed that they were respected and valued employees. To their surprise they find, instead, that management attempts to repress them, often by challenging their competence and trying to have them fired. What emerges then is a struggle in which each side attempts to discredit the other. Usually, one of the most attractive courses for whistleblowers to re-establish their dignity and reclaim their good names is to go to some external agency.

After the long and personally costly process that often unfolds, the whistleblowers come to the awareness that they have experienced how the organization normally operates. In addition to this awareness, whistleblowers who succeed often do so by getting others to join with them. Both their new awareness and their roles as agents of collective resistance are key elements in the transformation of the whistleblower to a new political consciousness. This change is reflected in the fact that many times, whistleblowers become increasingly active in a variety of other political causes.

In short, the experiences are associated with changes in one's political consciousness thereby altering a person's propensity to resist in other arenas. These changes in subjectivity are missed if one follows the seemingly standard paths of viewing the whistleblower as either 'bad apple' or as a 'saintly' individual who more than other people is willing to sacrifice him/herself for the common good. One way of guarding against these simplistic perspectives is to approach whistleblowing in much the same way we have suggested viewing other forms of resistance – grounded observation of the individual's experiences and actions informed by fine-grained analysis of the local context.

When we take all of these papers together we obtain a special view of resistance that is missing in existing labour process theory.

This view challenges us to abandon traditional perspectives that restrict the study of resistance to those struggles among large-scale entities whose members share a common cause. Instead, we are driven to explore how concrete local situations interact with the subjectivity of agents involved in complex power–resistance relations. Of course this does not mean that more global issues play no role or that they can be ignored. Indeed, they do play a role in shaping local situations and they are affected by local situations.

Further, viewing resistance in this way is consistent with an assumption that it is not some pathological aberration but the product of rationally coherent strategies and objectives. No grand collective consciousness or shared interests or special proclivity for self-sacrifice need be posited. This view implies a somewhat particular methodological stance. Inquiry demands examination of the concrete local situation in which individuals find themselves. The expressions of resistance and the social actors at whom they are directed will vary widely over space and time.

We believe that this collection represents an important step in reconceptualizing 'resistance' in a way which is necessary for viewing organizations of the late twentieth century. Theoretically, this reconceptualization has the space for individual agency and subjectivity, recognizing the crucial role played by events at the local level that affect both agency and subjectivity. Further, it recognizes the sweep of more global political-economic systems that help to shape local-level events.

In the final chapter, 'Power Relations and the Constitution of the Resistant Subject', *Stewart Clegg* reflects on the earlier chapters and advances a theoretical overview for the study of resistance that encompasses insights from each of the chapters. Such a theory demands analysis of the consciousness of the individual, the nature of the social organization, and the capability of the individual to draw on the resources of the collectivity. Clegg introduces several dimensions to help us conceptualize the major components of the central concepts and uses them to integrate and analyse the previous chapters. The resulting framework is especially valuable as it weaves together concepts of resistance, subjectivity and power.

In general, there has been a lacuna not only in labour process research but also in other social science literatures regarding the study of resistance. While this has been changing somewhat lately in the broader social science disciplines, a large knowledge-gap concerning workplace resistance still remains in labour process theory and other areas of organizational social science. This collection should help to fill the void. We expect that its primary value will be in assisting social scientists in conceptualizing and investigating resistance and relating it to existing theories of power and subjectivity. It may, however, be of some interest to lay persons. They may find comfort, a challenge or a threat from the evidence that people can and do indeed take greater control over their own lives, even in large-scale bureaucratic organizations.

REFERENCES

Aronowitz, S. (1978) 'Marx, Braverman and the Logic of Capitalism', *Insurgent Sociologist* 8(1): 126–46.

Braverman, H. (1974) *Labor and Monopoly Capital*, New York: Monthly Review Press.

Burawoy, M. (1979) *Manufacturing Consent*, Chicago: University of Chicago Press.

Burawoy, M. (1985) *The Politics of Production*, London: Verso.

Camus, A. (1956) *The Rebel*, New York: Vintage Books.

Camus, A. (1960) 'L'étranger', in *The Collected Fiction of Albert Camus*, London: Harnish Hamilton.

Collinson, D.L. (1992) *Managing the Shopfloor: Subjectivity, Masculinity and Workplace Culture*, Berlin: de Gruyter.

Edwards, R. (1979) *Contested Terrain*, New York: Basic Books.

Elger, A. (1979) 'Valorisation and deskilling: A critique of Braverman', *Capital and Class* 7: 58–99.

Foucault, M. (1980) *Power/knowledge: Selected Interviews and other writings 1972–77*, edited by Colin Gordon, Brighton, Sussex: Harvester Press.

Foucault, M. (1982) 'The subject and Power', in Dreyfus, H. and Rabinow, P. *Michel Foucault: Beyond Structuralism and Hermeneutics*, Brighton, Sussex: Harvester Press.

Friedman, A.L. (1977) *Industry and Labour: Class Struggle at Work and Monopoly Capitalism*, London: Macmillan.

Garfinkel, H. (1967) *Studies in Ethnomethodology*, Englewood Cliffs, New Jersey: Prentice-Hall.

Gartman, D. (1978) 'Marx and the Labor Process: An Interpretation', *Insurgent Sociologist* 8(2–3): 97–108.

Giddens, A. (1978–1979) 'The Prospects for Social Theory Today', *Berkeley Journal of Sociology* 23: 201–23.

Gordon, D., Edwards, R., and Reich, M. (1982) *Segmented Work, Divided Workers: The Historical Transformation of Labor in the United States*, Cambridge: Cambridge University Press.

Henriques, J., Hollway, W., Urwin, C., Venn, C. and Walkerdine, V. (1984) *Changing the Subject: Psychology, Social Regulation and Subjectivity*, London: Methuen.

Hodson, R. (1991) 'The Active Worker: Compliance and Autonomy at the Workplace, *Journal of Contemporary Ethnography* 20: 47–78.

Jermier, J.M. (1981) 'Infusion of Critical Social Theory into Organization Analysis', in Dunkerley, D. and Salaman, G. (eds) *International Yearbook of Organization Studies, 1981*, London: Routledge.

Jermier, J. M. (1983) 'Labor Process Control in Modern Organizations: Subtle Effects of Structure', *Journal of Business Research* 11: 317–32.

Jermier, J. M. (1985) ' "When the Sleeper Wakes": A Short Story Illustrating Themes in Radical Organization Theory', *Journal of Management* 11(2): 67–80.

Jermier, J. M. (1988) 'Sabotage at Work: The Rational View', in DiTomaso, N. (ed.) *Research in the Sociology of Organizations* 6: 101–134.

Jermier, J. M. (1991) Critical Epistemology and the Study of Organizational Culture: Reflections on *Street Corner Society*, in Frost, P., *et al.* (eds) *Reframing Organizational Culture*, Newbury Park, California: Sage.

Knights, D. (1990) 'Subjectivity, Power and the Labour Process', in Knights, D. and Willmott, H. (eds) *Labour Process Theory*, London: Macmillan.

Knights, D. and Collinson, D. (1985) 'Redesigning Work on the Shopfloor: A Question of Control or Consent', in Knights, D., Willmott, H. and Collinson, D. (eds) *Job Redesign: Critical Perspectives on the Labour Process*, Aldershot: Gower.

Knights, D. and Collinson, D. (1987) 'Disciplining the Shopfloor: A Comparison of the Disciplinary Effects of Managerial Psychology and Financial Accounting', *Accounting, Organizations and Society* 12: 457–77.

Knights, D. and Willmott, H. (1983) 'Dualism and Domination: An Analysis of Marxian, Weberian and Existentialist Perspectives', *Australian and New Zealand Journal of Sociology* 19: 33–49.

Knights, D. and Willmott, H. (1985) 'Power and Identity in Theory and Practice', *The Sociological Review* 33: 22–46.

Knights, D. and Willmott, H. (1989) 'Power and Subjectivity at Work: From Degradation to Subjugation in Social Relations', *Sociology* 23: 535–58.

Littler, C. (1982) *The Development of the Labour Process in Capitalist Societies*, London: Heinemann.

Littler, C. and Salaman, G. (1982) 'Bravermania and Beyond: Recent Theories of the Labour Process', *Sociology*, 16: 215–69.

Marx, K. (1967/1972) *Capital*, New York: Dutton.

Nichols, T. (1980) *Capital and Labour*, Glasgow: Fontana.

Nichols, T. and Beynon, H. (1977) *Living with Capitalism*, London: Macmillan.

Nord, W. (1974) 'The Failure of Applied Behavioral Science: A Marxian Perspective', *Journal of Applied Behavioral Science* 10: 557–78.

Nord, W. (1977a) 'A Marxist Critique of Humanistic Psychology', *Journal of Humanistic Psychology*, 17: 75–83.

Nord, W. (1977b) 'Job Satisfaction Reconsidered', *American Psychologist* 32: 1026–35.

Nord, W. and Jermier, J. M. (1994) 'Overcoming Resistance to Resistance', *Public Administration Quarterly* 12, 17: 396–409.

Ollman, B. (1971) *Alienation: Marx's Critique of Man in Capitalist Society*, London: Cambridge University Press.

Sturdy, A., Knights, D. and Willmott, H. (1992) *Skill and Consent: Contemporary Studies in the Labour Process*, London: Routledge.

Thompson, P. (1986) *The Nature of Work: An Introduction to Debates on the Labour Process*, London: Macmillan.

Thompson, P. (1990) 'Crawling from the Wreckage: The Labour Process and the Politics of Production' in Knights, D and Willmott, H. (eds) *Labour Process Theory*, London: Macmillan.

Tucker, J. (1992) 'Everyday Forms of Employee Resistance', *Sociological Forum* 8: 25–45.

Wardell, M. (1990) 'Labour and Labour Process', in Knights, D. and Willmott, H. (eds) *Labour Process Theory*, London: Macmillan.

Weeks, J. (1981) *Capital and Exploitation*, Princeton: Edward Arnold.

Willmott, H. (1990) 'Subjectivity and the Dialectics of Praxis: Opening up the Core of Labour Process Analysis', in Knights, D. and Willmott, H. (eds) *Labour Process Theory*, London; Macmillan.

1

STRATEGIES OF RESISTANCE

Power, knowledge and subjectivity in the workplace

David Collinson

Following the extensive criticism of Braverman's (1974) neglect of labour resistance, more recent critical analyses of organizations have increasingly turned their attention to the manufacture of consent, the (self-)disciplining of subordinates and the outflanking of resistance. While recognizing the importance of these themes, this chapter highlights the need to retrieve the analytical and empirical significance of workplace resistance. In seeking to contribute to a more detailed consideration of oppositional practices, the following chapter highlights the important role played by different knowledges in the articulation of resistance. It also identifies two distinct oppositional strategies that are shaped by particular subjective orientations to power, knowledge and information. 'Resistance through distance' describes the way in which subordinates try to escape or avoid the demands of authority and to 'distance' themselves, either physically and/or symbolically, from the organization and its prevailing power structure. By contrast, in 'resistance through persistence' subordinates seek to demand greater involvement in the organization and to render management more accountable by extracting information, monitoring practices and challenging decision-making processes. These different strategies, which are by no means exhaustive of possible resistance practices, are elaborated through two detailed case studies drawn from completed research projects. The paper concludes that resistance remains a persistent, significant and remarkable feature of contemporary organizations which requires further detailed examination by critical writers.

INTRODUCTION

Throughout the twentieth century, employee resistance has been a primary analytical concern of organizational scholars as well as a pervasive feature of labour process practices. Managerialist writers have explored various ways to eliminate or minimize employee recalcitrance and resistance (e.g. Taylor, 1947; Kreitner, 1986). Organizational psychologists have outlined different strategies designed to overcome resistance to change processes (e.g. Lewin, 1951, Kotter and Schlesinger, 1979; Plant, 1987; Dunphy and Stace, 1988). Industrial relations writers have examined strike patterns (Hyman, 1989) while industrial sociologists have focused upon output restriction on the shopfloor (e.g. Mayo, 1933; Roy, 1952; Walker and Guest, 1952; Goffman, 1959; Lupton, 1963; Klein, 1964; Brown, 1965; Ditton, 1976; Emmett and Morgan, 1982); workplace crime (Mars, 1982); industrial sabotage (Taylor and Walton, 1971; Brown, 1977; Dubois, 1979; Linstead, 1985; Jermier, 1988; Sprouse, 1992) and the way that informal practices often contravene formalized policies (Gouldner, 1954).

Labour process writers have made a distinctive contribution to this debate by highlighting the irreducible interrelationship between employee resistance and managerial control (e.g. Friedman, 1977; Nichols and Beynon, 1977; R. Edwards, 1979; Beynon, 1980; Cressey and Maciness, 1980; Littler, 1982; Edwards and Scullion, 1982; Storey 1985; Thompson and Bannon, 1985; P.K. Edwards, 1990). Emphasizing the extensive power asymmetries in contemporary organizations, these critical studies have explored the way that resistance is very much a *response* to practices of managerial control. In so doing, they have sought to overcome the neglect of labour resistance and subjectivity, for which Braverman (1974) has been heavily criticized. Yet despite this attention, important analytical questions about resistance remain underexplored. For example, why and how does resistance emerge? What discourses and practices constitute resistance? What resources and strategies are available to those who resist? How do we evaluate whether resistance is effective or ineffective? What are the consequences of resistance? Rather than address such questions, however, recent critical analyses of worker behaviour have tended to turn their attention to the manufacture of consent, the (self-)disciplining of subordinates and the outflanking of resistance (e.g. Burawoy 1979, 1985; Manwaring and Wood, 1985; P.K. Edwards, 1986; Clegg, 1989;

Rose, 1989; Knights and Sturdy, 1990; Sewell and Wilkinson, 1992; Sturdy, Knights and Willmott, 1992; Willmott, 1993; Grey, 1993). Although these studies are analytically important, some of them tend to neglect or underemphasize the significance and complexity of workplace resistance. This is illustrated by the recent contribution of Clegg (1989), whose influential earlier work concentrated on control and resistance in the labour process (Clegg and Dunkerley, 1980). Increasingly, however, he has been concerned with the way that workplace resistance is 'outflanked', a term he draws from Mann (1986).[1]

In seeking to explain 'why the dominated so frequently consent to their subordination and subordinators' (Clegg, 1989: 220), Clegg draws upon both Foucault's (1977) arguments that knowledge and information are key aspects of power in organizations and on Burawoy's use of the game metaphor.[2] On the one hand, he contends that subordinates are often 'ignorant' (Clegg, 1989: 221) of power in terms of: strategy construction, the negotiation of routine procedures, rules, agenda setting, protocol and assessing the resources of the antagonist. Consequently, 'it is not that they do not know the rules of the game; they might not recognize the game, let alone the rules' (p. 221). Clegg argues that subordinates often have little knowledge of others who are equally powerless and with whom alliances could be constructed. On the other hand, he acknowledges that outflanking can also result from subordinates having extensive knowledge. Subordinates may know only too well that the associated costs of resistance are 'far in excess of the probability of either achieving the outcome, or if achieved, the benefits so obtained' (p. 222). Hence, Clegg concludes that outflanking is the result of two quite extreme and contrasting situations. Either subordinates have too little information and knowledge, or they possess highly accurate and predictive knowledge concerning the future outcomes of resistance.[3]

Yet, is it the case in this period of late-modernism that subordinates are so easily outflanked? Are they so willing to consent to their subordination? Are they so lacking in knowledge and information that they are powerless or conversely so knowledgeable that they can always predict the detrimental consequences of their oppositional practices? To address these questions, this chapter draws on Clegg's focus on knowledge and power but in a way that seeks to retrieve the analytical and empirical significance of workplace resistance. This is not to reject the importance of the manufacture of consent/compliance or the outflanking of resistance. Rather it is to question the analytical primacy increasingly ascribed to these practices and to argue for a much more detailed examination of the conditions, processes and consequences of workplace resistance.

The following paper is primarily concerned to highlight two different strategies of dissent and opposition. These are illustrated below by exploring two empirical case studies drawn from completed research projects, that are re-examined here in the light of a specific focus upon knowledge and resistance. First, I argue that specific forms of knowledge are a crucial resource and means through which resistance can be mobilized. Knowledge in organizations is multiple, contested and shifting.[4] Employees may not possess detailed understandings of certain bureaucratic/political processes, but they often do monopolize other technical, production-related knowledges that facilitate their oppositional practices.

Second, I argue that it is not in any simple sense merely the possession, or ownership of particular knowledges that determines consent, outflanking or resistance, as Clegg seems to imply. Rather, it is also the way that these knowledges are deployed in particular organizational conditions and practices. The data reveal two quite different *subjective* strategies of workplace resistance that are shaped by particular orientations to knowledge, information and to those in authority. In the first case, men workers' routine resistance practices concentrate on *restricting information* from managers. They seek to escape or to avoid the demands of authority. I term this strategy 'resistance through distance'. The second case explores a woman's resistance to a particular managerial promotion decision. The more formalized processes of her challenge to managerial decision-making are informed by the converse strategy of *extracting information* from management. This oppositional strategy I term 'resistance through persistence'. These examples are by no means exhaustive of possible resistance strategies. What they reveal are the limited possibilities available to those who engage in resistance through distance and the greater viability and effectiveness of oppositional practices designed to render management more accountable by extracting information, monitoring practices and challenging decision-making processes.

Third, it is suggested that these arguments raise important issues about the subjectivity of subordinates in relation to power, knowledge and resistance that have tended to be neglected (see also Knights 1990; Thompson 1990; Willmott 1990, Collinson, 1992a). This chapter seeks to demonstrate that oppositional practices are significantly shaped, not only by power, knowledge and specific organizational conditions, but also by the particular subjectivities of employees and of those in more senior hierarchical positions. These subjectivities are invariably creative and knowledgeable, but also multiple, shifting, sometimes fragmentary, often inconsistent and frequently contradictory (see also Kondo, 1990).

Drawing on this analysis, the chapter concludes by arguing that much of the critical literature on employee behaviour tends to overstate either consent or resistance and to separate one from the other. Within these polarized perspectives, employee resistance is frequently treated either as all but non-existent or alternatively as all-pervasive. Yet neither approach adequately accounts for the multiplicity of oppositional practices in various workplaces. Resistance and consent are rarely polarized extremes on a continuum of possible worker discursive practices. Rather, they are usually inextricably and simultaneously linked, often in contradictory ways within particular organizational cultures, discourses and practices. Resistance frequently contains elements of consent and consent often incorporates aspects of resistance.

Hence, in an effort to contribute to the critical analysis of resistance, compliance and consent in the labour process, this chapter highlights the significant interrelationship between power, knowledge/information[5] and subjectivity. In doing so, it follows a tradition of labour process thinking which has emphasized how the appropriation and monopolization of knowledge constitutes a key control strategy of scientific management (Taylor, 1947; Braverman, 1974). Much of the post-Braverman labour process debate has continued to examine this relationship between power and knowledge in terms of the politics of managerial control and deskilling strategies (see e.g. Manwaring and Wood, 1985; Zuboff, 1988). Equally, feminist contributions have highlighted how job-related skills and knowledge are often 'saturated with sex' (Phillips and Taylor, 1980) in ways that not only reflect but also reinforce men's power and the gendered division of labour both in paid work and in the domestic sphere (Cockburn, 1983; Davies and Rosser, 1986; Walby, 1986, 1990). Yet, few studies have attended to the way that resistance is a condition and consequence of particular knowledges and subjectivities.

29

STRATEGIES OF RESISTANCE

The following sections re-examine two in depth case studies on workplace resistance drawn from separate research projects conducted in UK organizations during the 1980s. The first study explored the shopfloor culture of an all-male engineering factory (see Collinson, 1992a), while the second examined sex discrimination in the recruitment process (see Collinson et al., 1990). The class and gender issues arising in the first case of an all-male shopfloor are somewhat different from the second case study, which is drawn from the white-collar context of an insurance company. Here the workplace contained a gender mix and the oppositional practices examined below concentrate on resistance conducted by women.

Although quite distinct, the two cases also share certain commonalities. Both focus upon workplace resistance and both illustrate the importance of the strategic manipulation of knowledge and information in oppositional discursive practices. In each case, knowledge is contested and managers seek to retain and restrict information to enhance their control within the organization. Both companies had recently been taken over by US multinational corporations that in turn were beginning to have a significant influence on their respective corporate cultures. Moreover, strong trade unions with high membership levels were present in each company.

More detailed descriptions of the research objectives and methods that informed these projects are outlined in the appendices of the respective texts from which they are drawn. Suffice it to say here, that both projects used semi-structured in-depth interviews in order to explore the accounts of the research respondents. A distinctive methodological feature was the use of return interviews which facilitated the development both of trust relations and of a longitudinal analysis of events in the organizations. Extensive return interviews were conducted with certain respondents in both studies, who became key informants of 'insider' information (see Collinson, 1992b: 105). Interviews were supplemented by the observation of work relations, social interactions and of particular practices (e.g. production in the first case and selection interviewing in the second). In addition to these qualitative methods, company documents were examined and quantitative measures were collected (e.g. workforce profiles). The following discussion seeks to re-examine some of the research findings in a way that highlights both the consistent and distinctive patterns of resistance in each case and the interrelationships between workplace resistance, power, knowledge and subjectivity.

RESISTANCE THROUGH DISTANCE

The first research project was conducted between 1979 and 1983 within the Components Division of a private heavy vehicle manufacturing company located in a predominantly working-class Lancashire town in the north-west of England. During this period, 64 of the 229 manual workers in this division were interviewed, all at least twice and some on innumerable occasions. Interviews were also conducted with four managers in the production and personnel departments. On the shopfloor, the social relations were particularly localized, familial and informal. The factory had always been a place where whole families of men had worked, one generation providing an engineering apprenticeship to the next. As a result, the all-male shopfloor was characterized by a strong class and gender based community spirit that had largely remained intact despite a merger in 1970 and a takeover by a US transnational corporation in 1974.

This community spirit, however, did not translate into a harmony of interests within the organization as a whole. The research revealed a great deal of mistrust, defensiveness and insecurity on the shopfloor. Initiatives by the new owners intended to generate employee confidence and consent merely exacerbated workers' suspicions and provided the resources for shopfloor resistance. The managerial initiatives of a corporate culture campaign and a collective bonus scheme failed to address and change the negative aspects of work that were most important to shopfloor workers. Their subjective experience of manual employment consisted of being treated, first as commodities that could be hired and fired according to managerial discretion, second as 'unthinking machines' who were excluded from all strategic discourses and decision-making and finally as 'second-class citizens' whose terms and conditions of employment were inferior to all other occupational groups within the company. Hence, for shopfloor workers, in particular, interrelated material and symbolic insecurities were built into the employment relationship. These insecurities covered many aspects of work such as pay, employment stability, job control and even personal status and identity. The workers experienced themselves as controlled, commodified and stratified labour.

The corporate culture campaign which emphasized teamwork and communication was widely dismissed on the shopfloor as 'yankee bullshit' and 'propaganda'. The more management tried to adopt a 'personal' approach, the more convinced were shopfloor workers that this was part of a 'yankee plot' simply designed to improve productivity. Equally, the bonus scheme had the effect of strengthening workers' economic orientation to work. As a consequence these new initiatives reinforced workers' practices of resistance through distance that took multiple forms on the shopfloor. Workers' determination to 'distance' (Goffman, 1959) themselves as much as possible both symbolically and physically from managers, the organization and from shopfloor job requirements was the medium and outcome of a deeply embedded *counter-culture* on the shopfloor. Central to this counter-culture was a specific emphasis upon working-class masculinity that provided a primary sense of shopfloor identity and dignity for its members.

In response to the corporate culture campaign, shop stewards, for example, insisted that 'we don't have a relationship with management . . . they live in a different world from us, think differently and act differently'. Wary of being incorporated by a highly personal managerial approach, shop stewards refused to call managers by their first name as the latter requested, rejected their offers of lifts in cars and of cigarettes or cigars, and declined to have meetings with individual senior managers in the absence of other shop stewards who could witness the interaction. The shop steward in the axle department summarized the counter-cultural values of 'resistance through distance':

> We want to keep separate from them. We don't want to get personal. This 'call me Barney'[6] bullshit. . . . The further away management are the better. We've nothing in common with them.

These formalized negotiation strategies with senior managers were mirrored by the informal discursive practices of the shopfloor culture where resistance and self-differentiation were simultaneously articulated. Indeed, workers' concern to redefine their identities in a more positive way than that formally ascribed by the organization was an important condition and consequence of their oppositional discursive practices. As I will suggest, however, these subjective attempts to secure culturally validated and differentiated identities significantly limited workers' otherwise radical-sounding oppositional practices of resistance through distance.

Workers' particular notions of what constitutes valuable knowledge played a key role in these dual processes of resistance through distance and identity construction. Most workers emphasized the social and organizational importance of production and engineering. They were quick to elevate the 'practical' and 'commonsense' knowledge that they believed was a condition and consequence of manual labour over the more abstract and theoretical forms of knowledge found in the middle-class world of white-collar work and management. For many, the latter was simply an unproductive 'paper chase' and 'pen pushing' that had little or no relevance to the important realities of manufacturing heavy vehicles. Equally, the whole idea of promotion was widely rejected because it would mean incorporation, compromise and conformity. The few manual workers who had been promoted were dismissed as 'yes men' for having sacrificed their independence, autonomy, even their manhood in hierarchical conformity. It was widely believed that 'Blokes are made to change' once they were promoted.

Hence the men symbolically inverted the class-based hierarchy of the organization (see also Stallybrass and White, 1986). They redefined shopfloor work as a site of real, authentic and experiential knowledge, a belief that facilitated their resistance and self-differentiation. Part of this knowledge was derived from the workers' past experience of being treated as disposable commodities. This is illustrated by the following statement of one worker who rejected the corporate culture campaign:

> They give the impression we work together when it suits them,
> but when it gets rough, we're the ones who get it.

This class-based awareness of the ever-present possibility of disposability informed many workers' distancing from the incorporatist objectives of the corporate culture campaign. Providing a sense of power and identity for members of the counter-culture, these technical and social shopfloor knowledges emphasized manual workers' engineering skills and their 'real life' experience of organization.

These knowledges also facilitated a whole series of oppositional practices of resistance through distance in which shopfloor workers restricted the flow of technical and social information up the hierarchy by deploying their engineering and dramaturgical skills (Goffman, 1959). In seeking greater control over job and self, workers sought to manipulate the commodity status of their labour by using their knowledge of the labour process to appropriate and privatize 'public' space, time and production on the shopfloor. Their oppositional practices were intended to 'exploit' the interrelated material and symbolic spaces that were available to them as commodified labourers. The bonus scheme, in particular, became an important 'weapon' of resistance (Scott, 1985) through which workers could secure a degree of job control. Although management expected the bonus to generate employee flexibility and enhance productivity, it was actually reconverted by workers into a resource of inflexibility and output restriction.

The bonus scheme reinforced the widespread shopfloor view that 'management can't have what they don't pay for'. Having maximized bonus, shopfloor workers frequently refused to produce further. When negotiating times with the rate fixer, workers used their technical knowledge and engineering skills to mystify output potential. One 57-year-old turner in the machine shop illustrated workers' strategies of resistance using the bonus scheme. During his 40 years' experience in engineering he had developed many 'tricks of the trade' and shortcuts on jobs. Proud of his engineering skills, he believed he could handle 'any job on a lathe'. In exercising some control over production and the 'effort bargain', he invariably mystified and concealed his technical knowledge and skills when negotiating a time with the rate fixer, as he revealed:

> I do 400 of these a week. I always get them to do when they're needed. The time I got for this job from the rate fixer was eight minutes. But I can do them in two. Why should I worry? It pays to know your job. . . . You can't tell them what you can do or else you'd be doing three men's jobs for one man's wages.

Behind the appearance of conformity that he constructed when negotiating with the rate fixer, he maintained a deeper oppositional sense of self-determination. By manipulating the rate fixer, he could accumulate what different writers have called a 'kitty' (Burawoy, 1979), a 'bank' (Walker and Guest, 1952) or a 'stash' (Goffman, 1968). This comprised a private storage box concealed within his locker where he accumulated output in advance of it being required, which in turn enabled him to have some control over his production levels. This ability to mystify his potential output and to 'kid' the rate fixer, was a real source of personal pride and self-validation. It confirmed his technical skills, knowledge and experience. By restricting information, he was also able to exercise some control over his output and to avoid any intensification of his labour.

This example demonstrates how working the bonus system reinforced a very narrow, limited and defensive form of resistance that was concerned with the politics of controlling output, concealing information and producing false impressions of the individual for those in authority. Central to this resistance through distance was shopfloor workers' technical engineering skills and their social skills of appearance management which together enabled them to restrict the flow of knowledge and information back up the hierarchy. By controlling and managing production and information in this way, workers were able to appropriate both time and space. The toilets became an important 'back region' (Goffman, 1968) through which these processes of subversive appropriation could be enacted. Axle department workers spent a considerable amount of time in the toilet each afternoon. They too had negotiated favourable times for their work with the rate fixer. Since their bonus was calculated on a collective basis (i.e. the number of axles daily assembled by the 12 men), they had agreed amongst themselves to work 'flat out' in the morning to create some free time in the afternoon. In their view, the success of this resistance confirmed their skills and knowledgeability in exercising control over working times. Accordingly, these oppositional practices had the effect of validating identity and differentiating self. The toilets constituted a free space in which time could be appropriated and surveillance could be escaped.

In addition to controlling output, workers' management of knowledge and information facilitated their production of 'foreigners'. These were products for personal consumption that had no connection with lorry manufacture. Here workers used their technical and social knowledge to intensify production for their personal use. One winter, for example, when heavy snow fell in the Lancashire area, workers elicited the help of colleagues to create sledges for their children. Collective sharing and pooling of engineering knowledge also included extensive car maintenance that was conducted during working hours using company tools and equipment. Several men owned caravans and a reciprocal support network had developed of caravan parts and maintenance that had saved some workers enormous sums of money when compared with commercial repair costs. Such practices overlapped with more covert forms of workplace theft which included stealing materials, tools, car/lorry batteries and petrol.

In contrast with Burawoy's (1979) findings, the bonus scheme at this company proved to be a central site of conflict and resistance in everyday shopfloor relations (see also Knights and Collinson, 1985). Bonus payments were calculated by management who aggregated together the production figures of individual departments in order to measure productivity across the plant. Only managers had access to these aggregated factory-wide data that formed the basis of the weekly payout, and their control of this information was an equally important feature of conflict on the shopfloor. Unable to monitor bonus calculations, many workers believed that managers were withholding important information: they were as one worker put it, 'managing by mushroom'.[7] Consensus and consent were rarely in evidence as shopfloor workers insisted that managers were 'fiddling the figures'. Shopfloor cynicism and suspicion was fuelled by an oscillating weekly bonus payout, the widespread failure to understand how the figure was calculated and the uneven flow of production. Often individual departments would reach their necessary production targets, but would rarely receive full bonus after the collective payment had been averaged out with the other sections of the plant (see Collinson, 1992a, for elaboration). Paradoxically, the relaxation of controls in the guise of the bonus scheme rebounded on managers by reinforcing the workers' belief in managerial manipulation – the very perception and rumours that the corporate culture campaign was designed to eliminate. The managerial concern to generate flexibility and control over the production process through the manipulation of bonuses was merely reconverted by workers into a resource of inflexibility and resistance through distance.

Yet these diverse practices of resistance should neither be overstated nor romanticized. They were also shot through with unresolved contradictions, conflicts, ambiguities and unintended consequences. Resistance through distance and the concealment of information had only limited effectiveness as a means of dissent. This particular oppositional strategy simultaneously incorporated elements of compliance and consent that severely threatened the possibilities and effects of resistance. It failed to challenge and thus actually reinforced the commodification of labour and managerial control. By merely seeking to secure a degree of personal discretion and autonomy in and around the edges of their formally controlled and commodified position, these manual workers resisted in ways that simultaneously accommodated themselves to the sale of their own labour power. Their resistance failed to question and thereby remained confined within the commodity status of labour. Workers' contradictory search for security on the shopfloor actually reinforced the commodification of their labour and, paradoxically, reproduced their own material and symbolic insecurity. Hence, resistance, compliance and consent co-existed on the shopfloor, sometimes in the very same discursive practice.

In resistance through distance, workers sought to deny any involvement in or responsibility for the running of the organization. They often treated paid work in the 'public' sphere as a sacrifice for leisure and domesticity in the 'private' sphere, retaining a strong sense of separation between these two lifeworlds. Yet the illusory and precarious character of this public/private separation was frequently demonstrated when managers exercised their prerogative and discretion. In 1983, management announced extensive redundancies and a partial plant closure. Redundancies 'bring home' to workers the real interdependence between their 'private' and 'public' lives. Paradoxically, despite the ever-presence of shopfloor opposition and resistance to authority, when management announced large-scale redundancies, no actual resistance emerged. While some have argued that to 'take the money and run' was a 'rational surrender to inevitability' (Ackers and Black, 1992: 192), this was certainly not the view of the shop stewards' committee, which had tried to encourage their members to resist the decision or at minimum to demand higher redundancy settlements.

The redundancy process confirmed workers' experience and awareness of their own disposability as manual workers. Equally, it was characterized by their uncritical acceptance of managers' technical financial expertise and knowledge. Managers provided the shopfloor with extensive accounting information to justify the redundancies, releasing much more data than they had ever done in relation to the collective bonus. Shopfloor workers failed to question these figures despite some inherent inconsistencies in the data (see Knights and Collinson, 1987, for further discussion). Interrelated with workers' assumptions about managers' technical knowledge as accountants was their widespread acceptance of managerial prerogative. Although many workers routinely insisted that 'it's management's right to manage', they did not see this as an expression of compliance or consent. Rather it was a central assumption of their resistance through distance. Most workers were convinced and regularly insisted that managers were entirely responsible for the organization. For many shopfloor workers, the problem was that managers refused to accept this responsibility for which they were handsomely rewarded. One of the most oppositional shop stewards insisted,

> Management manage, workers work. That's how it should be.
> You can't play both sides like the yanks try to.

Paradoxically, the widespread shopfloor insistence on managerial prerogative was viewed as an expression of opposition, critique and dissent. Yet this resistance through distance also had the contradictory effect of creating compliance and consent. Hence, resistance through distance can also incorporate an explicit discourse of consent, not only to labour commodification but also to the elite control of the enterprise. In taking for granted labour commodification and elite managerial control, workers' resistance in this factory comprised a contradictory and ambiguous set of discursive practices that shifted over time and according to circumstances. Resistance, compliance and consent were simultaneously embedded in a shifting combination of contradictions, ambiguities and unresolved paradoxes and tensions on the shopfloor.

These contradictions and tensions sometimes collapsed into division, conflict and acrimony. Internal shopfloor conflicts occurred, for example, between workers who criticized colleagues for failing to work hard enough to maximize bonus. Conflict also resulted when workers sought to confirm their identity by differentiating themselves from colleagues as well as managers and white-collar workers. In such cases, the counter-cultural discourse of collectivism was revealed to be highly fragile and liable to collapse. This was particularly so since workers often looked to foremen, managers and even shop stewards to discipline recalcitrant workers and those believed to be 'not pulling their weight for the bonus'. Hence, the precariousness of shopfloor collectivism was a condition and consequence of a widespread worker belief in the need for managers to exercise discipline. In practice, it was shop stewards who usually found themselves having to exercise discipline over highly indifferent workers.

The union was committed to protecting jobs and maximizing wages. In seeking to achieve the latter, shop stewards often had to discipline recalcitrant workers.[8] This inevitably generated conflict and antagonism between stewards and some members. The ensuing internal divisions within the union were intensified by the stewards' policy of prioritizing the security of jobs over and above the maximization of pay. So, for example, when jobs were threatened, the shop stewards' committee successfully persuaded management to reduce or suspend bonus instead of announcing redundancies. This, however, generated a great deal of criticism from some shop-floor workers who were antagonistic to the stewards for reducing their take home pay. Hence, the contradictory nature of resistance through distance was reflected and reproduced in the practices of shop stewards and their sometimes acrimonious relations with union members. (In the second case study below the absence of such tensions or conflicts within the trade union was an important basis on which more effective resistance could be mobilized.)

This first case study has highlighted the importance of social and technical knowledge as a medium for the articulation of workplace resistance. It demonstrates how shopfloor workers sought to restrict information and knowledge as part of a consistent strategy of resistance through distance. Workers' counter-cultural practices were intended to appropriate time, space, knowledge and production on the shopfloor. Some of these practices had important effects in the organization, not least in influencing managerial strategies. They also provided workers with an albeit precarious sense of control over their working lives.

Yet although this oppositional culture was a routine and pervasive feature of shopfloor practices, it also contained significant ambiguities, ambivalences and paradoxes. Many of these oppositional practices of distancing are best seen as short-term 'escape attempts' (Cohen and Taylor, 1992) providing only temporary relief from the incessant pressures and insecurities of shopfloor production and subordination (Collinson, 1993). Resistance was confined within the commodity status of labour and was shaped, at least in part, by workers' pervasive concern to secure a positive sense of identity. Workers did not seek to obtain greater information about the company, to influence strategic decision-making or to make suggestions about production-related matters. In their eyes, this would have both contradicted their sense of 'independence' and identity as shopfloor workers and created the danger of co-optation and incorporation. They steadfastly insisted that management had the full responsibility for managing the enterprise. Hence, within workers' discursive practices, resistance, compliance and even consent were simultaneously embedded. Paradoxically, workers' resistance through distance reinforced the legitimacy of hierarchical control, left managerial prerogative unchallenged, and increased their vulnerability to disciplinary practices. This in turn suggests that it is not merely the absolute quantity of knowledge and information that significantly shapes the possibility for and effectiveness of resistance. Rather, it is the way in which this knowledge is used within particular power relations. The next case study illustrates this argument further, where far from restricting information, subordinates sought to extract it from management – an approach that proved to be both more strategic and effective.

RESISTANCE THROUGH PERSISTENCE

The second case study is drawn from the white-collar setting of the UK insurance industry. It concentrates on issues of gender discrimination and is drawn from a larger research project on sex discrimination in the selection process funded by the UK Equal Opportunities Commission (see Collinson *et al.*, 1990). This project examined selection practices in 64 workplaces. It revealed that resistance through distance was the most common response of many women who believed that they may have been victims of gender-based discrimination. Rather than formally challenge potentially unfair selection decisions, women candidates often denied any interest in working for the recruiting organization. They would simply look elsewhere for employment. In the external labour market, this response is hardly surprising given that candidates have not as yet made a career investment in the company. Moreover, external recruitment is a process shrouded in a veil of secrecy about which most candidates frequently have very little information and in which managerial prerogative is extensive.

The research found that where resistance to sex discrimination was relatively effective, it was more likely to be articulated in promotion practices and in organizations that had a strong trade union presence. In such cases, women often had more power, knowledge and commitment to challenge promotion decisions perceived to be unfair. Again, knowledge and information were vital. Unlike external candidates, internal applicants often either had or could easily obtain information concerning: who the other candidates were, and their background and skills, who the interviewers were and their selection criteria, the culture and history of the organization and the background to the particular vacancy. In order to develop these themes, I will now examine one specific promotion exercise which illustrates the dynamics of a more effective form of resistance. The detailed data presented below are based on two interviews with the job candidate herself, three with her local trade union representative and three with the general secretary of the trade union. The two union officials also provided extensive documentation related to this case, including, most importantly, copies of minutes of all the formal meetings that took place during this process (see also Collinson, 1992b). This documentation proved to be an invaluable source of information from which to piece together the discourses and practices of control and resistance that comprised the case.

The company in which this internal vacancy arose, had been taken over five years earlier by an American multinational corporation. The new corporate culture that was evolving out of this changed ownership structure included a strong public commitment to equal opportunities and an even stronger sensitivity to the possibility of bad publicity regarding gender or ethnicity. In consequence, the corporate personnel team had disseminated an equal opportunity policy statement throughout the company. Line managers had received guidelines on good equal opportunity practices, detailed forms to be completed during selection exercises and head office training courses in equal opportunity principles and procedures.

This particular promotion case took place in the motor department of a main branch situated in the north of England. In October 1986, Jane Bamber (a pseudonym to preserve confidentiality), was a grade-six motor clerk who applied for a grade-seven vacancy. Although Jane was interviewed and seriously considered, she was unsuccessful, but was told that she was 'next in line' for a grade-seven post. At the beginning of March 1987, Jane informed the company that she was pregnant. Soon afterwards, two grade-seven vacancies were advertised. Jane applied but was not interviewed. Yet, she was totally mobile and the only person in the department who had received an 'A' for her work performance in her annual appraisal in both the previous years. Jane also knew that she was the applicant with the highest educational qualifications. A woman who was not mobile and who had been rejected outright for the October vacancy and a man who had received a warning after being criticized by clients were appointed. When Jane requested an explanation, the superintendent gave no reason for her outright rejection except that he could not support her application and refused to discuss the matter further.

At this point, Jane might have decided to resist by taking her full entitlement of statutory maternity leave and then resigning from the company. Alternatively, she could have decided to remain in employment but with a different, less committed orientation to her work and to the company. But rather than choose a strategy of resistance through distance,[9] Jane decided to challenge management's refusal to justify their promotion decision. She sought to extract further information from them concerning their criteria and decision-making processes. This form of resistance was facilitated by the fact that as an internal candidate, Jane was familiar with the company, its practices and its management. She was also a local union representative. Jane's willingness to pursue the case was significantly influenced by her knowledge and experience of local union practices and of representing other members. Indeed, her determination was also reinforced by the strength of the national union and its commitment to equal opportunity principles. Hence Jane contacted a senior national official of the trade union who was also based at this main branch when not performing union duties.

The national union official arranged a meeting between the branch administration manager, Jane and herself at which she requested information about the formal rejection criteria in Jane's case. None had so far been provided. The manager could give no adequate explanation for the decision because he was unaware of the specific details of the case. He stated that selection decisions were largely the responsibility of the superintendent. The manager had great difficulty in trying to explain why, although the clerk had been a serious contender for the previous vacancy in October, she could not even be recommended or considered in the following March. After assuring Jane that her pregnancy had no impact on the decision, the administration manager adjourned the meeting to allow him to consult with the superintendent.

When the meeting was reconvened, the manager affirmed his complete support for the decision of the superintendent. He outlined the five formal reasons to justify Jane's rejection sent to him in writing by the motor superintendent. These were as follows:

1 Jane did 'not demonstrate the personality to take on the job'. She 'needed to display a greater desire to move beyond grade seven' and 'needed to improve her communication with trainee inspectors'.
2 Jane had 'never been fully committed' and 'allowed personal issues to interfere with her work'.
3 She was reputed to have made a critical comment about the company to a colleague.
4 She had shown no commitment to work overtime.
5 She had not begun to sit for her professional insurance examinations.

Ostensibly, these justifications seemed plausible, logical and difficult to challenge. The manager had avoided any mention of Jane's pregnancy in his formalized account. However, the information that management had very reluctantly provided proved to be useful in resisting their decision. At this point, the union official adjourned the meeting to discuss the points raised with Jane.

In fact the women were able to use the managers' disciplinary discourses and rationalizations to undermine the validity of the promotion decision. Extracting further information from management was an essential part of this resistance strategy. When she requested the meeting to be reconvened, the union official asked the administration manager to arrange an afternoon appointment because of Jane's morning sickness. In fact, the meeting was arranged for nine o'clock in the morning, which was construed by both women as a deliberate attempt by the manager to secure a tactical advantage. Prior to the meeting, the union official gave Jane three pieces of advice based on her experience of negotiations and representing cases. First, she told Jane not to respond to the manager if he tried to talk to her directly and added that she would do all the talking. Second, they would not criticize either of the two successful candidates but would simply concentrate on the decision-making processes in order to discover the managers' thinking about Jane's application. Third, she said that if Jane should start to feel nauseous she should on no account leave the room and if necessary should be sick on the managers' new office carpet.

During the meeting, the union official argued that the criteria outlined by management at the previous meeting were vague, inconsistent and incorrect. In response the manager began to talk directly to Jane. Using a highly personalized and paternalistic discourse, the older man asked Jane, 'Now why has it come to this? Surely we can resolve this problem without these formalities?'. Jane failed to respond except to become increasingly nauseous and seemingly about to throw up. At this point, it might be expected that the two women would have been forced to leave the room apologetically and defensively. Yet far from this, the union representative did not even acknowledge that the managers' carpet was in grave danger of being tarnished. Not surprisingly, the administration manager became disconcerted and called for another adjournment. No subsequent meetings were timetabled for this early in the morning. The union official had been able to draw upon and convert what appeared to be a managerial tactic of control and discipline into an effective tactic of resistance thereby shifting power from the manager to the subordinates.

At the reconvened meeting, the union official challenged each of the five justifications provided by the superintendent. The first point about personality was contradicted by written reports received from insurance brokers concerning Jane's work performance and communication skills. Jane had received excellent assessment reports which commented on the supervisory qualities that she had shown in motivating and guiding young trainee inspectors. Second, the view that Jane was not fully committed was contradicted by her outstanding assessment reports. Third, regarding the reputed critical comments, the union representative argued that it was completely untenable to base promotion decisions on hearsay. Moreover, Jane totally denied making these particular remarks. Fourth, statements regarding Jane's overtime record were incorrect since she had actually worked an extra ten hours in both January and February 1987. In addition, the union representative argued that commitment to overtime was not a valid criterion for making promotion decisions. Finally, that Jane had not begun to sit her professional examinations (although she had always intended to do so) was completely irrelevant anyway, it was argued, since neither had the two appointees. The union representative concluded that clearly these five justifications were based on incorrect information and thus could not be the real reason for Jane's rejection: 'so if these are not the formal criteria, because they can't be the criteria, what are the criteria?' she asked.

So far, the union strategy had sought to extract more detailed information from management about the formal selection criteria. This was a necessary precondition for resistance. However, it was by no means sufficient to translate a grievance into a successful challenge. Other more strategic and political knowledges and practices were now needed. Despite the union's counter-arguments, the administration manager refused to revise or even reconsider the decision. He stated that legally binding offer letters had already been sent to the successful candidates, there were no other vacancies and the branch manager had ratified the superintendent's decision which he also continued to support.

As the local management still refused to reconsider their decision, the trade union representative referred the case to the company's corporate personnel department. She implied that strong grounds existed for the case to be taken to the Equal Opportunities Commission. In the changing corporate climate senior personnel managers were very concerned about these possible developments. As a result, the latter placed extensive 'discreet' pressure on the local managers to upgrade the clerk regardless of whether another vacancy actually existed. Local managers knew that any promotion for Jane would exceed their staffing levels agreed with head office. This new grade-seven salary would be an additional unbudgeted cost that local management would have to cover from other financial sources within their branch. In addition, a change in the decision would lead to a loss of face for the local managers. They were therefore extremely reluctant to reverse their decision. However, as a result of the knowledge and resilience of the clerk, the experience and persistence of the trade union representative and her ability to expose the contradictions of the managers' rationalizations combined with the informal pressure by corporate personnel, the local managers eventually conceded that the clerk would be upgraded. Jane Bamber took statutory maternity leave and subsequently returned to work after the minimum period of absence.

This case study reveals how during the grievance procedure managers' strategies of control, particularly through their attempts to restrict information, had the effect of reinforcing the determination of both the clerk and the union representative to persist in their resistance against this promotion decision. The superintendent's initial failure to offer any explanation for the clerk's rejection alerted her to the possibility that she was probably being unfairly treated.

45

Her suspicions were compounded by inconsistencies and inaccuracies in the managers' formal rationalizations. Once these contradictions were exposed, the managers' continued refusal to reverse their decision and their failure to offer an adequate explanation confirmed to the clerk that behind these formal discourses, the managers' hidden concern was her pregnancy (see also Martin, 1990).

The decision to arrange a crucial meeting in the early morning appeared to both women to constitute a managerial control strategy. However, this practice had precisely the opposite effect, because it merely strengthened the clerk's resolve to resist. To be effective, the woman's resistance had to be informed, extremely persistent and determined. A central strategy was the securing of more detailed technical information from managers about their decision-making process. Using various local and strategic knowledges, the clerk and the trade union representative were then able to press for the decision eventually to be overturned. In the power struggles that ensued, specific overlapping knowledges were crucially important factors in strengthening this resistance, which in turn eventually resulted in local management being outflanked.

In addition to the information extracted from local management during the grievance process, Jane had the *technical and organizational* knowledge concerning much of this specific selection exercise which reinforced her critical appraisal of those events. She was aware of the promotion criteria, the credentials of the other candidates, her own past performance and the superintendents' assurances of her future promotion. She had also observed the managerial practices leading up to this specific selection decision. To Jane, therefore, management was relatively visible throughout the exercise. She was, of course, also familiar with past selection practices in the branch. Such detailed, localized and historical knowledge is usually unavailable to external candidates.

The trade union official had considerable knowledge, understanding and experience of the bureaucratic formalities of the grievance procedure, having represented union members throughout the country over several years. This was combined with strategic knowledge concerning the politics of resistance which enabled her to counter the intended effects of management's disciplinary practices. By requesting the formal criteria for Jane's rejection, the union representative rendered management's practices even more visible and accountable. She could therefore expose the contradictions and inconsistencies in the managements' formal promotion decision and use the company hierarchy against the branch-level management by going 'over their heads' and taking the case direct to corporate personnel. This information would otherwise never have come to the attention of personnel specialists at corporate level.

Furthermore, the union official was able to suggest that the Equal Opportunities Commission might be interested in the details of the case. Her legal knowledge of sex discrimination cases made her confident about the relative merits of pursuing the grievance. This suggestion resonated with a growing sensitivity in the ranks of corporate managers regarding equal opportunities that reflected the 'culture change' being introduced by the new American multinational owners of the insurance company. Indeed, the anti-discrimination legislation itself was a precondition for and legitimation of the employees' attempts to monitor and challenge management's decision-making about promotion. Prior to this legislation, such scrutiny of internal selection decisions by subordinates would never have been accepted by management.

The Equal Opportunities Commission research project un-covered several similar examples of persistent resistance where national-level trade unionists were able to exploit divisions between different levels of the managerial hierarchy in order to challenge and overturn unfair decisions. Unlike employees working in a specific location, national union officials have access to and knowledge of corporate managers. In Jane's case, social knowledge was an important precondition for effective resistance through persistence. Both women had some knowledge of the personalities and preferences of managers at local level which facilitated their ability to identify discrepancies, gaps and inconsistencies in the selection practices. The union representative knew corporate managers who were willing to examine the formal documents of the case and to rectify the position. Relatedly, the two women trusted each other. They were long-standing work colleagues, both from the north of England. Discussions with both women revealed a close gender-based identification between them. The trade union representative had two children of her own and understood some of the difficulties of managing paid work and pregnancy. Equally, Jane had confidence in the ability and commitment of the union representative and was therefore willing to follow the advice and guidance given to her throughout the procedure. Hence, the case also reveals a gendered form of knowledge that facilitated the effectiveness of their resistance.

Finally, some knowledge of or about self also appeared to be critically important for withstanding the tremendous psychological pressure involved in resistance through persistence. Jane's case illustrates the intensification of power struggles and strategies that often occur as the grievance procedure progresses. Jane had to withstand the cumulative pressures of managerial strategies of control, discounting and personalism; the fear of subsequent victimization by different supervisory levels and the on-going disciplinary discourses of both men and women work colleagues, many of whom insisted that Jane was 'going too far'. This required extensive determination, fortitude and conviction. Trade union support was very helpful, but this in itself was unlikely to have been enough. Crucially important here was Jane's belief in the legitimacy of her grievance and her determination to reject the pejorative definitions of identity ascribed to her by managers, supervisors and even colleagues.

Those seeking to discipline subordinates and colleagues frequently seek to dismiss their resistance by imputing negative motives. So, for example, derogatory labels or identities such as 'trouble-maker', 'whinger', 'chip on their shoulder', 'jealous' and 'looney feminist' frequently have significant symbolic and disciplinary impact on those considering resistance. Hence, in addition to issues of power, knowledge and information, definitions of identity and subjectivity are an important feature of workplace struggles. On the one hand, the anticipation of these negative identities might be a crucial limitation on explicit oppositional practices. Yet, on the other hand, disciplinary practices can actually reinforce resistance through persistence by intensifying the determination of the aggrieved. This is most likely where those who resist are not dependent on authority for identity confirmation. Rather, they are confident in the legitimacy of the specific case and refuse to reduce the negotiations to issues of personality. Jane's case illustrates some of the difficulties facing individual resisters who may experience much greater visibility than those involved in collective action. It also demonstrates how subordinates can outflank disciplinary processes by engaging in resistance through persistence.

CONCLUSION: RESISTANCE, KNOWLEDGE, POWER AND SUBJECTIVITY

What are the implications of the foregoing analysis for a critical understanding of workplace resistance and employee behaviour? Certainly, the analysis suggests that subordinates have available a variety of options, knowledges, cultural resources and strategic agencies through which they can and do initiate oppositional practices. Workplace resistance may seek to challenge, disrupt or invert prevailing assumptions, discourses and power relations. It can take multiple material and symbolic forms, and its strength, influence and intensity are likely to be variable and to shift over time (Brown, 1992). Resistance constitutes a form of power exercised by subordinates in the workplace.

Employees resist despite their subordinate and insecure organizational position and despite their never having full information or knowledge of future consequences. Dissatisfaction, disenchantment and frustration pervades the lives of many employees in contemporary organizations. Those at the lower levels of hierarchies often feel particularly vulnerable, unfairly treated and unacknowledged and most excluded from decision-making procedures. Their sense of grievance and insecurity frequently translates into oppositional discursive practices. While these practices may not always be revolutionary or even effective in the sense of securing significant organizational change, it is equally overly simplistic to suggest that resistance is 'so frequently outflanked'. Accordingly, the current analytical concentration on consent or outflanking is in danger of neglecting this crucially important feature of routine organizational practices.

Workplace resistance crucially draws upon various forms of knowledge. In practice subordinates have extensive knowledge which may not be shared with those in more senior positions, and which can be used as an important 'weapon of resistance' (Scott, 1986). Like resistance, knowledge itself can take multiple forms in organizational life. Oppositional practices are usually informed by the strategic exercise of particular knowledges which may be, for example, technical, bureaucratic and procedural, social, regional, cultural and historical, legal, economic, strategic/political and/or about self. These knowledges should neither be understated nor overstated when examining the discursive practices of subordinates. They are likely to overlap, be somewhat indeterminate, partial and shifting and often be couched in ambiguity, uncertainty and insecurity. Equally they may be highly specialist and narrow or more tacit and difficult to objectify (Polanyi and Prosch, 1975; Kusterer, 1978; Manwaring and Wood, 1985; Davies and Rosser, 1986; Lazega, 1992). They might even be used in ways that express cooperation and consent rather than resistance (Manwaring and Wood, 1985). Nevertheless, these various knowledges can be an important condition and consequence of resistance. Whether specific practices are best defined in terms of resistance or consent or both will be determined by the particular power relations and by employees' subjective orientation, commitments and indeed motivation and determination.

This focus on employee knowledge therefore raises issues about subjectivity. The foregoing case studies display two quite distinct subjective orientations to the acquisition and use of information and to authority in organizations. Resistance through distance involves a denial of involvement or interest in key organizational processes. It is very much an 'escape attempt' (Cohen and Taylor, 1992). In the engineering factory, knowledge and information were concealed by subordinates who engaged in defensive practices that sought to minimize their involvement in the company, while embellishing an oppositional sense of gender and class-specific identity and maximizing their economic return from work. Resistance through persistence, by contrast, may involve the acquisition of further information and knowledge in order to develop a critical analysis of organizational practices. In the insurance case study, this critical analysis was presented in such a strategic and determined way that an, albeit small, amount of organizational change was generated. Both companies were experiencing cultural change initiated by new American owners. While the shopfloor workers totally rejected the new corporate culture in their organization, the women insurance workers used the culture change as a means of justifying their monitoring and challenging of managerial practices. Resistance through persistence proved to be a much more effective oppositional strategy to conventional power relations. (See also McBarnet, *et al.*, 1993 for a similar kind of analysis regarding the disclosure and strategic acquisition of financial information.)

Whatever form resistance takes, however, it is always inextricably linked to organizational discipline, control and power. Resistance is rarely equal to control, neither is it necessarily successful nor fundamentally subversive in its effects (Henriques, *et al.*, 1984). Yet resistance cannot be examined as if it were separate from workplace discipline and control. Oppositional practices often draw upon the very forms of control that generate resistance in the first place. Indeed, control and resistance can be so mutually reproducing that they actually constitute one another. This is particularly likely where subordinates engage in resistance through distance. Moreover, it should be remembered that resistance is not always the rationally organized result of strategic planning and instrumental calculation. Opposition might be expressed through humour using ambiguity, irony and satire. It may be a spontaneous reaction to a particular event, possibly expressed in anger and frustration. Alternatively, it might not be an entirely conscious act but instead could be expressed in what Giddens terms 'practical consciousness' (Giddens, 1979: 148). Here even those who resist might not identify, explain or even recognize their actions as explicitly oppositional. Such practices are unlikely to be effective forms of resistance given the disciplinary processes that characterize contemporary organizations.

While control frequently generates resistance, as various labour process writers have demonstrated, resistance may also reinforce a managerial concern with further controls, as Taylor's (1947) work illustrates. Both control and resistance can therefore become intertwined within an organizational vicious circle in which power is exercised through mutually-reproducing strategies and counter-strategies.[10] Hence an unintended and contradictory consequence of both resistance and control might be the reproduction of one another (Collinson, 1992a). Having said that, resistance will not reproduce conventional power relations in any simple, mechanical and predetermined way but will have a variety of important organizational effects, many of which cannot be specified outside of particular workplaces and industries. Indeed resistance through persistence has the potential to overcome these mutually-reinforcing vicious circles by outflanking disciplinary practices.

An important feature of the oppositional strategies examined in the foregoing case studies is the overlapping and mutually embedded character of consent, compliance and resistance. In each case, resistance was circumscribed by elements of ambiguity, consent and compliance. Even the most critical and radical workers in the engineering factory supported managerial prerogative. Although in their view this was consistent with their oppositional discourses, it simultaneously expressed an ambivalence and acceptance of the prevailing power asymmetries of the company. Resistance through distance was contained *within*, rather than *against*, the idea of hierarchy and authority.

Ostensibly, resistance through persistence in the insurance company was relatively more effective, since an unfair decision was successfully challenged and overturned, which in turn had the effect of promoting equal opportunity issues throughout the company. Yet, here again, resistance was limited. It constituted a partial challenge to, but was also paradoxically confined within the principle of managerial prerogative. While it would be inaccurate to dismiss or reduce this resistance to some notion of 'outflanking', equally it would be inappropriate to overstate its radical intentions and/or effects. The employee's demand for meritocratic treatment in promotion can be interpreted simultaneously as an expression of both resistance to patriarchical control practices and of consent to conventional career progression and to the legitimacy of hierarchical organization. The case displays the rationality, knowledgeability and determination of those who resisted. Yet underpinning these strategic practices was a set of co-existent and partly incompatible and unresolved views about hierarchy and management. As in the engineering factory, managers were heavily criticized and attacked, but a fundamental and collective challenge to the prevailing organization of production seemed highly unlikely.[11]

Few studies in the literature on resistance and consent adequately account for these shifting ambiguities, ambivalences, confusions, partial knowledges, inconsistencies, multiple motives and paradoxical effects that comprise the subjective reality of organizational power relations. Indeed, a common problem with a great deal of the current critical literature on employee behaviour is its failure to address adequately the way in which conventional power relations are *subjectively* experienced, reproduced, challenged and sometimes even reversed in workplace practices.[12] When exploring these subjective dimensions, it is important for organization theorists to recognize that, on the one hand, all those involved in the labour process at all hierarchical levels are likely to be skilled, knowledgeable and creative actors in both a social and technical sense (Giddens, 1979). Subjectivity should therefore not be neglected. On the other hand, subjectivity is also simultaneously a specific, historical product embedded within particular conditions and power relations. It is ambiguous, fragmentary and multiple, sometimes non-rational, often contradictory (Henriques *et al.*, 1984) and frequently characterized by anxiety and uncertainty. Hence subjectivity should neither be subordinated to, nor treated as sovereign and privileged above, the analysis of power. Subjectivity and power are inextricably interwoven in all organizational practices (see also Knights and Vurdubakis, ch. 5 of this volume).

Yet, in the literature, either employee subjectivity and knowledgeability are downgraded and treated as the determined outcome of the particular workplace 'rules of the game' (e.g. Burawoy, 1979, 1985; Clegg, 1989; Mills and Murgatroyd, 1991) or else workers are seen as highly rational, knowledgeable and strategic in their subversive discursive practices (e.g. Willis, 1977, 1980; Scott, 1985). Both perspectives provide at best a partial analysis of workplace practices that is limited by a tendency to overstate either consent and compliance or dissent and resistance and to separate the latter from the former. I will briefly explore examples of each approach in turn.

Clegg's (1987) empirical analysis of the behaviour of joiners on a building site illustrates the tendency to overstate consent and to separate it from resistance. He described how joiners regularly stopped work on the pretext that the weather was 'inclement'. Drawing on Burawoy's game metaphor, Clegg argued that the joiners played these 'games' of work stoppage in order to 'put pressure on the management to increase control and thus more efficiently exploit them' (Clegg 1987: 65). According to Clegg, this was because the workers were unable to maximize their bonus since management failed to provide material and supplies in a timely manner. The 'inclemency rule' was the joiners' way of putting pressure on to management. He concluded that these workers 'happily collude in intensifying their own subjection' (p. 65). Yet this analysis fails to explore the accounts of the joiners themselves.[13] The author's own interpretation tends to be somewhat derogatory of the joiners in emphasizing their deliberate willingness to collude in their own subjection. No mention is made of resistance, even though the workers' strategies were consistent with an oppositional economic instrumentalism that sought to maximize bonus by improving the flow of supplies. In short, an alternative reading of Clegg's example would be that it illustrates the complex, contradictory and simultaneous expression of workplace resistance and consent.[14]

By contrast with this analysis, several of the most valuable qualitative studies of resistance tend to overstate and/or romanticize oppositional practices. These analyses are informed by overly-rationalist and essentialist assumptions regarding agency, subjectivity and human action. For example, in his study of Malaysian peasant resistance, Scott (1985) argued that although the peasants are forced to conform in their actions, they still resist in their discourses, thoughts and ideas. Mitchell (1990) rejects Scott's emphasis on the internal mental autonomy of peasants because it presupposes that there is a social sphere 'where the play of power does not penetrate, where discourse becomes authentic' (Mitchell 1990: 564). Such analyses according to Mitchell seek to uncover 'a collective self that is the author of its own cultural constructions and actions . . . a site of "essential truth"' (p. 564). Overly-rationalist and essentialist assumptions about subjectivity and resistance take for granted the notion of a pre-existing selfhood that is authentic, self-produced and sustained against an objective, oppressive and material world (see also Scott, 1990). Accordingly, the identities and counter-culture of the subordinated are left unquestioned and an exaggerated radicalism is imputed to their class cultural practices.

Overly-rationalist assumptions regarding subjectivity and resistance are also found in Willis's (1977, 1980) examination of the counter-cultural practices of a group of English working-class kids known as 'the lads'. Willis argues that they see through the dominant ideology of equal opportunity, its claim to evaluate individuals objectively and its legitimization of prevailing hierarchical relations. Although their 'penetrations' currently remain partial, Willis sees in the counter-culture the 'potential here for a not merely partial and cultural but a total social transformation' (Willis, 1977: 137). Willis's study highlights the agency and creativity of highly subordinated individuals in a class-ridden society and also displays some of the contradictory outcomes of their creative discursive practices of resistance.

However, Willis seems to overstate the knowledgeability of the lads and to exaggerate the extent of their partial 'penetrations' of class inequality. Like Scott, he assumes that subordinates' counter-culture contains an authenticity or existential truth that differentiates it from the objective, oppressive and material world of class inequality and capitalist domination. In the absence of any critical analysis of the lads' subjectivity, their motivations and proud boastings, Willis fails to recognize that their oppositional practices could simultaneously constitute acts of conformity to the expectations of the counter-cultural group. Class society reinforces identity problems or status anxieties particularly for those in subordinated positions (Sennett and Cobb, 1977). A great deal of the lads' behaviour can be interpreted not so much as an entirely rational critique of class inequality, as Willis suggests, but rather as a defensive/aggressive means of constructing a more positive sense of self or group identity than that provided by the school.

Hence those who engage in collective forms of resistance are likely to do so for a multiplicity of different, often individualistic reasons. Some radical writers, however, have neglected this complexity and the defensiveness, fragility and precariousness that frequently characterizes collective practices. In searching for 'pure' and 'authentic' forms of resistance, they have also tended to deny or understate the possible organizational significance and effects of individual forms of resistance. Yet, in certain cases, individual opposition might be more significant than collective resistance. For example, Jane Bamber's face-to-face and highly-visible resistance with management was not only more tenacious, traumatic and dangerous than the concealed, escapist and patriarchal strategies of shopfloor workers, but was also more effective in generating organizational change. For Jane, this sustained challenge to her superiors was indeed a radical act of defiance. Not only was Jane's approach important in enhancing her working life, but it may also have been the most appropriate strategy for establishing and sustaining further organizational change. Such oppositional practices should therefore not be ignored or under-estimated by critical organization theorists. Neither, of course, should they be romanticized nor treated as the existential expression of a rational resisting subject.

The assumptions about human agency and subjectivity under-pinning the work of Scott, Willis and other writers on resistance have been critiqued by Kondo (1990: 218–25). She argues that current notions of resistance and accommodation are inadequate particularly because they assume a wholly rational subject whose views would be consistent and uncontradictory were it not for the influence of dominant ideologies. Kondo highlights a failure in the literature to recognize that opposition is usually mitigated by elements of collusion and compromise, and that compliance can contain unanticipated subversive effects.[15] Rejecting the notion of a 'pristine space of authentic resistance' (p. 224), a realm of meaning beyond power relations, discourse or law, Kondo argues that actors should be seen as 'multiple selves whose lives are shot through with contradictions and creative tensions' (p. 224). She therefore rejects conventional notions of a fixed, static and singular identity and the simplistic assumption in the work of Scott and Willis that their respondents are 'true resisters' (pp. 220, 323). The subjective dimension cannot be reduced to an exclusive focus on labour resistance (Knights, 1990).

Challenging the dominant views of subjectivity and power found in analyses of resistance, Kondo outlines her ethnographic study of a family-owned Japanese factory to reveal the embedded character of consent, compliance and resistance. She describes how the subversive discourses of men and women shopfloor workers which often highlight managerial inconsistencies, can themselves be caught in contradictions and ironies, simultaneously legitimizing as they challenge dominant organizational and gendered discourses. In these workplace practices, characterized by ambiguity, paradox and shifting power relations, individuals construct multiple selves that are gendered, ambiguous and fragmented. Kondo's account reveals many of the ironies and ambiguities that are a condition and consequence of the crafting of selves within shifting fields of power. It therefore makes an important contribution to the critical analysis of workplace power, knowledge and subjectivity with its emphasis on the overlapping character of consent, compliance and resistance.[16]

What is missing from her analysis is any examination of the anxieties and insecurities that are frequently the medium and outcome of the subjective search to craft one or more selves through interwoven practices of control, resistance, compliance or consent. While technical and strategic knowledge is an important precondition for effective resistance, the subjective ability to deal with the disciplinary pressures and ensuing anxieties, ambiguities and uncertainties of conflict are equally crucial. A capacity to handle the pressures is at least in part derived from a recognition that the paradoxical search to secure particular social identities is likely to intensify rather than eliminate insecurity and anxiety (Knights, 1990; Collinson, 1992a). Hence identity concerns may not only facilitate but also constrain oppositional practices. Nonetheless, issues of identity are always likely to be one feature of the multiple motives that invariably inform human action. Where oppositional practices are shaped *predominantly* by identity – seeking motives, however, they are likely to be characterized by greater self-consciousness, anxiety and defensiveness which in turn will lead to less-effective forms of resistance. Two propositions follow. First, the more concerned individuals are with crafting selves, the less effective will be their oppositional practices. This is illustrated by the shopfloor workers' resistance through distance. Conversely, resistance is likely to be more effective when those involved are less concerned with the construction and protection of identity and more committed to the issues on which their opposition is based. This seemed to be the case in the second example of resistance through persistence. Hence, oppositional strategies that seek to increase employee involvement in organizational processes and to render managerial practices more visible and accountable have greater effectiveness than those primarily concerned with distancing.

To conclude, this chapter has been concerned to highlight the analytical importance of workplace resistance and to explore some of its interconnections with knowledge, power and subjectivity. Workplace resistance remains a persistent, significant and remarkable feature of modern organizations. Subordinates do continue to resist and articulate their dissatisfaction in innumerable ways despite considerable disciplinary barriers and insecurities. As we have seen, the commodification of labour not only reflects and reinforces managerial and hierarchical control, but also intensifies extensive material and symbolic insecurity for those in subordinate positions. The ever-present possibility of losing one's job is a significant discipline and disincentive to resist or challenge managerial practices (see also Littler, 1990). Job insecurity has intensified in many countries over the past decade as market processes have increasingly impacted on occupations and industries and unemployment rates have grown.

These insecurities and barriers to resistance are reinforced by the organizational structures of multi-divisional and multinational companies. In these large and powerful corporations primary decision-making processes are usually undertaken far away from operating units, and often in another country (see Ramsay and Howarth, 1989). Consequently, within these conglomerates, it is not merely labour, but operating units and even whole companies that are disposable. When combined with the additional pressures of domestic responsibilities and the need to provide for children and to finance a mortgage, dissatisfied employees may well decide to just 'grin and bear it' and to accommodate to the status quo in order to guarantee a wage or salary.

Where employment or income are so precarious, career advancement is often perceived to be both an escape from the most vulnerable jobs at the bottom of the organization and a means of securing greater pay and status. Career structures invariably characterize contemporary organizations. Yet these structures constitute another significant barrier to the mobilization of any form of dissent because aspiring individuals will frequently perceive extensive career damage arising from opposing those who also make decisions regarding their hierarchical progress or who would be asked to provide references and testimonies regarding their work performance. Resistance can generate reprisals.[17] In addition, conformity or compliant practices often have self-fulfilling effects. If the majority of work colleagues are unwilling to oppose management, those who would resist are aware that their actions have even less chance of being effective. The conformity or compliance of the many thus frequently disciplines the oppositional practices of the few.

As the second case study demonstrated, the marginalization of those who resist is further reinforced by the likely managerial response which typically will seek to negate the legitimacy of the particular grievance being articulated and to emphasize the so-called 'personality problems' of those who dissent. Negative motives may be imputed to the dissenters in order to discredit their legitimacy. While current systems and practices of control and discipline are deemed to be normal and legitimate, oppositional behaviour is thereby treated as aberrant, deviant and unjustifiable. In such discursive struggles, managers are in an advantaged position because they often have the material and symbolic resources and information to facilitate the widest dissemination of their definition of reality. Practices of resistance through distance are especially likely to reinforce subordinates' vulnerability to these disciplinary processes.

In what appear to be increasingly disciplinary and insecure employment conditions, it is remarkable indeed that strategies of workplace resistance continue to characterize organizational practices. This chapter has examined some of the organizational conditions, processes and consequences of resistance. It has identified two consistent and distinctive patterns of resistance that, while not being exhaustive of possible oppositional practices, might well have a broader applicability.[18] Highlighting how these different oppositional practices are shaped by specific power relations, knowledges and subjectivities, the foregoing analysis suggests that it is resistance through persistence in particular that has the potential to counter and even outflank disciplinary practices within contemporary organizations. Although workplace resistance does not always constitute a fundamental challenge to conventional power relations, it is a crucially important feature of organizational life which therefore requires further detailed conceptual and empirical examination by critical scholars of organizations.

NOTES

1 In Clegg's most recent work, *Modern Organisations* (1990), workplace resistance is rarely mentioned at all. The relationship between power and resistance is addressed in more detail in *Frameworks of Power* (1989). However, much more attention is paid here to the way that resistance is outflanked than to oppositional practices themselves.

2 Burawoy's (1979; 1985) emphasis on the way that consent is manufactured and reproduced within the labour process has been enormously influential. His study of workers' involvement in the game of 'making out' has significantly shaped assumptions within the labour process literature regarding not only resistance but also employee behaviour, their discursive practices, counter-cultures and subjectivities more broadly. The result has been a tendency to assume that in late modern organizations conflict and oppositional practices are being replaced by forms of organization that are effective in generating employee consent, compliance and/or subordination. If shopfloor workers can so easily be absorbed into game playing and believe that their immersion in making out is 'freely chosen' (1979: 29) then, as writers on the labour process, we need not spend precious time researching resistance because the data will simply not be there. In what follows, I argue that this approach overstates employee consent in the labour process to the neglect of compliance and resistance. (For other critiques, see Clawson and Fantasia, 1983; Knights and Collinson, 1985; Knights, 1990; Davies, 1990; Collinson, 1992a and footnote 14).

3 Clegg's approach to outflanking appears simultaneously to understate and overstate the knowledgeability of subordinates. The latter viewpoint rests on a set of highly rationalistic assumptions regarding subjectivity in which subordinates are seen as totally rational, calculative and instrumental with extensive skills of prediction. Yet those who resist are rarely, if ever fully aware of the consequences of their actions. While, they may fear intensified discipline, material and symbolic reprisals and victimization, these anxieties are merely expectations or anticipations of possible consequences. They may or may not be accurate. Clegg cites the rather atypical example of Nazi extermination camps to argue that inmates would not organize resistance for fear of failure and certain death. Yet the personal experience of Primo Levi (1987a, 1987b) suggests that forms of resistance did occur even in these brutalizing conditions. In such cases, resistance could even take the form of suicide. Death becomes one

means of escaping from the horror. Burrell (1984) has also revealed how homosexual relationships still emerged despite attempts by the Nazis to ensure their eradication. Perhaps a better example of how knowing can limit workplace resistance is in the case of managers who provide trade union officials with confidential, 'off the record' information that cannot be used or communicated to members. This often has the effect of reducing the possibility of resistance. However, Clegg's analysis at best provides only a partial account. The relationship between subjectivity and resistance can be the exact opposite of that which he suggests. In some cases 'not knowing' may facilitate resistance and the determination to see a challenge through. There are significant material and symbolic costs and pressures associated with resistance, many of which may be unfamiliar to those who decide to resist. In such cases initial ignorance could facilitate resistance rather than impair it (see also Rothschild and Miethe, ch. 4 of this volume). Yet in Clegg's analysis, there is no space for these non-rational aspects of subjectivity and motivation. Indeed, there is no analytical space for the examination of motives whatsoever (see also note 13 below).

4 While workers may not be fully cognizant of bureaucratic procedures, they often control technical, performance-related knowledge. It was precisely this control that Taylor sought to eliminate through scientific management principles (see also Manwaring and Wood, 1985; Davies and Rosser, 1986). Moreover, in his earlier work, Clegg (1979) himself highlighted workers' 'discretionary knowledge power' as a facilitator of workplace resistance. Ten years later, however, he talks of subordinates being 'ignorant' rather than about various types of knowledge producing different effects. Multiple knowledges have an important role within oppositional practices, as the case studies will outline later.

5 Since a great deal of resistance draws on a thorough knowledge of the technical and social organization of production, securing data on resistance can be difficult for researchers of organizations who may not possess such detailed information and understanding about routine practices. Equally, in some cases employees' statements are more oppositional than their practices. In other cases, it is not so much what respondents say, but more how they act that reveals grievances and workplace tensions. Hence, resistance often occurs at a highly informal, concealed and subterranean level that is deeply embedded in organizational practices. A great deal of time, effort and perseverance is necessary for researchers to develop the relationships of trust and familiarity that would make employees willing to reveal their covert practices of resistance. Like managers, employees may have strong reasons for restricting information to outside researchers. Hence, we often find considerable resistance to the study of resistance in organizations.

6 This was the headline on the first edition of the new house magazine designed to herald the culture change in the organization. It refers to the American managing director who is encouraging people to recognize management's open door policy.

7 He elaborated, 'what they do is, they keep us in the dark and then shit on us occasionally. That's how you grow mushrooms!'

8 Paradoxically, resistance through distance could also include managerial practices undertaken by shop stewards and workers. Indeed, workers' knowledge in various ways resulted in them managing the production process despite their oppositional discourses. Moreover, some workers managed their own businesses outside work. For example, one worker ran an off-licence selling alcohol and confectionery and another owned a fish and chip shop. The ways in which shopfloor workers managed production are elaborated in Collinson (1992a).

9 In an insurance office, as on the shopfloor of an engineering factory, resistance through distance can take many forms. For example, Jane could have: avoided dealing with telephone enquiries; spent longer periods in the toilet, picked up files off her desk under the pretext of researching a difficult problem and then left the department to talk with friends in other areas (see Collinson, 1993). Generally, Jane could have worked much more slowly than she had done previously and for which she had received strong praise in her annual appraisals.

10 Accordingly, what is an exercise of power/control and what is an exercise of resistance becomes difficult to disentangle. This is particularly so since resistance is not merely the prerogative of those most subordinated in organizations for even managers can engage in oppositional practices (see LaNuez and Jermier, ch. 8 of this volume, Collinson *et al.*, 1990). However, particular practices are invariably located in specific conditions of power asymmetries and inequalities which in turn largely determine whether they are best seen as an exercise of power or of resistance.

11 It could be argued that this contradictory and mutually embedded character of consent and resistance is simply a condition and consequence of the contradictory nature of the capitalist labour process in which conflict and interdependence co-exist (Cressey and Macinnes, 1980; Hyman, 1987). However, as Knights (1990) has argued in his criticisms of Cressey and Macinnes, an explanation of the reproduction of these contradictory features of employee behaviour requires a critical analysis of subjectivity as well as power.

12 The foregoing case-study material was presented in order to explore the relationship between resistance and knowledge in particular. There was not the space to develop a more detailed analysis of subjectivity (see Collinson, 1992a). Suffice it to say here, that viewing subjectivity as contradictory, ambiguous and shifting has important methodological and analytical implications. Case studies cannot claim to constitute an objective representation of 'organizational reality'. Such notions of objectivity deny the phenomenological processes and power relations at work in the conduct of research (see Collinson, 1992b). Hence the foregoing empirical analysis was merely one version amongst several that could have been presented. When presenting case study material it is therefore important to be explicit in outlining one's assumptions and analytical framework. It is then for the reader to decide on the plausibility of the argument by critically examining the coherence and

integration of the theoretical and empirical analysis. The value of case study material lies in its potential to question the validity of more abstract constructs while also illustrating and 'breathing life' into these analytical themes.

13 This neglect, however, is justified by Clegg in his later work (1989) where he highlights the methodological problems of trying to access 'the internal mental and intentional well-springs of another's causal actions' (p. 3). He argues that intention should not be associated with 'the private mental states of persons' (p. 210) but rather with 'currently "fixed" representations for making sense of what people do' (p. 210). For Clegg, since these 'vocabularies of motive' (Mills, 1940) are determined by current social rules (Clegg, 1989: 10), it is to an examination of rules and structures which we should turn. He contends that any resource to the actor's own account as an explanation will be fundamentally flawed (p. 3). While acknowledging that there is no perfect access to the subjective accounts of respondents (or of oneself, for that matter), I would reject this view. To argue that actors' accounts have no explanatory value is to reproduce the deterministic analytical perspective for which Braverman has been so heavily criticized and to derogate the subject in Giddens's (1979) terms. Even if accounts are to some extent rationalizations of practices, they may still shape future conduct (Mills, 1940: 907) and are nonetheless instructive and useful in innumerable ways. A reliance on these accounts would be problematic, but a recourse can enhance our understanding of organizational processes. Indeed, some of the most valuable studies of organizations in the past 20 years have been ethnographies that have taken accounts into consideration and examined them critically, locating them within broader conditions and consequences. It seems strange that Clegg acknowledges the 'embodied agency of subordinates' (p. 194), but then rejects any value in actors' accounts and rationalizations as at least a partial explanation of their discursive practices. Paradoxically, Clegg's position does not seem to restrict him from imputing (overly rationalist) motives and intentions on to those about whom he writes.

14 Like Clegg, Burawoy's analysis of employee consent fails to examine workers' accounts of their practices (see Collinson, 1992a). *Manufacturing Consent* is a study of observed workplace practices by a researcher tied for long periods to a particular machine. It therefore does not explore the subtleties and complexities of worker subjectivity, meaning and discourses that are the condition and consequence of these practices. Far from privileging subjectivity as some have claimed, Burawoy neglects it both empirically and analytically. Although Burawoy (1979: 229) is critical of Marxism and Althusserian structuralism for their reduction of 'wage labourers to objects of manipulation; to commodities bought and sold in the market' (p. 77), Burawoy's own account tends towards a deterministic analysis that derogates workers who are seen to be embroiled in and hoodwinked by the game of 'making out' and the wider capitalist society. In various places, and particularly in the footnotes, Burawoy does acknowledge his neglect of any discussion of subjectivity or what he terms 'explicit

psychology' and 'theory of human nature' (pp. 125, 157, 237). However, he seeks to justify this omission on the grounds that, 'presenting individuals as carriers or agents of social relations . . . captures the essential quality of existence under capitalism. Within such a context psychology can be reduced to a theory of needs: how capitalism generates needs, what these needs are in the different phases of its development, and whether capitalism can satisfy the needs it produces' (p. 236). In Burawoy's analysis, then, agency is reduced to an essentialist needs theory determined by the functionalist requirements of surplus value appropriation in an all-pervasive capitalist system. Social forces are given complete analytical primacy whilst human agency and subjectivity are neglected.

15 In the engineering factory, those workers who articulated a more explicit discourse of consent also criticized certain managers for their failure to live up to the 'hard but fair' image that they held of the ideal-typical authority figure. In their eyes, 'real' managers should be tough but reasonable. This negation of individual managers has been termed 'idealized substitution' by Sennett (1980). In this process, particular managers or leaders were criticized, but in ways that implicitly confirmed the legitimacy of hierarchy and control. As a result, many of these workers decided to stop informing supervisors and managers on ideas to improve working materials and product design. In addition, consent was often interpreted by these workers as a form of opposition to the majority of colleagues who they argued were intent on 'causing trouble' or 'skiving' from work.

16 Feminist ethnographies have demonstrated how the resistance of organized male labour can simultaneously constitute forms of oppression against women (e.g. Cockburn, 1983, 1991; Walby, 1986). Seeking to exclude or segregate women in order to protect the male 'breadwinner wage', men workers' resistance is clearly revealed to be a simultaneous exercise of power and control over women.

17 For example, Stanley Adams and his wife suffered severe consequences for his whistleblowing. In 1973, before resigning as world-product manager of the Swiss-based drug company, Hoffman-La Roche, Adams revealed the multinational's involvement in illicit price fixing, market sharing with competitors and oppressive control of the worldwide vitamin market. Roche was subsequently fined $430,000 by the European Economic Community. However, the company accused Adams of industrial espionage and treason. He was arrested in Switzerland, charged and given a three-year suspended sentence. During Adams's detention, his wife committed suicide (Adams, 1984; Madeley, 1986). More recently, a spate of 'whistleblowing' in UK public-sector organizations in the 1980s has resulted in the government considering the introduction of 'gagging clauses' into employment contracts, for example in the National Health Service.

18 Michael Muetzelfeldt and Jill Graham have both suggested certain similarities between the two strategies of resistance explored in this chapter and Hirschman's (1970) categories of 'exit' and 'voice'. Hirschman argues that in responding to organizational decline,

individuals will either resign/escape from (exit) or try to change (voice) products, conditions or processes which they find objectionable. Focusing heavily upon consumer behaviour, however, this perspective fails to acknowledge the distinctive nature of power relations *within* employment. Its economistic orientation is based on a rationalistic and voluntaristic notion of the subject that ignores the social and cultural dynamics of workplace power relations. This in turn reflects and reinforces Hirschman's underestimation of the costs *and* overestimation of the possibilities of *both* exit and voice (see also Ahrne, 1990; Flam, 1993). His rather static and one-dimensional categories do not allow for the possibility of more subtle, multiple, ambiguous and contradictory employee discursive practices such as resistance through distance which combines elements of both exit and voice. Hence I would argue that similarities with Hirschman's approach are actually more superficial than they might at first appear.

REFERENCES

Ackers, P. and Black, J. (1992) 'Watching the Detectives: Shop Stewards' Expectations of Their Managers in the Age of Human Resource Management', in Sturdy, A., Knights, D. and Willmott, H. (eds) *Skill and Consent*, London: Routledge, pp. 185–212.

Adams, S. (1984) *Roche Versus Adams*, London: Jonathan Cape.

Ahrne, G. (1990) *Agency and Organization*, London: Sage.

Beynon, H. (1980) *Working for Ford*, Harmondsworth: Penguin.

Braverman, H. (1974) *Labour and Monopoly Capitalism*, New York: Monthly Review Press.

Brown, G. (1977) *Sabotage: A Study in Industrial Conflict*, Nottingham: Spokesman Books.

Brown, R. (1965) *Social Psychology*, New York: Free Press.

Brown, R.K. (1992) *Understanding Industrial Organisations*, London: Routledge.

Burawoy, M. (1979) *Manufacturing Consent*, Chicago: Chicago University Press.

Burawoy, M. (1985) *The Politics of Production*, London: Verso.

Burrell, G. (1984) 'Sex and Organisational Analysis', *Organization Studies* 5(2): 97–118.

Cohen, S. and Taylor, L. (1992) *Escape Attempts*, London: Routledge.

Clawson, D. and Fantasia, R. (1983) 'Review Essay: Beyond Burawoy: The Dialectics of Conflict and Consent on the Shopfloor', *Theory and Society* 12(3): 671–80.

Clegg, S.R. (1979) *The Theory of Power and Organisation*, London: Routledge & Kegan Paul.

Clegg, S.R. (1987) 'The Power of Language and the Language of Power', *Organization Studies* 8(1): 60–70.

Clegg, S.R. (1989) *Frameworks of Power*, London: Sage.

Clegg, S.R. (1990) *Modern Organisations*, London: Sage.

Clegg, S.R. and Dunkerley, D. (1980) *Organisation, Class and Control*, London: Routledge & Kegan Paul.

Cockburn, C. (1983) *Brothers*, London: Pluto Press.

Cockburn, C. (1991) *In the Way of Women*, London: Macmillan.

Collinson, D.L. (1988) 'Engineering Humour: Masculinity, Joking and Conflict in Shopfloor Relations', *Organization Studies* 9(2): 181–99.

Collinson, D.L. (1992a) *Managing the Shopfloor: Subjectivity, Masculinity and Workplace Culture*, Berlin: Walter de Gruyter.

Collinson, D.L. (1992b) 'Researching Recruitment: Qualitative Methods and Sex Discrimination', in Burgess, R. (ed.) *Studies in Qualitative Methodology*, vol. 3, Greenwich, Connecticut: JAI Publications, pp. 89–122.

Collinson, D.L. (1993) 'Introducing On-Line Processing: Conflicting Human Resource Policies in Insurance', in Clark, J. (ed.) *Human Resource Management and Technical Change*, London: Sage, pp. 155–74.

Collinson, D.L., Knights, D. and Collinson, M. (1990) *Managing to Discriminate*, London: Routledge.

Cressey, P. and Macinnes, J. (1980) 'Voting for Ford: Industrial Democracy and the Control of Labour', *Capital and Class* 11, 5–33.

Davies, C. and Rosser, J. (1986) 'Gendered Jobs in the Health Service: A Problem for Labour Process Analysis', Knights, D. and Willmott, H. (eds) *Gender and the Labour Process*, Aldershot: Gower, pp. 94–116.

Davies, S. (1990) 'Inserting Gender into Burawoy's Theory of the Labour Process', *Work, Employment and Society* 4(3): 391–426.

Ditton, J. (1976) 'Moral Horror versus Folk Terror: Output Restriction, Class and the Social Organisation of Exploitation', *Sociological Review* 24: 519–44.

Dubois, P. (1979) *Sabotage in Industry*, Harmondsworth: Penguin.

Dunphy, D.C. and Stace, D.A. (1988) 'Transformational and Coercive Strategies for Planned Organisational Change', *Organization Studies* 9(3): 317–34.

Edwards, P.K. (1986) *Conflict at Work: A Materialist Analysis of Workplace Relations*, Oxford: Basil Blackwell.

Edwards, P.K. (1990) 'Understanding Conflict in the Labour Process: The Logic and Autonomy of Struggle', in Knights, D. and Willmott, H. (eds) *Labour Process Theory*, London: Macmillan, pp. 125–52.

Edwards, P. and Scullion, H. (1982) *The Social Organisation of Industrial Conflict*, Oxford: Basil Blackwell.

Edwards, R. (1979) *Contested Terrain: The Transformation of the Workplace in the Twentieth Century*, London: Heinemann.

Emmett, I. and Morgan, D.H.J. (1982) 'Max Gluckman and the Manchester Shop-floor Ethnographies', in Frankenberg, R. (ed.) *Custom and Conflict in British Society*, Manchester: Manchester University Press, pp. 140–65.

Flam, H. (1993) 'Fear, Loyalty and Greedy Organizations', in Fineman, S. (ed.), *Emotions in Organizations*, London: Sage, pp. 58–75.

Foucault, M. (1977) *Discipline and Punish*, London: Allen & Unwin.

Friedman, A.L. (1977) *Industry and Labour*, London: Macmillan.

Giddens, A. (1979) *Central Problems in Social Theory*, London: Macmillan.

Goffman, E. (1959) *The Presentation of Self in Everyday Life*, Harmondsworth: Penguin.

Goffman, E. (1968) *Asylums*, Harmondsworth: Penguin.

Goffmam, E. (1961) *Encounters*, Harmondsworth: Penguin.

Gouldner, A.W. (1954) *Patterns of Industrial Bureaucracy*, New York: Free Press.

Grey, C. (1993) 'A Helping Hand: Self-discipline and Management Control', delivered at the *11th Annual Labour Process Conference*, Blackpool, March.

Henriques, J., Hollway, W., Unwin, C., Vein, C., Walkderdine, V. (1984) *Changing the Subject*, London: Methuen.

Hirschman, A.O. (1970) *Exit, Voice and Loyalty*, Cambridge, Mass.: Harvard University Press.

Hyman, R. (1987) 'Strategy or Structure? Capital, Labour and Control', *Work, Employment and Society* 1(1): 25–55.

Hyman, R. (1989) *Strikes*, London: Macmillan.

Jermier, J. (1988) 'Sabotage at Work: The Rational View', in DiTomaso, N. and Bacharach, S. (eds) *Research in the Sociology of Organisations*, vol. 6, Greenwich: Connecticut, pp. 101–34.

Klein, J. (1964) *The Study of Groups*, London: Routledge & Kegan Paul.

Knights, D. (1990) 'Subjectivity, Power and the Labour Process', in Knights, D. and Willmott, H. (eds) *Labour Process Theory*, London: Macmillan, pp. 297–335.

Knights, D. and Collinson, D.L. (1985) 'Redesigning Work on the Shopfloor: A Question of Control or Consent?', in Knights, D., Willmott, H. and Collinson, D. (eds) *Job Redesign*, Aldershot: Gower, pp. 197–226.

Knights, D. and Collinson, D. (1987) 'Disciplining the Shopfloor: A Comparison of the Disciplinary Effects of Managerial and Financial Accounting', *Accounting, Organisations and Society* 12(5): 457–77.

Knights, D. and Sturdy, A.J. (1990) 'New Technology and the Self-Disciplined Worker in Insurance', in Varcoe, I., McNeil, M. and Yearly, S. (eds) *Deciphering Science and Technology*, London: Macmillan, pp. 126–54.

Kondo, D. (1990) *Crafting Selves: Power, Discourse and Identity in a Japanese Factory*, Chicago: Chicago University Press.

Kotter, J.P. and Schlesinger, L.A. (1979) 'Choosing Strategies for Change', *Harvard Business Review*, March/April.

Kreitner, R. (1986) *Management*, Boston: Houghton Mifflin.

Kusterer, K. (1978) *Know How on the Job*, Boulder: Westview Press.

Lazega, E. (1992) *Micropolitics of Knowledge: Communication and Indirect Control in Workgroups*, New York: Walter de Gruyter.

Levi, P. (1987a) *If This is a Man*, London: Abacus.

Levi, P. (1987b) *If Not Now, When?*, London: Abacus.

Lewin, K. (1951) *Field Theory: Social Science*, New York: Harper & Row.

Linstead, S. (1985) 'Breaking the Purity Rule: Industrial Sabotage and the Symbolic Process', *Personnel Review* 14(3): 12–19.

Littler, C.R. (1982) *The Development of the Labour Process in Capitalist Societies*, London: Heinemann.

Littler, C.R. (1990) 'The Labour Process Debate: A Theoretical Review 1974–1988', in Knights, D. and Willmott, H. (eds) *Labour Process Theory*, London: Macmillan, pp. 46–94.

Lupton, T. (1963) *On the Shopfloor*, Oxford: Pergamon.

McBarnet, D., Weston, S. and Whelan, C. (1993) 'Adversary Accounting: Strategic Uses of Financial Information by Capital and Labour', *Accounting, Organizations and Society*, 18(1): 81–100.

Madeley, J. (1986) 'Whistle-blower Paid High Price', in Frost, P.J., Mitchell, V.F. and Nord, W.R. (eds) *Organisational Reality: Reports from the Firing Line*, Glenview, Illinois: Scott, Foresman & Company, 228–30.

Mann, M. (1986) *The Sources of Social Power, Vol. 1: A History of Power from the Beginning to A.D. 1760*, Cambridge: Cambridge University Press.

Manwaring, T. and Wood, S. (1985) 'The Ghost in the Labour Process', in Knights, D., Willmott, H. and Collinson, D. (eds) *Job Redesign*, Aldershot: Gower, pp. 171–98.

Mars, G. (1982) *Cheats at Work*, London: Allen & Unwin.

Martin, J. (1990) 'Deconstructing Organizational Taboos: The Suppression of Gender Conflict in Organizations', *Organization Science* 1(4): 339–59.

Mayo, E. (1933) *The Human Problems of an Industrial Civilization*, New York: Macmillan.

Mills, A.J. and Murgatroyd, J.J. (1991) *Organisational Rules: A Framework for Understanding Organisational Action*, Buckingham: Open University Press.

Mills, C.W. (1940) 'Situated Actions and Vocabularies of Motive', *American Sociological Review* 5: 904–13.

Mitchell, T. (1990) 'Everyday Metaphors of Power', *Theory and Society* 19(5): 545–78.

Nichols, T. and Beynon, H. (1977) *Living with Capitalism*, London: Routledge & Kegan Paul.

Phillips, A. and Taylor, B. (1980) 'Sex and Skill: Notes Towards a Feminist Economics', *Feminist Review* 6: 79–83.

Plant, R. (1987) *Managing Change and Making It Stick*, London: Fontana.

Polanyi, M. and Prosch, H. (1975) *Meaning*, Chicago: Chicago University Press.

Ramsay, H. and Howarth, N. (1989) 'Managing the Multinationals: The Emerging Theory of the Multinational Enterprise and Its Implications for Labour Resistance', in Clegg, S.R. (ed.) *Organisation Theory and Class Analysis*, Berlin: Walter de Gruyter, pp. 275–97.

Rose, N. (1989) *Governing the Soul*, London: Routledge.

Roy, D. (1952) 'Quota Restriction and Goldbricking in a Machine Shop', *American Journal of Sociology* 57(5): 427–42.

Scott, J.C. (1985) *Weapons of the Weak: Everyday Forms of Peasant Resistance*, New Haven: Yale University Press.

Scott, J.C. (1990) *Domination and the Arts of Resistance: Hidden Transcripts*, New Haven: Yale University Press.

Sennett, R. (1980) *Authority*, London: Secker & Warburg.

Sennett, R. and Cobb, J. (1977) *The Hidden Injuries of Class*, Cambridge: Cambridge University Press.

Sewell, G. and Wilkinson, B. (1992) '"Someone to Watch over Me":
Surveillance, Discipline and the Just-in-time Labour Process', *Sociology*
26(2): 271–89.

Stallybrass, P. and White, A. (1986) *The Politics and Poetics of
Transgression*, London: Methuen.

Storey, J. (1985) 'The Means of Management Control', *Sociology* 19(2):
193–211.

Sturdy, A., Knights, D. and Willmott, H. (1992) (eds) *Skill and Consent*,
London: Routledge.

Sprouse, M. (ed.) (1992) *Sabotage in the American Workplace*, San
Francisco: Pressure Drop Press.

Taylor, F. (1947) *Scientific Management*, New York: Harper & Row.

Taylor, L. and Walton, P. (1971) 'Industrial Sabotage: Motives and
Meanings', in Cohen, S. (ed.) *Images of Deviance*, Harmondsworth:
Penguin, pp. 219–45.

Thompson, P. (1990) 'Crawling from the Wreckage: The Labour Process
and the Politics of Production', in Knights, D. and Willmott, H. (eds)
Labour Process Theory, London: Macmillan, 95–124.

Thompson, P. and Bannon, E. (1985) *Working the System: The Shop Floor
and New Technology*, London: Pluto Press.

Walby, S. (1986) *Patriarchy at Work*, Cambridge: Polity Press.

Walby, S. (1990) 'Theorising Patriarchy', *Sociology* 23(2): 213–34.

Walker, C.R. and Guest, R.H. (1952) *The Man on the Assembly Line*,
Cambridge, Mass.: Harvard University Press.

Willis, P.E. (1977) *Learning to Labour*, London: Saxon House.

Willis, P.E. (1980) 'Shopfloor Culture, Masculinity and the Wage Form', in
Clarke, J., Critcher, C. and Johnson, R. (eds) *Working Class Culture*,
London: Hutchinson, pp. 185–98.

Willmott, H. (1990) 'Subjectivity and the Dialectics of Praxis: Opening up
the Core of Labour Process Analysis', in Knights, D. and Willmott, H.
(eds) *Labour Process Theory*, London: Macmillan, pp. 336–78.

Willmott, H. (1993) 'Strength is Ignorance; Slavery is Freedom: Managing
Culture in Modern Organizations', *Journal of Management Studies*,
30(4): 215–552.

Zuboff, S. (1988) *In the Age of the Smart Machine*, New York: Basic Books.

2

THE SOURCES AND LIMITS OF RESISTANCE IN A PRIVATIZED UTILITY*

Julia O'Connell Davidson

INTRODUCTION

This chapter is concerned with the response of clerical workers to the restructuring of office work in one region of a privatized British utility, which will be referred to as National Utility (NU). This restructuring was broadly consonant with widely documented changes to the organization of clerical work in banking, insurance, building societies, financial services companies and major utilities in both Britain and the USA (Barras and Swann, 1983; Storey, 1986; Batstone *et al.*, 1987; Lane, 1988; Baran, 1988; Gapper, 1989); that is, it involved both extensive computerization and the introduction of functionally flexible teamwork. Certain commentators might be tempted to locate this concoction of new technology and flexible work organization in the context of 'post-Fordist' analyses of work organization; they might hope to find evidence of new patterns of accommodation or resistance in response to the 'new order' that we are supposedly entering (see, for example, Communist Party of Great Britain, 1988). At NU, however, these changes did not represent any profound break with the past. Indeed, Crompton and Reid's (1982: 175) description of clerical deskilling precisely captures NU's objectives. Management here sought to fragment, standardize and simplify clerical tasks; to centralize control over the planning and pacing of work which had, until then, rested with the clerks; and to diminish the organization's dependence upon any individual clerk's experience and acquired knowledge. Likewise,

* The author gratefully acknowledges the support of the Economic and Social Research Council (ESRC). This chapter draws on a Bristol University-based research project which examined restructuring and changing employment relations in the utilities (ESRC award number R000231466). The author is also indebted to Theo Nichols for his comments on innumerable drafts of this chapter.

there was nothing that could usefully be termed 'post-Fordist' or 'post-modern' about the responses of these clerical workers to change. Unhappy with the effects of new technology and with the increased intensity of working that teamwork threatened, these workers mounted various forms of action to impede management. They offered organized and informal, and collective and individual, resistance to change, but none of their actions, from walk-outs through passive resistance to acts of sabotage, mark any significant break with the history of labour protest in Britain.

This resistance was one of the factors which forced management to slow down the pace of change, yet, ultimately, it did not force management to abandon or modify its plans. Today these clerks are all undertaking on-line processing in multi-functional teams. Because there are few studies documenting clerical workers' opposition to computerization,[1] this chapter focuses upon why a workforce which was previously characterized by management as 'very accommodating' attempted to resist change, rather than upon why they failed in the mission. However, though the focus is on why these workers attempted to obstruct management's plans, the extremely limited nature of their success also has implications for theories of control and 'resistance', especially for the contention that worker subjectivity is a determining force in the organization of the labour process (Knights, 1990). For although features of any given firm's labour process itself can sometimes generate a willingness or wish to resist management, whether this wish is translated into action, and what form this action takes, and how effective this action is, are all powerfully constrained by broader political, institutional and economic factors. Clerical workers at NU sought to resist change in a period when organized labour was severely weakened by almost a decade of legal assault by a right-wing government; when their newly privatized employer was facing both more intense competition and more intense pressure to maintain profitability than ever before; and when labour market conditions were not especially favourable to them. Their attempts to resist change were also hampered by problems of communication and coordination within their union. More than anything else, these objective, structural factors constrained the form that resistance could take and set the limits to what it could achieve.

The chapter is structured as follows. After outlining the management objectives behind the restructuring of clerical work, it documents the response of clerical workers to change, exploring why computerization and the introduction of functionally flexible teamwork provoked such a strong reaction from the workforce. It then moves on to briefly describe the practical expression which clerical workers gave to their sentiments. It looks at how the existing industrial relations machinery and problems of coordination and communication within the main clerical union impeded effective formal action, and describes some of the informal resistance mounted by clerks. Finally, the chapter considers events at NU in relation to labour process analyses of control, resistance and subjectivity.

RESTRUCTURING CLERICAL WORK: MANAGEMENT OBJECTIVES

In 1989, when this research was conducted, National Utility had an operating profit of around £1,000m. and employed some 80,000 people, 60 per cent of whom were involved in clerical work. NU was organized as a number of regions, headed by semi-autonomous boards. The regions were divided into a number of geographical districts, each of which undertakes the company's key operational functions – supplying the utility, installations, repairs and services, and marketing and sales. These functions have traditionally been strictly demarcated. Clerical work arose in connection with all of NU's operations, and until recently, was organizationally attached to the particular function it served. Clerical work in the districts was not only characterized by strict functional demarcations, but also by a fairly detailed division of labour, so that each clerk undertook a specific and limited range of function-related tasks.

In terms of clerical employment, NU, like other public utilities, had traditionally offered most of its clerical staff what might be considered 'standard' direct employment, namely full-time, permanent employment, although some use had always been made of part time and temporary workers. The majority of clerical employees at NU were female, whilst supervisors were predominantly male. Although these women without doubt provide cheaper labour than would an all male workforce, it would be mistaken to characterize them as a peripheral workforce simply because they are women. As Lane (1988: 85) notes, female white collar workers are generally significantly better off than female manual workers, even though they may be disadvantaged in relation to their male colleagues. Moreover, within the utilities, both male and female clerical workers are typically well unionized and enjoy a good package of non-statutory employment benefits, a seniority-based pay and promotion structure and a fairly high degree of job security.

Throughout the 1980s, successive Conservative governments pursued a privatization programme which sold off nationalized industries and public utilities. By privatizing the utilities, the Government created massive corporations with monopolies over utility supply. However, the privatization proposals also involved the liberalization of the markets for appliance retailing, repair and servicing, which the utilities had, until then, also enjoyed a monopoly over. Both privatization and the liberalization of appliance markets made NU management increasingly concerned to cut costs.[2] Existing employment relations and the functionally specialist division of labour were held to foster inefficiency (for example, they led to the duplication of work, porosity in the working day, and extensive overtime working during peak periods – see O'Connell Davidson, 1990, for a more detailed account of these problems). The prime objective of the restructuring documented in this chapter was to reduce staffing levels and labour costs by reducing labour porosity. To this end, management sought to break down functional and task demarcations and traditional employment patterns. This involved transforming office work both through computerization and through the introduction of multi-functional teamworking.

In the early 1980s an integrated computer system, known as the New Office Systems Strategy (NOSS), which standardized and coordinated the activities of the different clerical functions was developed. NOSS consisted of a series of programmes or 'systems' designed to deal with particular clerical operations – Appliance Retailing, Utility Supply, Credit Utility and so on – all of which were fed into the region's mainframe computer. The systems were designed as a number of 'screens' to be called up on the VDU either to input or to extract information. Once a function was computerized, instead of operating manual systems (filling out job vouchers or order forms, taking them to other departments, filing and so on) clerks undertook on-line processing. For some clerks this meant calling up the appropriate screen to deal with the customer's query or request, and translating the information given by the customer into a form that could be accepted by that screen. For those clerks involved in planning the work of manual and craft employees, on-line processing meant that their job now basically consisted of transferring information from one screen on to another. NOSS automated certain routine clerical tasks, and standardized and routinized those which remained. It was, in the words of one NU manager, 'designed to deskill clerical work'.

The new computer systems were intended to facilitate three main changes to clerical work and employment. First, management wished to reduce staffing levels, and this would be more easily achieved if routine clerical tasks were automated. Second, management wished to make greater use of part-time and temporary staff. Previously, investment in training non-standard employees was seen as under-utilized, but because NOSS simplified routine activities it made it possible to use part-timers and temporary staff to process daily, monthly and seasonal peaks in clerical work without incurring substantial training costs. The use of part-time staff was attractive to management because it would reduce labour porosity since the hours part-timers work can be more precisely matched to the workload. A further advantage of using part-time staff for peak-smoothing work was that additional hours worked by part-timers were paid at plain time, rather than at overtime rates. Finally, deskilling clerical work in this way meant that full time permanent staff could undertake a wide range of tasks, instead of being limited to a small number of complex and functionally specialist activities. Management argued that the wider the range of operations that each clerk could perform, the less 'idle time' there would be.

Getting clerks to undertake a wider range of tasks entailed the reorganization of office work in each district – basically the introduction of multi-functional teamworking, which was known as the 'Beta' structure. Under the Beta structure, clerks were to be attached to a particular 'Geographical Team', which would deal with all clerical work arising in a particular geographical area, instead of being attached to a particular function. Thus, clerks would no longer simply undertake a narrow range of function-specific tasks. Whilst being primarily committed to particular tasks and duties, they would now also be expected to be cognizant with a broader range of clerical operations and functions in order to facilitate functional flexibility within geographical teams. The Beta structure, in combination with NOSS would thus enable management to reduce 'idle time'. NOSS had simplified and standardized clerical tasks, so that it was technically possible for clerks to master a wider range of activities, whilst the Beta structure would push clerks to work across the full spectrum of clerical functions. This would mean that clerks could be matched to the workload; when a clerk finished with the Sales work, he or she could immediately move on to Finance work, or to Supply work, and so on, as required.

The Brighton Labour Process Group observed that reintegration of fragmented tasks through job enlargement actually presupposes deskilling (1977: 20). Certainly at NU, functionally specialist clerks could not be cheaply transformed into multi-functional workers without first reducing the complexity of clerical work. The standardization and simplification of clerical work through computerization and the introduction of functionally flexible teams were therefore seen by NU management as inextricably linked.

Expenditure on NOSS was substantial – one manager involved in its design and implementation estimated the cost at around £7 million. Management therefore had a strong incentive to implement change on schedule. The NOSS Beta structure was to have been in place by mid-1989, however, its full implementation was delayed by almost eight months. This was partly a consequence of technical and managerial problems, but the implementation of NOSS Beta was also hampered by resistance on the part of clerical staff. The following sections examine the sources of this resistance and the factors which constrained the form that resistance could take. It draws on a case study undertaken in one district office, which will be called Eastvale South, between August 1989 and January 1990. The study involved a survey of 53 clerks in the Eastvale South office, unstructured interviews with clerks, managers and trade union representatives, and searches of management and trade union literature.[3]

THE SOURCES OF RESISTANCE

It was noted above that the restructuring of clerical work at NU was above all designed to reduce staffing levels and labour costs by reducing labour porosity. To this end, clerical work was computerized and management sought to break down functional and task demarcations and traditional employment patterns. As will be seen below, both technological and organizational change generated resistance from clerical workers. The new computer systems generally made clerical work more frustrating and time consuming; clerks were unhappy with the routinization of aspects of their work;

they also resented being asked to work more intensively and across functions without any financial reward for so doing. There was widespread condemnation of management for attempting to rush through change 'on the cheap'. Though management attempted to 'sell' change by claiming it would improve customer service, clerks came to see the search for profits as the real motive behind the restructuring, and this heightened their opposition to management plans.

Computerization and its discontents

The restructuring of clerical work at NU was informed by a clear set of objectives, and regional management had formulated a detailed strategy for achieving those ends. District managers were not only presented with precise instructions as to how to implement NOSS Beta, but also with targets for 'staff savings' and reductions in operating costs to be made on the back of the new systems and structure. Yet adapting the model to the real conditions of the workplace proved something of a nightmare for both district and regional management. In practice, change was a more complex process than top management had anticipated.

Plans for computerization were introduced to clerks with assurances from Personnel Managers that NOSS would ease and simplify their workload, and met with little opposition. But in practice, a catalogue of design faults and software problems meant that computerization had quite the reverse effect on their work. This is one reason why further changes were resisted. To begin with, there were problems with the mainframe computer located at the region's headquarters, which proved unable to cope with the volume of input. It would frequently 'go down', and since all the records pertaining to certain types of work were stored on the mainframe, with no manual back-up system, when this happened most clerks could not work at all. While the computer was down, work in many sections built up, adding to the backlog of work caused by low staffing levels, high sickness rates and absenteeism. However, the malfunctions of the mainframe computer appear almost insignificant next to the problems with the software.

As noted above, NOSS is a package of systems designed as a number of 'screens' to be called up on the VDU either to input or to extract information. One of the most common problems with the software was that the screen either did not ask for, or did not have room for, all the relevant information. For example, when job vouchers came back from engineers who had fitted appliances, the details of the job should have been entered into the system. However, as one clerk explained:

> We have such a limited space on the VDU to fill in details that, say an engineer goes out and fits an appliance and a number of parts as well . . . you only have room to put one part on. So you have to put, 'Fitted one appliance, etc.' But when a customer queries the account, you can't just say, 'Oh yes, we fitted the appliance and some other things, but I don't know what they were'. So then someone has to look up the job voucher that is filed away as paperwork, which all takes ages.

This kind of problem was widespread – in the survey, over 80 per cent of staff reported that the screens they worked with did not ask for, did not have room for, or did not provide, all the information necessary to process customer requests or job vouchers. This in turn increased the number of clerical errors made, and to add to the confusion, there was often no facility for amending screens once they had been filled out. Clerks therefore had to supplement the systems with separate manual records detailing corrections and amendments, which effectively doubled their work.

Problems also arose where control over planning was taken away from the clerk and vested in the computer. For example, service-works clerks used to use job sheets to plan out the engineers' appliance repair and servicing work manually. Clerks would consult these sheets, which showed how many jobs had been booked in for how many engineers, and decide when to give a customer an engineer's appointment. In 1989, this task was computerized. The computer system worked by allocating a standard length of time for each job (long and short jobs are supposed to average out) and stopped booking in jobs when all the labour available on a given date had been planned out. So when a customer asked the clerk to arrange for an engineer to call, instead of consulting job sheets and making a decision, all the clerk now did was to tap in a request for the job on the VDU, and the system would offer an engineer's appointment. If the customer agreed to that date, the clerk confirmed the appointment and the engineer's time was booked up within the system. Instead of receiving and processing requests for work, all the clerk now did was to mediate between the computer and the customer.

But the system did not work. To begin with, it continually over-scheduled work. This was partly because it failed to make allowances for sickness, absenteeism and turnover rates amongst engineers, and partly because it was absurd to make appointments on the basis of an average, standard time. When two consecutive jobs took longer than the standard time, the third job had to be cancelled, which put the engineer's schedule out for the rest of the week. More often than not it took months, rather than days or weeks, for the jobs to average out to the standard time, meanwhile backlogs of work built up and the computer system blithely continued to offer appointments which could not possibly be kept.

The problem was compounded by the fact that this over-scheduling was not visible to the clerks, since information about the engineers' daily schedules was now locked inside the system. Each morning, the computer printed out all the jobs vouchers for that day. It was only then that everyone knew how many jobs had been booked in for engineers for the day. Under the old manual system, clerks had been able to forestall such problems. One clerk explains:

> You can't just flick through the paperwork and say 'That's a six-hour job and he'll need someone to give him a hand because it's a heavy job. There's no way he'll get on to another appointment that day', because all that information is buried in the machine and you don't know any more.

When the job vouchers for the day were printed out and the over-planning was revealed, the clerks would have to phone customers to break appointments. The volume of this work was such that a temporary job title – 'broken appointments clerk' – was created. This clerk spent all day cancelling appointments, but still could not cope with the volume of calls to be made. It is not hard to imagine how unrewarding and demoralizing this task was, and in the words of one clerk 'we have customers phoning in complaining all the time . . . we want to give them a good service, but we can't, and we're the ones taking all the flak'. Again, this type of problem was widespread with over 80 per cent of clerks surveyed stating that the system they worked with prevented them from working effectively. One clerk summed up:

> The main thing about these new systems is that they make work so frustrating. They were designed 'up there' . . . . Management didn't come down to the grass-roots and ask us

what our jobs entailed, what problems needed to be got round.

Managers involved in the design of the systems accepted that there were some major problems, but they claimed it would not be cost effective to modify systems more than once a year. Thus, staff were often left working with seriously defective systems for up to 12 months before any attempt was made to correct them.

The new systems, in themselves, thus often made clerical work more frustrating and time consuming. Because a distinguishing feature of most clerical work at NU is that it involves direct contact with customers, any problems which slowed down the processing of work were doubly stressful, since clerks had to try to appease disgruntled customers whilst simultaneously attempting to clear backlogs of work.

Even if these systems failures were corrected, it is still uncertain whether NOSS would meet an unreserved welcome, for working with VDUs profoundly changes the nature of clerical work. NOSS effectively tied clerks to their work station for the bulk of the working day, since integrated systems largely removed the need to move around the office. For many clerks, the only legitimate reasons for leaving the work station were now either to get a cup of coffee or to go to the toilet. The use of VDUs was resented most strongly by those clerks whose jobs were already very monotonous, that is, clerks who processed the most standard and routine work, such as orders for appliances. As with Glenn and Feldberg's (1979) study of office work, computerization had not increased worker autonomy. The common sentiment was that working with VDUs reduced them to a mere appendage of the machine – as one Sales clerk said, 'You feel like a robot, continually thumping out calls . . . you're just part of the machine'. Although certain very monotonous tasks had been automated by the systems, the remaining tasks were often perceived to have been made more boring by computerization, which has standardized the way that clerks must work. Instead of filling in forms by hand, which allowed clerks to vary the sequence and respond creatively to idiosyncratic customer requests or details, the screens forced them to work to a preset order.

Braverman (1974: 333) quotes a clerical worker using computer systems in 1961 as complaining that 'We are working for the machine now'. Almost 30 years on, at NU clerks were reporting similar experiences. One observed that 'You've got to do what the computer says. Before we used to be able to work round problems by ourselves, now we can't. . . . The computer is our boss now'.

Opposition to the Beta structure

It has been seen that NOSS, the first phase of restructuring, generated much discontent. Management had promised that new office technology would ease the clerks' workload, but in practice it increased and complicated it. Further, NOSS diminished the degree of discretion clerks exercised over their work, and bound them more securely to their work stations. It was into this setting, then, that personnel managers introduced the idea of the second phase of restructuring, the introduction of functionally flexible teamworking. Again, management was liberal with promises, claiming that the Beta structure would 'improve standards of service for customers' and offer staff 'opportunities for personal development and job enrichment'. Perhaps unsurprisingly, these promises were greeted with scepticism by the clerks, and management's plans met with strong opposition. Yet this did not reflect a fundamental hostility to the principle of changing the existing mode of work organization. These workers were aware of the inadequacies of the rigidly functional structure, and because of the high level of customer contact, they had a clear interest in an improved standard of service. In fact, the majority of staff agreed with management that customers should not have to deal with numerous different functional sections in the office during the course of one transaction. They wanted to see better coordination both within and between functions, and a higher standard of customer service. However, the majority of staff did not believe that the new Beta structure, as it stood, would fulfil these objectives. They argued that management not only wished to introduce sweeping changes far too quickly, but also wished to do so 'on the cheap', that is, with insufficient training and with inadequate staffing levels.

NU was not renowned amongst clerical employees for a strong tradition of, or commitment to, staff training. Many clerks observed that in periods of over ten years, they had received no training other than the initial two weeks of on the job training, which consisted of watching another clerk working (or 'sitting-by-Nellie'), and an eight-hour course introducing them to VDUs. One clerk who had recently joined NU explained:

> When you come here and . . . people ring in and say all these different words about appliances, you think, 'What the hell are they on about?' . . . When I came here, they just said to me, 'Sit next to her, watch her, and then you do it'. That isn't training . . . it's just humiliating. You never know the answer so you have to keep asking all the time.

Management insisted that once the systems were 'de-bugged', computerization would so dramatically reduce the amount and complexity of clerical tasks that only minimal training would be required in order to become fully cognizant with each particular function. The clerks did not share this confidence. Quite apart from the fact that each computer system had its own idiosyncrasies and mnemonic codes which clerks had to learn in order to operate it, they argued that the computer systems could not completely expunge the need for acquired, function-specific knowledge. As one clerk explained:

> The customers . . . don't know all the technical jargon, they rely on you. So they explain the problem as best they can, and its up to you to interpret what they want from that. If you don't understand yourself all the different things involved, you don't know the right questions to ask. So then you can't extract the necessary information and you haven't a hope of getting it sorted out.

Managers told the clerks that when the Beta structure was introduced they would not immediately be expected to be fully polyvalent. Instead individual clerks within a team would specialize in their old function, and gradually learn the tasks associated with new functions from their colleagues. Yet as presented to the clerks, the Beta structure was designed to stop customers from experiencing the frustration of dealing with a number of different clerks, none of whom knew anything about the workings of different departments within the office. If clerks working in the teams were not to have the detailed knowledge and experience of the full range of functions, then, the clerks argued, the Beta structure would have done nothing to address this problem. Without comprehensive training to make all clerks fully polyvalent, the end result of Beta for the customer would be little different from the existing system. Instead of being passed from 'pillar to post' across sections, they would be passed from 'pillar to post' within the teams. This would simply make clerical work more frustrating.

Managers assured them that adequate training would be provided. The clerks, however, believed that the low staffing levels in the office would mean that even the minimal level of training perceived by management as 'adequate' would not be forthcoming. Clerks concluded that they would not be trained, but simply 'thrown in at the deep end'. They felt that customer service was already suffering because of a staff shortage, and that switching to the Beta structure would not improve this situation. It was difficult to see how moving people into geographical teams would improve matters by cutting out idle time when there was no idle time in the first place. Another clerk noted:

> The idea is that if you get a lull you will start doing somebody else's work, so you'll never stop. But with the staff shortages we never get a lull ever anyway, so I don't see how it will work at all really.

Even if these problems had all been miraculously solved, clerks at Eastvale South would still have been unhappy with management's proposals for the Beta structure since management was offering no improvements to the employment package in exchange for greater flexibility on their part. They did not see why they should be expected to take on a training role and expand their skills and job knowledge for the same basic pay and conditions. In the survey, over 80 per cent of district clerks wanted to be upgraded in recognition of their wider brief. They also observed that teamworking would intensify working, and argued that management should make some sort of concession in exchange for productivity improvements gained through clerks working harder.

Making contradictions manifest

It has been shown that a range of design faults and systems failures meant that computerization increased the number of tasks associated with many operations, and generally made clerical work more difficult and frustrating. Given that the majority of clerks are directly exposed to customers, anything which complicates or slows down the service and leads to customer dissatisfaction is, in itself, enough to generate substantial hostility. But, perhaps more importantly, the problems and systems failures threw into sharp relief certain features of the work process which had previously been largely obscured from view.

As successive problems with the systems emerged, it became clear to the staff that the people who had designed the systems had an inadequate knowledge of the content of clerical work, and had assumed it to be far less complex than it was in reality. Somewhat ironically, the introduction of systems intended to simplify and standardize clerical work actually drew the clerks' attention to the fact that they provided the company with a kind of expertise that cannot easily be written into a computer programme. As one clerk noted, 'Each section involves knowledge that has to be picked up, that can't be built into the systems'. This was because, although a great deal of the clerical work was routine and specifiable in advance, a portion was not. The non-routine work could not easily be separated out and handled by specialist clerks, since it was an integral part of the daily workload. Clerks had to be capable not only of undertaking the mundane, pedestrian tasks, but also of processing atypical work. A supply clerk explained:

> As well as the routine stuff, I have to sort out problems and emergencies. . . . Today, I had a woman on the phone who was absolutely hysterical. . . . The real difficulty was getting the information out of her, and you need to understand the function to know what questions to ask. Now that sort of thing is not actually classified as part of my job. It's not routine and it's not in the job description, but it actually takes up over half my day.

The computer technology involved could only deal cheaply with standard, predictable work. Although management talked of building prompts into the screens to reduce the degree of function specific knowledge required to operate them, the fact remained that, at that moment, to design a system capable of responding to *all* possible variations and emergencies would have been enormously costly. It would have defeated the whole object of NOSS, which was to reduce the costs associated with clerical work. Clerks argued that while routine clerical operations could be standardized and computerized, clerical workers would always need a substantial degree of acquired, firm-specific knowledge in order to deal with problems and emergencies. As another clerk put it; 'It's alright when everything's running smoothly, but it's when things go wrong that you can't cope if you don't understand the job properly'.

It is patently obvious that these clerks were not, and that management did not intend them to become, 'skilled' in the sense that a time-served craftworker may be. But it is also clear that management had always depended upon the clerks' acquired, firm-specific knowledge, and that when management spoke of 'deskilling', it was referring to the reduction or elimination of this dependence. The paradox was that in attempting to do so, NOSS actually revealed to the clerks the extent of NU's dependence upon the emergency reserve of knowledge they provided. One of the unintended consequences of computerization, then, was to reveal both to management and to staff the importance of the clerks' contribution to the work process:

> I don't think we realized before just how much management depends on us knowing about the job . . . . [Management] obviously thought all we did was pen pushing, so they thought all we'd have to do was just tap stuff into the computer instead. They thought they knew all what we did, they said, 'We know the procedures, we've got it written down'. I think it's been a bit of a shock to them to find out they didn't know, that procedure is not necessarily how you do the job, job descriptions can't cover everything.

Although the systems made the significance of acquired and firm-specific knowledge more obvious, they were simultaneously removing elements of control and discretion from clerical work. Initially, design faults made this a fairly disastrous move. However, many clerks feared that ultimately, once the systems were perfected, computerization would render clerical staff more easily substitutable. In this sense, computerization also made manifest the conflict of interests between management and staff. One clerk observed:

> The new systems are just trying to take away everything from the job, to tunnel it down until there's no thought left it in, so they could pick someone off the street and bring them in to replace us. They want to create systems that even a bloody chimp could use.

Another commented:

> They'd like to turn us into a sausage factory. . . . All you are is the thing that links the customer to the system. You ask the right questions so what the customer wants can be tapped into the machine, that's all your job is. If the consumer could get direct to the system, there would be no need for half of us to be here at all.

In part, how threatened clerks felt by computerization depended on the function in which they worked. There was considerably less need for acquired knowledge when dealing with orders for appliances or processing bills than there was when dealing with utility supply or queried accounts. Yet clerks often expressed *both* a belief that there were limits to how far their work could be specified in advance, and therefore limits to standardization and deskilling *and* the opinion that management was attempting to reduce them to a mere appendage of the machine. They saw that the new systems had already encroached on the discretionary content of their work, simplifying and standardizing tasks in such a way as to facilitate greater use of part time and temporary staff and making all clerks more readily disposable. They therefore held somewhat contradictory views on computerization, but the key point here is that both of these perceptions intensified their resistance to change. The fact that management had not anticipated, and did not fully appreciate, the problems which standardization and deskilling created reduced its legitimacy (management was 'out of touch', 'autocratic', a bunch of 'Yes Men, covering their own backs', and so on). The fact that management sought to make workers more readily disposable, and to replace full-time permanent employees with part-time and temporary workers made clerks very aware of the fact that management's interests conflicted with their own: 'I used to think that managers and staff were part of a team, but with the new systems coming in it is very much like being on opposing sides.' It also made many clerks see their relationship to NU in a new light. The company's rhetoric about 'caring' for employees was less potent when set against its growing preference for temporary and part-time contracts, and its drive to reduce staffing levels. As one clerk commented:

> People here are just another resource as far as management is concerned, a resource to be manipulated for the gain of the company, something they'll invest in or drop as it suits them, not something they have a commitment to.

Similarly, the proposals for functionally flexible teamworking sharpened the clerks' perceptions of contradictions in the work process. The importance of 'customer care' and 'customer service' had been key features of management's ideological armoury, and seemed, in the past, to be effective in winning a fairly high degree of consent to managerial authority and particular forms of work organization. It was probably no coincidence that plans to reorganize clerical work were introduced in tandem with an advertising campaign stressing the company's commitment to customer care, and an internal campaign exhorting employees to identify more closely with the customer's needs. Management attempted to 'sell' the new structure to the staff by claiming that its sole purpose was to improve standards of service for the customer. However, the fact that management was perceived as wishing to introduce the Beta structure 'on the cheap' (minimizing on staff training and keeping staffing levels low, pressing on with inadequate systems because of the expense involved in correcting them quickly and so on) undermined the claim that change was primarily intended to improve service. In the survey, over 70 per cent of all staff agreed with the statement that 'the real purpose of the Beta structure is to cut costs, cut staffing levels and increase profits'. As one clerk observed, 'All this has really proved to us that at the end of the day, the only thing that matters to management is profit'. This was of enormous significance for workers who dealt so constantly and directly with the customer. Management was forcing them to provide an unsatisfactory service, and the quality of their working lives was immediately and dramatically affected.

The essence of what happened at NU is well captured by Hyman's (1987: 43) observation that 'Employers require workers to be *both* dependable *and* disposable'. In implementing NOSS Beta, management unintentionally revealed this to clerical workers. It exposed them to the fact that management was dependent upon their knowledge and understanding as human participants in the work process, and yet would prefer to treat them as a mere commodity, to be taken on and dropped at will. At the same time, by making the profit motive manifest in a work environment which has traditionally sought consent through a 'service' ideology, management undermined its own legitimacy. Change momentarily illuminated facets of the employment relation which were normally obscured from view, and this was one reason why a normally fairly acquiescent workforce was motivated to resist management's plans for change.

RESISTING CHANGE

It has been seen that NOSS Beta generated opposition for a number of reasons. The effects of computerization upon clerical work were

widely disliked; clerks resented being asked to accept job enlargement without being offered any financial reward in exchange; they
were under pressure not only from backlogs of work, but also from
a barrage of abuse from dissatisfied customers; they were angered
to find management apparently attaching far greater priority to cost
cutting and profit maximization than to either customer service or
protecting employment security. However, a desire to resist management is not automatically translated into effective opposition, even
amongst well-unionized workers such as these. This section looks
at how resistance manifested itself, and why it took the forms it did.

Organized resistance: official forms

It was not until the beginning of 1989 that the unions were given any
really detailed information about how NOSS and the office reorganization would affect their members. At this point regional officials
from the main clerical union entered into negotiations over its
implementation. The union side won some important concessions
during these discussions but were unable to reach an agreement on
the grading of district clerks, who formed the vast majority of
administration staff. The union side's position was that district clerks
should be upgraded in recognition of their wider brief. Management
replied that although district clerks would be multi-functional in the
new geographical teams, the amount and complexity of work in
each function had been reduced by the new systems, so that on
balance, no more was being required of clerks.

Since negotiations had ground to a halt by August 1989, with
neither side being prepared to move on the grading of district clerks,
the union decided to hold a consultative ballot. Some 75 per cent of
the region's staff rejected the Beta structure on the consultative
ballot. The union formally declared a dispute with NU at the end of
September, and balloted its members again, this time asking
whether they would refuse to cooperate with the introduction of
Beta and be prepared to take strike action on one day per week, on
dates to be arranged. The result was for industrial action, but this
time with a much smaller majority.

However, no formal industrial action was ever taken. To understand why clerks were unable to mount effective resistance to
change through their union it is necessary to consider the nature of
the industrial relations machinery in the utilities, and a number of
factors internal to the union itself.

Industrial relations at NU are based upon the principals of the Whitley Report. Negotiating machinery is two tiered, with a National Joint Council (NJC) to negotiate the broad terms and conditions of employment (salary scales, gradings, shift patterns, health and safety, etc.) and Regional Joint Councils (RJCs) to negotiate the details of work organization and job descriptions within the parameters set by the NJC. Until privatization, NU management adopted a basically 'constitutionalist' approach to industrial relations, and it was rare for regional managements to introduce changes which undermined the spirit, far less the letter, of national agreements. In this context, the two-tier system was generally held to be effective.

In 1988, NU management initiated national-level review talks on flexible working with the clerical unions. It was seeking a broad package of changes, including functional flexibility, cooperation with new working practices and technology, greater staff mobility between locations, shift and week-end working, and much more. At national level, the union was concerned to achieve two things during these talks. First, it wished to negotiate a package which would protect its members from any harmful consequences of change – for example, to ensure that new technology would not be used to down-grade and deskill workers. Second, it hoped to win some major concessions in return for flexible working, including a no-redundancy agreement, agreements on payments and shift patterns, better annual leave, childcare allowances, and so on.

The national union believed it was in a fairly strong position to win these concessions, except for the timetabling of the talks. The problem was that the review talks were set to continue until mid-1990, and it was not until the end of that year that NU and the unions would actually enter into formal negotiations over flexible working. In the meantime, national union officials did not want regional union officers to strike any deals with regional management over flexibility, since this would undermine the national union's position when it finally got to the negotiating table. As a national official put it, 'If we're not careful, the employers will have no incentive to reach a national agreement, because they will have got it through in the regions on the cheap'.

The ambitions of the national union could only be realized if regional union officials adopted a strictly defensive position, deflecting management initiatives for flexibility. Thus the regional union faced a very real dilemma in its negotiations over NOSS Beta, since there was a great deal of overlap between the type of flexibility management was proposing at national level, and the type of flexibility entailed by NOSS Beta. The regional officials felt themselves to be 'piggy in the middle', with management eager to reach an agreement over the Beta structure, members keen to take industrial action in order to force some concessions from management in exchange for flexible teamworking, and the national union insisting that no agreements on flexibility should be reached.

The regional union therefore felt unable to authorize industrial action on the basis of the second ballot, and referred the matter to the union's national-level Emergency Committee. Since the national-level union's prime concern was to impede any regional agreements on flexibility, the Emergency Committee deferred making a decision and instructed regional officials to try to stall management as best as they could. This was an almost impossible task, particularly given that the introduction of flexible working practices was the culmination of a process of change (the introduction of NOSS) which had been underway for several years. Regional officials tried to slow management down by insisting on fuller consultation with the membership before the introduction of the Beta structure, but despite their efforts the Beta structure was imposed on Eastvale South in February 1990, and on other district offices later that year.

In short, then, the existing industrial relations machinery was ill-suited to deal with a regional management which was (probably deliberately) bypassing national negotiations. However, these problems should not have been insuperable, and it is possible that clerical workers would have been able to mount some form of resistance through their union had it not been for other problems of coordination and communication within the union itself.

Communication between national, regional and local level officials appeared to be less than adequate. For example, when a national official was interviewed during the course of this research, he was unaware of the details of the dispute over NOSS Beta, and did not know that management had already eliminated job demarcations within functions at Eastvale South and other district offices:

> They might think [flexibility within functions] is in, but I'm not convinced it is. There are a number of disputes in [that region] and I'm not sure what's happening with them. . . . I would dispute whether they've really done away with demarcations.

Even regional officials did not appreciate the full nature or extent of restructuring until after the second ballot, when closer consultation with local branches began. Local union representatives saw this lack of communication between branch and regional officials (as well as a lack of training in union matters) as having been a general problem for many years. For example, one ex-representative commented:

> I didn't get the chance to support my fellow workers because I didn't have the knowledge because I had no training. Three years with no back up, no training, no support. They just used me as a mailing point really. They never asked me what my members thought or what they wanted. There was no contact.

These problems became even more apparent during the course of the dispute. Union representatives at Eastvale South did not even know why no formal industrial action was taken after the second ballot. When asked about the dispute, one representative said:

> I think national deferred because they didn't know exactly what we were going to strike about. I've been told there's people in our own union that don't particularly want us to go on strike, but I'm not sure what's going on.

Another representative remarked:

> I don't really know to be honest. They say the union is only as strong as its members, and the members have asked for strike action and they weren't given it. I don't know why exactly.

Meanwhile, the rank-and-file members were becoming increasingly frustrated by the inaction of the union. Clerks said that the unions had not 'explained things well enough', that the two ballots were 'a fiasco', that the union was 'sitting on its bum while management does whatever they want'. However, despite their frustration, many clerks still felt unable to vocalize their demands at branch meetings, largely because they found these meetings intimidating. Though the majority of these clerks were female, all the representatives at Eastvale South at the time of the dispute were male, and at branch meetings, in the words of one clerk, 'it tends to be the men that have their say'. Furthermore, most clerks, both male and female, felt disempowered by their lack of general knowledge about trade union activities and procedures, and this contributed to their reluctance to make demands of the union. This point is illustrated by the comments of one young woman who had recently joined the union:

When I joined I just got this plastic wallet with all this information . . . I read through it, understood bits, didn't understand
other bits . . . no one sort of said 'We do this and that, and we
can do this for you' . . . they just give you the pamphlet and I
suppose they think you'll pick it up as you go along. But I still
don't really understand. I know they fight for us and stuff, but
whereas at these meetings there's a few that stand up and
speak their minds, I wouldn't do that, because I don't know
much about the unions. I stand in the back row and keep my
mouth shut. I'm worried about this Beta structure, so I've been
to all the meetings, but to be honest, I don't understand what
they're on about.

In short, even though a majority of clerks actively wanted to
strike, for a number of reasons no formal action was taken against
the Beta structure. Resistance did take other forms, however.

Organized resistance: unofficial forms

In many district offices, informal action against NOSS Beta was
mounted by the clerks. At Eastvale South, there were two unofficial
walk-outs in November 1989, and staff in two other district offices
also staged walk-outs the following month. At Eastvale South, the
walk-outs lasted no more than a couple of hours, but since they took
place during the peak hours of work they caused considerable
disruption. Local union representatives at Eastvale South also designed a programme of informal action to impede the introduction
of the Beta structure. To make the shift to multi-functional teamworking, management had to get clerks both to learn new tasks, and
to take on a training role, teaching others about their specialism.
Although their employment contracts were loosely specified in
terms of the range of tasks they could be asked to perform, there
was no provision requiring clerks to train others, since all training
was supposed to be offered by the training department. However,
the training department was numerically small and underfunded
and did not have the resources to train clerks to be fully
multi-functional. This gave the clerks the power to hamper the
implementation of the Beta structure by simply refusing to
cooperate with the training programme. Management could not
compel them to train each other, since this fell outside their job
specifications. As one union representative explained, 'It's tit for tat.

If someone says to a clerk "Can you train this person?", I advise them to say no. They're not paid to train other people.' This tactic was effective in slowing down the introduction of the Beta structure. Management responded by targeting training resources on one district at a time, which meant that the imposition of the Beta structure had to be staggered rather than simultaneous, but the clerks' refusal to train each other did not ultimately prevent the introduction of functional flexibility.

Other forms of resistance

Resistance also took less organized, more individualistic forms. To begin with, some instances of 'sabotage' were reported. By assiduously filling in all the details of a customer request, instead of using abbreviations or summarizing, some clerks found that certain screens could be overloaded so that they retained no information at all. They experimented with various other ways of making the system lose information. There were also cases of clerks in-putting obscenities on their VDUs (generally in reference to their district manager) and at least one case of a clerk taking job vouchers home and hiding them instead of in-putting the information on the VDU. Instances of 'sabotage' were not numerically large (only four out of 30 clerks interviewed admitted to, or professed knowledge of, such action), but are significant amongst a workforce which prides itself on customer care and service. These acts of sabotage, like other forms of resistance, appeared to be as much a protest against the idea that profit should take precedence over service, as against wages or conditions. Each of the four clerks who spoke of sabotage linked it in some way to the perceived shift in management's commitments (away from customer service and towards profit maximization) which was noted above. This draws attention to a limitation in Rudolph Rocker's view that 'the whole import of sabotage is actually exhausted in the motto, for bad wages, bad work' (quoted in Brown, 1977). One clerk nicely illustrated Jermier's (1988) point that 'sabotage is usually a rational choice, but is not without its regrets' when she said:

> I know I shouldn't muck about with the screens because it's the customer that suffers, but then I think 'Well, if management doesn't care tuppence, why should I?'.

Again, however, it is important to note that there are external factors which constrain workers' choices about how to resist. The new office technology had also made it far easier for management to monitor the workforce. NOSS now recorded every stroke of the keyboard made by each individual clerk. Obscenities could be traced back to their author (this led to the dismissal of one clerk), and likewise, mistakes (either genuine or deliberate) could be identified. Although this potential for control had, thus far, only been used in disciplinary cases, clerks were well aware of it and this may have made sabotage appear a less viable form of resistance than it might otherwise have done. NOSS's surveillance potential also made certain forms of 'passive resistance', such as working more slowly or taking more frequent breaks, less viable. For example, a system had been installed which allowed supervisors to continually monitor the performance of telephone enquiry operatives. The number of calls which each clerk had answered in the past half hour and during the entire day could be displayed on the supervisor's monitor, and if a call continued for longer than five minutes this was indicated on the supervisor's screen. The supervisor could then 'listen in' on the call, which ensured, in the words of one supervisor, 'that the girls [weren't] taking personal calls'. It seems reasonable to suppose that this kind of visibility would make certain forms of resistance less attractive options.

Clerks and union officials claimed there had also been a growth in absenteeism and staff turnover, though management declined to estimate by how much either of these had increased. However, in the survey, over 60 per cent of staff said that they would leave NU if they could find an equally well-paid job elsewhere, which gives some indication of the degree of dissatisfaction amongst the clerks. It also indicates the importance of external, structural factors in shaping the form which resistance takes. A majority of clerks in the office may have *wished* to 'vote with their feet', but this desire could only have been translated into action if labour market conditions had been extraordinarily favourable to them.

In summary, then, computerization and plans to introduce multi-functional teamwork generated a strong desire to resist amongst clerical workers at NU. It was difficult for them to mount effective opposition through their union, not simply because of problems with the existing industrial relations machinery, but also because of problems of coordination and communication within the union itself. They therefore had to find alternative ways of expressing their opposition and attempting to obstruct management, and in the final instance, their efforts were of limited success. These developments are considered in relation to theories of control and resistance below.

ON CONTROL AND RESISTANCE MORE GENERALLY

The case-study material presented above could be interpreted in several different ways. For example, the fact that management's plans to simplify and reduce the clerical workload had quite the reverse effect in practice, and the fact that in attempting to reduce the organization's dependence on the acquired knowledge and experience of the individual worker management inadvertently made this dependence manifest, could be explored in terms of the Weberian insight that social action often has unintended consequences. Another approach might lay particular emphasis on NU management's ineptitude (both in terms of planning and implementing change), considering this in relation to Marxist analyses of management's role in creating worker disaffection through its own technical incompetence (Nichols, 1986; Williams *et al..*, 1983). Other commentators, meanwhile, might be primarily concerned with the nature of the deskilling process to which the clerks were subjected. The question of whether they were skilled in the first place could stimulate a lengthy theoretical discussion centring, yet again, on the definitional problems associated with the term 'skill' (Braverman, 1974; Pollert, 1981; Manwaring and Wood, 1985; Jenson, 1989; Jones, 1989). This paper has focused on the sources and limits of clerical resistance, however, and the discussion will therefore centre on debates about control and resistance within the labour process tradition.

Although Braverman explicitly stated that *Labour and Monopoly Capital* was concerned with labour as a class in itself, rather than for itself (1974: 27), both admirers and critics have argued that to focus on labour solely as an object of capital leads to a distorted view of the capitalist labour process. As Elger (1982: 24) observed, such conceptualizations underline capital's capacity 'to reorganize the labour process, degrade the labourer and propel her/him from sector to sector', but forget 'that the working class remains an active agency in the capital relation'. The underestimation of the strength and importance of worker resistance to capital's control strategies in Braverman's work has provoked two main lines of criticism.

First, there are those for whom 'resistance' is synonymous with class struggle. For them, Braverman's analysis fails to reveal class struggle as a dynamic in the historical development of the labour process, and consequently neglects how capital, as a class, is forced to transform the production process and adopt new control strategies as a response to worker resistance (e.g. Edwards, 1979; Clawson, 1980). This kind of analysis is not without theoretical problems. As a number of commentators have observed (Littler and Salaman, 1984; Wardell, 1990; Knights, 1990), resistance here is implicitly conceived as one side of a control–resistance dualism, wherein workers are driven to resist by the same sort of ineluctable, functional imperative which drives capital to seek ever greater direct control over labour. Taken to an unacceptable extreme, such a view would reduce both managers and workers to mere bearers of structurally determined historic roles.

Second, there are those who explicitly treat 'resistance' as a variable, rather than universal, force at the point of production which management must adjust to, and can adjust to in a number of different ways (Friedman, 1977; Littler, 1982; Littler and Salaman, 1984). Yet even in those cases where claims about the significance, impact and consequences of 'resistance' are more cautious, the term itself remains problematic. The problem is that 'resistance' is a residual category. It can encompass anything and everything that workers do which managers do not want them to do, and that workers do not do that managers wish them to do. It can take in both collective and individual actions; it can embrace actions that are specifically designed to thwart management (such as strikes and work-to-rules), and those which may not be (such as absenteeism).

Resort to such an essentially residual category of analysis can easily obscure a multiplicity of different actions and meanings that merit more precise analysis in their own right. Whatever the adequacy of the above case study as a factual record, for example, it is true that workers' reactions to the changes taking place at NU were implicitly counted as resistance, whether they involved minor acts of sabotage, threats of strike action, refusal to cooperate actively with management, or simply quitting the organization.

It is important to catalogue different forms of resistance (Friedman, 1977; Littler, 1982; Edwards and Scullion, 1982; Edwards, 1990) and to note that workers' capacity for resistance is not undifferentiated. But it is also of both political and theoretical significance to ask whether management must *always* adjust to all types of resistance

94

(individualized and collective action, 'legitimate' acts such as quitting and 'illegitimate' acts such as sabotage, and so on) and to consider whether different forms of resistance elicit different responses.

Another feature of the above case study that merits attention in this more general discussion is that it serves to underline the fact that 'resistance' is not always or only a reaction to increased managerial control over the work process itself. Because clerks at NU saw the organization as fulfilling a socially useful function, the strengthened emphasis on profit at the expense of service was also deeply resented and contributed to the intensity of opposition to management's plans. In other words, workers' subjective states, and so how willingly they cooperate with management's objectives, are not simply affected by the immediate work situation as the control-resistance couplet suggests.[4]

Oddly enough, given that the control–resistance model was developed in response to a supposed omission in *Labour and Monopoly Capitalism*, this is a point which Braverman himself fully appreciated. He observed that workers' subjective states are not only affected by the organization of the labour process and forms of supervision over it, but also reflect their previous history, the general social conditions under which they work, the particular conditions of the enterprise and the technical setting of their labour (Braverman, 1974: 57). To this list we could add their evaluation of the social usefulness of the organization's product or service, and their assessment of whether or not the employing organization is predatory in its pursuit of profit.

Workers are subjective beings not automatons and they are, therefore, capable of mounting various forms of resistance. But it is important to see that this blindingly obvious truism (still sometimes triumphantly unfurled as if it were a revelation in some parts of the labour process literature) can only take us so far. For example, it is by no means certain that a more adequate concept of workers as subjects would contribute much to an understanding of the restructuring of the clerical labour process at NU. Recently, it has been implied that worker subjectivity is a determining force in the organization of the labour process (Knights, 1990), in the sense that workers collude with, and so reproduce, the structures and social practices that dominate them. The extreme political and theoretical implications of such a position cannot be explored here, except to note that they are antithetical to the Marxist tradition which informs labour process theory. This chapter can merely point out that subjective impulses are mediated by wider political, institutional and economic factors.

Changes to the organization of the labour process can (but do not always) provoke strong sentiments of opposition, but whether these are translated into action, and the form this action takes, and how successful this action is, all depend on a number of other factors. To begin with the most obvious, not all workforces are equally well unionized, and even amongst highly unionized workers, such as NU clerks, factors internal to their union can facilitate or inhibit certain forms of resistance. Labour market conditions can also be more or less favourable to workers who wish to resist management tactics. Bray and Littler have observed that,

> in general, we can say that the labour market structure sets the agenda of the control relationship. . . . This is because the ultimate form of managerial control is the power to threaten loss of employment, a relation which, in part, defines the nature of wage labour.
>
> (1988: 569)

By the same token, the labour market structure will impact on the form and intensity of resistance. Conditions within any given industry must also affect what workers decide to do about their discontents. National Utility had slashed its clerical and retailing workforce by over 30 per cent in the years between 1981 and 1989. This fact was not overlooked by clerks as they considered how best to resist and when to acquiesce.

Moreover, any subjective wish to resist is located in a broader historical and political context. It is true that resistance cannot be conceptualized as an automatic response to the stimulus of control, but neither can a lack of resistance be simply interpreted as active consent (or as 'constitut[ing]' a social practice' in order to reaffirm a 'subjective identity' as Knights (1990) would have it). Quitting a job, for example, is not a viable form of resistance if legislation such as the master and servant laws are in operation and workers can be imprisoned for breach of contract;[5] neither is it an option for most workers during periods of high unemployment. In circumstances where resistance could lead to dismissal, blocked promotion or financial hardship, whether or not workers choose to engage in particular forms of resistance must be determined as much, if not more so, by the workers' assessment of the *objective* consequences of such actions as by their subjective feelings about the work itself.[6]

Equally significant, on the management side of the equation strategies and responses to resistance are also influenced by wider political and economic features. Where labour markets are slack and the political climate more than usually favourable to the employer, there may be no need to modify the design of the labour process or soft pedal on the introduction of new technology as a response to worker resistance. As witnessed by events in the newspaper and docking industries, it is sometimes possible to simply dispense with the old, recalcitrant labour force.

At NU, the strength of worker resistance was a factor that contributed to management's decision to slow down the implementation of NOSS Beta, but it did not force management to abandon the plan. NU management clearly did not believe it was necessary or possible to jettison NOSS Beta, and this may have been partly because its goal was actually to replace large sections of the traditional clerical workforce with 'a new breed of employees'; namely part-time workers, 'mums with small children who want to work irregular hours, a few hours a day and less in the summer when the kids are on holiday', complemented by graduate trainees 'who are looking for a complete career package'. If the supply of the type of labour preferred by management outstrips the demand, resistance on the part of the existing workforce is hardly likely to be a determinant force in shaping the labour process.

In conclusion, the immediate work situation of clerical workers at NU was not the sole source of resistance – their subjective state was also shaped by their commitment to supplying a socially useful service, and their belief that privatization had made NU predatory in its pursuit of profit, as well as those factors listed by Braverman (1974: 57). The form that their resistance took, and the limits to what it could achieve, were above all constrained by the political, institutional and economic context in which their actions were set.

The broader implication of all this is simply that any theory of resistance or subjectivity which does not locate the subject firmly in the context of historical and objective constraints is more likely to intensify the 'crisis' of labour process theory than to revitalize it.

NOTES

1 The lack of data on clerical resistance could be because management have 'soft peddled' on fully exploiting the control potential of new office technology (Storey, 1986), or because it has offered various

financial 'sweeteners' to accompany the introduction of on-line processing and cross-functional teamworking (Batstone *et al.*, 1987), or
because white-collar workers are less likely to enter into non-pay
disputes with their employer (Carter, 1979), or simply because their
reactions have not been widely documented.

2 The bulk of NU's clerical work did not arise from utility supply, but from
   appliance retailing, repair and servicing. Anticipation of competitive
   pressures following the liberalization of this market made office work a
   key target for restructuring.

3 This case study formed part of a larger ESRC funded, Bristol University-
   based research project into restructuring and employment relations in
   the utilities. This project was structured as a number of case studies at
   NU as well as at a water authority which was preparing for privatization.
   Clerical work at Eastvale South was selected as one of these case studies
   for the following reasons. The Eastvale South office is the largest of the
   region's eight district offices, and NU management had selected it to
   pilot the Beta structure. Thus, when the research was planned in 1987,
   NU management told me that by 1989 clerical work in this office would
   be fully computerized and completely multi-functional, whereas other
   district offices would still be in the process of change. Eastvale South
   therefore promised to provide the opportunity to explore the responses
   of clerical workers to both new technology and flexible forms of work
   organization. (In practice, of course, for reasons set out in this chapter,
   clerical workers at Eastvale South were not yet working in functionally
   flexible teams when I arrived to undertake fieldwork. Instead, they
   were in dispute with their employer.)

Between August 1989 and January 1990 I visited the Eastvale South
office regularly. NU management were cooperative with the research. I
was given access to observe clerks working and was able to conduct 25
interviews of 40 minutes to one hour in duration, both in the formal
setting of a private office, and in the more informal setting of the
canteen. Data of a more systematic nature were obtained through a
survey. The questionnaire sought clerks' views on working with VDUs;
on NOSS; on the Beta structure; on the grading dispute; and further
attempted to measure job satisfaction and morale by asking whether
clerks would leave NU for an equally well-paid job elsewhere. It was
given to all clerks present in the office on the morning of the survey.
This amounted to 63 clerks (out of a workforce of about 80). Some 53
questionnaires were completed, a response rate of 84 per cent.

I was able to interview all the supervisors and district managers at the
office, as well as those senior managers from the regional headquarters
who were involved in the design and implementation of NOSS Beta.
The District Administration Manager gave several interviews over the
six-month fieldwork period, so that it was possible to discuss the
progression of the dispute with him. National, regional and local trade
union officials were also interviewed. Once again, repeat interviews
were obtained in order to discuss the progress of the dispute. Both NU
management and trade union officials were helpful in providing me
with relevant documents.

Although fieldwork for this particular case study ended in January 1990, I continued to undertake fieldwork in other functions in National Utility until August 1990, which meant that I was able to keep in touch with developments in the Eastvale South office.

4 This point also underlines the need for caution when dealing with sweeping claims about a 'new realism' on the part of workers. Consider, for example, Knights' (1990: 328) unsubstantiated and uncritical claim that 'The "New Right" clearly *appeals to* – and is productive of – the materials and symbols that confirm the subjective identities of *a majority of the population*, such that it can claim their willing submission to its power and truth effects' [emphasis added].

5 Price notes that master and servant law was a major weapon of industrial discipline throughout the eighteenth and much of the nineteenth century. It 'provided a convenient instrument for quick punishment or intimidation over a wide variety of offences ranging from neglecting work to refusing overtime . . . it was particularly useful for enforcing the employment contract . . . where long-term hiring remained common. . . . And its breach of contract clauses were used to order the twisters and rovers back to work in the Preston strike of 1853–4' (1986: 42). In other words, it made virtually all forms of resistance, even passive resistance, criminal offences.

6 Knights (1990) ignored the significance of a weakened labour market and strengthened legal constraints on trade unions for labour's capacity to resist restructuring in arguing that workers 'readily accepted' state-led interventions to curb the power of organized labour, and 'willingly submitted' to New Right policies (pp. 327–8). If a decrease in organized resistance to capital during a period of economic recession, high unemployment, soaring mortgage interest rates, and legal assault on trade unions can be taken as evidence of 'willing submission' and 'ready acceptance' on the part of the majority of the workers, then Conservative governments since 1979 could be accused of soft peddling on industrial reform. Using such logic, all that needs to be done to achieve virtually unanimous consent and industrial harmony is to make all forms of organized resistance criminal offences.

REFERENCES

Baran, B. (1988) 'Office Automation and Women's Work: The Technological Transformation of the Insurance Industry' in R. Pahl (ed.) *On Work*, Oxford: Blackwell.

Barras, R. and Swann, J. (1983) *The Adoption and Impact of Information Technology in the UK Insurance Industry*, Report No. TCCR-83-014, London.

Batstone, E., Gourlay, S. and Moore, H. (1987) *New Technology and the Process of Labour Regulation*, Oxford: Clarendon Press.

Braverman, H. (1974) *Labour and Monopoly Capital*, New York: Monthly Review Press.

Bray, M. and Littler, C. (1988) 'The Labour Process and Industrial Relations: Review of the Literature', *Labour and Industry*, 1, (3): 551–87.

Brighton Labour Process Group (1977) 'The Capitalist Labour Process', *Capital and Class*, 1.

Brown, G. (1977) *Sabotage: A Study in Industrial Conflict*, Nottingham: Spokesman Books.

Carter, R. (1979) 'Class, Militancy and Union Character: A Study of the Association of Scientific, Technical and Managerial Staffs', *Sociological Review* 27 (May): 297–316.

Clawson, D. (1980) *Bureaucracy and the Labor Process*, New York: Monthly Review Press.

Communist Party of Great Britain (1989) *Manifesto for New Times*, London: CPGB.

Crompton, R. and Reid, S. (1982) 'The Deskilling of Clerical Work', in S. Wood (ed.) *The Degradation of Work?* London: Hutchinson.

Edwards, R.C. (1979) *Contested Terrain*, London: Heinemann.

Edwards, P.K. and Scullion, H. (1982) *The Social Organization of Industrial Conflict*, Oxford: Blackwell.

Edwards, P.K. (1990) 'Understanding Conflict in the Labour Process: The Logic and Autonomy of Struggle' in D. Knights and H. Willmott (eds) *Labour Process Theory* London: Macmillan.

Elger, A. (1979) 'Valorisation and Deskilling: A Critique of Braverman', *Capital and Class* 7 (Spring): 58–99.

Elger, A. (1982) 'Braverman, Capital Accumulation and Deskilling', in S. Wood (ed.) *The Degradation of Work?* London: Hutchinson.

Friedman, A. (1977) *Industry and Labour. Class Struggle at Work and Monopoly Capital* London: Macmillan.

Gapper, J. (1989) 'Team-work System is Studied as Model in US', *Financial Times* December 89.

Glenn, E. and Feldberg, R. (1979) 'Proletarianizing Clerical Work: Technology and Organizational Control in the Office', in A. Zimbalist (ed.) *Case Studies on the Labor Process*, New York: Monthly Review Press.

Hyman, R. (1987) 'Strategy or Structure: Capital, Labour and Control', *Work, Employment and Society* 1 (1): 25–57.

Jenson, J. (1989) 'The Talents of Women, the Skills of Men: Flexible Specialization and Women' in S. Wood (ed.) *The Transformation of Work?* London: Unwin Hyman.

Jermier, J. (1988) 'Sabotage at Work: The Rational View', *Research in the Sociology of Organizations*, vol. 6, pp. 101–34.

Jones, B. (1989) 'When Certainty Fails: Inside the Factory of the Future', in S. Wood (ed.) *The Transformation of Work?* London: Unwin Hyman.

Knights, D. (1990) 'Subjectivity, Power and the Labour Process' in D. Knights and H. Willmott (eds) *Labour Process Theory,* London: Macmillan.

Lane, C. (1988) 'New Technology and Clerical Work', in D. Gallie (ed.) *Employment in Britain*, Oxford: Blackwell.

Littler, C. (1982) *The Development of the Labour Process in Capitalist Societies*, London: Heinemann.

Littler, C. and Salaman, G. (1984) *Class at Work*, London: Batsford.

Manwaring, T. and Wood, S. (1985) 'The Ghost in the Labour Process' in D. Knights, H. Willmott, and D. Collinson (eds) *Job Redesign: Critical Perspectives on the Labour Process*, Aldershot: Gower.

Nichols, T. (1986) *The British Worker Question*, London: Routledge & Kegan Paul.

O'Connell Davidson, J. (1990) 'The Road to Functional Flexibility: White Collar Work and Employment Relations in a Privatized Utility', *Sociological Review* 38(4): 689–711.

Pollert, A. (1981) *Girls, Wives, Factory Lives*, London: Macmillan.

Price, R. (1986) *Labour in British Society*, London: Croom Helm.

Storey, J. (1986) 'The Phoney War? New Office Technology: Organization and Control', in D. Knights and H. Willmott (eds) *Managing the Labour Process*, Cambridge: University Press.

Wardell, M. (1990) 'Labour and the Labour Process', in D. Knights and H. Willmott (eds) *Labour Process Theory*, London: Macmillan.

Williams, K., Williams, J. and Thomas, D. (1983) *Why Are the British Bad at Manufacturing?*, London: Routledge & Kegan Paul.

3

LEARNING THE SCORE

The duality of control and everyday resistance in the temporary-help service industry

Heidi Gottfried

Drawing on labour process and feminist theories, this chapter uses a dialectical approach to examine management strategies to secure workers' compliance with workplace control, and the forms of workers' resistance to that control when work is no longer location-specific, time-bound and male dominated. The data were culled from a five-month study using both participant observation of the intake process at four temporary-help service firms and interviews with temporary workers. Temporary clerical workers, who would seem to be the most susceptible to control and the least likely to have the organizational resources and opportunities to engage in resistance, participate in everyday acts of resistance that are individually engaged and immediate responses to the unequal power relations inherent in capitalist production and patriarchy. Evaluating traditional understandings of control and resistance against a changing work environment, the chapter discusses how a new spatiality of work transforms authority relations and organizational structures that in turn shape and limit control and resistance. Women's work culture enables a range of resistance practices, but in so doing, it contributes to accommodation by preparing women for unskilled, low-paid and unpaid domestic labour.

INTRODUCTION

The recent shift from industrial production to service work is a compelling reason to reassess research on control in the workplace. Contemporary research on workplace control centres around an examination of the capitalist labour process as revived by Braverman (1974). Seventeen years after the publication of *Labor and Monopoly Capitalism*, his work continues to play an important in defining the terms of debate. While labour process theorists acknowledge a debt to Braverman for refocusing attention on the labour process, many criticize his work for economic determinism (Burawoy, 1985) and for insufficient attention to resistance (Hodson, 1991; Knights and Willmott, 1990).[1] Recent contributors to the debate call for a dialectical approach which 'examines the deep structures that impact the interplay of administrative control and worker resistance' (Jermier, 1988: 105). A dialectical approach improves labour process theory, but the changing economic landscape poses a challenge to the adequacy of labour process concepts to explain worker conduct within an emergent pattern of contingent work – a pattern that promises to be one of the major shifts in the organization of work (Coyle, 1986, cited in West, 1990: 264).

Contingent employment, which uses workers on an as-needed basis, includes part-time, subcontracting and temporary work (Christopherson, 1987: 6). Workers employed by temporary-help service (THS) firms represent a growing portion of the US workforce in general, and among office workers in particular.[2] THS firms dispatched about 760,000 temporary workers on a daily basis to workplaces nationwide in 1985 (Pollock, 1986),[3] up from only 20,000 in 1956 (Gannon, 1984). Clerical work accounted for much of this growth, representing 60 per cent of all THS employment (Hartmann and Lapidus, 1989).[4] Despite the growth of this population, labour process studies continue to assume a traditional work setting with a prototypical male worker.

The movement towards a service economy, and the increasing reliance on contingent workers in industrial production have taken a gendered form (Beechey and Perkins, 1985; West, 1990). Contingent work has been the fate of many women, for both new entrants into the labour force as well as those seeking reemployment (Appelbaum, 1987). Women compose 62 per cent of all temporary workers (Howe, 1986), and nine out of ten temporary clerical workers (Christensen and Murphree, 1988). The almost exclusive recruitment of women to fill temporary clerical positions suggests the need to recast labour process theories in light of gender dynamics.

Drawing on labour process and feminist theories, this chapter examines management strategies to secure workers' compliance with workplace control, and the forms of workers' resistance to that control when work is no longer location-specific, time-bound and male dominated. Temporary clerical workers, who would seem to be the most susceptible to control and the least likely to have the organizational resources and opportunities to engage in resistance, participate in everyday acts of resistance that are individually engaged and immediate responses to the unequal power relations inherent in capitalist production and patriarchy. Evaluating traditional understandings of control and resistance against a changing work environment, the chapter discusses how a new spatiality of work transforms authority relations and organizational structures that in turn shape and limit control and resistance.

CONTROL AND RESISTANCE IN THE LABOUR PROCESS

Work within capitalism is both an economic and a political activity involving the production of goods and services and the exercise of power.

> Patterns of power in relations of production reflect the differential distribution among individuals and groups of the ability to control their physical and social environment and, as part of this process, to influence the decisions which are and are not taken by others. This ability is typically founded on privileged access to or control over material and ideological resources. Thus ownership and control over the means of production involve immense power, since it carries the ability to admit or exclude those who depend on employment for their living.
>
> (Hyman, 1975: 88)

Ownership and control over the means of production and the power they confer are, to use Edwards' (1979) phrase, a contested terrain creating both the necessity for capitalist control over the labour process and the possibility for its transformation.

The necessity for capital's control over the labour process stems from the contradictory nature of capitalist production. Social relations between capital and labour are antagonistic as surplus value is produced by labour and appropriated by capital. While capitalism as a system compels workers to obtain employment for wages, individual capitalists face the problem of extracting labour from the labour power of workers. The economic compulsion to sell their labour power to capitalists in exchange for wages does not guarantee that workers will perform at their potential once they are on the payroll. This discrepancy between what the capitalist buys (labour power) and the requirements of production, referred to by

Littler (1982: 31) as 'the central indeterminacy of labor potential', creates the imperative for capitalists to control the labour process (R. Edwards, 1979: 12).

Capital's attempts to solve the indeterminacy of labour potential, and thereby secure surplus value, have centred on control strategies that conjoin time and effort. Control on the shopfloor regulates work intensity (e.g. speed or the length of the working day) by minimizing the amount of unperformed potential labour time. In THS work, time and effort become dissociated. THS firms profit from time on-the-job (e.g. the number of hours at a placement site) leaving control over effort to the client (this will be discussed more fully below).

Indeterminacy creates an imperative for control, but does not dictate any specific form control must take (Thompson, 1990). Following P.K. Edwards (1990: 130) control refers to a system of regulation that permits some form of behaviour and tends to rule out others, its parameters can be summarized in the concept of 'frontier'. The frontier of control does not derive from an objective logic of capitalist development, but rather 'arises from the activities of both "sides" and embraces informal and formal elements' (P.K. Edwards, 1990: 130); control is the outcome of struggle. Delimiting this struggle and its effects remain a major project for labour process theory, raising the question: How much and to what extent do workers' actions matter, not only for the reproduction of capitalist social relations, but also for shaping and ultimately transforming them?

Research on resistance identifies constant and continuing conflict as 'normal' features of work organizations and workers' conduct.

> Despite the major efforts of senior executives to legitimize the activities, structure and inequalities of the organization and to design and install 'foolproof' and reliable systems of surveillance and direction, there is always some dissension, some dissatisfaction, some effort to achieve a degree of freedom from hierarchical control – some resistance to the organization's domination and direction.
>
> (Salaman, 1979: 145)

Resistance implies agency in the context of power relations, where agency can be understood in terms of consciousness or action, whether structurally or subjectively determined, either collectively or individually engaged.[5]

105

In class analyses and conventional organizational- and industrial-relations studies, resistance has been developed as a political concept, with a focus on institutional-level struggle among (formally or informally) organized collectivities. The emphasis has been on the structural dimensions and institutional relations characterizing the resistance of labour to economic and political control and exploitation (Hyman, 1987), sometimes examined in terms of worker recalcitrance, opposition and non-compliance (Edwards and Scullion, 1982).

Other contemporary theories of resistance have taken a 'bottom–up' perspective and focus on the cultural significance of everyday acts of resistance. Following in the tradition of ethnographic studies of underclass groups (Chicago school) (Anderson, 1923; Kornblum, 1974; Roy, 1959) and cultural studies of workers' cultures and subcultures (Birmingham school) (Clarke *et al.*, 1976; Willis, 1990), this work explores the complex mediations of the dichotomy accommodation/resistance accomplished by workers in the workplace and the myriad tactics of survival that refuse assimilation, incorporation or inculcation (Willis, 1974). Contrary cultural definitions are always in play, reflecting the structural difference between the material position, outlook and everyday life-experience of the different classes (Clarke *et al.*, 1976: 42).

Cultural studies reconceptualize the social formation 'as a structure of relatively autonomous levels of social practices, giving ideology and culture a central and determining influence that could not merely be explained as the displaced trace of other forms of social practice' (Grossberg and Nelson, 1988: 7). Society generates cultural diversity and differentiation through multiplication of social worlds and logics, points of antagonism proliferate, creating a plurality of subject positions (Hall, 1988). Hall continues that we:

> lack an overall map of how these power relations connect and of their resistances. Perhaps there isn't, in that sense, one 'power frame' at all, more a network of strategies and powers and their articulations – and thus a politics which is always positional.
>
> (Hall, 1988: 27)

This rejection of the singularity of subject positions, and the impulse to move away from deterministic accounts, however, only multiplies the problem. Brennan (1989: 13) asks whether this current emphasis on negotiation, ambivalence and what Laclau and Mouffe

(1985) call a 'pluralism of subjects' constitutes a paradoxical re-fashioning of liberalism's own illusion about itself. The redefinition of politics within the ideological struggle displaces politics, removes class from its determining function and fails to theorize the articulation of different structural positions.

Sharing cultural studies' focus on the formation of work cultures, socialist-feminist theory can provide a map to connect various oppressive relations – particularly capitalism and patriarchy, but also including racism, heterosexism[6] and imperialism – conceptualized either as independent systems that reinforce each other (Hartmann, 1981) or as parts of a unitary system (Sargent, 1981). Socialist-feminism casts women as subjects in a double sense. Women are *authors* of their own histories; and as historical agents, women have the potential of seeing themselves, and not solely through the eyes or the image which a masculine culture has defined for them. But as historical subjects, women are also *subjected* to structures of domination. Structures are gendered to the extent that advantage and disadvantage, exploitation and control, action and emotion, meaning and identity are patterned through and in terms of a social distinction between male and female, masculine and feminine (Acker, 1990; Game and Pringle, 1984).

Structures of domination generate the grounds for resistance, but do not determine the repertoire of actions once and for all time or on a day-to-day level. Resistance can be mapped on a continuum marked at one end by institutionalized labour conflict which involves more expansive capital and labour relations, definitive forms of organization and manifest conflict at both the institutional and shopfloor level. Workers' strikes, both official and unofficial, are examples of institutional labour conflict. On the other end of the continuum is resistance that takes place on a local, immediate and often informal level. This might be called everyday forms of resistance, including covert and subtle forms like restriction of output and rule violations, or more illicit, subterranean forms like sabotage and theft (Edwards and Scullion, 1982; Jermier, 1988). Jermier sums up the connection between 'seemingly petty and unheroic' worker resistance and larger class struggles:

> Workers are no less class actors because they avoid open confrontation with coercive instruments of capital, the mass strike, and even contract strikes in favor of subterranean protest.
>
> (Jermier, 1988: 121)

Taking gender struggle as an orienting problematic, feminists have criticized the gender-neutral conceptualizations of labour resistance developed in class analysis or models of organizational control (Ferguson, 1984; Milkman, 1985). While studies of worker strikes have made the experiences of male, blue-collar workers as the model, feminist scholars have found a qualitative difference between women's and men's resistance experiences. Kaplan's (1982) concept of a life-nurturing orientation as the instigating and organizing principle in women's political, collective action develops an important counterpoint to the male-dominated assumptions about large-scale labour resistance. Costello (1987) finds women's labour solidarity to be fragmented and subverted by class affiliations as well as familial and domestic responsibilities and expectations. Or women may weave domestic rituals and celebrations of women-centred events (e.g. marriages or the birth of a child) into an ensemble of practices that constitute an oppositional culture to resist management control (Westwood, 1985). The family/work nexus determines the conditions under which women and men sell their labour power, and offers clues to understanding practices performed in, or absent from, the workplace.

The complex mediations between accommodation and resistance set limits on transformative capacities of women's work cultures. The appropriation of femininity or womanhood can be an expression of resistance as well as accommodation (Anyon, 1983; Brittan and Maynard, 1984; McRobbie, 1981). Valli (1986) shows how women becoming clerical workers use a culture of femininity to resist impositions of wage labour, but in doing so, they tacitly consent to and confirm their subordination, preparing themselves for unskilled, low-paid and unpaid domestic labour.

Many studies from a feminist perspective – including this one – suggest that women often engage in less visible forms of resistance that take place on, and are rooted in, everyday life. Institutional labour conflict depends on a high degree of worker market power (control over the supply of labour power) and worker production power (control over sources of uncertainty in the labour power). Any group able to maintain a shortage of labour power (worker market power) – whether real or manipulated – possess some leverage over production decisions (worker production power). Sex segregation, which relegates women to secondary labour market jobs (minimal job security and unstable employment), lowers their market and production power, thereby minimizing their participation in institutional labour conflict.

The discussion above located the dynamics of control and resistance in capitalist work organization. Studies of resistance apply different approaches, but have tended to privilege class over gender, ignore gender altogether as a principle orienting resistance activities, or allow the possibility for multiple subject positions without naming these positions or theorizing their connections. Socialist-feminists have proposed alternative conceptualizations that retain cultural studies' sensitivity to agency but that theorize the subjection of women as well.

The dialectical relationship between control and resistance can be best explored when situated in historically specific cases and contexts. The requirements of capitalist production dictate only the need for control and the existence of conflict, but not the forms control and resistance take. These forms reflect past struggles for control and current resolutions to these struggles. To delineate contemporary forms of and interplay between administrative control and worker resistance, we turn to an examination of the particular conditions in the THS industry.

DATA AND METHODS

The data were culled from a five-month study using both participant observation of the intake process at four THS firms (two large national firms and two local firms) located in a medium-sized mid-western city in the United States, and interviews with 18 temporary workers. Coregistration (the trade's term for being retained by multiple temporary-help service suppliers) with the four THS firms produced two clerical work assignments: a placement at a university department lasting four days and a placement at a florist spanning five consecutive days.[7] The assignments came from each of the two largest THS firms in the United States. Time between job placements was spent waiting to receive telephone assignments and calling each firm once a week to enquire about new jobs. Additional visits to one firm, for training on a personal computer, allowed me to observe others during their intake process.

The intake process served as the initial port of entry into THS work. THS firms use an intake process as a means of selecting employees and establishing the rules to be followed in the absence of direct supervision. Each prospective employee takes an array of tests to provide information about past work experience and is observed during this intake process. To secure entry, I kept my identity hidden from both employers and coworkers. This meant omitting information about my advanced education as well as my intended research plans, and having a friend relay calls to me at my office. Other labour process studies have favoured the use of hidden observation because it increases the likelihood of entry into the workplace and of being able to experience work as an insider (Cavendish, 1982). Secrecy, however, is not without its critics or problems. The participant observer must consider ethical dilemmas, weighing the potential benefits for the affected community against the possibility of injuring any party to the research.

Field notes catalogued the intake procedures of each THS firm (lasting from two hours to half a day), detailed the labour process at the two placement sites and recorded my experiences at the end of each working day. The participant observer's immersion in a context opens up ways of seeing that can reveal practices 'unnoticed' through the use of other methods (Smith, 1987), especially more subtle and less visible forms of control and resistance (Gottfried and Sotirin, 1991). This immersion, however, limits disclosure of some 'social facts'. Participant observation emphasizes detailing of events at the expense of describing actors' meaning systems (Jermier, 1988: 118) and occurs within work situations where atomization and fragmentation, characteristic of many labour processes including temporary clerical work, tie workers to their job precluding the participant observer from much social intercourse (Knights and Collinson, 1985: 205). Taking sides, whether the worker's – as in this case study – or management's, limits the participant observer's access to the other. Furthermore, there is no way of knowing management's real intentions; they can only be inferred from observations and employer documents (Graham, 1991: 1).

To compare my workplace experiences with those of others, I held conversations[8] with three male and 15 female temporary clerical workers who were identified through a modified snowball sampling technique.[9] These respondents, ranging in age from 25 to 35, pursued temporary work as an interim strategy either while looking for more permanent employment or while between jobs, possessed a high degree of skill (including high levels of literacy, some college education and upper-level typing speeds), generally relied on their own income for subsistence, and all but two had no children. They differed from the demographic profile of the temporary workforce overall in that female respondents tended on average to be younger and have fewer children, but shared a sub-cultural background (see Table 3.1).[10]

CONTROL AND RESISTANCE AT WORK

The frontier of control: a duality of structures

Flexible specialization has become a catch phrase of the 1990s to define a new spatiality of work, signalled by a shift from Fordist to post-Fordist production processes (Jenson, 1989; Jessop, 1988). Post-Fordism replaces Fordist production methods (task fragmentation, functional specialization, mechanization and assembly line) with a 'social organization of production based on work teams, job rotation, flexible production, integrated production complexes' (Kenney and Florida, 1988: 122). Flexibility associated with post-Fordism entails the breakdown of hierarchical work organization and the decentring of regulation which disperses control functions to individuals and small groups of workers. Such a concept includes both temporal and spatial dimensions often left out of traditional labour process theory, but post-Fordism does not precisely describe the 'flexibility' inherent in THS work.

Table 3.1 Demographic characteristics of THS employees and other members of the labour force

		Minorities %	*Age*	*No. of children*	*MNS* %
Women					
THS	(n = 160)	21.0	34.2	1.59	44.0
Others	(n = 372)	17.0	37.3	1.52	49.0
Men					
THS	(n = 160)	29.0	32.0	1.17	30.0
Others	(n = 372)	9.0	39.0	1.73	73.0

Source: Data are sample means (except per cent where noted) calculated from May 1985 Current Population Survey, by Lapidus (1989).

Notes: MNS = Married, not separated.
OTHERS is a random sample of men and women in the labour force.

111

THS work alters standard assumptions about spatiality and temporality in the organization of capitalist production. Whereas in traditional work settings spatiality is circumscribed and workers are unified under one roof, temporary work occupies an institutional space that spans multiple locations. Temporary workers perform their tasks at widely distributed work sites and are no longer situated in immediate proximity to their THS supervisors. For these workers, management of production and management of labour reside in separate organizational domains. Temporality has entailed a standard of working time historically fixed in terms of hours and days; now time discontinuities characterize the intermittent use of temporary labour power.

These changing spatial and temporal dimensions present new problems of conceptualizing and actualizing control over and resistance by workers. Indeterminacy of labour potential, a problem for all capitalists, is exacerbated by these changes. Consequently, THS firms develop a frontier of control for regulating struggle among workers dispersed across multiple job sites. This operates on two institutional levels: (1) a decentralized level, whereby the THS firms indirectly control workers by dispersing responsibility for control to individual workers,[11] and (2) a bureaucratic level, whereby the THS firm rationalizes jobs in the organization's hierarchy delimiting a set of tasks, competencies and responsibilities (Gottfried, 1991). The firm, along with its clients, attempts to secure the temporary clerical worker's compliance by applying a double layer of management which subjects workers to overlapping systems of sanctions imposed by and between the firm and the client.

THS authority relations differ from those in more commonly studied manufacturing industries. There is a *duality of structures* describing the presence of contradictory structural elements underlying THS authority relations in place of unitary control objectives: bureaucracy coexists with decentralization based on contradictory organizational rationalities. Because of this duality, the ideal-typical concept of bureaucratic control (R. Edwards, 1979) only loosely applies. Service-sector employment, especially temporary jobs, do not offer the same bureaucratic rights and protections that have developed through worker struggles in the manufacturing sector. The frontier of control in the THS industry, like its bureaucratic counterpart, seeks worker identification with the goals of capitalist production and loyalty to the firm, but relies on a different ensemble of institutional practices to accomplish these twin goals.

THS control shares with post-Fordism a mode of regulation that disperses control functions and articulates different forms of control into an overall system. In contrast to post-Fordism, there are no work teams to monitor worker behaviour. While temporary workers are a prototypical workforce in the Marxian sense – they sell their labour power in exchange for wages and exercise no authority over other workers – they supply highly flexible labour power, perhaps more so than workers in any other work setting. Temporary clerical workers are close to being part of the reserve army of labour,[12] are subordinate to two or more organizations, are recruited to perform 'deskilled' work and are predominately women. These workers exist in the margins between wage and non-wage work. While flexibility is built into the THS labour force, it must be sustained by both, and between, the firm and the client.

Learning the score

The first layer of management involves an intake process during which prospective employees learn to work 'responsibly' without direct supervision. Mechanisms of control principally take ideological and symbolic forms that construct temporary work as 'women's work'. The temporary clerical is subject to the second layer of management by the client who relies on traditional control mechanisms to keep workers in line.

The intake process is one of the few times THS managers have sustained contact with their employees. Each firm uses direct observation, interviews and graded tests to collect information about the applicant's basic clerical skills and to check reliability. They monitor the applicant's performance in a 'simulated office setting' while the applicant is expected to take careful note of the surroundings. An orientation booklet sums up the purpose of the interviewing and testing process: '[the intake process] evaluates not only office skills, but important intangibles too. Things like how you will work under pressure or unsupervised'. The brochure of a large THS firms states that 'Predictable Performance not only makes you more confident and efficient, it makes you more valuable to our customers'.

Two of the largest firms emphasize timed tasks and tests during their intake process. One large firm also administers a standardized test to tap the applicant's behavioural responses in a variety of high-pressured work situations. To use time efficiently, applicants are expected to pick up information embedded in typing tests and in encounters with their supervisors. In the two smaller firms, the typing test both evaluates secretarial skills and instructs the applicant about the proper behaviour for temporary workers in the absence of the firm's supervision.[13]

Mechanisms of control attempt to construct temporary work as 'women's work'. Hochschild (1983) relates women's work to a type of labour performed focusing on emotional labour. Those who perform emotional labour in the course of giving service are like those who perform physical labour in the course of making things; both are subject to the rules of mass production, but what is being mass produced is a smile, a feeling, a relationship. This affective production commodifies the worker such that certain feminine characteristics (e.g. charm, poise, courtesy, personality and appropriate dress) become associated with the performance of women's work.

Affective production is present in THS firms which commodify workers by selling not only a set of competencies but also a gendered subject to a client in the same way that a manufacturing firm subcontracts standardized parts from a supplier. When clients purchase the labour power of a temporary worker, they expect a person whose conduct and demeanour conform to extant organizational norms. The production of gendered subjects principally utilizes symbols that express and reinforce femininity, taking forms in dress and conduct, rather than the performance of emotional labour. However, temporary clericals who come in contact with the clients of the client may be called upon to perform emotional labour. Nevertheless, emotional labour plays a smaller role in the production of gendered subjects in temporary clerical jobs than in other female-typed jobs since it implicates social relationships absent from THS work.

A proper feminine appearance plays a central role in the process of symbolically constituting the temporary clerical worker as a gendered subject. For example, dress codes are signifying practices which narrowly define gender differences. Supervisors communicate proper feminine appearance in explicitly assigning appropriate dress for each assignment. One firm defines 'appropriate' attire for women as a dress to be worn on the first day of an office assignment. Another firm's brochure stresses first impressions. 'First impressions are often lasting impressions. That is why it is important how you present yourself on the first day of your assignment'.

Dress codes mean more than merely 'looking nice', they reinforce feminine qualities that foster competition between temporary clerical workers for a presumed male audience (bosses or customers). On one assignment the supervisor gave us the option of wearing casual clothes. We ignored the explicit instruction, and arrived in either business suits or professional dresses, indicating the significance of gendered self-portrayal in our calculus of 'appropriate' job performance. The style of dress seemed peculiar in a job context that never came in contact with the public. In place of the smile frozen on the faces of flight attendants is a 'uniform' style of dress that encodes femininity.

Gender symbols and ideologies both foreground women's identities as mothers–wives or as sex objects abstracted from the family/work nexus to affect control (Beechey and Perkins, 1985: 251–2); and they present the family/work nexus to women as a trade-off between family obligations on the one hand, and wage labour on the other. The trade-off is expressed in management's emphasis on what Collinson (1987) calls the 'mutual reciprocal and voluntary nature' of temporary clerical work. This is effective as an ideological control mechanism because it resonates with presumed gender differences in work commitments and expectations, especially with regard to women's responsibility for both child-rearing and housework. While THS firms expect to tap a portion of their female labour pool already formed in and constrained by family obligations, they must construct traditional gender appearances at the workplace regardless of a woman's marital status.

THS firms promote gender differences using various mechanisms. One large THS firm projects this message through a slide presentation. The narrator fixes the meaning of the images by characterizing the workplace as 'a place to meet interesting people'. Such descriptions discursively encode the workplace as either a dating service for an implied single woman whose main concern is finding a suitable marriage partner, or an outlet for an implied married woman from the solitude of domestic work. In the course of the 'sex games' played at work, female temporary clericals are encouraged to develop a split identity, simultaneously imagining themselves as wage-workers and as women. The maintenance of temporary clerical work as women's work involves the representation of wage employment in terms of gendered activities outside the workplace. By invoking commitments to non-employment concerns (e.g. family, marriage, leisure) juxtaposed against employment mandates, the THS firm precariously balances the contradictory principles of self-reliance, on the one hand, and loyalty on the other.

At the client, the fragmented nature of the clerical labour process permits easy movement of temporary clerical workers into and out of work, and atomizes work relations by keeping the temporary worker detached from other workers – whether or not the temporary worker is isolated from or working alongside either permanent or temporary clericals. Temporary clerical work individualizes employment relations, eliminating the basis of comparison (e.g. office average) by which a temporary clerical worker can measure output to determine a fair day's work.

Both placements exhibited this fragmented labour process. The first placement at a university department physically separated me from other employees. At the second placement, a florist employed 25 temporary clerical workers during a Mother's Day holiday rush. Despite the addition of this legion of workers, the florist slotted people into one of three positions with minimal on-the-job training. Telephone operators received a brief orientation; a sheet with a sample script served as a guide. CRT operators and Mercury dispatchers (operators of a computer used to transmit flower orders) similarly began working after a short review of the sequencing of data entry. Although the work flowed unevenly, few people strayed from their work stations. None of us knew each other nor did we have the chance to learn or to establish group norms.

As others have found, computer-based technologies relieve on-site supervisors from monitoring workers closely (Barker and Downing, 1980; R. Edwards, 1979). In this example, the florist incorporated 25 temporary clerical workers without having to change its management structure. Technical control is particularly effective because temporary clerical workers have no recourse to collectively established routines for regulating output.

THS firms establish control through gendered ideological mechanisms during the intake process. Prospective employees leave the intake process supplied with materials detailing the conditions of employment, reminding the new employees of their contractual obligations and stipulating the rules of on-the-job behaviour (e.g. dress codes and supervisory protocols) that the applicant must follow in the absence of direct management. Continuous enforcement of these rules, however, presents problems for THS firms. The client relies on traditional control mechanisms (e.g. technical control) to regulate temporary workers' behaviour. These dual layers of management, originating in and extending between the firm and the client, are uncoordinated and contradictory.

The duality of control structures erects formidable barriers against agency, but the contradictory nature of joint control creates a space for agency.

The limitations of joint control

Contracting temporary help from firms presents problems of worker control for the client. Since clients appropriate surplus labour, they face the problem of actually extracting labour from the labour power of a worker. The threat of disposability and the absence of job rights pressure temporary workers to intensify their labour, but the client has few other sanctions to enforce productivity levels. Moreover, any loyalty a temporary worker may feel is directed towards the THS firm.

While the client and the firm share a goal of controlling workers, dualistic control involves linking together control strategies of the client and of the THS firm that have contradictory goals. The firm and clients share a common interest in ensuring an adequate supply of cheap labour (i.e. minimizing variable capital). Their interests diverge at the point of production. On the one hand, the client derives profits from control over the worker's *work intensity*. On the other hand, the firm generates profit from control over the worker's *time at work*. Consequently, the client profits more when work is complete in a short amount of time (increased effort), the firm if the same work takes more time. While both the firm and client extract shares of surplus value produced by labour, the THS extracts shares from both the client and the worker. This conflict between the firm and client, among THS firms, between labour and capital, and the contradictions embedded in dualistic control, gives workers a space for resistance.

Everyday acts of resistance among temporary clerical workers

Much of resistance theory and research predicates the possibility of resistance on people having opportunities to build collective awareness and solidarity with other people. Some add a further condition that workers need 'substantial control over the labour process before the means of restricting effort can become feasible or even thinkable' (Edwards and Scullion, 1982: 271). The existence of resistance in the THS industry, despite the absence of these preconditions, suggests the need to modify conventional assumptions. Solidarity cannot be forged easily in the bonds between clerical workers (Costello, 1987; Gottfried and Fasenfest, 1984). Although temporary clerical workers are not part of a collectivity from which to learn and to enact resistance rituals, they creatively improvise from accumulated experience which becomes the repository of knowledge and the pragmatic grounds for resistance.

As people 'produce culture' at work, they generate a set of practices and ideas that run counter to hegemonic ones, setting up alternative ways of 'making sense' (Cockburn, 1985: 167), if only in embryonic form (Gramsci, 1971: 327). Alternative ways of making sense inform resistance that occurs as everyday acts rooted in, and directed against, power relations experienced on the shopfloor. Resistance involves actions carried out by subordinate groups (defined, for example, by class, gender or race) that undermine or disrupt the objectives of corresponding dominant groups.[14] In the capitalist firm, resistance may include specific actions to block capital accumulation (slow-downs, work-stoppages, etc.) or other actions that articulate orientations contrary to hegemonic ones (e.g. symbolic). These actions are expressions of workers' 'normal' conduct, regardless of solidaristic conditions.

The ubiquity and importance of resistance in the experiences of wage-workers invites a tendency to find resistance everywhere and celebrate it unreflectively (Milkman, 1985). Consequently, conceptualizations must consider the dialectic relation between resistance and accommodation, and its potential to fragment as well as unite women workers. By analysing the frontier of control, we can identify forces which shape both the repertoire of resistance, and the circumstances under which it arises (Edwards and Scullion, 1982: 271). Resistance is not simply a reaction to control, it also constrains and alters its frontier. A dialectic approach mandates examination of the deep structures that impact the subtle interplay of administrative control and worker resistance (Jermier, 1988: 105).

As one of the most vulnerable groups of workers, temporary clerical workers have minimal access to resources necessary for mobilizing collective actions or institutional labour conflict. Their resistance is constituted as everyday acts, individually engaged, informal, immediate, local, and often invisible; are defensive, accommodative actions; and involves a limited withdrawal of cooperation with management, ranging from work-to-rule to sabotage.[15]

The refusal to make adjustments (insisting on 'work-to-rule') constitutes a withdrawal of cooperation since workers suspend adaptation games (like Burawoy's making-out) that maintain productivity levels. Because management informally sanctions adaptation games, this form of non-compliance is not subject to punitive legal reprisal. As a form of resistance it allows workers to remain on-the-job continuing to work while throwing a proverbial wrench into the production machinery by disrupting work flow and slowing down work intensity. Work-to-rule, however, is a defensive action.[16] This form of resistance leads to accommodation by failing to challenge the rules of the game.

Work-to-rule implies that workers possess detailed knowledge of organizational policies and procedures in order to subvert them. The limited tenure inherent to temporary clerical work would seem to prevent temporary workers from working to rule. While temporary clerical workers may lack knowledge of specific work rules, their accumulated experience becomes a repository of knowledge for use in this form of resistance.

An incident during my placement at the university department illustrates the ability of temporary clerical workers to work-to-rule. On one of my first days on-the-job I discovered a discrepancy in the copy editor's instructions. When this error was brought to my supervisor's attention, she responded, 'They paid good money for a copy editor to correct the text', and instructed me, 'not to read for meaning of the text, but instead just type it'. This recourse to the authoritative expert and denigration of my knowledge based on the authority of experience left me less willing to make the usual adjustments. My response was to work-to-rule: typing the words without regard for their meaning.

Withdrawal of cooperation also can take symbolic expressions and gendered forms, such as the appropriation of femininity in the service of resistance. For example, styles of dress can subvert dress codes by projecting individuality. Temporary clerical workers interpret dress codes for their own purposes such as stretching the meaning of 'appropriate' by wearing slacks on the first day of a new job despite the recommendation to 'dress for success'. Those with the longest accumulated experience as temporary clerical workers are most likely to appropriate styles of dress to resist prepackaged gendered identities. Without the culture developed in the social relations between co-workers, only past practice remains to guide temporary clerical worker's resistance. Yet again, resistance is accommodative in that appropriation of gendered symbols stays within the narrow limits of femininity.

The possibilities for more illicit, subterranean forms of resistance like sabotage and theft have been enhanced by computerization giving workers the ability to shut down entire systems with minimal effort. A skilled computer operator can damage a system by unleashing a program virus, erase files or forget to save one or many documents in whole or in part. There is increasing evidence of computer-based sabotage by clericals subject to technical control (Gottfried and Fasenfest, 1984).

Among resistance tactics common to clericals are the many ways they find to reappropriate control over space, movement and time (e.g. taking extra time in the bathroom, misfiling, forgetting to correct typos) to disrupt organizational routines (Judith Ann, 1970). Temporary workers may put in more 'real' time than permanent clerical workers since the former have less (or at least don't feel they have) ability to engage in non-productive activities such as chatting in the halls or taking long coffee breaks. The relative absence of solidaristic conditions makes it difficult for temporary clerical workers to resist by extending their control over time and space.

As modes of daily activity, resistance provides women with ways of negotiating individually felt social conflict or oppression. This activity remains just that, individual, fragmented and isolated from the group (Brittan and Maynard, 1984). Such resistance focuses on the wage–effort bargain and the frontier of control, and rarely touches the more 'global' issues of ownership, appropriation and distribution of surplus value.[17] Accommodation is not without resistance but resistance often produces accommodation as well. Workers' adaptation games can disrupt production as well as promote capitalist objectives, but resistance remains accommodative as long as workers continue to play by the rules of the game.

CONCLUSION

This case study of the THS industry reveals a frontier of control that differs from those operating in more commonly studied manufacturing industries. Theories of control must take account of the burgeoning service sector. Service jobs do not offer the same bureaucratic protections that have developed through worker struggles in manufacturing. Temporary workers are subject to a double layer of management, combining bureaucratic and decentralized control mechanisms. Control is not necessarily a succession of discrete management systems that embody a single organizational logic; bureaucracy coexists with decentralization rooted in opposing organizational logics. Contrary to expectations, particularistic distinctions like those based on gender have not disappeared with the increased use of bureaucratic control.

Capitalism may not operate like an impersonal machine geared to the extraction of surplus value and indifferent to the sorts of people absorbed (Davies, 1990: 401). Gender not only identifies the incumbents who are queued up for temporary clerical positions, but also provides a way to encode and decode meaning. Womanhood, as expressions of femininity and the family/work nexus, informs the gendered ideologies that THS firms use to construct women's work and the resistances that women clerical workers pursue to subvert that control. The incorporation of gendered mechanisms in the frontier of control empowers women as women, not only as workers, to engage in resistance practices. Women's work culture defines a range of resistance practices abstracted from these gendered forms, but in so doing, it contributes to accommodation by preparing women for unskilled, low-paid and unpaid domestic labour.

The frontier of control is inherently contradictory, creating problems of and possibilities for worker resistance. Theories of resistance have focused on collective, institutional labour conflict because of the assumed social character of the labour process and the emphasis on traditional work settings. Despite extreme individuation, temporary clerical workers negotiate and resist the multiple layers of management. Resistance occurs as part of everyday life in a society structured by antagonistic social relationships. It remains defensive, accommodative and intermittent.

Learning the score implicates workers in the regulation of production, but also contributes to a repository of knowledge which becomes the pragmatic grounds enabling worker resistance. As people produce culture at the workplace, they generate practices and ideas that run counter to those which are hegemonic. While everyday activities on the shopfloor generate counter-hegemonic practices, these practices may take less visible forms – especially among contingent workers like temporary clericals. Labour process theorists have not conceptualized adequately the disruptive potential of these seemingly mundane and less visible practices that constitute everyday acts of resistance. Theorists could turn their attention now to the structuration of power based on knowledge produced in micro-settings (shopfloor). This would enable deeper understanding of the subtle interplay of administrative control and worker resistance as they unfold within post-Fordist production processes.

NOTES

1 Others offer a more sympathetic reading; for example, Wardell argues 'that critics have failed to recognize, or have chosen to disregard, Braverman's appreciation of the dialectical relationship between action and structure' (cited in Knights and Willmott, 1990: 25). This renewed interest in rehabilitating Braverman has given more coherence to labour process theory; a debate that all too often has taken place in 'the vacuum of the shopfloor' (Manwaring and Wood, 1985: 175).

2 Between 1963 and 1979, temporary-service employment in the United States increased by 725 per cent compared with only 58 per cent in non-agricultural jobs (Christopherson, 1987). In a two year period (1982-84), the number of new temporary employees on the payroll rose by 70 per cent to make it the fastest growing segment among industries with 50,000 or more employees (Carey and Hazelbaker, 1986).

3 In 1985 employment estimates of temporary workers varied from: 455,000 in the Current Population Survey; 689,000 in the Current Employment Statistics (Howe, 1986); and 939,000 in the National Association of Temporary Services (Hartmann and Lapidus, 1989). Hartmann and Lapidus note that all these numbers are taken at a single point in time, and thus don't reflect the cumulative impact of changes in the size of the temporary labour force on the economy.

4 Health-care services recently surpassed clerical work as the fastest-growing category of temporary employment (Gannon, 1984).

5 Much of this section on resistance is the product of collaborative work with Patty Sotirin (1991); also see Sotirin, 1993 and Sotirin and Gottfried, forthcoming).

6 Heterosexism refers to the 'enforcement of heterosexuality for women as a means of assuring male right of physical, economical, and emotional access' (Rich, 1984: 416).

7 Throughout the text *firm* refers to the temporary-help service employer while *client* refers to the job site employer.

8 A conversation is an unstructured mode of talk that can elicit the respondents' frames of reference. More in-depth interviews, however, would be necessary to capture these workers' meaning systems.

9 These conversations took place during the annual conference of the National Association of Working Women held in 1985.

10 Clerical workers tend to be white women while women of colour and men seeking temporary work are tracked into the non-clerical lines of employment such as light manufacturing. All respondents were white except for one black male respondent.

11 Like Friedman's (1977) concept of 'responsible autonomy' or Burawoy's (1985) concept of 'making-out', the maintenance of managerial

authority involves getting workers to identify with the competitive aims of the enterprise so that they will act 'responsibly' with a minimum of supervision.

12 Temporary workers come closest to being part of the stagnant segment of the reserve army of labour – characterized by irregular, casual, marginal employment relations, who in Marx's words, furnish to capital 'an exhaustible reservoir of disposable labour power' (cited in Braverman, 1974: 388).

13 For a more detailed discussion of the THS intake process see Gottfried (1991).

14 I owe John Jermier and Walter Nord for their helpful comments towards the development of this definition of resistance.

15 Pioneering efforts to organize women workers in India's 'informal economy' indicate the possibility for building associations of and collective resistance among a vulnerable class of workers. Although the success of the campaign remains in a balance, the Service Employees International Union's Justice for Janitors Campaign organized black women employed by third-party janitorial firms to collectively oppose one of the largest real estate magnates in Atlanta (Hurd and Rouse, 1989). Organizing temporary workers will require unions to address and confront the conditions that compel women to become temporary workers.

16 When the airline machinists followed the compendium of rules to slow the departure and arrival of planes, this action signified a strategic, organized response arising out of dwindling bargaining power – the inability to stop airline traffic.

17 Thompson (1990) makes this distinction between struggles of resistance and struggles of transformation.

REFERENCES

Acker, J. (1990) 'Hierarchies, Jobs, Bodies: A Theory of Gendered Organizations', *Gender and Society* 4: 139–58.

Anderson, N. (1923) *The Hobo*, Chicago: University of Chicago Press.

Anyon, J. (1983) 'Intersections of Gender and Class: Accommodation and Resistance by Working Class and Affluent Females to Contradictory Sex-Role', in S. Walker and L. Barton (eds) *Gender, Class and Education*, New York: The Falmer Press.

Appelbaum, E. (1987) 'Restructuring Work: Temporary, Part-Time and At-Home Employment', in H. Hartmann (ed.) *Computer Chips and Paper Clips*, Washington, DC: National Academy Press.

Barker, J. and Downing, H. (1980) 'Word Processing and the Transformation of the Patriarchal Relations of Control in the Office', *Capital and Class*, Spring: 64–99.

Beechey, V. (1987) *Unequal Work*, London: Verso Press.

Beechey, V. and Perkins, T. (1985) 'Conceptualizing Part-Time Work', in B. Roberts, R. Finnegan and D. Gallie, (eds) *New Approaches to Economic Life*, Manchester: Manchester University Press.

Braverman, H. (1974) *Labor and Monopoly Capitalism*, New York: Monthly Review Press.

Brennan, T. (1989) 'The State and (Cultural) Revolution: Ideology is for Other People', unpublished paper.

Brittan, A. and Maynard, M. (1984) *Sexism, Racism and Oppression*, London: Basil Blackwell.

Burawoy, M. (1985) *The Politics of Production: Factory Regimes under Capitalism and Socialism*, London: Verso Press.

Carey, M. and Hazelbaker, K. (1986) 'Employment Growth in the Temporary Industry', *Monthly Labor Review*, 109: 37–44.

Cavendish, R. (1982) *Women on the Line*, London: Routledge & Kegan Paul.

Christensen, K. and Murphree, M. (1988) 'Introduction', in Department of Labor (ed.) *Flexible Work Styles*, Washington DC: United States Department of Labor.

Christopherson, S. (1987) 'The Mobile Workforce', *High Flex Society Working Papers*, Roosevelt Center for American Policy Studies, Washington, DC.

Clarke, J., Hall, S., Jefferson, T. and Roberts, B. (eds) (1976) 'Subculture, Cultures and Class: A Theoretical Overview', *Resistance Through Rituals: Youth Subcultures in Post-War Britain*, London: Hutchinson.

Clawson, D. and R. Fantasia (1983) 'Beyond Burawoy: The Dialectics of Conflict and Consent on the Shop Floor', *Theory and Society* 12(5): 671–80.

Cockburn, C. (1985) *Machinery of Dominance: Women, Men and Technical Know-How*, London: Pluto Press.

Collinson, D. (1987) 'Picking Women': The Recruitment of Temporary Workers in the Mail Order Industry', *Work, Employment and Society* 3: 371–87.

Costello, C. (1987) 'Working Women's Consciousness: Traditional or Oppositional', in C. Groneman and M. B. Norton (eds), *'To Toil the Livelong Day': America's Women at Work, 1780-1980*, Ithaca, NY: Cornell University Press.

Coyle, A. (1986) *Dirty Business: Women's Work and Trade Union Organization in Contract Cleaning*, Birmingham: West Midlands Low Pay Unit.

Davies, S. (1990) 'Inserting Gender into Burawoy's Theory of the Labour Process', *Work, Employment and Society* 4: 391–406.

Edwards, P.K. (1990) 'Understanding Conflict in the Labour Process: The Logic and Autonomy of Struggle', in D. Knights and H. Willmott (eds) *Labor Process Theory*, London: Macmillan.

Edwards, P.K., and Scullion, H. (1982) *The Social Organization of Industrial Conflict: Control and Resistance in the Workplace*, Oxford: Basil Blackwell.

Edwards, R. (1979) *Contested Terrain: The Transformation of the Workplace in the Twentieth Century*, New York: Basic Books.

Ferguson, K. (1984) *The Feminist Case Against Bureaucracy*, Philadelphia: Temple University Press.

Friedman, A. (1977) *Industry and Labour: Class Struggle at Work and Monopoly Capitalism*, London: Macmillan.

Game, A. and R. Pringle (1984) *Gender at Work*, Sidney: George Allen & Unwin.

Gannon, M. (1984) 'Preferences of Temporary Workers: Time, Variety, and Flexibility', *Monthly Labor Review* 107: 26–8.

Gottfried, H. (1991) 'Mechanisms of Control in the Temporary Help Service Industry', *The Sociological Forum* 6(4): 699–713.

Gottfried, H. and Fasenfest, D. (1984) 'The Role of Gender in Class Formation: A Case of Female Clerical Workers', *Review of Radical Political Economics* 16: 89–104.

Gottfried, H. and Sotirin, P. (1991) 'Research For Women: Notes Toward the Development of a Liberatory Research Project', unpublished paper.

Graham, L. (1991) 'Production Control: A Case Study of a Japanese Automobile Plant', unpublished PhD thesis, Purdue University.

Gramsci, A. (1971) *Selections from the Prison Notebooks*, translated by Q. Hoare and G.N. Smith, New York: International Publishers.

Grossberg, L. and Nelson, C. (eds) (1988) 'Introduction: The Territory of Marxism', in *Marxism and the Interpretation of Culture*, Urbana: The University of Illinois Press.

Hall, S. (1988) 'Brave New World', *Marxism Today*, October, pp. 24–9.

Hartmann, H. (1981) 'The Unhappy Marriage of Marxism and Feminism', in L. Sargent (ed.) *Women and Revolution: A Discussion of the Unhappy Marriage of Marxism and Feminism*, Boston: South End Press.

Hartmann, H. and J. Lapidus (1989) 'Temporary Work', *Working Paper 29*, Institute for Women's Policy Research, Washington, DC.

Hochschild, A. (1983) *The Managed Heart: The Commercialization of Human Feeling*, Berkeley: University of California Press.

Hodson, R. (1991) 'The Active Worker: Compliance and Autonomy at the Workplace', *Journal of Contemporary Ethnography* 20(1): 47–78.

Howe, W. (1986) 'Temporary Help Workers: Who They Are, What Jobs They Hold', *Monthly Labor Review* 109(11): 45–7.

Hurd, R. and Rouse, W. (1989) 'Progressive Union Organizing: The SEIU Justice for Janitors Campaign', *Review of Radical Political Economics* 23(3): 70–5.

Hyman, R. (1975) *Industrial Relations: A Marxist Introduction*, London: Macmillan.

Hyman, R. (1987) 'Strategy or Structure? Capital, Labour and Control', *Work, Employment and Society* 1(1): 25–55.

Jenson, J. (1989) ' "Different" but not "Exceptional": Canada's Permeable Fordism', *Canadian Review of Sociology and Anthropology* 26(1): 69–94.

Jermier, J. (1988) 'Sabotage at Work: The Rational View', in S. Bacharach and N. Ditomaso (eds) *Research in the Sociology of Organizations*, Greenwich, CN: JAI Press.

Jessop, B. (1988) 'Regulation Theory, Post-Fordism and the State: More than a Reply to Werner Bonefield', *Capital and Class* 34: 147–68.

Judith Ann. (1970) 'The Secretarial Proletariat', in R. Morgan (ed.) *Sisterhood is Powerful: An Anthology of Writings from the Women's Liberation Movement*, New York: Vintage Books.

Kaplan, T. (1982) 'Female Consciousness and Collective Action: The Case of Barcelona', *Signs*, 7: 545–66.

Kenney, M. and Florida, R. (1988) 'Beyond Mass Production: Production and the Labor Process in Japan', *Politics and Society* 16(1): 121–58.

125

Kornblum, W. (1974) *Blue Collar Community*, Chicago: University of Chicago Press.

Knights, D. and Collinson, D. (1985) 'Redesigning Work on the Shopfloor: A Question of Control or Consent', in D. Knights, H. Willmott and D. Collinson (eds) *Job Redesign: Critical Perspectives on the Labor Process*, London: Gower.

Knights, D. and Willmott, H. (eds) (1990) 'Introduction', in *Labor Process Theory*, London: Macmillan.

Laclau, E. and Mouffe, C. (1985) *Hegemony and Socialist Strategy: Toward a Radical Democratic Politics*, London: Verso.

Lapidus, J. (1989) 'The Temporary Help Industry and the Operation of the Labour Market', unpublished PhD dissertation. University of Massachusetts-Amherst.

Littler, C. (1982) *The Development of the Labour Process in Britain, Japan and USA*, London: Heinemann.

McRobbie, A. (1981) 'Just Like a Jackie Story', in Angela McRobbie and Trisha McCabe (eds) *Feminism for Girls: An Adventure Story*, London: Routledge & Kegan Paul.

Manwaring, T.P. and Wood, S. (1985) 'The Ghost in the Labour Process', in D. Knights, H. Willmott and D. Collinson (eds) *Job Redesign: Critical Perspectives on the Labour Process*, London: Gower.

Milkman, R. (ed.) (1985) 'Women Workers, Feminism and the Labor Movement since the 1960s', in *Women, Work and Protest: A Century of US Women's History*, Boston: Routledge & Kegan Paul.

Olesen, V. and Katsuranis, F. (1978) 'Urban Nomads: Women in Temporary Clerical Services', in A. Stromberg and S. Harkess (eds) *Women Working*, Palo Alto, CA: Mayfield.

Pollock. (1986) 'The Disposable Employee in Becoming a Fact of Corporate Life', *Business Week*, (15 December), pp. 52–6.

Rich, A. (1984) 'Compulsory Heterosexuality and Lesbian Existence', in A. Jaggar and P. Rothenberg (eds) *Feminist Frameworks*, New York: McGraw Hill.

Roy, D. (1959) 'Banana Time: Job Satisfaction and Informed Interaction', *Human Organization*, 18: 158–68.

Salaman, G. (1979) *Work Organizations: Resistance and Control*, London: Longman.

Sargent, L. (ed.) (1981) *Women and Revolution: A Discussion of the Unhappy Marriage of Marxism and Feminism*, Boston: South End Press.

Smith, D. (1987) *The Everyday World as Problematic: A Feminist Sociology*, Boston: Northeastern University Press.

Sotirin, P. (1993) 'Workplace Resistance: A Feminist Reframing', PhD dissertation, Purdue University.

Sotirin, P., and Gottfried, H. (forthcoming) 'Women, Work and Resistance', in K. Borman and P. Dubeck (eds) *Encyclopedia of Women and Work*, New York: Garland.

Thompson, P. (1989) *The Nature of Work: An Introduction to Debates on the Labor Process*, New York: Humanities Press.

Thompson, P. (1990) 'Crawling from the Wreckage: The Labour Process and the Politics of Production', in D. Knights and H. Willmott (eds) *Labor Process Theory*, London: Macmillan.

Valli, L. (1986) *Becoming Clerical Workers*, Boston: Routledge & Kegan Paul.

Wardell, M. (1990) 'Labour and Labour Process', in D. Knights and H. Willmott (eds) *Labor Process Theory*, London: Macmillan.

West, J. (1990) 'Gender and the Labour Process: A Reassessment', in D. Knights and H. Willmott (eds) *Labor Process Theory*, London: MacMillan.

Westwood, S. (1985) *All Day, Every Day: The Factory and the Family in the Making of Women's Lives*, Urbana: University of Illinois Press.

Willis, P. (1990) 'Masculinity and Factory Labor', in J. Alexander and S. Seidman (eds) *Culture and Society: Contemporary Debates*, Cambridge: Cambridge University Press.

Willis, P. (1974) *Learning to Labor: How Working Class Kids Get Working Class Jobs*, New York: Columbia University Press.

4

WORKING WITH NATURE

Organic farming and other forms of
resistance to industrialized agriculture*

Carolyn P. Egri

The contemporary farm crisis (economic, social and ecological)
provides the background for an exploration of the forms and targets
of resistance of family farmers to industrialized agriculture in North
America. Drawing from sociological research on agrarian protest as
well as findings from a research study of family farmers in British
Columbia, this paper analyses the resistance to industrialized agriculture by two types of family farmers – those who practise an
industrial (conventional) system of production and those who
advocate and practise sustainable agriculture (organic farming). In
comparison to the struggles of resistance of conventional family
farmers, the ideological and practical resistance of organic family
farmers appears to offer significantly more potential for a transformation of the labour process of industrialized agriculture. However,
as illustrated by the current organizational power and politics within
the organic farming community in British Columbia, the course of
revolutionary change is not without its own challenges.

INTRODUCTION

Over the past 50 years, the North American agricultural sector[1]
has undergone a scientific-technical revolution which, as a whole,
rivals that which occurred during the nineteenth-century
Industrial Revolution in both scope and depth. In essence, there
has occurred a transformation of agri*culture* into industrial agri-
business such that

---

* I would like to thank John Jermier, Walter Nord, Peter Frost, Clive Gilson, Dev
Jennings and Nancy Langton for their helpful comments on earlier drafts of this
chapter.

American agriculture has increasingly emphasized industrial values and assumed the characteristics of industrial organization. Farms have become more specialized, relying on the prescriptive application of standard technologies, producing on a large-volume basis, using sophisticated machinery that limits the farmer's ability to adapt or change. Farms increasingly rely on perpetual debt to foster expansion. Most important, as competition for land among expanding farms increases land values, the tendency is to separate farm ownership from farm operation.

(Strange, 1984: 117)

The introduction of modern industrial values, practices and technologies has been a mixed blessing for the family farmers who comprise over 94 per cent of the farm operator population. The promise of industrial agriculture for family farmers has been that these new technologies and practices would increase output productivity, the efficiency of labour and profits. Based on traditional economic indices, such gains have indeed been recorded for the agricultural sector as a whole (Carr, 1988; Kendrick, 1983). Operating efficiencies resulting from the substitution of capital for labour[2] have been instrumental in reducing Canadian farm employment from 1,246,622 in 1941 to 486,000 in 1987 while meeting the food needs of a growing population (11,506,700 in 1941 to 27,296,855 in 1991) (Sanford Evans Statistical Service, 1944; Statistics Canada, 1989, 1991b).

However, as identified by Strange, these outcomes have come at a price for the family farmer. New agricultural technologies and practices have provided the leverage for agribusiness and governments to institute a capitalist mode of production in agriculture which fragments the production of food into three stages: (1) the manufacture and provision of instruments of production (tools, machines, chemicals, seeds, etc.); (2) the raising of food and fibre (farming); and (3) the processing, distribution and marketing of farm products (Goss, Rodefeld and Buttel, 1980). When one considers that the first and third stages are dominated by off-farm oligopolistic agribusiness interests (Doyle, 1985; Smith, 1987; Weir, 1987), this division of function and labour challenges the neopopulist 'myth' of the family farmer as an independent and autonomous commodity producer operating within a competitive market system of private property (Banaji, 1980; Davis, 1980; Martinson and

129

Campbell, 1980; Vogeler, 1981). In reality, the movement towards an industrial system of agricultural production has significantly diminished the financial and technological discretion and autonomy of the individual farmer.

The industrial process of capital accumulation and concentration has also transformed the landscape of the North American countryside. Concomitant with the decrease in farm employment over the past 50 years, there has been a 62 per cent decrease in the number of Canadian farms (64 per cent decrease in the number of US farms) and a 152 per cent increase in average farm size (Hay and Basran, 1988; National Research Council, 1989; Sanford Evans Statistical Service, 1944; Statistics Canada, 1991a).[3]

This exodus from farm employment and rural communities has not been entirely voluntary. Despite enviable increases in productivity and production output, the majority of family farmers in Canada and the United States lead a perilous financial existence. The 'cost–price squeeze' of depressed prices for farm output[4] exacerbated by surplus production and government intervention, inflated prices for production inputs, and high-interest servicing costs on farm debt has made farm foreclosures increasingly common in the agricultural sectors of both countries (Auer, 1989; Comstock, 1987; Giangrande, 1985; US Dept of Agriculture, 1987). Despite government subsidies, commodity and income support programmes,[5] the 'farm crisis' which started in the late 1970s has only gained momentum. A recent report of the House of Commons agriculture committee estimates that in 1989, 19 per cent of Canada's 250,000 farm operations were considered insolvent and $5 billion of Canada's $22 billion farm debt was unserviceable (Wilson, 1991).[6] Where once a rarity, the majority of modern farmers and family members (53 per cent of all farms in Canada; 75 per cent in the United States) now need to seek off-farm employment to supplement farm income (Bollman and Smith, 1988; National Research Council, 1989).

Given the severity of the contemporary farm crisis, what evidence is there of challenges or resistance to industrialized agriculture in North America? What evidence is there of what Thompson (1990: 119) defines as struggles of resistance which 'focus on the wage–effort bargain and the frontier of control in work relations' or struggles of transformation which 'embody goals which are directed in some way at the relations of production and reproduction' and/or an integration of both?

In terms of agents of resistance and/or transformation, three groups are evident: (1) family farmers, (2) organic farmers and (3) hired agricultural labour and tenant farmers. One would expect there to be resistance amongst the family farmers who have experienced and witnessed the destructive economic and social repercussions of the movement towards industrialized agriculture. No longer the independent petty commodity producers of the past, several contend that the majority of family farmers who have adopted an industrial system of production (i.e. conventional farmers) have been transformed into a *de facto* rural proletariat (e.g. Davis, 1980; de Janvry, 1980; Vogeler, 1981).[7] While there have been isolated incidents of collective action by conventional family farmers in response to economic distress, there appears to be little evidence of a pattern of wholesale resistance or struggles of transformation which challenge the ideology and institutional structure of industrialized agriculture (Danbom, 1979; Flora, 1990; Troughton, 1989).

It is proposed that family farmers who practise organic farming are amongst the most active agents of resistance to transform the relations of production and reproduction of industrialized agriculture. Under the banner of the sustainable agriculture movement, this small but growing number of family farmers are advocating and practising alternative agricultural production systems which resist industrialized agriculture at both ideological and practical levels. In contrast to conventional family farmers who adhere to the industrial model of agricultural production, the everyday resistance of organic farmers is informed by a vision of a post-industrial ecologically sustainable system of family farming in which farmers are once again agrarian craftspersons.

Historically, hired agricultural labourers and tenant farmers have been disadvantaged and exploited within industrial agricultural production systems and therefore are also agents of resistance (Bolaria, 1988; Friedland, Barton and Thomas, 1981; Shields, 1988; Vogeler, 1981). While the resistance of hired agricultural labourers (in particular, the formation of farmworkers unions to alter exploitative wages and working conditions) and of tenant farmers to industrialized agriculture is a rich arena for study, it is beyond the scope of the present study.

Instead, this chapter focuses on the experiences and actions of conventional family farmers and organic family farmers within modern industrialized agriculture. Of particular interest are the differences between conventional and organic family farmers in terms of their resistance to the capitalist labour process. What are their targets for change? To what degree are their goals transformational? What forms are their resistance to industrialized agriculture taking? Is there evidence of passive resistance in the form of exit, denial or avoidance protest? Or alternatively, is resistance in the forms of confrontation or retribution? Finally, to what degree is their resistance an individual or collective phenomenon?

To date much of the theoretical and empirical literature on the labour process and resistance has been concerned with the industrial and service sectors (Braverman, 1974; Burawoy, 1985; Knights and Willmott, 1990; Littler, 1982). Only recently has a critical neo-Marxist perspective been adopted by rural sociologists to study the labour process in modern industrialized agriculture (Buttel, Larson and Gillespie, 1990; Buttel and Newby, 1980; Davis, 1980; Mann, 1990; Strange, 1988; Vogeler, 1981). Thus far, empirical studies of resistance to industrialized agriculture have focused primarily on that of hired agricultural labour in North America (e.g. Bolaria, 1988; Friedland, Barton and Thomas, 1981; Shields, 1988; Thomas, 1985) and on agrarian resistance in peasant societies (e.g. Adas, 1986; Scott, 1986; Wolf, 1969).

In regards to modern family farmers in North America, the farm crisis of the 1980s has stimulated research on the impacts of rapid technological change, state intervention in agricultural production, marketing and research, and the growth of vertically integrated oligopolistic agribusinesses under monopoly capitalism (Banaji, 1980; Davis, 1980; de Janvry, 1980; Friedland, Barton and Thomas, 1981; Goss *et al.*, 1980; Hedley, 1981; Vogeler, 1981). The study of resistance of family farmers to industrialized agriculture has primarily focused on rural social movements to influence government policy during periods of financial crisis (Danbom, 1979; Davis, 1980; de Janvry, 1980; Troughton, 1989; Vogeler, 1981). However, less attended to by rural sociologists has been family farmers' everyday political and economic struggles for control at the point of production; much less family farmers' personal beliefs, motivations and experiences which inform their acts of resistance. Further, as identified in their extensive overview of the sociology of agriculture, Buttel *et al.* (1990: 184), 'there is a need to better understand the agriculture–environment nexus, particularly in terms of the socioeconomic significance of the environmental contradictions of agriculture and of how environmental mobilization may affect agricultural structures and policies'. What little research that has focused on these questions has been conducted in Europe, not North America (Buttel *et al.*, 1990).

One intent of this chapter is to address these gaps in the literature by using an integrative approach to understand the dynamics of family farmer resistance to modern industrialized agriculture. Following the suggestions of a number of labour process theorists (e.g. Burawoy, 1985; Littler, 1990; Strinati, 1990), the approach taken is one which attends to the economic, social and political dimensions (and their interrelationships) of the labour process. The next section of this chapter presents an analysis of family farmer movements for social and economic changes within agriculture. Of particular interest is the degree to which such collective action has not (and why) constituted real resistance to the labour process of industrialized agriculture.

The subsequent section focuses on the emergence of the sustainable agriculture movement as a potentially powerful force for revolutionary social, economic and environmental change to industrialized agriculture. How the sustainable agriculture movement represents ideological and practical resistance to industrialized agriculture will be considered. The implications of this resistance for society and industrial agribusiness, as well as for agrarian craftsmanship, will also be explored.

However, a full understanding of the labour process and resistance to industrialized agriculture is incomplete without attending to the experiences, motivations and actions of the family farmers themselves. As proposed by Knights, there is a need to 'bring the subject back in' to labour process theory for 'an understanding of consent as much as resistance, gender and race as well as class, and market forces at the same time as relations at the point of production' (Knights, 1990: 298). With this admonition in mind, the results of a research study of conventional and organic family farmers currently underway in British Columbia, Canada will be presented.[8]

Briefly, 57 organic farmers (47 male, 10 female) and 37 conventional farmers (35 male, two female) were interviewed in 1991. In addition to personal background and farm production and practice data, information has been gathered concerning their experiences as farmers, the degree to which they access and trust various information sources, their perceptions of agrichemicals and organic farming, their beliefs concerning environmental issues, and what they identify as the critical issues in agriculture. For members of farming organizations (organic and conventional), information is being gathered concerning organizational goals, issues, activities and processes as well as organizational leadership.

As will be demonstrated, the differences in intents and actions between conventional and organic family farmers and their organizations are significant and yield a deeper understanding of the dynamics of resistance at the point of production. Given that the primary focus of the research project is on organic farmers and their organizations, the remaining sections of the chapter will be devoted to the special challenges of battling the status quo of industrialized agriculture. One of the highlights of this segment is the politics of resistance within the organic farming community which, in many respects, mirrors the struggle between Marx and Bakunin over the means and ends of social and political revolutionary change (Gouldner, 1985).

Finally, the chapter will conclude with a discussion of how this study of resistance to industrialized agriculture relates to labour process theory and studies of resistance in non-agricultural settings.

RESISTANCE TO INDUSTRIAL AGRICULTURE

The structural crisis within agriculture (in terms of overproduction and financial distress) indicates a growing divergence of interests between the majority of family farmers and industrial agribusiness. What evidence is there of resistance to the capitalist mode of production in industrial agriculture in North America and what forms has it taken?

The history of rural social movements documents the unique challenges of organizing collective resistance amongst a geographically dispersed and heterogeneous farm population (Danbom, 1979; Davis, 1980; de Janvry, 1980; Troughton, 1989; Vogeler, 1981). One obstacle to collective resistance has been the strength of the neopopulist 'myth of the family farm' which appeals to the liberal capitalist 'values of independence, egalitarianism, agrarianism, entrepreneurship and puritanism' (de Janvry, 1980: 165). Within this ideological context, collective action by the majority of farm organizations has focused on obtaining greater economic benefits and security for individual producers whilst denying the need for radical structural changes in production practices or the relations of production of industrialized agriculture.

One outcome of the widespread subscription to the neopopulist

134

myth has been the fragmentation of farmers into numerous farm interest groups representing separate commodity groups, geographic regions and political ideologies (Browne, 1988; Forbes, 1985; Robinson, 1989). In Canada, there are over 10,000 local, provincial and national farmer organizations including 449 cooperatives, marketing agencies, unions, trade associations and federations (Forbes, 1985). Amongst the most influential in government and industrial circles are the conventional farming organizations (e.g. in Canada, the Canadian Federation of Agriculture and in the United States, the American Farm Bureau Federation) and those representing agribusiness interests. The primary focus of their actions has been to protect and sustain their members' interests by lobbying for increased government intervention (price support and commodity programmes, trade barriers, tax policies) in ways which support the existing industrialized system.

While garnering high public support and visibility through their unconventional tactics, the grassroots agricultural reform organizations (such as the National Farmers' Union in Canada and the American Agriculture Movement in the United States) have proven to be less influential in guiding government policy or restructuring the agricultural sector. Historically, groups concerned with agricultural alternatives such as rural communities, farmworkers' rights, conservationists, environmentalists and consumers have been even less well organized and funded (Browne, 1988; Forbes, 1985; Robinson, 1989; Strange, 1988).

When it has occurred, collective confrontational action within North American agriculture has generally taken place during periods of financial crisis such as the US Grange movement in the 1870s and the economic depressions of the 1930s, 1970s and 1980s. For example, in response to the increasing number of US farm foreclosures during the 1930s, the Farm Holiday Movement involved direct action in the form of a general strike to withhold farm produce. The national farmers' strike which started in 1977 in Colorado, quickly spread to 30 states within a year and culminated in 1979 with the American Agriculture Movement's 'tractorcade' in Washington, DC (Robinson, 1989; Strange, 1988).

In Canada, the financial distress exacerbated by recent developments in the international grain trade war has prompted the organization of numerous farmer protest rallies during the autumn of 1991. Thus far, over 25,000 farmers have attended nine rallies in the Prairie provinces and Ontario (Duckworth and Sproat, 1991;

Schuettler, 1991; Sproat, 1991). The largest rallies have been in Regina, Saskatchewan, where 7,000 farmers participated and in Winnipeg, Manitoba with 5,000 farmers in attendance. A new interprovincial farmer grassroots coalition, the Concerned Farmers of Canada, is organizing a large-scale farmer 'trek' to Ottawa to underscore the severity of the farm crisis and to present their demands for additional farm-level financial assistance, a new national agricultural policy and a renewal of political efforts to resolve the international grain trade war (Shein and Swihart, 1991). Although on the agenda, whether these farm protests will culminate in a farmer strike remains to be seen.

On an individual level, the National Farmers' Union's local farm crisis committees continue to assist individual farmers in severe financial distress (Jenkins, 1991; Pugh, 1987). The focus of these committees is to prevent farm foreclosures by assisting individual farmers in their negotiations with financial institutions and when necessary, using confrontational methods. Amongst the more unique methods are the 'Penny Auctions' which take place when farmers declare bankruptcy and surrender their assets to a financial institution. At these events, financial institutions are denied full value from the sale of farm assets and goods when local farmers (by prior informal agreement) at the auction bid only 1 penny per item and then sell back their purchases to the bankrupt farmer. However, the main focus of groups such as the National Farmers' Union and Concerned Farmers of Canada remains on lobbying governments to augment farm income stabilization programmes and government subsidies (domestic and export), price support and commodity production control programmes.

One distinctive feature of the Canadian agricultural sector is the predominance of producer-initiated commodity marketing boards as a vehicle for supply management (Troughton, 1989). In 1984–5, 56 per cent of total farm cash receipts were controlled by marketing boards.[9] Although instigated to protect producers from the threat of agribusiness oligopolies in processing, marketing and distribution, the primary beneficiaries of the marketing board system have not been the family farmers. As demonstrated by Troughton (1989), the institutionalization of supply management under the marketing board system has accelerated the industrialization of agriculture thereby enhancing the power of multinational agribusiness oligopolies to control production and to extract surplus value from farm producers.

Together, the neopopulist myth of the family farm and the result-ant fragmentation of the farm producer population have served to constrain the widespread development of a class consciousness which would inform economic, social and political changes to capit-alist systems. For the majority of family farmers locked into existing industrial production systems, there is little attention or credence given to the need for a radical restructuring of current political and social relationships within the agricultural sector (Danbom, 1979; Davis, 1980; Vogeler, 1981) or aligning with other social movements (Strange, 1988). Threats of dismantling government subsidy and crop insurance programmes are met with vocal resistance by farmers and their organizations (Allen and Elliott, 1988; Petit, Rossmiller and Tutwiler, 1988).[10] Instead, the collective efforts of the large majority of conventional family farmers entrenched in industrial agricultural systems is to increase government intervention programmes and to retain current mechanisms which support industrial agriculture's production, marketing and distribution systems (Flora, 1990; Strange, 1988; Vogeler, 1981).

However, for the majority of family farmers, this represents a fundamental contradiction in that industrial agriculture threatens their long-term individual economic survival. The enigma of American agriculture is that

It is productive but troubled. It is desperate, but supports the status quo. It frequently issues calls to 'get the government out of agriculture', but regularly fights prolonged battles to protect farm programs with complicated rules, regulations, and subsidies. It is modern and progressive, but stuck in the mud.

(Strange, 1988: 14)

These contradictions surface in my research interviews with con-ventional farmers who consistently rail against unfair competition (e.g. the Canada–United States Free Trade Agreement and govern-ment subsidies) whilst voicing support for commodity marketing boards and government-sponsored farm income and commodity price support programmes. Despite their espoused belief in free competitive market principles, conventional farmers frequently express satisfaction with their commodity organizations' efforts in lobbying government agencies to obtain greater economic benefits and financial security.

In summary, the record of farm protest amongst conventional family farmers gives credence of Marx's dismissal of agriculture as

137

the site for reactionary politics and his prediction of the demise of farmers as petty commodity producers (Goss *et al.*, 1980; Mann, 1990). Farm protest has primarily focused on remedying the symptoms of the current economic and technical systems rather than the structural causes of experienced distress and threat. Therefore one could argue that the response of the majority of family farmers to industrialized agriculture has been financially motivated with little evidence of class consciousness.

However, there is a growing minority who subscribe to a class-dialectic model of social change (Whitt, 1979) in their challenge and resistance to the technologies, practices and relations of production of industrialized agriculture. It is with the advocates and practitioners of sustainable agriculture alternatives that we see the genesis of a class consciousness which challenges the dominant status quo.

IDEOLOGICAL AND PRACTICAL RESISTANCE TO INDUSTRIAL AGRICULTURE: THE EMERGENCE OF ENVIRONMENTALLY SUSTAINABLE ALTERNATIVES

Every advance in capitalist agriculture is an advance in the art, not only of robbing the worker, but also of robbing the soil; such progress therefore leads in the long run to the ruin of the permanent sources of this fertility [of the soil].

(Marx, 1930: 547)

Within industrial agriculture, the capitalistic drive towards the exploitation of labour also extends to the extraction of surplus value from the forces of Nature.[11] One of the legacies of 50 years of industrial technologies and intensive-farming practices has been the degradation and pollution of land, water and air resources (e.g. Canter, 1986; Merrill, 1976; World Commission on Environment and Development, 1987). As warned by Marx and by Engels (in Braverman, 1974: 16), the capitalist process of transforming the forces of Nature systemically destroys Nature by depleting and degrading natural resources thereby threatening the very foundations of agriculture. Thus, capitalism in advanced societies creates an *ecological crisis* which intensifies the capitalist crises of over-accumulation and reproduction (Gorz, 1980).

In response to the environmental and socio-economic repercussions of industrialized agriculture, there are those who advocate an

138

alternative system of agricultural production. The sustainable agriculture movement is one which resists and challenges the current materialist and hierarchical model of industrial agriculture at both ideological and practical levels. Ideologically, sustainable agriculture is an integral part of the environmentalist agenda for social and political change (Bookchin, 1990; Commoner, 1990; Devall and Sessions, 1985). In opposition to modern capitalist society where institutional and industrial elites dominate, the ideology of sustainable agriculture is informed by a model of society based on local autonomy and control, self-regulation and self-sufficiency.

Perhaps what most distinguishes sustainable or organic agriculture from industrial agriculture is best summarized by Wendell Berry:

> The mentality of organic agriculture is not a technological mentality – though it does concern itself with technology. It does not merely ask what is the easiest and cheapest and quickest way to reach an immediate aim. It is, rather, a complex and radical attitude toward the problem of our relationship to the earth. It is concerned with the long-term questions of what humans need from the earth and what duties and devotions humans owe the earth in return for the satisfaction of their needs. It understands that the terms of a lasting agriculture are not human terms, that the final terms are nature's, that an agriculture – and for that matter, a culture – that holds in ignorance or contempt the truths and the mysteries of nature is doomed to failure, for it is out of control.
>
> (Berry, 1976: 15)

Under the umbrella of sustainable agriculture, four of the most prominent approaches within North America are organic farming, regenerative agriculture, ecological agriculture and bio-dynamic agriculture (Gips, 1987; Oelhaf, 1978). While some advocate developing in parallel to existing conventional agriculture, others are less hesitant to challenge the status quo in their call for a restructuring of current linkages between agribusiness, government and individual family farmers.

The modern *organic farming* movement originated in England with the work of Sir Albert Howard in the 1930s and was continued by Lady Eve Balfour and the Soil Association of England. Later, organic farming would be introduced to North America by J.I. Rodale. The primary focus of organic farming is on enhancing soil health and fertility through the use of naturally derived materials (composted organic material, leguminous crops, etc.) rather than synthetic man-made ones. Under the organic production system, the use of synthetic chemical pesticides and fertilizers is prohibited. Cultural practices such as crop rotations, intercropping, companion planting, cover corps and green manures are used to control for weeds and pests and to provide soil and plant nutrients. The organic approach is perhaps the most widely accepted one in North America and is often used as the basic operating definition of producer certification programmes. It is estimated that 1 per cent to 2 per cent of the farm population in Canada and the United States are currently operating as organic farm producers (Hill, 1989; US Dept of Agriculture, 1980).

A recent offshoot of organic farming is *regenerative agriculture*. Regenerative (meaning to renew or restore) agriculture holds a less stringent definition of 'organic' and allows for the use of reduced levels of pesticides and fertilizers to achieve a minimal reliance on non-renewable resources (Gips, 1987). As such, regenerative agriculture represents an approach which combines both organic and conventional agricultural practices thereby potentially appealing to a broader audience.

Ecoagriculture, or *ecological agriculture*, builds on the growing concern about environmental pollution caused by the use of synthetic inputs in agriculture. It is a framework for agriculture which incorporates environmental, ecological and socio-economic variables in the production process (Altieri, 1987; Commoner, 1990; MacRae *et al.*, 1989). Ecoagriculture advocates often target agribusiness interests as the primary villains who promote the excessive use of non-renewable toxic chemicals in agricultural production. They also assert that there is an urgent need for a reconceptualization of agricultural production as only one part of an interdependent holistic environmental, social and cultural system.

Bio-dynamic agriculture is the oldest organized alternative agriculture discipline in the world. Although a small segment of the North American organic farming movement, bio-dynamics has become a significant force in Europe through its farmer-researcher network and international marketing organization (Koepf, 1989). Inspired by Austrian philosopher Rudolph Steiner in the 1920s, bio-dynamics (meaning 'life force') advocates a system which integrates spiritual and aesthetic values with agricultural practice (Koepf, 1989; Tompkins and Bird, 1989). The underlying anthroposophical philosophy of

140

the bio-dynamic approach stresses the need for spiritual unity between cosmic and terrestrial forces. In addition to practising organic farming methods, special bio-dynamic preparations are used (in a manner similar to homeopathic medicine) to 'influence' life processes in plants, soils and composts. Another unique feature of bio-dynamic agriculture is the scheduling of planting times in accordance with astrological signs and lunar rhythms (or cycles).

In summary, sustainable agriculture first resists industrialized agriculture at an ideological level. Where industrialized agriculture's relationship with Nature is one of desired dominance and control, the approach of sustainable agriculture is not one of subservience but rather of a profound respect for the intricacies and power of natural systems of life. This philosophy informs resistance to industrialized agriculture at a practical level in codes of conduct which advocate: (1) the substitution of imported fertilizers derived from non-renewable petrochemical resources with organic fertilizers produced within on-farm closed systems; (2) the substitution of synthetic chemical control of weeds and pests with biological and cultural controls; (3) resistance to highly mechanized production through the practice of reduced tillage systems; and (4) resistance to intensified large-scale monoculture operations through the practice of diversified medium- and small-scale farm operations. (Given the predominance of organic farming within the North American sustainable agriculture movement, the term 'organic farming' will be used henceforth to represent the spectrum of sustainable agriculture approaches.)

The more labour-intensive nature of organic farming coupled with the rejection of large-scale specialized production units reduces the organic farmer's need to invest in expensive capital equipment. As a result, the organic farmer is less indebted to financial institutions for capital to finance asset acquisitions (land and equipment) and operating expenses (MacRae *et al.*, 1988). Product diversification at the level of the individual production unit also reduces the organic farmer's reliance on government controlled (and politically influenced) commodity price and production programmes. As yet, the majority of organic food is being sold either independently at the farm gate or directly to retailers and consumers (Oelhaf, 1978). For the majority of organic producers, there is an increased measure of security against exploitation from the existing vertically integrated food processing, marketing and distribution industries. As the organic food industry has matured, however, there have emerged organic farming cooperative wholesale distribution and marketing vehicles which operate in parallel to those serving conventional producers thus increasing the potential for the appropriation of surplus value by off-farm entities.

There would also be a number of socio-economic changes if organic production systems became the norm rather than the exception. Organic farming practices are more labour intensive (Lockeretz *et al.*, 1976; Oelhaf, 1978) thereby creating an opportunity to stem out-migration from rural communities. There would be a greater number of farms and increased farm employment as small- and medium-sized labour-intensive farms became more economically viable. The decreased demand for agrichemical inputs would also mean a dislocation in the synthetic chemical fertilizer and pesticide industry (MacRae *et al.*, 1990). It is predicted that for the individual family farmer there would be an increase in net income due to an increase in crop prices, a reduction in production costs, lower asset requirements and debt loads (Langley, Heady and Olson, 1982; Lockeretz *et al.*, 1976; MacRae *et al.*, 1990).[12]

Thus, we see the potential power of the passive resistance of organic farming (primarily through denial and avoidance protest) to effect transformations at societal and local levels as well as at the point of production.

THE ORGANIC FARMER AS CRAFTSPERSON

In each craft, the worker was presumed to be the master of a body of traditional knowledge, and methods and procedures were left to his or her discretion. In each such worker reposed the accumulated knowledge of materials and processes by which production was accomplished in the craft. . . . The most important and widespread of all crafts was, and throughout the world remains to this day, that of farmer.

(Braverman, 1974: 109)

While Braverman's conception of the craftsperson has often been criticized as being romantic (Knights, 1990; Littler, 1982), his identification of farmer as craftsperson is one which is fundamental to the neopopulist view of the family farmer. Palmer (1975) asserts that technological innovation reduces the autonomy of the skilled craftsperson and is the primary force driving craftsmanship out of industry. It can also be argued that under industrialized agriculture,

142

farmers' traditional craftsperson role has been compromised through their reliance on the technologies developed by capitalist agribusiness and traditional scientists (Hightower and DeMarco, 1987; MacRae *et al.*, 1989). Overall, the requirement of farmers under industrialized agriculture to be technical specialists places at risk the traditional body of knowledge and tacit skills of agricultural production whilst reducing individual control of their production role and the labour process (Wardell, 1990).

In contrast, does organic farming represent the re-emergence of the farmer as agrarian craftsperson? At present, the practice of sustainable agriculture as a holistic and integrated system of production is generally regarded as requiring a higher level of management ability and skill (Lockeretz, 1990; MacRae *et al.*, 1990). The successful use of organic biological production inputs and cultural practices requires personal knowledge in both their production and application. Furthermore, the organic farmer who foregoes the purchase of these products of reductionistic science retains proportionately more control over the entire production process cycle. Thus, the potential for the separation between knowledge and practice, ownership and managerial control is less for the organic farmer.

Organic farming is not a return to pre-industrial agriculture but rather the on-site development of sophisticated organic systems which integrate pre-conventional methods with modern knowledge and technologies (MacRae *et al.*, 1990; National Research Council, 1989). Given the relative lack of academic and government research and advice on organic farming as well as the recognition of specificity required for the adaptation of farming techniques to local conditions, many organic farmers are required to become experimental researchers and independent masters of their craft as illustrated by the following statement by an organic farmer in British Columbia:

> Organic farming is to take Mother Nature as your guardian. She makes no mistake whatsoever. However, Mother Nature has all the time and you as farmers have not much time – you are only here for a short time. So She allows you to bend, stretch, curve but not break her rules. If you go by that, you'll do well. So what does that mean to you? That means you observe, the most basic thing is to observe. And you never stop observing and then you learn her laws. If you observe

closely, you will see that Nature has a balance. If you go hand in hand with her, you're fine. And that's where your skill comes in.

Another feature of organic farming which parallels that of the craftsperson is the operation of organic farming associations as guilds. Although there are no restrictions on the independent use of organic farming methods, membership in an organic farming association is mandatory in order to qualify for certified organic status. To be certified as organic under OFPANA (Organic Foods Production Association of North America) guidelines, the land must be worked under an organic production regime for a minimum of three years before the food produced on that site can be represented as certified organic.[13] During this 'transitional' period and subsequent to achieving certified status, organic farmers are subject to on-site operational audits conducted by their association's certification committee. In deciding whether to accept a farmer on to their certification programme, the actions, practices and beliefs of the applicant are evaluated.[14] Given the practical impossibility of supervising farmers on a daily basis, a significant degree of trust and confidence that the farmer will not violate the organic standards is required. This normative control to ensure that the maintenance of standards of conduct is very similar to that of the craftsperson's guild.

The educational or apprenticeship function of the craftsperson guild also appears to parallel that of organic farming associations. In addition to obtaining legitimation through the certification process, organic farmers in British Columbia often cite one reason for membership as being the opportunity to meet with and learn from other organic farmers as part of their ongoing technical development. This has been confirmed by these organic farmers' judgements of a variety of agricultural information sources (other farmers, farming organizations, mass media, government, educational institutions, agribusiness and contracting companies) in terms of relevance and trustworthiness. For organic farmers, the most frequent external sources of relevant and trustworthy information are other organic farmers, their organic farming organizations and organic farming publications. In contrast, conventional farmers utilize information from a much greater range of sources. Interestingly, one of the greatest differences between organic and conventional farmers is their relative ranking of government sources of information (agriculture extension agents and publications). While conventional farmers rank government sources first on the dimensions of relevance and trustworthiness, organic farmers rank government sources fifth in relevance and fourth in trustworthiness. This finding suggests that compared to conventional farming associations, organic farming associations have a greater role to play in the development and dissemination of production knowledge amongst their members.

Thus through their legitimation and educational functions, organic farming associations may be facilitating the re-emergence of the farmer as agrarian craftsperson.

BATTLING THE STATUS QUO: PRACTISING AND ORGANIZING ORGANIC FARMING

In concert with the increasing public activism concerning environmental issues and governments' interest in sustainable agriculture, the organic farming movement is growing within North America (Hill and MacRae, 1990; National Research Council, 1989). However, there remain significant technical, practical, institutional and social obstacles to operating outside of the mainstream.[15]

One question asked of organic farmers in British Columbia concerns why they have decided to follow a different course from their conventional counterparts. As found in other surveys of organic farmers (Blobaum, 1983; Conacher and Conacher, 1983; Hill, 1984; US Dept of Agriculture, 1980), many of those interviewed have also practised conventional farming and their reasons for converting to organic farming are diverse, rational and subjective. Some say it is the only logical way in which to ensure the long-term productive potential and health of the soil whilst remedying the damage wrought by the use of conventional products and practices (chemicals, monoculture and other specialized practices) on the natural environment. Others say that they were looking for a viable means of reducing operating costs by eliminating expensive production inputs such as synthetic chemical fertilizers and pesticides. Several report of their experience with the negative effects of synthetic chemical pesticides on their personal health, the health of their families and wildlife.

One principle difference between the organic and conventional farmers found in this research study is the strength of their beliefs and opinions concerning environmental issues. As revealed by their responses to an Ecological Opinion Survey questionnaire which measures beliefs concerning environmental issues, organic farmers are proving to be more environmentally 'radical' than their conventional counterparts.[16] Specifically, organic farmers are less control oriented in terms of humankind's relationship with Nature, are more critical of the negative consequences of growth and technology and believe that not enough attention is being given to environmental issues in society.[17]

The degree to which organic farmers differ from conventional farmers is further demonstrated by their responses on survey questionnaires concerning the use of synthetic agrichemicals in agriculture and their perceptions of organic farming.[18] As expected, organic farmers are more critical in their assessments of the risks associated with the use of synthetic chemicals as one important technological facet of industrialized agriculture. Organic farmers view agrichemicals as more dangerous to the natural environment, to food safety and to their personal health than do conventional farmers. Organic farmers are also more likely to disagree with conventional farmers' beliefs in the economic necessity of agrichemicals to ensure high productivity and to reduce crop losses due to pests and diseases.[19]

However, there are a number of apparent paradoxes in the responses of the conventional farmers. For example, while conventional farmers believe that agrichemicals are now restricted to carefully tested compounds, they agree with organic farmers (although not to the same degree) that the use of agrichemicals endangers the health of farmworkers. Apparently, conventional farmers are able to discount the potentially negative personal health effects of agrichemicals and are willing (or feel compelled) to trade off these effects in order to secure the economic benefits from their usage. This is not to say that there is a complete absence of ecological consciousness amongst conventional farmers. There are a number of farmers in this study and elsewhere (National Research Council, 1989) who are experimenting with new techniques of soil conservation and biological and cultural methods of pest control (e.g. Integrated Pest Management). However, the primary focus of these experiments has been to make incremental adjustments to existing practices, rather than engaging in a systemic-level transformation of an industrialized mode of production. In contrast, organic farmers appear to be more willing to endure the accepted short-term economic costs associated with organic farming (such as the increased crop losses due to weeds and insect pests; the greater labour effort required by organic methods) in the belief that their course of action is, in the long term, environmentally sustainable and financially viable.

As these results demonstrate, the ways in which organic and conventional farmers construct the realities of industrialized agriculture and organic farming are distinctly different. Their perceptions, beliefs and motivations are important to understanding the underlying dynamics of resistance to industrialized agriculture. On the one hand, conventional farmers tend to focus on the economic aspects of agricultural production thus informing their resistance to remedying the financial dislocations created by industrialized agriculture whilst denying the need for or validity of environmentally informed systemic-level changes. On the other hand, the overriding concern of organic farmers appears to be the environmental consequences of industrialized agriculture. Unlike the case for conventional farmers, the organic farmers' stronger subscription to the environmentalist ethic results in fewer contradictions. Thus, for organic farmers there is a higher congruence between ideological beliefs and personal practice and actions – a unity which is proving to be an essential prerequisite for battling the status quo of industrialized agriculture.

The modern struggle for revolutionary change

There are a number of organic farmers who view their practice of organic farming as part of a grassroots social movement to replace centralized institutional control of food production and distribution with decentralized and self-sufficient economic and political bioregions. As self-described 'anarchists', it is these organic farmers who espouse an ideological belief system which is most closely aligned with the philosophies of deep ecology (Devall and Sessions, 1985) and social ecology (Bookchin, 1990). This position is most clearly illustrated in the statement of one member of a regional organic farming association in British Columbia who wrote in a newsletter critique of current developments within the organic farming community,

> [The organic agriculture movement] is not about mass marketing or world trade or inflated prices or establishing authoritarian institutions or engaging government bureaucracies or organizing an industry. On the contrary, it stands very much

opposed to all this. It is about transforming human society and it is about healing the earth.

Organic agriculture has to do with down-sizing farms; with restoring human scale to food production; with returning people to the land.

As the champions of a radical alternative to the status quo, these individuals see themselves at the vanguard of a new social and economic order in which the minority tradition of Thomas Jefferson, Henry Thoreau and Walt Whitman prevails. In contrast to the dominant form of community in industrial-technocratic Western societies, this minority tradition espouses decentralized, non-hierarchial and democratic authority (as opposed to centralized and bureaucratized authority of the dominant social order); local autonomy, self-responsibility and communalism within small-scale communities (as opposed to competitive individualism in bureau-cratized communities); self-regulation (government regulation); simplicity of wants (consumerism); and a definition of community which encompasses all human, animal and plant life (an anthro-pocentric definition of citizenship) (Devall and Sessions, 1985). In its most radical form, organic farming is framed as part of a socio-political revolution to replace capitalism and the nation-state which supports it with truly participative democracy and ecologically sustainable communities which seek a holistic integration with Nature (Bookchin, 1990; Gorz, 1980).

In what ways have these values surfaced in the formation and operation of the organic farming organizations which are being studied? The majority of these organizations are less than five years old and are still in the midst of organizing. Initially formed to provide for the informal exchange of information about organic farming within each geographic bioregion and operating in relative isolation, each association appears to have followed a similar pattern of development. While continuing to provide a venue for education and information sharing, the next step has been the estab-lishment of committees to develop regional organic certification standards. As non-profit societies, the organic farming associations have operated solely on a non-profit voluntary basis with the only paid staff members (with the exception of two associations which have hired part-time administrators) being verification officers who review applications for grower certification and inspects applicants' farms. One notable feature of these organic farming associations (in comparison to conventional farming organizations), is the greater visibility and involvement of women farmers in organizational formation, operation and leadership roles.

In 1989, an umbrella group called the Alliance of British Columbian Organic Producers Associations (ABCOPA) formed to provide a linkage between the various bioregional groups. Within this umbrella group and the majority of bioregional associations, there is evidence of the social agendas of deep ecology and social ecology emerging in their egalitarian, participative and full consensus decision-making processes. For example, one of the more radical regional associations does not have elected officers (only spokespersons) or a formal organizational structure thereby eschewing any semblance of hierarchy. With the exception of two of the more ideologically moderate associations, consensus decision-making is the *modus operandi* of these organizations. Although several members of ABCOPA have commented that full consensus consumes an inordinate amount of time and energy and can frustrate the quick resolution of issues, suggestions to compromise (i.e. instituting an 80 per cent majority rule) have been met with vocal opposition and rejected.

Most distinctive is the importance these individuals attach to the *process* of interaction, sometimes to the extent of overriding the content of outcomes or resolution of issues. This is perhaps reflective of the practice of organic farming itself. Unlike industrial agriculture where the primary concern is with productive output (with the ends justifying the means), the process by which food is produced is pre-eminent for organic farmers. The emphasis on process also surfaces in the enforcement of organic certification standards which involve the auditing of the production process (i.e., methods of soil and plant nutrition, pest control) rather than the testing of products for banned/restricted chemicals. The assumption is that if the process is ecologically sound, then the product which results will be also.[20]

Currently, there is a political and ideological contest within the British Columbian organic farming community which is reminiscent of the struggles between Marx and Bakunin within the International Workingmen's Association from 1864 to 1872 (Gouldner, 1985). Like modern-day Bakuninists, members of the more ideologically radical organic farming associations (the current majority in ABCOPA) envision their organizations operating like 'Bakuninist conceptions of small autonomous communities coming together voluntarily in federated systems' (Gouldner, 1985: 170). Unlike the nineteenth-century Bakuninists though, these individuals do not regard direct action or violence as necessary ingredients for effecting revolutionary change within agriculture. Instead, they advocate passive resistance, withholding support for the status quo by working outside of industrialized agriculture and avoiding contact with those they view as part of the politically corrupt industrial system. They see the ecological crisis created by industrialized agriculture (and its institutional elite) as providing the impetus for the inevitable transformation of agricultural production. They are confident that as the ecological crisis becomes more severe, conventional farmers will become convinced of the necessity for change and will join the organic farming movement.

Spokespersons for these organic farming associations oppose any semblance of cooperation with those they view as adversaries (i.e. government institutions, conventional producer organizations and agribusiness) in their quest for social, political and technological reform. For these actors there can be no compromising (either in thought or action) the long-term objective of revolutionary change. The response of one regional member who opposes the current provincial government initiative to implement organic certification regulatory standards is illustrative:

> We, once the proud renegades of agriculture, are now laying the groundwork for the 'organic industry' to coopt the organic movement, and in the process are inviting into our lives an alarming degree of external control and scrutiny.

For those who hold this view, the government's motives are suspect despite official statements to the contrary. (In fact, the genesis of the provincial government's Food Choice and Disclosure Act remains a mystery and the subject of much speculation. One thing is certain, though, the legislation was not the result of lobbying by any of the existing organic farming organizations. Yet the only use of this enabling legislation to date has been to set up a regulatory system for organically produced food.) Their scepticism is given credence by the close historical alliance between government agricultural agencies, agribusiness and conventional agriculture organizations (Browne, 1988; Forbes, 1985).[21] Distrust of government agencies is also fuelled by the lack of practical support for organic farming such as government research and advice (in publications and by farm advisory representatives) on alternatives to synthetic chemical and

150

mechanical prescriptions for production problems (MacRae *et al.*, 1989; McEwen and Milligan, 1991). These organic farmers contend that the linkages between government agencies, conventional producers and agrichemical manufacturers remain strong and often only 'lip-service' is being accorded to supporting environmentally sustainable agriculture. Consistent with this view, ABCOPA rejected the government offer of a grant to develop provincial certification standards and elected independently to develop a set of organic production guidelines.

In contrast, members of two of the more ideologically moderate organic farming associations believe that social, economic and political change can be attained by working within the existing political system. Viewing themselves as pragmatists, they are less reluctant to develop alliances with the existing institutional elites in government and in industry. Instead, they regard the commercialization and institutionalization of organic farming as an industry, as a positive step. Furthermore, they contend that government accreditation is essential for exporting their products to Europe and the United States – a motive generally viewed as environmentally suspect by those committed to the ecological principle of bioregional self-sustainability.

Significantly, the majority of members in these two associations subscribe to the less radical schools of organic farming. One of the associations identifies with the regenerative agriculture school (in both name and membership) which advocates the reduction, rather than total elimination of petrochemical production inputs. (However, their organic certification standards are consistent with those of the OFPANA guidelines.)[22] The process of decision-making within these two organizations is that of majority rule rather than consensus decision-making. They view themselves as pragmatists rather than founders of a new social and economic order and see government as a potential ally in the promotion of organic farming as a commercially viable industry operating in parallel to the conventional agri-food industry. What appears to be less important to these actors is the revolutionary potential of organic farming as a social and political movement.

Despite charges by other ABCOPA members that they have been co-opted by the dominant societal elite and instructions to stop, the two moderate organizations have accepted government funds and have worked closely with government officials to develop provincial certification standards. They deny that they have been co-opted and contend that these short-term compromises are necessary in order to achieve the long-term goal of an environmentally sustainable agriculture. Notably, in drafting the new standards, representatives of these two associations have purposefully edited out any statements or references to the philosophical objectives of organic farming. Under this new regulatory model, the provincial government's ministry of agriculture would have the power to audit individual organic farming associations to ensure that their certification standards met with the provincial r¬gulations. In order to ensure conformity amongst associations, one option being considered is a government education programme and review process for verification officers. Both of these provisions run in direct opposition with the philosophy of the majority of bioregional associations which subscribe to the environmental principles of self-regulation and local autonomy.

In 1991, these two organizations created a new provincial organic producers' association to work with the government in the development and operation of the new provincial accreditation system and organic production standards (Certified Organic Associations of British Columbia, 1992a, 1992b). With the assistance of government ministry representatives, they have drawn up an organizational constitution which would establish an umbrella association that closely mirrors the structure and decision-making process of the existing provincial body for the conventional food industry. The membership of the new Certified Organic Associations of British Columbia (COABC) would consist of

> one representative of each participating certification agency having members certified under these [provincial] regulations; one representative from each wholesale/retail/distributor/ processor association which markets organic food products; one representative of a consumer and/or environmental advocacy association; one representative from BCMAFF [British Columbia Ministry of Agriculture, Fisheries and Food].
> (COABC, 1992a: Section 4.3.2.)

While the consumer/environmental representative and government representative will sit on the COABC Board of Directors in a non-voting advisory capacity, their inclusion as well as that of a wholesale/retail/distributor/processor representative is a feature which has been rejected by the radical bioregional associations.

While envisioning that individual bioregional associations would remain operationally independent, the architects of this new association see it also working with government agencies to develop marketing and educational programmes to promote organic products as a 'niche' market. A new provincial 'British Columbia Certified Organic' stamp would be introduced to indicate conformity with the provincial regulations (BCMAFF, 1992). This may make redundant the efforts of bioregional organic associations to develop their own stamps which reflect their individual identities. However, the rationale for reproducing the existing institutional structure of conventional agriculture without the revolutionary rhetoric of radical environmentalism is that it will be easier to convince existing conventional farmers either to convert to organic farming or at least to modify their production systems to be more environmentally sustainable.

One acknowledged repercussion of this initiative could be the complete dissolution of ABCOPA or the reduction of its role as the representative body for the provincial organic farming community. Initially, the political strategy of the breakaway organizations was to try to convince the more 'moderate' bioregional organizations to join the new association thereby leaving out the 'anarchists' and 'back to the landers' whom they view as obstructing the progress of the organic farming industry. This strategy was subsequently amended to try to convince all bioregional associations to sign on to COABC in support of the new provincial regulations. Following a series of meetings with individual bioregional associations and two intensive (and at times, acrimonious) meetings involving ABCOPA, COABC and BCMAFF representatives, in May 1992 a taskforce comprised of representatives of five bioregional associations was established to review the proposed regulations. As of the fall of 1992, the remaining five bioregional associations and the biodynamic society have chosen not to participate in the process of implementing a provincial certification programme.

In summary, what initially started out as an independent grassroots movement which resists the status quo in farming philosophy and practice, is now undergoing a crisis of identity and direction. What then is the long-term revolutionary potential of organic farming in British Columbia given these latest developments? Despite the initial radical environmentalist agenda of the majority of the founding members in all of the organic farming associations, pressures to institutionalize the organic farming movement in British Columbia appear to be succeeding. From the literature on technological and social innovation, we learn that innovations which are *perceived* to be incremental and *perceived* not to threaten existing power relationships are easier to implement and are less likely to evoke resistance to change (e.g. Frost and Egri, 1991; Weick, 1984). Thus, the strategy of the more moderate associations to present organic farming as a politically neutral technological alternative to existing practices would appear to bode well for its acceptance within the wider agricultural community. Further, their acceptance of government plans to promote organically grown food products as a specialized niche market reduces the potential for economic conflict with large-scale conventional producers.

However, incremental innovations are also more vulnerable to the power of existing institutional elites to channel the process of change in ways which pre-empt fundamental deep structural changes in social and economic relationships. This raises some question regarding the ability (and will) of those working with the institutional elite in agriculture to resist abandoning the environmentalist agenda for radical social and political change. The government regulation of organic production may be a two-edged sword. On the one hand, it provides a measure of legitimacy to organic producers and protection against misrepresentation within the marketplace. On the other hand, the spectre of government regulation (and the scrutiny and inevitable record-keeping it entails) may serve to discourage those considering converting to organic farming thus limiting the growth of the movement for radical social, political and environmental change.

CONCLUSION

What then are the implications of this case study of resistance to industrialized agriculture for labour process theory and other studies of resistance? First, the current farm crisis in North America provides vivid confirmation of Burawoy's (1985) assertion that there are interrelated economic, social and political dimensions to the capitalist labour process and the resistance it engenders. The means by which industrialized agriculture became entrenched illustrates the power of institutional elites (agribusiness and governments) to use technological changes to create capitalist relations of production whilst eroding the craftsmanship of labour (as also found by Braverman, 1974; Littler, 1982; Noble, 1984). As is borne out by the record of governments' corporatist farm policies and programmes, this case study also confirms Strinati's (1990) assertion that the state is not a neutral party within monopoly capitalism.

Interestingly, the economic and overproduction crises of industrialized agriculture appear not to have provided sufficient impetus
for the creation of a unified social class consciousness amongst
family farmers to challenge capitalist relations of production. One
impediment to the development of class consciousness can be
traced to the adherence of family farmers to the illusory neopopulist ideal whilst another impediment is the transitional and
contradictory class locations of family farmers (Mooney, 1986;
Vogeler, 1981). However, as demonstrated in this case study of
resistance to industrialized agriculture, there is emerging a class
consciousness amongst organic family farmers who are responding
to the ecological crisis created by the capitalist system of production
(as predicted by Gorz, 1980).

It can be argued that an integrated class-ecological consciousness
is required to inform and focus the struggles of resistance to the
modern capitalist labour process in both agricultural and industrial
sectors. In an era where industrial capitalism is being championed
and embraced (most dramatically in the former States of the Soviet
Union and Eastern Europe), there is little critique of the negative
impact of capitalist systems on humans and the natural environment.
Whilst by no means universally accepted as yet, the environmentalist agenda for ecological, social, political and economic change
holds significant potential for generating and guiding ideological
and practical resistance to exploitative systems of production.
Furthermore, environmentalism may be a potent unifying force for
developing cooperative linkages between rural and urban agents of
resistance to challenge capitalist systems (Buttel, 1980).

The different responses of conventional versus organic family
farmers to the farm crisis created by industrialized agriculture
illustrates the importance of ideology and subjectivity in framing
and focusing struggles of resistance (Knights, 1990; Willmott, 1990).
It also leads one to reconsider Thompson's (1990) conclusion that
struggles of resistance and struggles of transformation can be considered separately. Without transformative intent, the struggles of
conventional family farmers to renegotiate economic benefits do
not appear to constitute real resistance to industrialized agriculture.
In reality, the efforts of conventional farmers and their organizations
have been constrained to reproducing existing capitalist relations of
production. In contrast, passive resistance informed by the more
integrated transformative goals (social, political, economic and ecological) of the organic farming movement appear to hold more

potential for effecting fundamental changes to industrialized agriculture. However, as is currently being experienced within the
British Columbian organic farming community, radical changes are
not inevitable or without conflict. Only time will tell whether the
potential of organic farming to revolutionize industrialized agriculture will be realized.

NOTES

1 The focus of this chapter is on agriculture in Canada and the United
States. While each is a sovereign state, the integration of both countries'
economies under the recent Canada–United States. Free Trade Agreement has only formalized the historically close economic, political and
cultural linkages between the two countries. Within Canadian and
American agriculture, development and issues have been primarily
influenced by North–South geographically defined interests (e.g. grain
production in the Great Plains of the American mid-west and the
Canadian Prairies). The dominance of US-based multinational corporations in Canada's agricultural inputs and equipment, food processing,
marketing and distribution industries also demonstrates the economic
integration of both countries' agri-food sectors (Troughton, 1989). For
these reasons, data and observations from both Canada and the United
States will be used, at times, interchangeably. In contrast, Mexico offers
a distinctly different model of agricultural development (historically,
politically and culturally) and therefore will not be included in this
chapter's analysis.
2 While investment in agricultural machinery and vehicles has increased
sevenfold (in constant dollars) from 1945 to 1985, the use of labour has
decreased by a factor of five. Labour efficiency since 1940 has increased
significantly in that the labour required to farm one acre of land
declined 75 per cent while farm output per acre has doubled with the
net result being that farm labour is now eight times more productive
than in 1940 (National Research Council, 1989).
3 The number of farms in Canada has declined from 732,715 in 1941 to
280,043 in 1991 (Sanford Evans Statistical Service, 1944; Statistics
Canada, 1991a). While area under farm production has remained
relatively constant, the size of the average Canadian farm has increased
from 237 acres in 1941 to 598 acres in 1991 (Hay and Basran, 1988;
Statistics Canada, 1991a). In the United States, the number of farms has
been reduced from 5.9 million in 1945 to 2.1 million by 1987 (National
Research Council, 1989). One result of the concentration of land assets
into larger holdings has been a concentration of food production with
30 per cent of the farms in Canada accounting for over 85 per cent of
gross farm receipts (Troughton, 1989). In the United States, 15–20 per
cent of all farms produce more than 80 per cent of food and fibre output
(National Research Council, 1989).
4 One agriculture policy objective of governments has been the provision

· of cheap food for urban populations (Danbom, 1979; Flora, 1990; Hightower and DeMarco, 1987; Strange, 1984). The success of their strategies is demonstrated by the fact that the percentage of family expenditures on food has declined from 18.9 per cent in 1969 to 14.2 per cent in 1986 (Statistics Canada, 1989: 5-38). A recent survey of food prices in Canada shows that over the past 10 years, real prices to farmers has remained relatively constant (the farm product price index has increased only 0.2 per cent while the farm input price index has increased 16.5 per cent) with the main beneficiaries of higher food prices being the retailer buying groups (Ferguson, 1991).

5 Government intervention in agriculture has taken the forms of extensive commodity supply and price support programmes, export subsidies, tax policies, the funding of agricultural research and development, and farm extension services (Flora, 1990; Hadwiger, 1982; National Research Council, 1989; Vogeler, 1981). Government subsidies to farm producers are a highly political issue both domestically and internationally. Based on a recent OECD report in 1990, 40 per cent of Canadian farmers' income and 30 per cent of US farmers' income comes directly or indirectly from governments. This compares to the European Community statistic of approximately 45 per cent. In terms of the total cost of subsidies to governments, there has been a steady increase over the past decade. The 1990 estimates of spending (in $US) on direct and indirect support to agricultural producers are: $6.46 billion (Canada); $35.93 billion (United States); $82.62 Billion (European Community) (*Western Producer*, 18 July 1991: 4).

6 In 1985 in the United States, 3 per cent of all farms were insolvent and an additional 18.9 per cent had a debt-to-asset ratio greater than 40 per cent (the threshold level beyond which an operation cannot serve debt and pay other operating costs) (US Dept of Agriculture, 1987).

7 In their analysis of the relative share of accumulated value accruing to capitalists (off-farm and industrial farms) and to family farm labour (hired labour and family members), Lianos and Paris (1972) found a tenfold increase in the exploitation of farm labour from 1949 to 1968.

8 This research study is the author's PhD dissertation project at the University of British Columbia.

9 The extent of marketing board control varies substantially between different commodity groups. For example, producers' receipts through marketing boards as a percentage of farm cash receipts in 1984–5 were as follows: 100 per cent of dairy products; 95 per cent of poultry; 83 per cent of grains (wheat, oats, barley, rye, corn); 83 per cent of eggs; 50 per cent of vegetables; 46 per cent of fruit; 65 per cent of hogs; 3 per cent of cattle (Troughton, 1989).

10 The history of farm policy and programmes has been one of a fundamental shift from populism to corporatism in support of the industrialization process. State price support and commodity programmes have served to promote capital accumulation into large-scale operations and favour the industrial agricultural production system which is highly specialized (functionally and regionally), mechanized and reliant on non-renewable natural resources. Not surprisingly, many

of these programmes were the result of lobbying by industrial agri-business groups and conventional farming organizations dominated by large-scale producers who have proven to be their greatest beneficiaries. (Allen and Elliott, 1988; McCreary and Furtan, 1988; Petit, Rossmiller and Tutwiler, 1988)

11 In this chapter, Nature is not meant to be anthropomorphized but rather to represent a holistic multiplicity of interdependent and interacting systems of life comprised of microbial, plant, animal, insect and inanimate entities.

12 Organic producers' operating costs are generally 10 per cent of assets versus 33 per cent for conventional producers (MacRae *et al.*, 1988). In addition to reducing expenditures for synthetic chemical production inputs, organic methods have lower asset requirements (fewer buildings, less technologically sophisticated equipment), therefore there is a lower debt-service load for capital investment. Energy requirements in terms of fossil fuels are significantly less (average 37 per cent) under the organic production regime (Lockeretz, *et al.*, 1976). When the observed price differential (10 per cent/50 per cent price premiums) for organic produce is taken into account, the net result of these economic differentials is that the overall profitability of both methods of production is essentially the same or favourable for organic products (Koepf, 1989; Lockeretz *et al.*, 1976; Oelhaf, 1978).

13 While the length of the transitional period has been largely at the discretion of the individual certifying organic association, three years is becoming the norm in North America. For example, in the United States, both California and Washington organic farming organizations are currently extending their one-year transitional period to three years. In Canada, three years will be the basis for the national standards. Within British Columbia, a few organic farming associations still retain a five year transitional period. The most stringent certification standards are those of the bio-dynamic farmers. International and domestic guidelines require five years' experience with bio-dynamic production systems before the granting of 'Biodyn' status, and seven years for 'Demeter' status.

14 There is an important distinction between the certification of land as being an organic production site and a farmer as being a certified organic grower. This may or may not coincide with the farmer's actual experience as an organic grower. In the event that the individual farmer is the one to instigate the land certification process, then his/her acceptance as a certified organic grower would coincide with the period of land certification.

However, if the farmer has purchased an already certified organic farm, then the retention of certified status is problematic. A few organic farming associations deal with this issue by assessing the purchaser's experience with and commitment to organic production methods and if judged to be sufficient by the certification committee, certified organic status for the land and product is continued. The majority of organic farming associations take a more cautious approach and require that the land revert back to 'transitional' status until the farmer has proven his/her expertise (and trustworthiness) as an organic grower.

15 These include the lack of technical information about organic methods; difficulties in developing marketing distribution networks for organically produced food; negative social pressures (non-supportive opinions of farm neighbours, agribusiness dealers, academic researchers); lack of adequate certification of organic products as such; as well as uncertainty about the impact of organic production methods on crop yields, weed problems, etc. (Blobaum, 1983; MacRae *et al.*, 1989, 1990; Oelhaf, 1978; US Dept of Agriculture, 1980).

16 The Ecological Opinion Survey is derived from the New Environmental Paradigm scale which measures the degree to which one subscribes to the New Environmental Paradigm of radical environmentalist philosophy or to the Dominant Social Paradigm of modern capitalist society (see Dunlap and Van Liere, 1978; Geller and Lasley, 1985; Kuhn and Jackson, 1989, for earlier versions of this scale). The Ecological Opinion Survey consists of 30 seven-point Likert-type scale items (strongly disagree to strongly disagree) measuring six scale factors: the negative consequences of growth and technology (eight items); the relationship between humankind and Nature (eight items); the limits to the biosphere (eight items); quality of life (four items); public attention to environmental issues (two items); and the role of government in environmental issues (two items).

17 Organic farmers ($N = 38$) more strongly subscribe to the New Environmental Paradigm than do conventional farmers ($N = 25$). In t-test comparisons on the six questionnaire factors, organic farmers were found to be significantly different from conventional farmers on *all* but the role of government in environmental issues. Statistical differences (two-tailed probability estimates) between organic and conventional farmers were as follows: negative consequences of growth and technology ($t = 3.86$; $p < 0.0005$); relationship between humankind and nature ($t = 3.38$; $p < 0.0005$); the limits to the biosphere ($t = 3.40$; $p < 0.001$); quality of life ($t = 5.00$; $p < 0.0005$); public attention to environmental issues ($t = 4.01$; $p < 0.0005$).

18 The survey questionnaire on the use of agrichemicals consists of 16 items rated on a seven-point Likert-type scale (strongly disagree to strongly agree). The questionnaire items provide an assessment of the environmental (seven items) and personal health (four items) risks associated with the use of synthetic agrichemicals as well as the financial risks (seven items) associated with their non-use.

The survey questionnaire concerning perceptions of organic farming consists of 11 items (rated on a five-point scale from strongly disagree to strongly agree) to assess four factors: economic viability, complexity, quality of organic food, and compatibility with work practices. Forty-eight organic and 36 conventional farmers completed this questionnaire as part of interview sessions.

19 Statistical comparisons between organic farmers ($N = 39$) and conventional farmers ($N = 27$) yielded significant differences on all three risk factors ($p < 0.0005$, two-tailed probability estimate) and 14 of the

16 questionnaire items. Compared to conventional farmers, organic farmers perceived agrichemicals to pose greater risks to the environment (t = 8.21) and to personal health (t = 8.23). In regards to the financial risks associated with the use of agrichemicals in production, conventional farmers perceived that agrichemicals reduced this risk factor significantly while organic farmers were less convinced of the financial necessity of agrichemicals (t = 8.24). For example, organic farmers felt that synthetic agrichemicals were less necessary to ensure high productivity or to reduce crop losses due to pests and diseases.

20 There is also a practical need for trust in the production process given the cost for an individual laboratory test for chemicals can cost $600 each.

21 In an interview with a provincial agriculture ministry employee, it was revealed that prior to implementation, the organic certification standards would be reviewed by the British Columbia Federation of Agriculture which represents the majority of conventional producers in the province.

22 Whilst members of the two more moderate organic farming associations do not differ significantly from the other organic farmers in British Columbia in terms of their opinions regarding environmental issues, they are more moderate in their stance on the use of agrichemicals. In fact, members of the moderate associations (N = 12) scored between the other British Columbian organic farmers (N = 27) and conventional farmers (N = 27) on the majority of items on the use of agrichemicals questionnaire (although only two items reached statistical significance at the p < 0.05 level). In terms of the agrichemical risk scale factors, members of the moderate organic farming associations were the same as other organic farmers in terms of perceptions about the personal health and financial risk factors. However, they saw a slightly lesser degree of environmental risk associated with the use of synthetic agrichemicals (t = 1.95; p < 0.071).

REFERENCES

Adas, M. (1986) 'From footdragging to flight: the evasive history of peasant avoidance protest in South and South-east Asia', *Journal of Peasant Studies* 13(2): 64–86.

Allen, K. and Elliott, B.J. (1988) 'The current debate and economic rationale for US agricultural policy', in M.A. Tutwiler (ed.) *US Agriculture in a Global Setting: An Agenda for the Future*, Washington, DC: National Center for Food and Agricultural Policy.

Altieri, M.A. (ed.) (1987) *Agroecology: The Scientific Basis of Alternative Agriculture*, Boulder, CO: Westview Press.

Auer, L. (1989) *Canadian Prairie Farming, 1960–2000: An Economic Analysis*, Ottawa: Supply and Services Canada.

Banaji, J. (1980) 'Summary of selected parts of Kautsky's *The Agrarian Question*', in F.H. Buttel and H. Newby (eds) *The Rural Sociology of the Advanced Societies: Critical Perspectives*, London: Croom Helm.

Berry, W. (1976) 'Where cities and farms come together', in R. Merrill (ed.) *Radical Agriculture*, New York: New York University Press.

Blobaum, R. (1983) 'Barriers to conversion to organic farming practices in the Midwestern United States', in W. Lockeretz (ed.) *Environmentally Sound Agriculture*, New York: Praeger.

Bolaria, B.S. (1988) 'The health effects of powerlessness: the case of immigrant farm labour', in G.S. Basran and D.A. Hay (eds) *The Political Economy of Agriculture in Western Canada*, Toronto: Garamond Press.

Bollman, R.D. and Smith, P. (1988) 'Integration of Canadian farm and off-farm markets and the off-farm work of farm women, men, and children', in G.S. Basran and D.A. Hay (eds) *The Political Economy of Agriculture in Western Canada*, Toronto: Garamond Press.

Bookchin, M. (1990) *Remaking Society: Pathways to a Green Future*, Boston, MA: South End Press.

Braverman, H. (1974) *Labor and Monopoly Capital*, New York: Monthly Review Press.

British Columbia Ministry of Agriculture, Fisheries and Food (1992) 'Organic Agricultural Products Certification Regulation. Draft 3 – August 14, 1992', Victoria, BC: BC Ministry of Agriculture, Fisheries and Food.

Browne, W.P. (1988) 'The fragmented and meandering politics of agriculture', in M.A. Tutwiler (ed.) *US Agriculture in a Global Setting: An Agenda for the Future*, Washington, DC: National Center for Food and Agricultural Policy.

Burawoy, M. (1985) *The Politics of Production*, London: Verso.

Buttel, F.H. (1980) 'Agriculture, environment, and social change: some emergent issues', in F.H. Buttel and H. Newby (eds) *The Rural Sociology of the Advanced Societies: Critical Perspectives*, London: Croom Helm.

Buttel, F.H. and Newby, H. (eds) (1980) *The Rural Sociology of the Advanced Societies: Critical Perspectives*, London: Croom Helm.

Buttel, F.H., Larson, O.F. and Gillespie, G.W., Jr (1990) *The Sociology of Agriculture*, New York: Greenwood Press.

Canter, L.W. (1986) *Environmental Impacts of Agricultural Production Activities*, Chelsea, MI: Lewis Publishers.

Carr, A.B. (1988) 'Agricultural information and technology: a continuum of change', in M.A. Tutwiler (ed.) *US Agriculture in a Global Setting: An Agenda for the Future*, Washington, DC: National Center for Food and Agricultural Policy.

Certified Organic Associations of British Columbia (1992a) 'Certified Organic Associations of British Columbia policy and structure (draft). Submission for regulation under B.C. Food Choice and Disclosure Act. Eighth Draft, 20.03.92'.

Certified Organic Associations of British Columbia (1992b) 'Certified Organic Associations of British Columbia production standards (Draft). 27 April 1992'.

Commoner, B. (1990) *Making Peace with the Planet*, New York: Pantheon Books.

Comstock, G. (ed.) (1987) *Is There a Moral Obligation to Save the Family Farm?*, Ames, Iowa: Iowa State University Press.

Conacher, A. and Conacher, J. (1983) 'A survey of organic farming in Australia', *Biological Agriculture and Horticulture* 1: 241–54.

Danbom, D.D. (1979) *The Resisted Revolution: Urban America and the Industrialization of Agriculture, 1900–1930*, Ames, Iowa: Iowa State University Press.

Davis, J.E. (1980) 'Capitalist agricultural development and the exploitation of the propertied laborer', in F. Buttel and H. Newby (eds) *The Rural Sociology of the Advanced Societies: Critical Perspectives*, Montclair, NJ: Allanheld, Osmun.

de Janvry, A. (1980) 'Social differentiation in agriculture and the ideology of neopopulism', in F.H. Buttel and H. Newby (eds) *The Rural Sociology of the Advanced Societies: Critical Perspectives*, London: Croom Helm.

Devall, B. and Sessions, G. (1985) *Deep Ecology: Living as if Nature Mattered*, Salt Lake City, UT: Peregrine Smith Books.

Doyle, J. (1985) *Altered Harvest: Agriculture, Genetics, and the Fate of the World's Food Supply*, New York: Penguin Books.

Duckworth, B. and Sproat, D. (1991) 'Organizer says farm rallies have served their purpose', *The Western Producer* 29(12): 4.

Dunlap, R.E. and Van Liere, K.D. (1978) 'The "new environmental paradigm": a proposed measuring instrument and preliminary results', *Journal of Environmental Education* 9 (Summer): 10–19.

Ferguson, R. (1991) 'Compare the share: Canadian farmers need a fair share of the consumer food dollar', Ottawa: R. Ferguson, MP, House of Commons.

Flora, C.B. (1990) 'Policy issues and agricultural sustainability', in C.A. Francis, C.B. Flora and L.D. King (eds) *Sustainable Agriculture in Temperate Zones*, New York: John Wiley & Sons.

Forbes, J.D. (1985) *Institutions and Influence Groups in Canadian Farm and Food Policy*, Toronto: Institute of Public Administration of Canada.

Friedland, W.H., Barton, A. and Thomas, R.J. (1981) *Manufacturing Green Gold*, New York: Cambridge University Press.

Frost, P.J. and Egri, C.P. (1991) 'The political process of innovation', in L.L. Cummings and B.M. Staw (eds) *Research in Organizational Behavior* 13: 229–95, Greenwich, CT: JAI Press.

Geller, J.M. and Lasley, P. (1985) 'The new environmental paradigm scale: a reexamination', *Journal of Environmental Education* 17(1): 9–12.

Giangrande, C. (1985) *Down to Earth: The Crisis in Canadian Farming*, Toronto: Anansi.

Gips, T. (1987) *Breaking the Pesticide Habit: Alternatives to 12 Hazardous Pesticides*, Minneapolis, MI: International Alliance for Sustainable Agriculture, Newman Center at the University of Minnesota.

Goss, K.F., Rodefeld, R.D. and Buttel, F.H. (1980) 'The political economy of class structure in US agriculture: a theoretical outline' in F.H. Buttel and H. Newby (eds) *The Rural Sociology of the Advanced Societies: Critical Perspectives*, London: Croom Helm.

Gorz, A. (1980) *Ecology as Politics*, Montreal: Black Rose Press.

Gouldner, A. (1985) *Against Fragmentation: The Origins of Marxism and the Sociology of Intellectuals*, New York: Oxford University Press.

Hadwiger, D.F. (1982) *The Politics of Agricultural Research*, Lincoln, NEBR: University of Nebraska Press.

Hay, D.A. and Basran, G.S. (1988) 'The Western Canadian farm sector: transition and trends', in G.S. Basran and D.A. Hay (eds) *The Political Economy of Agriculture in Western Canada*, Toronto: Garamond Press.

Hedley, M.J. (1981) 'Relations of production of the "family farm" ', *Journal of Peasant Studies* 9(1): 71-85.

Hightower, J. and DeMarco, S. (1987) 'Hard tomatoes, hard times: the failure of the land grant college complex', in G. Comstock (ed.) *Is There a Moral Obligation to Save the Family Farm?*, Ames, Iowa: Iowa State University Press.

Hill, S.B. (1984) 'Organic farming in Canada', *Ecological Agriculture Project Research Paper No. 4*, Ste-Anne de Bellevue, QUE: Macdonald College of McGill University.

Hill, S.B. (1989) 'Sustainable agriculture in Canada', Working Paper, Ecological Agriculture Project, Ste-Anne de Bellevue, QUE: Macdonald College of McGill University.

Hill, S.B. and MacRae, R.J. (1990) 'Organic farming in Canada', presentation to the 7th IFOAM Scientific Conference, Budapest, Hungary, 27-30 August.

Jenkins, P. (1991) *Fields of Vision: A Journey to Canada's Family Farms*, Toronto: McClelland & Stewart.

Kendrick, J.W. (1983) *Interindustry Differences in Productivity Growth*, Washington, DC: American Enterprise Institute.

Koepf, H.H. (1989) *The Biodynamic Farm: Agriculture in the Service of the Earth and Humanity*, Hudson, NY: Anthroposophic Press.

Knights, D. (1990) 'Subjectivity, power and the labour process', in D. Knights and H. Willmott (eds) *Labour Process Theory*, London: Macmillan.

Knights, D. and Willmott, H. (eds) (1990) *Labour Process Theory*, London: Macmillan.

Kuhn, R.G. and Jackson, E.L. (1989) 'Stability of factor structures in the measurement of public environmental attitudes', *Journal of Environmental Education* 20(3): 27-32.

Langley, J.A., Heady, E.O. and Olson, K.D. (1982) 'The macro implications of a complete transformation of US agricultural production to organic farming practices', in W. Lockeretz (ed.) *Environmentally Sound Agriculture*, New York: Praeger.

Lianos, T.P. and Paris, Q. (1972) 'American agriculture and the prophecy of increasing misery', *American Journal of Agricultural Economics* 54: 570-7.

Littler, C.R. (1982) *The Development of the Labour Process in Capitalist Societies: A Comparative Study of the Transformation of Work Organization in Britain, Japan and the USA*, London: Heinemann Educational Books.

Llambi, L. (1988) 'Small modern farmers: neither peasants nor fully-fledged capitalists?', *Journal of Peasant Studies* 15(3): 350-72.

Lockeretz, W. (1990) 'Major issues confronting sustainable agriculture', in C.A. Francis, C.B. Flora and L.D. King (eds) *Sustainable Agriculture in Temperate Zones*, New York: John Wiley & Sons.

Lockeretz, W., Klepper, R., Commoner, B., Gertler, M., Fast, S., O'Leary, D. and Blobaum, R. (1976) *A Comparison of the Production, Economic Returns, and Energy Intensiveness of Corn Belt Farms that Do and Do Not Use Inorganic Fertilizers and Pesticides*, St Louis, MI: Center for the Biology of Natural Systems, Washington University.

McCreary, I.L. and Furtan, W.H. (1988) 'Income distribution and agricultural policies', in G.S. Basran and D.A. Hay (eds) *The Political Economy of Agriculture in Western Canada*, Toronto: Garamond Press.

McEwen, F.L. and Milligan, L.P. (1991) 'An analysis of the Canadian research and development system for agriculture/food', Ottawa: Science Council of Canada.

MacRae, R.J., Henning, J. and Hill, S.B. (1988) 'Financing organic/ sustainable agriculture: current problems and new strategies', *Ecological Agriculture Projects Research Paper No. 5*, Macdonald College of McGill University, Ste-Anne de Bellevue, Quebec, Canada.

MacRae, R.J., Hill, S.B., Henning, J. and Mehuys, G.R. (1989) 'Agricultural science and sustainable agriculture: a review of the existing scientific barriers to sustainable food production and potential solutions', *Biological Agriculture and Horticulture* 6: 173–219.

MacRae, R.J., Hill, S.B., Mehuys, G.R. and Henning, J. (1990) 'Farm-scale agronomic and economic conversion from conventional to sustainable agriculture', *Advances in Agronomy* 43: 155–98.

Mann, S.A. (1990) *Agrarian Capitalism in Theory and Practice*, Chapel Hill, NC: University of North Carolina Press.

Martinson, O.B. and Campbell, G.R. (1980) 'Betwixt and between: farmers and the marketing of agricultural inputs and outputs', in F.H. Buttel and H. Newby (eds) *The Rural Sociology of the Advanced Societies*, Montclair, NJ: Allanheld, Osmun & Co.

Marx, K. (1930) *Capital, Vol I*, translated by E. and C. Paul, London: J.M. Dent & Sons.

Merrill, R. (ed.) (1976) *Radical Agriculture*, New York: New York University Press.

Mooney, P.H. (1986) 'Class relations and class structure in the Midwest', in A.E. Havens, P.H. Mooney and M.J. Preffer (eds) *Studies in the Transformation of US Agriculture*, Boulder, CO: Westview Press.

National Research Council (1989) *Alternative Agriculture*, Report of the Committee on the Role of Alternative Farming Methods in Modern Production Agriculture, Board on Agriculture, Washington, DC: National Academy Press.

Noble, D.F. (1984) *Forces of Production*, New York: Knopf.

Oelhaf, R.C. (1978) *Organic Agriculture: Economic and Ecological Comparisons with Conventional Methods*, New York: John Wiley & Sons.

Palmer, B. (1975) 'Class conception and conflict: the thrust for efficiency, managerial views of labour and the working class rebellion', *Review of Radical Political Economics* 7: 31–49.

Petit, M., Rossmiller, G.E. and Tutwiler, M.A. (1988) 'International agricultural negotiations: the United States and the European Community square off', in M.A. Tutwiler (ed.) *US Agriculture in a Global Setting: An*

Agenda for the Future, Washington, DC: National Center for Food and Agricultural Policy.

Pugh, T. (1987) *Fighting the Farm Crisis*, Saskatoon, SASK: Fifth House.

Robinson, K.L. (1989) *Farm and Food Policies and Their Consequences*, Englewood Cliffs, NJ: Prentice Hall.

Sanford Evans Statistical Service (1944) *Facts from the Census: 1941 and 1931*, Winnipeg, MAN: Sanford Evans Statistical Service.

Schuettler, D. (1991) 'Ontario farmers vow to march on Ottawa', *The Western Producer* 69(7): 3.

Scott, J. (1986) 'Everyday forms of peasant resistance', *Journal Peasant Studies* 13(2): 5–35.

Shields, J. (1988) 'The capitalist state and class struggle in the fruit and vegetable industry in British Columbia', in G.S. Basran and D.A. Hay (eds) *The Political Economy of Agriculture in Western Canada*, Toronto: Garamond Press.

Shein, E. and Swihart, R. (1991) 'Farmer coalition ready for Ottawa', *The Western Producer* 69(14): 4.

Smith, T. (1987) 'Social scientists are not neutral onlookers to agricultural policy', in G. Comstock (ed.) *Is There a Moral Obligation to Save the Family Farm?*, Ames, Iowa: Iowa State University Press.

Sproat, D. (1991) 'Saskatchewan farmers rally again', *The Western Producer* 69(13): 1.

Statistics Canada (1989) *Canada Year Book 1990: A Review of Economic, Social and Political Developments in Canada*, Ottawa: Minister of Supply and Services Canada.

Statistics Canada (1991a) 'Census overview of Canadian agriculture: 1971–1991', Catalogue 93-348, Ottawa: Statistics Canada.

Statistics Canada (1991b) 'Census divisions and census subdivisions: population and dwelling counts', Catalogue 93-304, Ottawa: Statistics Canada.

Strange, M. (1984) 'The economic structure of a sustainable agriculture', in W. Jackson, W. Berry and B. Colman (eds) *Meeting the Expectations of the Land: Essays in Sustainable Agriculture and Stewardship*, San Francisco: North Point Press.

Strange, M. (1988) *Family Farming: A New Economic Vision*, Lincoln, NEBR: University of Nebraska Press.

Strinati, D. (1990) 'A ghost in the machine?: the state and the labour process in theory and practice', in D. Knights and H. Willmott (eds) *Labour Process Theory*, London: Macmillan.

Thomas, R.J. (1985) *Citizenship, Gender, and Work: Social Organization of Industrial Agriculture*, Berkeley, CA: University of California Press.

Thompson, P. (1990) 'Crawling from the wreckage: the labour process and the politics of production', in D. Knights and H. Willmott (eds) *Labour Process Theory*, London: Macmillan.

Tompkins, P. and Bird, C. (1989) *Secrets of the Soil: New Age Solutions for Restoring our Planet*, New York: Harper & Row.

Troughton, M.J. (1989) 'The role of marketing boards in the industrialization of the Canadian agricultural system', *Journal of Rural Studies* 5(4): 367–83.

US Department of Agriculture (1980) *Report and Recommendations on Organic Farming. Report of the USDA Study Team on Organic Farming*, Washington, DC: US Government Printing Office.

US Department of Agriculture (1987) *Economic Indicators of the Farm Sector, National Financial Summary 1986*, Washington, DC: Economic Research Service.

Vogeler, I. (1981) *The Myth of the Family Farm: Agribusiness Dominance of US Agriculture*, Boulder, CO: Westview Press.

Wardell, M. (1990) 'Labour and labour process', in D. Knights and H. Willmott (eds) *Labour Process Theory*, London: Macmillan.

Weick, K.E. (1984) 'Small wins', *American Psychologist* 39(1): 40–9.

Weir, D. (1987) *The Bhopal Syndrome: Pesticides, Environment and Health*, San Francisco: Sierra Club Books.

Western Producer (1991) 'Trends in farm subsidies', 68(49): 4.

Whitt, J.A. (1979) 'Toward a class-dialectical model of power: an empirical assessment of three competing models of political power', *American Sociological Review* 44 (February): 81–100.

Willmott, H. (1990) 'Subjectivity and the dialectics of praxis: opening up the core of labour process analysis', in D. Knights and H. Willmott (eds) *Labour Process Theory*, London: Macmillan.

Wilson, B. (1991) 'Fifth of all farmers on the edge', *The Western Producer* 68(40): 3.

Wolf, E.R. (1969) *Peasant Wars of the Twentieth Century*, New York: Harper & Row.

World Commission on Environment and Development (1987) *Our Common Future*, New York: Oxford University Press.

5

FOUCAULT, POWER, RESISTANCE AND ALL THAT*

David Knights and Theo Vurdubakis

INTRODUCTION

It could be argued that a 'crisis' in labour process theory began almost simultaneously with its revival through Braverman's (1974) reconstruction of the original Marxian thesis. For while *Labour and Monopoly Capital*, suddenly caught the attention of a wide range of researchers, it also aroused intellectual controversy that continues to smoulder almost 20 years later. Much of the controversy occurred through Braverman's undermining of a whole tradition of industrial sociology (described as 'managerialist') because it was seen to reflect and reinforce the dominant interests of management over labour. A secondary literature then began to emerge voluminous enough to attract the ironical label 'Bravermania' (Littler and Salaman, 1982). Many students of workplace industrial relations are attracted to labour process analysis as a means of bringing to bear a critical edge to their work. The UMIST/ASTON labour process conferences, from which this volume arises, have contributed to the prolongation of the debate, and some might argue, to a weakening of whatever orthodoxies existed in this field. Indeed, the proliferation of studies subscribing to a multiplicity of distinct approaches ostensibly claiming to be pursued under the auspices of labour process analysis, has generated feelings of theoretical anomie with certain critics (e.g. Thompson, 1990) demanding a halt to further theoretical dilution in order to arrest the sense of crisis.

This chapter is concerned with only one aspect of labour process theory – the way in which the introduction of Foucault into the

* We acknowledge the critical comments of Hugh Willmott, Brian Bloomfield, Chris Grey, John Jermier and Walter Nord as well as participants in the 9th Labour Process Conference at UMIST, Manchester.

debate has generated the kind of controversy that sustains talk of a crisis. For some (e.g. Knights and Willmott, 1989; Dandeker, 1990; Sakolsky, 1992) Foucault is seen to provide a way out of the crisis, whereas for others resort to his work is nothing but a diversion, a clear symptom of the crisis itself (e.g. Thompson, 1991; Fine, 1979; Neimark, 1990; Armstrong, 1991). With respect to an analysis of the labour process, much of the value or otherwise of Foucault's work would appear to hinge on what one is to make of his account (or non-account) of resistance (e.g. Tanner *et al.*, 1992). As many of the early critics (Aronowitz, 1978; Edwards, 1979; Elger, 1982; Gartman, 1983; Stark, 1980) pointed out, resistance was a theoretical lacuna in Braverman's thesis and a discourse on resistance in the labour process debate has remained limited and undeveloped ever since (cf Burawoy, 1979, 1985; Knights and Collinson, 1985; Knights and Willmott, 1986, 1990; Turner, 1989). Moreover, there is by no means a consensus within the literature as to the meaning of, or significance which should be attributed to, resistance (see Knights and Willmott, 1990). In this context, both inside and outside the labour process debate, the absence of a Foucauldian theory of resistance provides critics with further evidence (if evidence was needed) of the invalidity of the approach.

Our response is motivated by the belief that these critiques, particularly when combined with a rhetoric of crisis, can too easily function as scare tactics, alibis as it were for avoiding direct engagement with the important (if unsettling) issues that (so-called) post-structuralist developments raise for labour process theorizing. In this sense then, this chapter constitutes an exercise in (to paraphrase Clifford Geertz, 1984) 'Anti-antiFoucauldanism'. This is not to imply that either Foucault or the 'Foucauldians' are beyond criticism – quite the contrary. Indeed, our aim is to preserve space within the labour process debate where the Foucauldian opus can be exploited fruitfully through work which can profit even while deviating from it (see Connolly, 1987). For the reasons outlined, the concern of this chapter is Foucault's notion of resistance.

It is our view that most of the critiques of Foucault tend to be rooted in dualistic understandings of the relationship between various subject–object polarities such as that between the individual and society, force and consent, power and powerlessness. Within such dualistic thinking resistance is perceived as one pole in a dichotomy where it is always opposite to and outside of power. By treating power and resistance as analytical conditions of each other's possibility such that 'each constitutes for the other a kind of permanent limit, a point of reversal', Foucault (1982: 225) goes some way towards deconstructing these dualisms. Moreover resistance, like power, is a socially constructed category. Resistance (power) consequently should not be treated as being simply 'out there', empirical data to be gathered and made available through value free enquiry. To treat resistance as self-evident is to miss the actual interpretive practices through which knowledge about it is acquired and communicated. Questions need to be raised as to how to recognize it; an examination is necessary of what qualifies or is disqualified as resistance and attention has to be given to the kind of knowledges that are invoked in this process. Attention needs to be paid to the framework within which conceptualizations of resistance and power are formed – the 'power of the language of power', as Clegg 1987: 68) put it. In other words, the constitutive effects of particular ways of speaking has to be addressed. This contrasts with the taken-for-granted status given to it in many labour process accounts where resistance is often deployed as simply a counter or 'corrective to mechanistic analyses of control' (Turner, 1990).

We need then to question the assumptions that render knowledge of resistance self-evident. These assumptions are readily exposed in examining a series of issues that appear to be raised when adopting a concept of resistance drawn from a reading of Foucault. More precisely, these issues concern specific objections to Foucault's conception of power which critics suggest preclude a theory or analysis of resistance. They revolve around three central questions: where is resistance to be 'located', who are its 'agents' and how can it be justified? Each of these questions, we argue, is usually asked from a dualistic perspective that presumes power to be held by the powerful and wielded over the powerless. From such a perspective, Foucault's argument that there is no position exterior to power–knowledge relations and that the latter constitute the very subjects that resist it, seemingly obliterates in a single stroke the space occupied by the agents of resistance and undermines its conventional justification. The chapter is, then, concerned to locate an analysis of resistance within the relations of power and knowledge to which Foucault draws attention; it argues, therefore, that those critiques seeking to return to the comfort of 'old certainties' regarding power and resistance are misplaced.

But why in a book on resistance in the labour process is it appropriate to concentrate on Foucault and secondary accounts or critiques of his work? Surely it might be objected that Foucault has contributed little to the discussion of the labour process. While this may be the case, Foucault, nonetheless, has been one of the vehicles through which a number of problems have been exposed in labour process theory. Take, for example, the early critique of Braverman's (1974) deterministic views of capital and his claimed attribution of omnipotence and omniscience to its managerial agents. In avoiding such determinism, labour process theorists have been in equal danger of slipping into voluntaristic perspectives where subjective action was the primary target of analysis. By refusing to choose between power as either centred in abstract structures (the determinism of functionalism) or as a possession of individual subjects (the voluntarism of 'action' theory) Foucault offers the promise of an escape from such dichotomies. It is this aspect of Foucault's various analyses to which labour process theorists (e.g. Knights and Collinson, 1987; Knights and Willmott, 1989; Sakolsky, 1992) have been most attracted. Not only can we avoid seeing subjects as separated from, yet determined by, the structures of power in which they are embedded, but an analysis drawing upon Foucault also enables us to examine labour process conceptions of control and resistance as differentially constituted by power–knowledge relations and discourses. Clearly many of Foucault's insights in this matter are also retrievable from the work of other social theorists such as Bachelard, Canguilhem, Bakhtin, etc. (see Gutting, 1989). Still, the work of Foucault has been the actual means through which these issues were posed in the context of the rethinking of the labour process debate and hence he can claim our special attention.

Before addressing the three central questions around which this chapter is constructed, we provide some background to the debate by offering a brief account of the differences between Foucault and his critics' conception of power. But we would first like to qualify our 'relation' to Foucault. There is a tendency in the literature to sustain Foucault the Author often for purposes of setting him in an intellectual competition with his presumed intellectual opponent, 'Marx'. We do not wish to subscribe to these preoccupations of seeking to find the Author behind the text; in (re)presenting or in vindicating the 'real Foucault' or even in 'revealing' what he 'really had in mind'. Even if we were so inclined, the non-static character of his work with its many unresolved questions, gaps, ambivalences and contradictions, resists such a closure. What is proposed here instead is a particular reading as the means whereby a theoretical object ('Foucault') is constructed, for purposes of discussion and critique. Such a reading necessarily emphasizes some aspects of the works under consideration while ignoring/suppressing others. Consequently this is not an attempt to replace 'misconceptions' with an 'authentic' reading. After discussing our misgivings about the conceptions of power to which critics of Foucault frequently subscribe, the remainder of the chapter examines the presuppositions behind their shared belief that his analysis removes the space, agency and justification for resistance.

SOME DOUBTS CONCERNING 'THEORIES OF POWER'

Theories of power have the tendency of setting themselves the task of clarifying 'the nature of power' (Hoy, 1981: 43). In other words, they are constituted as competing descriptions of what power is. Giddens (1976: 127) for instance, defines power as the capability of the actor 'to intervene in a series of events so as to alter their course' and as 'the capability to secure outcomes where the realisation of these outcomes depends on the agency of others' (1976: 111; 1979: 93). But he attempts to escape conventional dualistic ways of perceiving objective structures of domination as constraining subjective action or power by suggesting the opposite: that power operates when it utilizes the 'transformative capacity' of agents to achieve certain outcomes through the support of particular structures of domination (1979: 91–3). These formulations are indicative of a tendency to treat power as something that can be identified with a 'given' human 'capacity' or 'ability' and, despite Giddens's (1979: 91) claim to do otherwise, they privilege action in such a way as to remain caught on the horns of the dualistic dilemma from which they set out to escape. What is pertinent to the discussion at hand, is that this 'capability' to secure outcomes through the agency of others may vary greatly from context to context with respect to different means of action, agents, situational considerations and so forth. But as Hindess (1982: 272) notes, once this capability is seen as subject to specific conditions and means of action, it ceases to be a capability to secure or realize objectives and becomes nothing more than the ability to act in pursuit of such objectives. By invoking a generalized capacity of certain (individual and collective) subjects, theories of what power 'is' tend to deflect attention from a range of more pertinent questions; questions of 'how' power 'works' rather than who 'possesses' it: by means of what mechanisms, is this (attempted) access to the 'agency of others' made possible? We cannot assume that people enlist their efforts in the pursuit of the objectives of the 'powerful' simply because of the initial impetus given to such demands by their (powerful) source. 'Power' is after all the 'outcome', as it were, as well as the 'cause' of such a 'use' of others (Law, 1986a, 1986b; Foucault, 1982). What is therefore crucial are the specific means, techniques and mechanisms through which the compliance of 'agents' (in Giddens's sense) is generated, where this is the case.

Foucault (1982: 217) therefore distances his conception of power from questions of the 'capacity' to 'modify, use, consume or destroy' things.[1] To do otherwise is to transform power from a theoretical category into a platonic essence.[2] To the degree that Foucault avoids essentializing power (and he has occasionally been down this slippery slope) he does indeed constitute a break with tradition. 'Power' he argues is the name given to a certain coherency of social relations which in turn makes possible the construction of a 'grid of intelligibility' of the social order: 'one needs to be nominalistic no doubt; power is not an institution, and not a structure; neither is it a certain strength we are endowed with, it is the name one attributes to a complex strategical relationship in a particular society' (Foucault, 1981: 93). 'To put it bluntly, I would say that to begin the analysis [of power] with a "how" is to suggest that power as such does not exist. At the very least it is to ask oneself what contents one has in mind when using this all-embracing and reifying term' (1982: 217).

Besides drawing back from essentialist conceptions of power, Foucault also refrains from advancing a general 'theory' of power – much less a 'grand theory' of society, as a number of commentators (e.g. Dreyfus and Rabinow, 1982; Cousins and Houssain, 1984) have stressed. If he has something approaching a general thesis it is that relations of power are historically constituted configurations of practices. Power has thus to be understood in terms of its particular socio-historical settings and these settings can in turn best be understood in relation to the forms of power that define them (cf Taylor, 1984). Instead of a theory of what power 'is' he therefore offered a number of perspicuous examples (case histories) of particular techniques of power at work and of the characteristic features they display. Accordingly, Foucault proposed an 'analytics' (as opposed to an all embracing 'theory') of power: 'In studying these power

172

relations, I in no way construct a theory of Power' (Foucault, 1988: 38). His studies of the clinic, the asylum, prison, sexuality, and so on, were, he suggested, histories of specific power–knowledge configurations and did not amount to such a theory:

> I have tried to indicate the limits of what I wanted to achieve, that is, the analysis of a specific historical figure, of a precise technique of government of individuals and so forth. Consequently these analyses can in no way in my mind, be equated with a general analytics of every possible power relation.
>
> (Foucault, 1984b: 380)

Arguments, therefore, to the effect that Foucault's view of power is Eurocentric (Neimark, 1990: 107) are misplaced (see Hoskin and Macve, 1991). If no 'theory of power' with global pretensions is being proposed, only a direct empirical examination of particular sites could indicate whether or not these insights can be usefully utilized 'beyond' those spheres analysed by Foucault and theorists drawing upon his work.[3] The 'failure' to provide an all-inclusive general theory of power (e.g. Neimark, 1990: 108; Armstrong, 1991) is a problem only if one is committed to exactly those essentialist notions that Foucault calls into question.

A related argument is that Foucault appears to ignore the all too evident presence of instruments of coercion such as Lenin's (1970: 292) proverbial 'bodies of armed men' (Fine, 1979: 92). What is at issue is not the existence of these 'armed bodies' but whether all forms of analysis should ultimately have to refer to such organs of coercion. Among the modes of operation of power that have become salient in modern liberal-capitalist society, attempts to shape the wills, desires, interests and identities of subjects are far more typical and routine than coercive domination (Rose, 1987).[4]

What, then, is to be gained by abandoning essentialist conceptions of power? As has been suggested, certain hidden costs are incurred in the cases where those subscribing to a 'general theory of power' conceive it as a description of what power *is*. Such a theory entails a number of ontological commitments which compel it, however reluctantly, to reify the concepts thereby employed. Regarded in terms of possession or non-possession, power is something that the powerful (individuals, groups, classes) 'have' and the 'powerless' lack. A 'quantity theory' of power is implied: more of it prevails over less. It is not our purpose here to satirize such accounts.

(Effective critiques are in any case available elsewhere, e.g. Hindess, 1986; Foucault, 1980.) But theories of what power (or resistance) 'is' are meagre explanatory devices. They tend to obscure the issue of how these terms are given their specific content.

The grander the proposed theory, the more it attempts to account for, the greater the struggle to reduce the unexpected and the incoherent to its parameters. On the other hand, not aiming for such a theory has the advantage of opening up 'fields of analysis for specific intervention and work' (Harley and Roper, cited in Wickham, 1985: 178). As they continue, 'these fields may well overlap, but we reject the possibility of providing one field which exists as the key to unlock all others' (ibid). As Wittgenstein (1966: 17–20) argued in another context, 'the price to be paid for "our craving for generality" is a contemptuous attitude towards the particular case'. Accordingly, if we are to take seriously Foucault's argument on the decisive role of shifting configurations of institutional apparatuses and 'technical' procedures developed in response to a diverse range of 'local' concerns, we need to give up the craving for a theory of what power (or resistance) is 'in itself'. This is not to deny the use of theoretical generalization altogether. It is simply to reject those ontological commitments which prevent the diversity of power relations from being taken seriously as anything more than mere surface manifestations which theory must aim to unify through the identification and description of the essential 'nature of power'.

What is gained by reproblematizing resistance and power along the lines sketched out above? Labour process theory's concern with power is linked to its desire to trace oppression back to an original source. Having its origin in oppression, power cannot be seen as anything other than an imposition upon subjects who experience it as coercion, repression and denial. To 'identify' the power of management over workforce, doctor over patient, teacher over pupil, as but different instances of a common essence is, in our view, to embark upon a futile search for the *principle* that collects these instances together. Rather than seeing power as something held by the powerful and mechanistically enforcing conformity among the powerless, we believe it is more productive to attend to the practices, techniques and methods through which 'power' is rendered operable. By this we mean those contextually specific practices, techniques, procedures, forms of knowledge and modes of rationality that are routinely deployed in attempts to shape the

174

conduct of others. By seeing power as 'emanating' from a dominant centre such as the state, capital and its stewards and so on, we tend to obscure how instances of dominance by such centres are achieved in practice.

Having briefly outlined the ways in which Foucault's conception of power relations as forms of governance of fields of possible action breaks with tradition, we can now turn more directly to an analysis of resistance. If, as has been argued, a global, transcontextual 'Theory of Power' is eschewed, then a theory of resistance along the same lines is equally implausible. Power and resistance, we suggest, are best understood when examined in specific sites with definite socio-historical conditions of existence and means of operation. Foucault's critics tend to demand precisely the kind of global theories that he has been at pains to discard.[5]

POWER AND NOTHING BUT? THE WHERE, WHO AND WHY OF RESISTANCE

As has already been argued, the problem of resistance raised by critics of Foucault revolves around three questions that derive from their understanding of his conception of power. First if, as Foucault is supposed to claim, power is everywhere then where can resistance reside; how can there be any space for resistance? Second is the problem of who are to be the 'agents' of resistance: if power is constitutive of subjects, how can those self-same subjects become agents of resistance? Third is the question of why anyone should resist given the implications of Foucault's account of power. For if the only choice is between different power–knowledge regimes, what justification is there for resistance? These may be restated respectively as the problems of location, agency and justifiability:

1 If one is 'never outside power', is there any social space for resistance to occupy?
2 If subjectivity is an effect of power (the 'obedient subject') who are to be the agents of resistance and how can resistance ever be subversive of power? To what kind of 'liberating agency' does it have access?
3 In the absence of a theory of rights or objective interests even assuming that an explanation of resistance is after all possible, what can be the grounds of its justification? 'Why fight?' as Habermas (1986) put it.

There appears to be widespread agreement (e.g. Poulantzas, 1979; Giddens, 1982; Comay, 1986; Philip, 1983; Taylor, 1984) that Foucault's account runs into difficulties over these three related issues. All three lines of questioning (if one can call them that) highlight particular gaps, obscurities and inconsistencies in Foucault's references to resistance. In this we consider the 'justification' issue (item 3 above) to be of particular importance because it leads us directly to the political implications of subscribing to a Foucauldian account of resistance. But first we have to deal with the issues of 'location' (item 1) and 'agency' (item 2) as critiques referring to these problems tend to carry with them a 'baggage' of un-examined and questionable assumptions. Each of the three issues is considered in turn in order to discuss certain key presuppositions with which debate surrounding them is typically imbued.

SPACE FOR RESISTANCE

The 'problem' of the 'location' of, or space for, resistance has its origin in Foucault's (1984a: 94) claim that 'Relations of power are not in a position of exteriority with respect to other types of relationships . . . but immanent in the latter'. Consequently, 'It seems to me that power is "always already there", that one is never outside it, and there are no margins for those who break with the system to gambol in' (Foucault, 1980: 141). Strong language indeed! At the same time in what appears to critics to be a paradoxical move he states that

> there are no relations of power without resistances: the latter are all the more real and effective because they are formed right at the point where relations of power are exercised; resistance to power does not have to come from somewhere else to be real, nor is it inexorably frustrated through being the compatriot of power. It exists all the more by being at the same place as power; hence like power resistances are multiple and can be integrated into global strategies.
>
> (1980: 142)

As Poulantzas sees it, the world Foucault constructs is hermetically sealed: 'For if power is already there, if every power relation is immanent in itself, why should there ever be resistance? From where would resistance come, and how would it ever be possible?' (Poulantzas 1979: 148–9). Moreover if, as Foucault claims, resistance takes place so to speak, 'within' power, then resistance can offer no

176

escape. By drawing on Foucault, argue Tanner *et al.* (1992: 451), accounts of the labour process produce an even 'more entrenched picture of an ideologically subjugated working class'.

In identifying the paradox in these terms one takes on board a dualistic understanding of power and resistance. It means treating 'power relations' and the 'plurality of resistances' (Foucault, 1984a: 96) they generate in particular locales as if they were collapsible into two great aggregated heaps: Power versus Resistance. This dualistic view is implicit in for instance the making of 'externality to power' a necessary condition for resistance; that resistance must always be outside the mechanisms of power it opposes. The price for this is a certain totalization of power and resistance. While Foucault has (usually) been careful to stress the multiplicity of power relations – 'I hardly ever use the word "power" and if I do sometimes, it is always a short cut to the expression I always use: *relationships* of power' (1988b: 11, our emphasis) – many Foucauldians as well as anti-Foucauldians have elevated 'disciplinary power' into just such a totalizing and absolute phenomenon. However, Foucault provides no basis for doing so:

> when I speak of power relations, of the forms of rationality which can rule and regulate them, I am not referring to Power – with a capital P – dominating and imposing its rationality on the totality of the social body. *In fact there are power relations.* They are multiple and have different forms, they can be in play in family relations, or within an institution, or an administration – or between a dominating and a dominated class . . . *[power] is a field of analysis and not a reference to a concrete instance.*

> (1988a: 38, emphasis added)

Consequently, as Gordon (in Foucault, 1980: 246) points out, it would be a mistake to imagine some hyper-rationalist Leviathan where all relations and programmes of power merge into an all-pervasive monolithic regime of social subjection. If power relations were to manifest such omnipotence, then 'history would assume the form of a homogeneous narrative of perpetual despotism, and the subtleties of genealogical analysis would be entirely superfluous' (1980: 247). If we substitute for such a 'total system' a range of what Foucault (1984a: 380) described as 'localized' procedures, apparatuses and techniques – of which some have for socio-historical reasons been selectively developed, externalized and come to inform and organize the social – then there is no reason to assume that this ensemble comprises a seamless web. Why should 'powers' be coordinated and consistent with one another in producing their effects and why should the manifestation of tensions, contradictions or non-correspondences within power relations be excluded *a priori?*[6]

Power relations may compete, contradict as well as reinforce one another. There is no sense or justification in simply assuming the monolithic unity or even compatibility of all power relations (or forms of resistance) in a given locale. Indeed, the unintended consequences of various programmes, practices and discourses play a crucial role in bringing about shaping, limiting and transforming such relationships. Of course, specific power relations, procedures, apparatuses, and so on, may at certain times and in particular sites achieve together some measure of stability. Nevertheless this stability needs to be understood in terms of the specific conditions that made it possible in a given site (Knights and Collinson, 1987). We cannot *a priori* assume, as Foucault (1984b: 3) has pointed out, that any such stability is anything more than contingent and precarious. Power relations can make up an untidy mixture even within a single site (Foucault, 1991: 81). As Gordon (Foucault, 1980: 256) argues, apparatuses of power constitute 'fragile' structures in the sense that 'their instruments and techniques are . . . liable to forms of re-appropriation reversibility and re-utilisation not only in tactical re-alignments from "above" but in counter-offensives from "below"'. This fragility is often a reflection of precisely the spread of power apparatuses throughout society which allows one to talk of 'omnipresence' in that it relies upon a multiplicity of intricate institutional interdependences. It is precisely these interdependences that enhance the possibilities for 'local' disruptions. Ironically, if not unexpectedly, managerialist/prescriptive literature has been more sensitive than critical theorizing to such possibilities for disruption.

In the absence of a unitary monolithic Power there seems to be less reason to assume that resistance cannot operate 'from within', and therefore the problem of finding an external location or space for resistance dissolves. As Silverman (1987: 191–264) noted in his study of social relations in the clinic, one form patient resistance tended to take, was the 'playing' of power relationships against one another by exploiting the various tensions within the discursive relations (medical, moral, organizational, etc.) constitutive of that site. The 'tactical function' of the techniques and discourses of power, argues Foucault (1981: 100) is 'neither uniform nor stable.

Discourses are not once and for all subservient to power or raised up against it'. What we need to investigate therefore is the 'complex and unstable process whereby discourse can be both an instrument and effect of power, but also a hindrance, a stumbling block, a point of resistance and a starting point for an opposing strategy'. Discourses do not simply produce, transmit and reinforce power relations, they also threaten, expose and render them fragile (1981: 101). The stability of such discourses is always precarious if for no other reason than that they can never capture/fix their referent. The elements present within power–knowledge relations are always open to unauthorized rearticulations. Foucault (1979: 101–2) illustrates the point by drawing attention to how the nineteenth-century medicalization of homosexuality also established its naturalness (albeit as a form of pathology). The same categories of the medical disqualification of homosexuals were then effectively redeployed by the intended targets and their allies, enabling them to construct a 'counter-discourse' and to effect a form of 'social' requalification (Minson, 1986: 115). The reason for this is that 'power is only exercised over free subjects and only insofar as they are free . . . for where the determining factors saturate the whole there is no relationship of power' (Foucault 1982: 221). Consequently, 'at the very heart of the power relationships, and constantly provoking it, are the recalcitrance of the will and the intransigence of freedom' though, as Foucault (1982: 225) makes clear, 'from the moment [that confrontation] is not a struggle to the death, the fixing of a power relationship becomes a target – at one and the same time its fulfilment and suspension'. But power and resistance constitute for one another 'a kind of permanent limit' (p. 225) a point where it is possible for the relationship between antagonists to undergo a complete reversal.

Even if we were to accept, as Foucault proposes, that the binary division between resistance and power is an unreal one, that would still not be the end of the story. For Foucault took heresy a step further by claiming that power is also 'productive' of resistance. Particular exercises of power can therefore be understood in terms of the resistances they generate, confront, 'manage' or even promote (Minson, 1986). The elimination of resistance, in other words, is not a necessary feature of the exercise of power. Nor does resistance deprive relations of power of their opportunities to reconstruct themselves; indeed, it may stimulate technologies of power to reorganize, adapt and multiply. Donzelot (1979) for example, has shown how the 'discovery' of sites of 'resistance to education' outside the school itself enabled what he calls the 'tutelary complex' to be extended to those areas.

To use an example drawn from our own research[7] on the work of IT consultants and other expert 'agents of change', we have found the identification of sites of 'resistance to change' being used as crucial vehicles through which the services and expertise of consultants are sold, and spaces of intervention carved out in client organizations. So, for example, once the 'attitudes', skills and 'needs' of organizational members are identified/constituted as resistant or less than flexible with respect to the introduction, use and development of new technology, consultants have created not only a point of entry but also a 'problem' that their 'packages' are designed to resolve. Their intervention for purposes of transforming employee behaviour through programmes of technology assessment, training, awareness-raising and so on is rendered not only legitimate but also necessary by this exercise of power. In short, consultants readily constitute certain forms of conduct as 'resistance to technology' as this gives them some purchase on its reform by identifying a space in which expertise can be brought to bear in the exercise of power. Resistance consequently plays the role of continuously provoking extensions, revisions and refinements of those same practices which it confronts.

Another useful reminder of the possibilities for mutual appropriation and interdependence between practices of resistance and particular relations of power, is how practices and discourses that are in opposition at one level may be mutually supportive at another. In terms of the example cited earlier, while initially oppositionary, the social requalification of homosexuals does not destabilize but actually reinforces those power–knowledge practices (confessional, medical, educational, psychotherapeutic and so on) that produce 'sexuality' as a part of 'human nature' and categorize human subjects in terms of a sexual 'identity' (heterosexual, homosexual, bisexual or whatever). This formulation does not seek to deny the value of affirmations of the desire for difference. It does reveal, however, what one might call, the 'internal limits' of certain liberationist 'identity politics' where there is nearly always the temptation to privilege (and enforce) an 'authentic' identity and experience through the denial of ('internal') difference and the policing of 'external' boundaries of sexuality, ethnicity, colour, religion, gender and so on.

The resistance/non-resistance dichotomy has been an unfortunate feature in much of the literature on 'Foucault's theory of Power'. Foucault, the argument goes, emphasizes consent and ideological incorporation at the expense of force and compulsion (e.g. Fine, 1979: 92). The first problem with this formulation is its recreation of the consent/force dichotomy. Apart from obscuring the various possibilities of a common ground between the two, it also entails a reductive rationalistic view of the human subject (Therborn, 1980: 93–112). Subjects are assumed to relate to power relations in a conscious and consistent manner. They conform *either* because of ideological incorporation *or* because of physical compulsion. Either they resist or they acquiesce. By assuming such consistency, argues Gordon (in Foucault, 1980: 256–7), we obscure more than we reveal.

> The existence of those who seem not to rebel is a warren of minute individual strategies which counter and inflect the visible facts of overall domination, and whose purposes and calculations, desires and choices resist any simple division into political and apolitical.

Drawing the line between those social practices that represent resistance and those that indicate its absence, between the resisters and the acquiescent, is a political matter. Defining what is to count as Resistance – with a capital R – entails the inclusion/qualification of some practices and the exclusion/disqualification of others (as, for example, private rather than political; deviance rather than resistance, co-optation by, rather than transformation of, the system; apathy, sectarianism, etc. – see for instance Thompson (1990: 120); Burawoy (1979: 48); Nichols (1976); Willis (1977) and his various critics). The resistance/non-resistance division is constantly recast in the context of various political programmes as new classes of agents ('blacks', 'women', 'prisoners', 'the passive masses') and new classes of acts are included or excluded. Such programmes have therefore a constitutive rather than a purely 'representational' function: resistance acquires its status within specific political programmes and analyses. In this matter theories with a critical intent enjoy no special immunity.

A similar point could be made of Burawoy's (1979) account of the 'making out' game. Adopting a functionalist definition of resistance he dismisses such shopfloor practices as 'adaptation', and accords them the function of 'obscuring and securing surplus value' (p. 30).

Burawoy's critics on the other hand (e.g. Grzyb, 1981) viewing these same practices in terms of 'progressive potential', are able to celebrate them as constituting a worker rejection of labour's commodity status within capitalism. To recognize how resistance is as much constituted through as represented by a political programme and that its space is not eradicated by an all-pervasive and ubiquitous power is of increasing importance to labour process and other critical analyses of organizations.

This brings us back to Foucault's claim that power relations are not 'outside' other social relationships. Attempts to institute relationships that are uncontaminated, so to speak, by any form of power are consequently utopian in character (which does not mean they are devoid of value). On the other hand, power is not exhaustive of the content of such relationships; it is not the case that all social relationships are *nothing but* power relations. This is why a notion of power as 'everywhere' does not eradicate (as many critics suggest) the potential space in which resistance is to reside. Nor does it remove from that space the agents of resistance. It is to this issue we now turn.

THE PROBLEM OF AGENCY

For most variants of Marxism, there is a historically designated agent of resistance, for example, the proletariat (e.g. Lukacs, 1971), or the 'vanguard party' (e.g. Lenin, 1961). The various 'post-Marxisms', on the other hand, prefer to put their faith in the 'new social movements'. In every case, however, there is recourse to traditional notions of the subject as a precondition for any discussion of resistance. The possibility of losing that subject is consequently a major stumbling block for any coherent account of resistance along these lines. Yet Foucault's insistence that power relations are constitutive of subjects entails precisely such a loss. *Who*, then, after the loss of the subject does the resisting? asks Comay (1986: 116). Similarly, Giddens's (1981, 1982) critique of Foucault is also centred on his notion of the subject. Foucault, he argues, fails to acknowledge that 'human beings are always and everywhere knowledgeable human agents, though acting within historically specific bounds of the unacknowledged conditions and unanticipated consequences of their acts' (Giddens, 1981: 158–81). In Foucault's account however, 'human beings do not make their own history but are swept along by it'. The consequence is that Foucault cannot 'adequately acknowledge that those subject to the power of dominant groups are themselves knowledgeable human agents, who resist, blunt or actively alter the conditions of life that others seek to thrust upon them' (ibid.). The issue of resistance is to be settled, according to Giddens, via an invocation of abstract 'capacities' of subjects *qua* human agents. The problem with this account of resistance is that it emphasizes the abstract capacity of agents to secure transformations through mobilizing the agency of others rather than focusing upon the concrete struggles in which power relations are embedded and the mechanisms/knowledges in the particular sites of their exercise. Power is seen as a capacity that everyone shares at least in principle and the context in which it is exercised is treated as contingent and therefore not an obstacle to abstract theorization.

There are broad similarities here between Giddens's critique of Foucault and his (Giddens 1982: 197–8) critique of Braverman. Braverman's (1974) account, he argues, treats workers as if they were passive objects incapable of organizing and resisting. This, however, cannot be accepted: 'to be a human agent is to have power', even 'the most seemingly "powerless" individuals are able to mobilize resources whereby they carve out "spaces of control"'. While Giddens's conclusion may have merit, it is again founded on the same decontextualized, ahistorical notion of power as something all 'human agents' possess to a different degree. Significantly the terms 'human agents' and 'individuals' are used interchangeably. Also, while resistance is the focus of Giddens's critique of both Foucault and Braverman, the term is used simply as a synonym for the power possessed by subordinate groups.

Giddens's (subjectivist) assumption of a pre-given agent lies at the centre of this account of power and resistance. The agents of power relations are understood as having a stable existence *prior* to the social relations in which they are enmeshed. All such agents are seen as reducible to 'knowledgeable human agents' (or 'individuals') and their status as 'knowledgeable subjects' remains unaltered regardless of their location in networks of power. Since their capacity as agents of a generalized 'Power' is a straightforward consequence of their status *qua* human, agents are qualitatively indistinguishable from one another (Barbalet, 1986).[8]

Such an approach, we suggest, is not very helpful. Our disagreement with Giddens is not over the status of humans as agents of power relations but with the claimed ontological foundations of this status (Hirst and Woolley, 1982). Against the notion of a universal 'knowledgable human agent', for instance, we have Foucault's (1975) suggestion that human subjects may be bringing qualitatively different forms of knowledge into power relations. But this knowledge needs to be examined in the context of the power relations in which it was made possible and is used rather than in terms of some abstract notion of human capacity. This immediately turns attention to the differences between formal and subjugated knowledges and how these may be drawn upon in struggles within power relations. In *Pierre Rivière* (1975) Foucault contrasts the knowledge embodied in the formal (e.g. legal, psychiatric, criminological) discourses with the marginalized self-knowledges of the prisoner, the patient, the mad person and so on. Indeed, Foucault saw the rehabilitation of such marginal knowledges as constituting a critical resource for contesting domination. Clearly, therefore, Foucault's subjects are not the cultural dopes claimed by Giddens. Like Pierre Rivière and his narrative they are a presence within, rather than simply bearers of, discursive relations. They are active in both positioning themselves within such relations and in committing themselves to particular subject positions.

Power and resistance should not therefore be understood as having an origin in abstract 'human agents' but as having specific conditions of existence at particular sites: Power relations involve agents that are constituted in a specific form in particular locations as for instance workers, shop stewards, managers, accountants, trade unions, feminist groups, shareholders and so forth. To argue that the agents of resistance are constructed in this way does not mean that they are determined. Opposing construction to agency is to elaborate a false opposition. Construction does not imply the passivity of physical determination. On the contrary, construction is the very scene of agency, it makes intervention possible through participation (Butler, 1990). Power does not mechanically reproduce itself. It presupposes and requires the activity/agency of those over whom it is exercised. The acknowledgement that forms of individuality and subjecthood are constituted – unequally – under particular relations of power and knowledge in no way implies that these discourses and practices are incapable of being employed in a challenge to the subjectivities that are produced. As Foucault has argued, challenges to relationships of power can arise from within the very subject positions such relationships make available (Silverman, 1987: 203–32; Henriques *et al.*, 1984). Indeed, Foucault constitutes the task of (his own) critical enquiries as attempts to bring together 'erudite knowledge' with local 'discontinuous, disqualified, illegitimate' knowledges and memories which would make possible a historical knowledge of struggles and their tactical use by the subjects of these struggles (1980: 20).

Given the emphasis on the 'productive' character of power/knowledge practices and relations, it is worth remembering that these are diverse and their demands complex and inconsistent. Accordingly, the routine discourses and practices through which subjects are constituted (and constitute themselves) as, for instance, unitary autonomous individuals, are fraught with contradictions. Self-identity can therefore be realized only as a constant struggle against the experience of tension, fragmentation and discord. Subject positions are made available in a number of competing discourses (see previous section). Identity is thus of necessity always a project rather than an achievement (Knights and Willmott, 1985; Knights, 1990; Kerfoot and Knights, 1993). Also power has to work on recalcitrant material – otherwise as Foucault has pointed out, it would have no way of asserting its presence. Particular power regimes establish themselves by displacing/colonizing other such regimes, social relations and institutions. Technologies of power therefore encounter and work on terrain already occupied by a variety of social relations and forms of subjectivity. The unity of the (modern) self as a free responsible individual, is conditional upon the subjugation of whatever does not fit into this ideal order. As Derrida (1978) puts it, what is present is always parasitically dependent on that which is absent, denied or marginalized. Normality involves the attempted foreclosure of alternative possibilities of subjectivity. The self-conscious autonomous subject has to deal with the threat of 'otherness' within itself. Individuals seek both to expunge 'the other' in themselves and criminalize or treat it when manifested in others as irrationality, criminality or perversion. It is clear in turn that any resistance to such subjectification will draw upon the concrete experience of, and involve practical engagements with, the specific sites (prisons, factories, etc.) of normalization. The normality of the modern bourgeois subject is therefore rendered problematic to the extent that the marginalized others are able to speak.

If the various dualistic notions about resistance and power discussed above are to be rejected, then it is difficult to see why there should be any need for *an* agent of resistance to be designated in advance or independently of any context in which conflict or struggle takes place. Only the dogma of 'grand theory' or historicist interpretations of social change would insist on identifying such agents *a priori.*

The implications of this for labour process analysis and critical studies of organizations is that it brings out some of the possibilities inherent in the workplace ethnographies and other such empirical investigations with which it has recently been associated. For these constitute particularly fruitful means of examining how power and resistance occur in the particular circumstances of specific struggles and engagements without imposing on them the requirement to become merged in the name of the search for unity and continuity.

JUSTIFYING RESISTANCE

The paradox of Foucault's position is aptly summarized in Habermas's (1986) 'Why fight?' question. According to Habermas, Foucault's refusal to indulge in 'a naturalistic metaphysics which idealizes counter-power into a prediscursive referent' while commendable in itself also undercuts the grounds of his critique. Foucault, he feels, cannot offer any reason 'why' one does (or should) resist power. Many of Foucault's critics (e.g. Neimark, 1990) while in agreement with Habermas's critique, tend to be less careful in their formulation of the problem accusing Foucault of all the sins in the political spectrum from being a crypto neo-conservative to glorifying all forms of deviance.

We have already indicated that, in our view, a major part of the 'problem' lies in the unexamined totalizing assumptions that not just anti-Foucauldians but also Foucauldians (e.g. Lemert and Gillan, 1982) tend to bring into the discussion. Such assumptions are, for instance, the rhetoric of a Resistance (with a capital R) confronting Power (with a capital P) or the notion that this grand 'confrontation' can be theorized independently of the concrete sites and specific political struggles where it is embedded. These notions are in turn played out in arguments couched in binary terminology such as outside/inside (Power) resistance/non-resistance, control/consent and so forth. If power, resistance and their agents are seen as context-specific then we can have no justification for 'resistance in general'. Unless we assume *a priori* the 'evil nature' of power and the 'liberatory nature' of resistance, then there is little alternative to conducting a case by case, site by site assessment. Does all this mean that there are no great radical ruptures . . . [or] massive binary divisions then? Occasionally, yes [there are]. But more often one is dealing with mobile and transitory points of resistance, producing cleavages in a society, that shift about, fracturing unities and effecting regroupings . . . [like power] resistance traverses social stratifications and individual unities.

(Foucault, 1984a: 96)

Even in these local terms, what are the grounds for endorsing particular engagements? By refusing to find any good that can be universally affirmed, Taylor (1984) argues, Foucault cannot substantiate the normative judgements that he implicitly makes. For what good is critique if it is not the means to a better form of power? For Foucault the 'unmasking [of power relations] can only be the basis for a kind of local resistance within the regime . . . there is no question of a new form, just a kind of resistance movement . . . always local and specific, within the dominant form' (Taylor, 1984: 176). Foucault, of course, rejected this dilemma as false. For him there could be no 'ideal society'; there would always be dangers. Reform cannot be made a condition of critique:

> The necessity of reform must not be allowed to become a form of blackmail serving to limit, reduce or halt the exercise of criticism. Under no circumstances pay attention to those who tell you: 'Do not criticise since you are not capable of carrying out a reform'. That's ministerial cabinet talk. Critique doesn't have to be the premise of a deduction which concludes: this is what needs to be done. It should be an instrument for those who fight and refuse what is.
>
> (Foucault, 1981: 13)

Foucault's reluctance to draw up plans for institutional reform did not imply a rejection of, or hostility to, reform *per se*. Nor did it, as Taylor (1984: 175–81) seems to argue, suggest the impossibility of improvement. He did argue that such reforms were dangerous: 'my point is not that everything is bad, but that everything is dangerous which is not exactly the same as bad' (Foucault, 1984b: 343) 'Power is neither good nor bad in itself. Its something perilous' (cited in Gandal, 1986: 129).

Even conceding this issue, however, the question remains. To paraphrase Fraser (1981: 283) when are particular struggles to be endorsed? When is domination to be resisted? Taylor (1984) offers a solution. Our historically constituted subjectivity, he suggests, is the only ground for our choices:

> We have already become something. Questions of truth and freedom can arise for us in the transformation we undergo or project. In short we have a history. We [are] . . . related to a past that has helped define our identity, and a future that puts it again in question.
>
> (Taylor, 1984: 180)

We can endorse Taylor's conclusion but not the reasoning that has led to it. There is a hint of 'progressivism' there: 'It is not for nothing that we are the descendants and heirs of the people who so tortured Damiens' (ibid: p. 179). Maybe so, but as contemporary men and women, we are hardly short of skeletons in our own closets. Taylor's 'we' while claiming to be universal is constituted through, and under the authority of, a particular regime of power/ knowledge.

Taylor's solution, then, has a certain hidden cost. While he is right no doubt to argue that we are grounded in our historically given identity, in turning this point into an affirmation of this identity he has to push out of sight (and mind) the various 'unedifying processes' that closely shadowed its construction, precisely that which Foucault would force us to remember. Hence the difference between the two 'projects': Taylor embarks on the perfection of the identity now given to us, with endorsement of that identity being a necessary first step in the process; while Foucault embarked on a project of estrangement from that identity by rendering visible the various costs involved in how we become 'who we are' (e.g. Connolly, 1985). This then is where Foucault departs from Taylor, who is content to ground resistance in the moral experience of subjects whose historically constituted identity 'gives' them a certain competence to choose. By contrast, Foucault would wish to expose the conditions that rendered us 'who and what we have become' and might assist in a 'refusal of this kind of individuality which has been imposed on us for several centuries' (Foucault, 1982: 216). Here Foucault provides a philosophical underpinning for, if not a direct justification of, resistance in that he normatively defends 'struggles against the "government of individualization"' (p. 212). However, even this refusal is grounded in 'what we have become' as the only foothold available. Dreyfus and Rabinow make the following assessment of Foucault's understanding of the grounds from which he speaks:

The practitioner of interpretive analytics realizes that he him-self is produced by what he is studying; consequently he can never get outside it. The genealogist sees that cultural prac-tices are more basic than any theory and that the seriousness of theory can only be understood as part of a society's ongoing history. The archaeological step back that Foucault takes in order to see the strangeness of our society's practices does not mean that he considers these practices meaningless. Since we share cultural practices with others, and since these practices have made us what we are, we have, perforce, some common footing from which to proceed, to understand, to act. But the foothold is no longer one which is universal, guaranteed, verified or grounded.

(Dreyfus and Rabinow, 1982: 125)

The precariousness of the foothold is what makes the outcome of resistance as unpredictable as the conditions that make it possible.

Rather than advocating some 'Grand Gesture of Denial', Foucault looked to the local struggles of those who 'paid' the costs of par-ticular identity formations and subjectivities. That did not mean, however (to stretch the economic metaphor a bit further) that some general 'balance sheet' could be drawn up: opposition arises, he argued, out of the concrete experiences of certain forms of subjection: 'opposition to the power of men over women, . . . of psychiatry over the mentally ill, of medicine over the population, of administration over the way we live' (Foucault, 1984b: 379). Critique, he suggested, is a necessary part of such oppositional practice.

Are all such oppositional struggles worth endorsing and, if so, under what conditions? Don't all struggles contain the seeds for alternative, and not necessarily more attractive, power relation-ships? Foucault can offer no guarantee which would ensure that we are engaging in the right struggles, in the service of the humanity's true interests (Rouse, 1987). In an answer to a similar question about revolts, Foucault argued that 'One does not make the law' for those who risk themselves by revolting. 'Lets [therefore] leave this question open. There are revolts and that is a fact':

A delinquent puts his life into the balance against absurd punishments; a madman can no longer accept confinement and the forfeiture of his rights; a people refuses the regime which oppresses it. This does not make the rebel in the first case innocent, nor does it cure in the second, and it does not assure the third rebel of the promised tomorrow. One does not have to be in solidarity with them. One does not have to maintain that these confused voices sound better than the others and express the ultimate truth. For there to be a sense in listening to them and in searching for what they want to say, it is sufficient that they exist and that they have against them so much which is set up to silence them. A question of morality? Perhaps. A question of reality? Certainly. All the disenchantments of history amount to nothing: it is due to such voices that the time of men [sic] does not have the form of an evolution, but precisely that of a history.

(Foucault, 1987: 8)

It is Foucault's position *vis-à-vis* the notion of 'rights' that perhaps best illustrates both the normative grounds of his claims and his distance from, and similarity to, critics such as Taylor. Foucault's opposition to legitimations couched in terms of 'rights' is of course well known: 'Right should be viewed not in terms of legitimacy to be established but in terms of the methods of subjugation that it instigates' (cited in Keenan, 1987: 24). His whole project could in effect be interpreted as an attempt to reveal the micro-techniques and the subjugations that underwrite such formal rights. The vocabulary of rights could in turn be seen as a language of mystification guaranteed to keep such processes of domination invisible. Paradoxically, however, 'rights' are a condition of this critique. As Fraser (1989) has observed, the contrast between 'rights' and techniques of power is only possible and effective because they are 'rights'. Foucault admits that

When today one wants to object in some way to . . . all the effects of power and knowledge that are linked to them, what is it that one does, concretely, in real life . . . if not precisely appeal to this canon of right, this famous, formal right, that is said to be bourgeois, and which in reality is the right of sovereignty?

(Foucault, in Gordon, 1980: 108)

Here, critics argue, Foucault is contradicting himself. Moreover, since there is no readily available alternative source of legitimacy to 'rights', there is a clear danger that by questioning their foundation we have everything to lose and little to gain. Like Taylor's appeal to 'progress' discussed above, Foucault's critics at this point tend to reach out for the comfort of old certainties. But this cannot be accepted without question. What is the point in any critical enterprise if not to expose the risks and the stakes of any given set of terms and what they stand for ('rights', 'subject', 'resistance', etc.)?

As Keenan (1987) shows, Foucault is not just saying that we need to support human rights as well as problematize their foundations and transformation – but that this support and problematization should proceed simultaneously; that is to say, we need to remain sceptical at one and the same time precisely of those rights that we support (and perhaps campaign for), if only to avoid the kind of self-subjugation or project identification which stifles critical judgement.[9]

While Foucault does not provide a moral blueprint to guide us in our lives (and in this sense our attraction to Foucault is as a means of developing a more philosophically adequate sociology and not a philosophy *per se*), he suggests alternative possibilities for practice and ones that do not necessarily rely on existing formal mechanisms or ways of doing things. In this respect, he denies us the comfort of conventional orthodoxies, and this is just as well.

CONCLUDING REMARKS

In this chapter we have focused attention on the concepts of resistance and power and attempted to address three of the central questions which critics of Foucault raise in regard to his diversion from conventional understandings of power. While recognizing how the issues of space, agency and justification for resistance would appear problematical given the character of Foucault's conception of power, we have sought to show how these problems disappear once certain basic dualistic assumptions regarding power/resistance and agents/victims are discarded. First is the problem of what space resistance can occupy if power is everywhere, and here it was pointed out that, while pervasive, inasmuch as power can only be exercised in and through social relations, it can never be so total, coherent and exhaustive as to preclude resistance occurring within its own space. Second is the problem of agency, for if subjects are all constituted by power, who can be the agents of resistance? Here again it was argued that the agency of power is not mutually exclusive from the agency of resistance. It is not a matter of some people having power and others lacking it but the ways in which acts of resistance are also exercises of power and how the same set of agents can be involved in both exercising power and resisting its effects at one and the same time. Finally, we confronted the problem of justification. How can resistance be justified when there is no ideal or ultimate liberation on offer? Here the refusal to designate any particular social order as the ideal implicit in this critique has made Foucault's commitment appear at odds with his theoretical stance (Harvey-Brown, 1992). Reaction to this ambivalence by anti-Foucauldians has tended to be (predictably) dismissive (e.g. Neimark, 1990) while Foucauldians have often tended to find comfort in his personal record as a human rights activist (e.g. Gandal, 1986). Both responses are, we suggest, unsatisfactory. They tend to resolve the issue by reference to Foucault (the fetishized 'Author') himself and consequently miss the implications for critical theorizing more generally.

Foucault's ambivalence between affirmation and the suspicion of that affirmation is, we would claim, an (albeit extreme) manifestation of the burden borne by all critical theorizing. That is the inability to achieve a straightforward translation of the normative ideals that underwrite it into concrete plans for institutional arrangements. Specifying 'What Is to Be Done' carries with it the political imperative of decisional closure: critical theory must suspend all critique of what it authorizes. It must give up its questioning of that for which it claims to speak. In so doing, it betrays its emancipatory interest (to use Habermas's term) by attempting to render the decisions it authorizes immune to continued critical scrutiny. By blunting its critical edge, theory would simply reinstate the forms of power/knowledge it set out by opposing. Since there are no easy solutions to these dilemmas, critical theorizing must therefore resist excessive claims. As Foucault (1984b: 374) put it, 'the "best" theories do not constitute a very effective protection against disastrous political choices'. Great themes such as 'humanism', he added, can be appealed to in order to legitimate any end whatever. Accordingly, emancipation is not something that happens once critical theorizing has as it were, completed its task. On the contrary, critique constitutes the perpetual activity of inducing critical reflection, of opening up 'problems that are as concrete and general as possible' (p. 374). By seeking to develop an analytics of power–knowledge relations as they interact in particular contexts with specific 'movements, critiques, and experiences that call them into question' (p. 374), Foucault aimed to interrogate the mechanisms through which the taken for granted is produced. The value of the approach is also its limitation. It constitutes primarily a 'negative' tool, a means of deconstructing social processes that routinely prevent those caught in them from becoming genuine political agents.

In this chapter, we have addressed a number of issues. On the one hand, we have attempted to indicate the inadvisability of treating 'Foucault' as a 'catch all' social theory, as Foucauldians have sometimes tended to do. On the other hand, we hope to have shown that 'Foucault' does *not* constitute the 'fatal distraction' (Thompson, 1991) that must be stopped from leading labour process theorizing astray. Ritualistic denunciations of Foucault, the Foucauldians and all their works, have too often been used as alibis in order to avoid serious critical engagement with the substantive issues of this type of approach. Clearly, we believe that labour process analysis can benefit from a critical reading of Foucault's work in facilitating the development of theoretical and empirical analyses that go beyond the either/or of conventional dualistic accounts of resistance and power.

NOTES

1 For him '"power" designates relationships between partners' (Foucault 1982: 217) and although it must therefore always involve communication, the analysis of power cannot be reduced to a study of signs and the processes whereby meanings and norms are (re)constructed, as those influenced by social construction theory are often accused of doing. As Foucault puts it, 'Power relations, relationships of communication, objective capacities should not therefore be confused' (pp. 217–18).

2 A similar claim is made by Bentham (1962: 199) who argues that 'of nothing that has a place, or passes, in our minds can we give any account, otherwise than by speaking of it as if it were a portion of space with portions of matter . . . otherwise than in a way of fiction'. In Benthamite terminology, then, a (meaningful) discussion of a concept such as 'power' has to accord it the status of a material object (i.e. a thing that is possessed by, or distributed between, individuals, groups or institutions). While this type of reification constitutes a deeply ingrained social scientific habit, it should nevertheless be jettisoned.

3 Our own suggestion would be that since such work is concerned with the constitution and development of the social technologies characteristic of occidental modernity, its relevance for different socio-cultural contexts depends on the extent to which similar technologies have also been deployed in these contexts.

4 Consider for instance Turner's (1989) rejection of analyses of scientific 'power–knowledge': 'To put things quite simply, the state can lock up

scientists, forbid them to publish and refuse to pay their bills, and by doing so, assure that the "power" they posseses cannot be exercised. The state may not wish to suffer the consequences of such actions but it is the state that decides' (p. 557). In other words, more power always prevails over less. Note, before proceeding any further the assumption that 'power' can be safely treated as a possession of particular subjects (scientists, the state). But even if we granted Turner, for speed of argument, this formulation of what is at stake, the questions that remain are crucial. First, the ability to 'take' and carry out such decisions cannot be simply assumed as a straightforward 'capacity' of 'The State'. On the contrary it is the differential availability of mechanisms for coercive intervention, (and the forms of political calculation that inform them), that are constitutive of the different forms of 'State'. Hence the liberal state is one defined through the observance of formal limits to its capacity for coercive intervention. Overriding those limits implies the transition to another form of state (e.g. totalitarian, authoritarian, theocratic, etc.). Second, science and scientists are linked to the state through the deployment of a wide variety of routine mutually constitutive relationships, and of institutional relay points (think tanks, universities, systems of accreditation, research councils, and so on). Governmental interventions are effected through this complex network, as for example in current demands on humanities to conform more closely to a productivist/entrepreneurial ethos (Hunter, 1990; Connolly, 1985).

5 Which is not to say that Foucault's practice has always been consistent with his own injunctions.

6 In his discussion of the Panopticon, for example, Foucault (1981) points out the discrepancy between the plan and its take-up in practice. Criminals, he observes, 'stubbornly resisted the new disciplinary mechanism in the prison . . . the actual functioning of the prisons, in the inherited buildings where they established and with the governors and guards who administered them were a witches' brew compared with the beautiful Benthamite machine'.

7 Various aspects of this research is reported in Bloomfield and Vurdubakis (1994).

8 See, for instance, Cohen (1986: 128) who notes (approvingly) Giddens's 'commitment to a realist ontology of the actual social world' and also argues that the theory has a 'metaphysical core' (p. 129).

9 Consider, for example, the statement below which was part of a speech by Foucault delivered at the launch of a 1981 initiative in defence of the Vietnamese 'boat people': 'There exists an international citizenry, which has its rights, which has its duties, and which promises to raise itself up against every base of power, no matter who the author or the victims. After all, we are all governed and, to . . . that extent in solidarity the will of individuals must inscribe itself in a reality over which governments have wanted to reserve a monopoly for themselves – a monopoly which we must uproot little by little every day' (Foucault, cited in Keenan, 1987: 21). How were the rights Foucault talks about established in the first place? 'Who then commissioned us? No one. And that is precisely what established our right' (p. 21). What brings

everybody together is 'a certain shared difficulty in accepting what is happening' (p. 21). The moral ground the initiative claims for itself, while not 'new', has not been derived from the usual formal processes. And that constitutes new possibilities for practice.

REFERENCES

Aronowitz, S. (1978) 'Marx, Braverman and the Logic of Capitalism', *Insurgent Sociologist* 8(1): 126–46.

Barbalet, J.M. (1986) 'Power and Resistance', *British Journal of Sociology*, 36(1): 521–48.

Bentham, J. (1962) 'A Fragment on Ontology', in J. Bowring (ed.) *The Works of Jeremy Bentham*, Vol. 8, New York: Russell & Russell.

Bloomfield, B. and Vurdubakis, T. (1994) 'R-presenting Technology: IT Consultancy Reports as Textual Reality Constructions', *Sociology*, 28(2): 123.

Braverman, H. (1974) *Labour and Monopoly Capital*, New York: Monthly Review Press.

Burawoy, M. (1979) *Manufacturing Consent*, Chicago: University of Chicago Press.

Burwawoy, M. (1985) *The Politics of Production*, London: Verso.

Butler, J. (1990) *Gender Trouble: Feminism and the Subversion of Identity*, New York: Routledge, Chapman and Hall.

Clegg, S.R. (1987) 'The Power of Language, the Language of Power', *Organization Studies*, 8(1): 60–70.

Cohen, I.(1986) 'The Status of Structuration Theory: A Reply to McLennan', *Theory, Culture and Society* 3(1): 123–34.

Comay, R. (1986) 'The Repressive Hypothesis: Aporias of Liberation in Foucault', *Telos* 67.

Connolly, W. (1985) *Politics and Ambiguity*, Madison, New York: University of Wisconsin Press.

Cousins, M. and Houssain, A. (1984) *Michel Foucault*, London: Macmillan.

Dandeker, C. (1990) *Surveillance, Power and Modernity*, Oxford: Polity Press.

Derrida, J. (1978) *Writing and Difference*, London: Routledge & Kegan Paul.

Donzelot, Jacques, (1979) *The Policing of Families: Welfare Versus the State*, London: Hutchinson.

Dreyfus, H. F. and Rabinow, P. (eds) (1982) *Michel Foucault: Beyond Structuralism and Hermeneutics*, Brighton, Sussex: Harvester.

Durkheim, E. (1961) 'Moral Education', New York: Free Press.

Edwards, R. C. (1979) *Contested Terrain*, London: Heinemann.

Elger, T. A. (1982) 'Braverman, Capital Accumulation and Deskilling' in S. Wood (ed.) *The Degradation of Work?* London: Hutchinson.

Fine, B. (1979) 'Struggles Against Discipline: The Theory and Politics of Michel Foucault', *Capital and Class* 9: 75–96.

Foucault, Michel (1971) *The Birth of the Clinic*, London: Tavistock.

Foucault, Michel (1975) *I, Pierre Rivière, Having Slaughtered My Mother, My Sister and My Brother . . . A Case of Parricide in the 19th Century*, New York: Pantheon.

Foucault, Michel (1977) 'Discipline and Punish', London: Allen Lane, Penguin.

Foucault, Michel (1979) *The History of Sexuality Vol.1*. London: Allen Lane, Penguin.

Foucault, Michel (1980) *Power/Knowledge: Selected Interviews and Other Writings 1972–7* edited by Colin Gordon, Brighton, Sussex: Harvester Press.

Foucault, Michel (1982) 'The Subject and the Power', in H.F. Dreyfus and P. Rabinow *Michel Foucault: Beyond Structuralism and Hermeneutics*, Brighton, Sussex: Harvester, pp. 202–26.

Foucault, Michel (1984a) 'The History of Sexuality: An Introduction', London: Allen Lane.

Foucault, Michel (1984b) *The Foucault Reader*, edited by P. Rabinow, Harmondsworth: Penguin.

Foucault, Michel (1988a) 'The Ethic of Care for the Self as a Practice of Freedom', in J. Bernauer and D. Rasmussen (eds) *The Final Foucault*, Cambridge, Mass: MIT Press.

Foucault, Michel (1991) 'Questions of Method' in G. Burchell, C. Gordon and P. Miller (eds) *The Foucault Effect*, Brighton, Sussex: Harvester Wheatsheaf.

Fraser, N. (1989) *Unruly Practices: Power Discourse and Gender in Contemporary Social Theory*, Cambridge: Polity.

Gandal, K. (1986) 'Michel Foucault: Intellectual Work and Politics', *Telos* 67.

Gartman, D. (1983) 'Structuralist Marxism and the Labor Process: Where Have the Dialectics Gone', *Theory and Society* 12: 659–69.

Geertz, C. (1984) 'Distinguished Lecture: Anti-Anti Relativism', *American Anthropologist* 86(2).

Giddens, A. (1976) *New Rules of Sociological Method*, London: Hutchinson.

Giddens, A. (1979) *Central Problems of Social Theory*, London: Macmillan.

Giddens, A (1981) *A Contemporary Critique of Historical Materialism*, London: Macmillan.

Giddens, A. (1982) *Profiles and Critiques in Social Theory*, London: Macmillan.

Grzyb, G.J. (1981) 'Decollectivization and Recollectivization in the Workplace: The Impact of Technology on Informal Work Groups and Block Culture', *Economic and Industrial Democracy* 2: 455–82.

Gubrium, J. (1989) 'Local Cultures and Service Policy', in J. Gubrium and D. Silverman (eds) *The Politics of Field Research*, London: Sage.

Gutting, G. (1989) *Michel Foucault's Archaeology of Scientific Reason*, Cambridge: Cambridge University Press.

Habermas, J. (1986) *The Philosophical Discourse of Modernity*, London: Heinemann.

Harvey-Brown, J. (1992) *Reading the Ethnographic Text*, London: Routledge.

Harvey-Brown, R. (1992) *Writing the Social Text*, New York: DeGruyter.

Henriques, J., Hollway, W., Urwin, C. and Walkerdine, V. (1984) *Changing the Subject: Psychology, Social Regulation and Subjectivity*, London and New York: Methuen.

Hindess, B. (1982) 'Power, Interests and the Outcomes of Struggles', *Sociology* 16: 498–511.

Hindess, B. (1986) ' "Interests" in Political Analysis', in J. Law (ed.) *Power, Action and Belief*, London: Routledge, pp. 112–31.

Hirst, P. and Woolley, P. (1982) 'Social Relations and Human Attributes', London: Tavistock.

Hoskin, K.W. and Macve, R. (1988a) 'The Genesis of Accountability: The West Point Connection', *Accounting Organizations and Society* 13(1): 37–73.

Hoskin, K.W. and Macve, R. (1988b) 'Cost Accounting and the Genesis of Managerialism: The Springfield Armoury Episode', paper presented in the second IPA Conference, University of Manchester, July.

Hoy, D. C. (1981) 'Power, Repression, Progress: Foucault, Lukes and the Frankfurt School', *Tri Quarterly*, 52 (Fall): 43–63.

Keenan, J. (1987) 'Power/Knowledge: Reading Foucault on Bias', *Political Theory* 15:. 5–37

Kerfoot, D and Knights, D (1993) 'Management, Masculinity and Manipulation: From Paternalism to Corporate Strategy in Financial Services' *Journal of Management Studies* 30(4): 659–77.

Knights, D. and Collinson, D. (1985) 'Redesigning Work on the Shopfloor: A Question of Control or Consent', in D. Knights, H. Willmott, and D. Collinson (eds) *Job Redesign: Critical Perspectives on the Labour Process*, Aldershot: Gower.

Knights, D and Collinson, D. (1987) 'Disciplining the Shopfloor: A Comparison of the Disciplinary Effects of Managerial Psychology and Financial Accounting', *Accounting Organisations and Society*, Vol. 12, 5, pp. 457-477.

Knights, D and Willmott, H., editors (1986) *Gender and the Labour Process*. Aldershot: Gower.

Knights, D and Willmott, H (1989) 'Power and Subjectivity at Work: From Degradation to Subjugation', *Sociology*. 23/4: 475-483.

Knights, D and Willmott, H., editors (1990) *Labour Process Theory*. London: Macmillan.

Knights, D and Willmott, H (Forthcoming) *Management, Organization and Society*. London: Sage.

Law, J. (ed.) (1986a) 'Power, Action and Belief', London: Routledge & Kegan Paul, pp. 233–63.

Law, J. (1986b) 'On Power and Its Tactics: A View from the Sociology of Science', *Sociological Review*.

Lemert, C. C. and Gillan, G. (1982) *Michel Foucault: Social Theory and Transgression*, New York: Columbia University Press.

Lenin, V.I. (1961) 'What Is to Be Done', in *Collected Works*, Vol.5, Moscow: Progress.

Lenin, V.I. (1970) *The State and Revolution*, Moscow: Progress.

Littler, C. and Salaman, G (1982) 'Bravermania and Beyond: Recent Theories of the Labour Process', *Sociology* 16(2): 215–69.

Lukacs, G. (1971) *History and Class Consciousness*, London: Merlin (first published 1923).

Minson, J. (1986) 'Foucault's Conception of Power', in M. Gane (ed.) *Towards a Critique of Foucault*, London: Routledge & Kegan Paul.

Nichols, T. and Armstrong, P. (1976) *Workers Divided*, London: Fontana.

Neimark, M. (1990) 'The King Is Dead, Long Live the King?', *Critical Perspectives in Accounting* 1: 103–14.

Philip, M. (1983) 'Foucault on Power: A Problem in Radical Translation?' *Political Theory* 11(1): 29–52.

Poulantzas, N. (1979) *State, Power, Socialism*, London: New Left Books.

Rose, N. (1987) 'Beyond the Public/Private Division: Law, Power and the Family', *Journal of Law and Society* 14(1): 61–76.

Rouse, J. (1987) 'Knowledge and Power: Towards a Political Philosophy of Science', Ithaca, NY: Cornell University Press.

Sakolsky, R. (1992) 'Disciplinary Power in the Labour Process', in A. Sturdy, D. Knights and H. Willmott (eds) *Skill and Consent*, London: Routledge.

Silverman, D. (1987) *Communication and Medical Practice*, London, Sage.

Stark, A. (1980) 'Class Struggle and the Transformation of the Labour Process: A Rational Approach', *Theory and Society* 9: 89–130.

Tanner, J., Davies, S., O'Grady, B., (1992) 'Immanence Changes Everything: A Critical Comment on the Labour Process and Class Consciousness', *Sociology* 26(3): 439–54.

Taylor, C. (1984) 'Foucault on Freedom and Truth', Political Theory, 12(2): 152–83.

Therborn, G. (1972) 'The Ideology of Power and the Power of Ideology', London: Verso.

Thompson, P (1990) 'Crawling from the Wreckage: The Labour Process and the Politics of Production', in D. Knights and H. Willmott (eds) *Labour Process Theory*, London: Macmillan.

Thompson, P. (1991) 'The Fatal Distraction: Postmodernism and Organizational Analysis' paper delivered at the Conference on New Theories of Organisation, Keele University, 3–5 April.

Turner, K. (1990) 'The Fatal Attraction of the Obvious', paper delivered at the 8th Aston/UMIST International Labour Process Conference, Aston, Birmingham, 28–30 March.

Turner, S. (1989) 'Depoliticizing Power', *Social Studies of Science* 19: 533–60.

Wickham, G. (1985) 'Power and Power Analysis: Beyond Foucault?' in M. Gane (ed.) *Towards a Critique of Foucault*, London: Routledge & Kegan Paul.

Wickham, G. (1990) 'The Political Possibilities of Post-modernism', *Economy and Society*, 19(1).

Wittgenstein, L. (1966) *The Blue and Brown Books: Preliminary Studies for the Philosophical Investigations*, Oxford: Blackwell.

6

POSITIONING RESISTANCE AND RESISTING POSITION*

Human resource management and the politics of appraisal and grievance hearings

Terry Austrin

This chapter is concerned with the politics of human resource management in the finance sector. It takes as its starting point the literature on the transformation of work in the British finance sector (Knights and Sturdy, 1989; Knights and Morgan, 1990; Knights and Morgan, 1991). This literature uses the writings of Michel Foucault, to develop an analysis of self-discipline in the workplace. This analysis of self-discipline is reviewed and critiqued and an alternative, based upon fieldwork observation and interviews in the New Zealand finance sector, is put forward. This alternative focuses upon both management and unions as organizers of forms of talk or, more conventionally, employee voice. The forms of talk that the chapter addresses are those of appraisal and grievance procedures. I argue that these procedures, both of them central to the disciplinary practices of human resource management, are not one-dimensional. New forms of appraisal, for example, raise the issue of the use by unions of alternative forms of their own appraisal as a method of resistance. Far from producing self-disciplined workers and displacing collective resistance, human resource management is viewed as opening up a new agenda for unions.

INTRODUCTION

This chapter will both review and critique what I will term, the 'turn to Foucault' in the labour process debate. The central concern of the

* I would like to acknowledge and thank Geoff Fougere for his generous help and encouragement, and Mike Lloyd for his references. The extensive comments of the editors of this volume, John Jermier and Walter Nord, were also central in forcing me to clarify my argument. The paper was supported by the New Zealand Social Science Research Fund Committee and made possible by Barbara Pringle.

chapter is to present a different analysis of the constitution and consequences of what Foucault documents as a process of individualization and what has been referred to in labour process literature as the development of a self-disciplined worker (Knights and Sturdy, 1989; Knights and Morgan, 1990, 1991). The chapter focuses upon the techniques of appraisal and grievance hearings used by human resource management in the finance industry. I argue that these hearings, through which talk about the self is mobilized, can also be appropriated and deployed by employees in forms which have consequences for collective resistance.

The narratives of the self provided in appraisal and grievance hearings involve what I call identity 'talk'. This talk has become, as it has in the school (Ball, 1990) and in medicine (Armstrong, 1983), central to the sets of practices which constitute the workplace in the finance industry. Such talk involves constant negotiation of contexts and questions in which subjects are provoked or required to articulate accounts of their self. This process of negotiation will be referred to by the term 'positioning practices' (Davies and Harre, 1991). These practices both deploy and contest the discourses of human resource management in which they are constituted.

This representation of positioning practices, through the talk typical of appraisals and grievance hearings, is not meant to signify a totally new development. I argue, however, that the deployment of human resource management practices, requires that we recognize the emerging significance of the politics of these forms of talk. This significance is constituted, on the one hand, by the moves on the part of managers to deploy multiple forms of appraisal systems to maximize their own discretion and, on the other, by the constraint placed on their discretion by the need to institute grievance systems. This constraint arises from the increasing legal codification of work and individual rights in the workplace. Human resource management is therefore revealed as being, like all other forms of managerial control, a complex articulation of discretion and constraint.

The examples drawn upon to illustrate the argument will be, like the British work on the self-disciplined worker, taken from the finance industry. Empirical research on the industry was carried out in New Zealand between 1988 and 1991. The research involved a combination of extensive interviewing of workers and managers, and participant observation with union organizers and delegates from the finance union which organizes the industry. The argument presented constitutes a reflection upon the experience of research in a service industry in which the overwhelming majority of employees are women (Austrin 1991; 1992). This reflection was prompted by the current discussion of trade-union survival strategies in male manufacturing industries (Kochan, 1985; Kochan, Katz and McKersie, 1986; Badham and Mathews, 1989; Clegg 1990; Horst and Sabel, 1991). Like those discussions, it is presented as an attempt to locate (women) workers as 'practical experimentalists' (Clegg, 1990: 8) in an uncertain and contradictory world.

The chapter is split into four sections. The first section, presents and critiques the idea of the centrality of a self-disciplined worker in the finance industry. The second section, treats the changing function of performance appraisals. The third section, develops an argument concerning performance appraisals, resistance and new forms of unionism in the finance industry. This section draws upon the example of an alternative strategy of appraisal developed by women in the finance industry to resist male forms of categorization. The last section deals with changing practices of unionism and the politics of greivance hearings.

THE SELF-DISCIPLINED WORKER

The incorporation of Foucault into the labour process debate can be seen to be concerned with the problem of explaining both the deployment of managerial power, and the effects of this power in bringing about an end to collective forms of worker resistance. Analysis inspired by Foucault's writings dispensed with a focus on forms of resistance, previously represented in labour process literature as defensive struggles over gender and class boundaries, and in their place focused upon the generation of what it termed a 'self-disciplined worker'. This development in labour process analysis mirrored the wider concern in the literature on the organization of work with managerial strategy, but in this case the strategy was viewed, as in the rhetoric of human resource management, as constituting new subjects. These new subjects or self-disciplined workers are presented in the form of a new ideal type.

The representation of the self-disciplined worker is presented very clearly in writing on the new labour process in the British finance industry. In Knights and Sturdy's (1989) article, 'New Technology and the Self-Disciplined Worker in Insurance', the explanation of the development of this new worker is focused upon 'the constitution of labour subjectivity' and what the authors identify as positive responses to new technology. In their argument, self-discipline is presented as a new form of power generated from the capacity of new technology virtually to make direct management unnecessary (1989: 146). This generative form of power is contrasted with hierarchical forms of power characteristic of both the paternalism of the pre-computerized office and the machine technology of the factory (Collinson and Knights, 1986; Knights and Collinson, 1985; Pollert, 1981; Burawoy, 1979; Beynon, 1973; Nichols and Beynon, 1977).

The significance of this new form of power in the finance industry lies in its consequences for identity formation in the workplace. In the new computerized office, typical of the finance industry, workers are placed at individual work stations. They and their work are visibly accountable and as responsible workers they are obliged to exercise the power distributed to them:

Individual workers are, in short, invested with productive power. The dispersal of power in this way has the effect of making productive performance a particularly powerful obligation.

(Knights and Sturdy, 1989: 128)

According to Knights and Sturdy, this new context of work has two consequences. First it produces a positive response to new technology. Second, this response is grounded in the fact that the technology is individualizing or has individualizing effects. That is to say, workers are now visibly responsible as individuals for sets of specified tasks. In turn, their positive responses to the new technology are based upon the fact that as individuals they can control their own output.

This positive embrace of the new workplace is not, however, without its contradictions. The workers in the new workplace are physically divided from one another and, as they are no longer part of a restricted chain of work tasks, are more autonomous. This condition introduces what Knights and Sturdy refer to as a preoccupation with 'shifting', a process of constant repeated attempts to complete and control the individualized workload. Shifting is interpreted by Knights and Sturdy as 'reflecting the constitution of an individualised, compliant yet highly productive type of worker mentality' (1989: 146). Further, they argue that this concern with shifting intensifies workers' problems with self-worth and meaning.

More significantly, in this new context of isolation, these existential troubles find release, not through resistance to work, but rather through effective performance in the job.

Knights and Sturdy go on to argue that workers' problems of confirming self-worth eventually lead to ambivalence about the new technology. Further, the self-disciplined intensification of work associated with new technology has the effect of increasing frustration and the re-emergence of negative attitudes to work. These attitudes are manifested ultimately in the form of high turnovers of staff. The individualized, computerized labour process is therefore a site of seething individualized discontent.

Knights and Sturdy explicitly recognize their debt to Foucault in this analysis. His influence is also clearly articulated in a further analysis of the self-disciplined worker involved in insurance sales (Knights and Morgan, 1990). This examination of sales is an important step for labour process analysis which has traditionally been locked into discourses on the factory and office. Knights and Morgan argue that the internalized self-discipline of sales staff in insurance complements strategies of management control in the intensification of labour. Sales staff are directly employed and are driven by a simple piecework system of commission and persistency bonuses. Sales staff have targets on sales and no maximum limit on their earnings. Targets are described by Knights and Sturdy as part of a 'person's subjective competence' (Knights and Morgan 1990: 374). The achievement of targets therefore becomes a crucial component of subjective existence. In this analysis, targets operate as a form of discipline. They provide a mechanism for personal self-monitoring of progress and therefore operate as an individualizing technique. In this configuration of power, then, it is the establishment of targets, together with the individualizing effects of competitive struggles for prizes and symbolic recognition, which produces the self-disciplined worker.

It is clear that the novelty of these accounts of self-disciplined workers in the insurance sector, lies in the use of a version of Foucault's analysis of power. This power individualizes and, according to the self-discipline thesis, places employees in competition for the scarce rewards of social recognition. This condition is framed by the elementary fact that there are no guarantees that subjects will reach the standards by which they are judged. Thus, at one and the same time, individuals, whether working with information technology or under a regime of targets, are rendered more directly responsible and their identities become ever more problematical. Their self-consciousness ties them as subjects to identities which they are unable to confirm.

The terms of this new analysis can be seen to have recast Braverman's argument for one dominant form of power, expressed in the deskilling practices of scientific management, with another dominant form of power which controls through establishing a no-win game of struggle for individual identity. In both cases, however, power is described in ways that automatically produce discipline. Further, the transformation from Braverman's external form of discipline to Foucault's internal form is articulated at the expense of specific details of how work is actually organized and discipline systems operate. For example, in place of detail on disciplinary techniques we are informed that, in their struggles in work, individuals choose the security of an unspecified identity. This choice is represented as a resolution to the problem of the double bind of desire for independence and fear of isolation that the new type of work is supposed to establish.

In this form of explanation, then, the finance industry is represented as a site in which workers experience an enhanced freedom, in terms of both job design and reduced constraint by their fellow workers. This freedom, inscribed in the social organization of their work, demands their self-discipline and offsets all forms of collective action. The negative result of this freedom is expressed strategically in the form of workers choosing individually to exit their employment. The alternative political strategy that Hirschman (1970) refers to as voice, finds no place in this explanation. The self-disciplined worker, to play on Clegg again, would seem therefore to have very few of the qualities summed up in the term 'practical experimentalist'.

PERFORMANCE APPRAISALS AS CONTEXTS OF TALK

I argue in this section that what has been characterized as work carried out by self-disciplined workers utilizing information technology or working to performance targets, is in fact better understood as work which has been restructured by strategies of control developed under the broad heading of human resource management. The key to this restructuring is a form of power dispersal which does not flow directly from a logic of a utilization of new technology but is associated with it in so far as companies, which utilize information technology, deploy decentralized means of budgetary control to organize their service delivery. As a consequence of this decentralization, the more traditional office or retail outlet work is now geared to service delivery and, as a result, what was once organized as routine and bureaucratic functions, is now subject to performance criteria and differentiated payment systems which have always been associated with sales work. This strategy of decentralization is part of a deliberate marketing strategy which places new demands upon employees through an emphasis on customer service.

This different analysis of the development of work in the finance industry leads me to replace the issues of identity and self-discipline, that the turn to, or interpretation of, Foucault has presented, with a very different analysis of a potential politics of work that arises in this new managerial context. This revised analysis highlights the different concerns of the positions from which workers are required to speak by management and the positions that they, through their union, collectively construct themselves to speak from. In this section, emphasis will be placed upon the intensified deployment of performance appraisals as a central technique requiring workers to speak. In the following section I will develop the argument that workers also resist by attempting to develop different positions from which to speak. These positions will be referred to as alternative forms of appraisal carried out by the workers themselves.

For the purposes of this chapter, then, what is significant in the transformation of work in the finance industry is not that the new configurations of decentralization give rise to self-disciplined workers but, in the first instance, that decentralization is associated with new forms of managerial discipline. A central component of this discipline is the development of new forms of accountability, or appraisal, which stress a much more consumer-oriented focus.

The disciplinary technique of performance appraisal of workers in the finance industry is not new but, as a result of decentralization, has been reorganized by human resource management. Originally regular performance appraisal functioned to assist management in economic efficiency decisions concerning the deployment of individual staff. This hierarchical function remains, but through reorganization the technique has been supplemented with managerial concerns of the quality and effectiveness of performance of both individuals and complete units of work such as a retail outlet of a bank. This development of the appraisal function involves increases in the sources of information concerning individual performance, such as data from questionnaires filled out by consumers at point of sale. In one bank in New Zealand, in which management has adopted this 'consumer choice' model, referred to as 'speak out', customers are requested to assess performance and nominate a staff member who has been particularly helpful. This request is accompanied by an invitation to the customer to arrange an interview with the company to discuss the appraisal.

These new types of performance appraisal are used extensively in the finance industry and for the purposes of this article can be understood as the creation of new contexts of 'talk'. These new contexts of 'talk' involve a new form of questioning employees and middle management. Finance industry companies now invite their employees and middle managers to both give an account of themselves and set their own objectives in regular appraisal interviews. These interviews institutionalize both the means and support for the employees' views. This new model of appraisal can also involve employees being required to fill out appraisal forms on their managers.

What is new in these arrangements is that the accusatory form of control that marked the more paternal practices of the pre-computerized finance industry no longer functions. In the computerized finance industry, austere paternalistic judgements have been replaced with an increased volume of 'user friendly' communications and encounters. This replacement of what was often experienced as overt and intimidatory questioning does not, however, remove the surveillance function of appraisal. Further, the multiplication of sources of information on employees operates to heighten the ambiguity of their technique of both answering questions and performing their functions.

In the new form of appraisal, employees are required to judge their own performance, using pre-packaged items such as 'describe what you have done best or with greatest satisfaction during the review period' or 'describe your strengths'. This form of questioning positions employees to provide accounts of themselves, but how they should answer such questions, and how far they should go in asserting their strengths, is left ambiguous. This ambiguity involves both diffuse stress and risk. If employees are honest about their faults they risk censure. On the other hand, if they are dishonest they risk being found out.

Despite this ambiguity, this speech encounter (Dingwall, 1980) can take on a quasi-legal status. The appraisal requires that employees both disclose themselves and authorize or witness their accounts. On the employers' part it requires comment on the capability of the employee. These comments, together with the accounts of the employee's desires, are filed. Generally carried out on an annual basis, but sometimes as frequently as every three months, the appraisal system produces a cumulative text of self, a recorded agreement on the moral character and aims of the employee.

As part of the appraisal typically a manager or supervisor summons the employee, as if for an interrogation, and asks him or her to give elements of his or her biography. The context is framed as helping the candidate. The way in which this framing is accomplished can be seen in the following extract taken from a performance review carried out by a branch manager in a bank retail outlet. The manager notes that 'Joan has maintained a calm and intelligent approach to her job which has enabled her to achieve a consistently good level of output'. Clearly the discourse of the manager links her 'consistently good level' of performance (the interrogation part of the encounter) with praise for her display of a calm and intelligent demeanour (the therapeutic part of the interview). The manager's observations are then supplemented with comments from a higher order of power referred to as 'comment by the bank'. These additional comments ratify the encounter and may indicate that the employee's desires have been recognized. In Joan's case, the comments document the bank's appreciation of her efforts and that her request for another position has been noted and placed on record. The document has four signatures on it; those of the employee, her immediate supervisor, her manager, an agent of the bank (area or divisional manager) and a fourth, which indicates that the employee has received a copy of the text. This form of questioning can also be extended by formal and informal counselling sessions in which individuals are further encouraged to talk about and represent themselves. Such sessions would include drinks after work in the small personalized office and continual training sessions in which the self is at the centre.

I suggest that questions and texts of this sort, and not simply working in isolation with new technology or to targets, are a major component of the form of disciplinary power that human resource management deploys. Together with the ambivalent response of the self-disciplined worker to information technology and targets we have, then, the appraisal as a set of questions which involve the deployment of the twin discourses of interrogation and therapy.

The workplace in the finance industry, like the school, can now be seen, then, to be increasingly constituted as an examining technology (Jones, 1990: 75) geared to inciting individuals both to talk to and inscribe their biographies in texts in order to make them visible. At the centre of this examining technology is the extensive use of performance appraisal – required by management but also invested in by employees. Through this technique, employees (and increasingly customers) are positioned in an explicit managerial process of giving or disclosing information about themselves. For employees, this positioning demands the construction of psychologically informed narratives of the performing self. In turn these narratives of performance become the means by which persons constitute and represent themselves. However, rather than the production of a self-disciplined worker, I argue that they multiply the conscious play of discourses of the self. Such multiplication plays upon the issues of the boundaries which define workers and produces problems for collective resistance. At the same time, however, they have another important effect. They create a new space for resistance. In so far as such processes 'unfreeze' the hold of older discourses, new opportunities for collective forms of resistance to work are opened up.

TOWARDS A NEW UNIONISM: THE POLITICS OF APPRAISAL

Writing in the context of human resource management, Kochan, Katz and McKersie have suggested that the reconstruction of American unions requires a 'blending of traditional representation and newer participatory processes, along with perhaps additional, more individualized forms of voice and representation' (1986: 225). This agenda of union reconstruction and the issues of representation, participation and employee voice (Lewin and Mitchell, 1992) will be discussed in the following two sections with reference to, first, what I call a politics of appraisal. This discussion of appraisal is followed by an analysis of grievance hearings. I argue that in the context of human resource management, appraisal and grievance hearings are at the centre of new strategies of both managerial discipline and union resistance.

McHoul (1987a: 368) has argued that knowing the form talk takes is a prerequisite for understanding its place in the formation of power relations. In these terms a finance industry in which individuals are 'incited' to talk about themselves is very different from a finance industry in which this form of question and answer is not institutionalized. In the terms of the conversational analysts, employee voice systems can be seen to have promoted new speaking positions constituted as a new order of turn taking and entitlements (Atkinson and Heritage, 1984).

The new forms of talking, that human resource management has sponsored, involve not only assessment of the individual but also recognition of the increasing codification and legalization of work. For example, issues which impact upon the worker, such as health and safety, and race and gender discrimination, have now been codified and legitimated as resources in law. This new form of the politics of work has made the fine detail of the subject of work both a part of everyday discourse and, at the same time, a sphere in which expert knowledge is required for purposes of interpretation. The result of these developments is that if it occurs, resistance must take on a discursive form which deploys as resources the very texts that have codified work. In this context, a politics of appraisal can become a resistance strategy.

Such a resistance strategy requires a heightened reflexivity concerning the organization and control of work. This reflexivity can be most easily shown through the example of women's struggles against forms of male categorization. These struggles against male practices have typically involved women challenging or intervening in male discourses of work and significantly, as resistance strategies, they have also involved the deployment of questions and texts. In the 1970s and 1980s, these resistance strategies had the effect of destabilizing everyday definitions of the boundaries of work. The ambiguity that resulted placed the issue of what work actually 'is' on the political agenda. It is argued here that these struggles can be seen as the use and development of collective forms of appraisal of male practices.

An example taken from women's struggles in the New Zealand finance industry can help us understand how this development of alternative forms of appraisal was realized. In the first stage of the struggle for women's rights in work, women used a strategy of voice, or incitement to talk, extensively for organizing resistance to the effects of patriarchal practices which classified and subordinated women to men. These practices had established boundaries in work, like the removal of women from paid work on marriage and placed boundaries upon what could be spoken of, by whom and when. Resistance to these boundaries involved, therefore, resistance to being named and classified in particular ways. In the first instance, it required that these issues entered into everyday discourse.

In this case resistance involved not a search for, or affirmation of, identity but rather an opening up of multiple positions from which to speak. This process of 'opening up' required the replacement of a discourse of male professionalism with new discourses to mobilize women members. These new discourses were embedded in new sets of appraisal practices organized by the finance union in the early 1980s. Initially these took the form of women's seminars, with women from the finance industry telling of their experiences of patriarchal exclusion. This method of presenting 'cases' in intensely personalized forums was derived from the discourses employed and articulated by the women officers in the union.

These confessional sessions, which always ended with the song, 'Don't be too polite girls', the last verse of which runs, 'its not their balls we are after, it is a fair square deal', were used to construct a collective understanding of how women had been positioned in the finance industry. The talked-through experiences or 'reflexive biographies' (Giddens 1991), which utilized many different types of discourse and drew upon the shared humour of the women, were then used as a basis to mount a campaign against gender discrimination in the industry. The key to this form of resistance then, was not an agreement on identity but rather a combination of the use of seminars, as new types of union decision-making procedures, and the translation of narratives of experience into texts of appraisal on women's positions.

The women's seminar format, in which women's experiences were the topic, can be seen as a process of information exchange which drew upon the knowledge of women members, in order to appraise the process of the male order of positioning in finance industry work. As a form of resistance this type of appraisal required collective efforts to address and recognize socially constituted experiences of ways of talking. The example makes clear, however, that in order to resist claims made by management, the women were drawn into constructing and presenting narratives about themselves. In this case their 'sex discrimination talk' (Brown, 1991) opened the way for positioning their own narratives within male discourses. Further, it was their active construction of new positions and new discourses, about their selves, which constituted a collective appraisal of both themselves and the institutions which employed them. The seminars were powerful. The woman union officer who organized the seminars described them as, 'the most humbling experience of my life'.

This model of resistance to gender discrimination constitutes a very useful example of a new politics of appraisal which supplements the traditional union functions of inspection and advocacy. While these functions remain, if unions are to survive then their function as organizers of such forms of talk becomes increasingly important. This shift in function may require unions to take on more participatory styles of organization. Such styles shift the emphasis from representation of members to participation and increase the role of the union as interpreter of its members' experiences. In the case of the women in the finance industry, the union agenda provided for the construction and presentation of narratives of the self.

This type of development requires us to view unions as monitoring agencies concerned with the appraisal of all forms of work relations. The different discourses they are able to develop on this subject are, however, intrinsically grounded in providing their members with positions from which to speak. In the case reviewed, the repositioning of the women's narratives opened up the possibility of pursuing personal grievance issues on the grounds of gender discrimination. The same type of repositioning could be used to open up other isssues of relevance to workers.

TOWARDS A NEW UNIONISM: THE POLITICS OF GRIEVANCE HEARINGS

Grievance hearings are concerned with the issue of ambivalence inherent in the classification of both persons and actions. This ambivalence refers to the fact that who one is can only be articulated from specific speaking positions. Grievance hearings should also be seen, then, as providing for forms of speech exchange concerned with establishing such positions. Viewed in this way, workers are not concerned to use grievance hearings to discover or enforce their identities but rather because they have a need to be placed in positions in which they can speak to and answer specific claims made about their selves. When those claims are phrased in necessarily vague terms like 'not performing', the necessity for such speaking positions should not be considered surprising.

Judgement and resistance to judgement have always been central to the way in which work is organized. However, as judgement becomes more and more geared to the psychological profiles of employees, their rights to pursue and present their own accounts become more and more critical. Employees therefore have an interest in the range of codification that can be drawn upon in grievance hearings. The latter is crucial, for it is the range of codification which serves as a resource for individuals to construct positioning possibilities and therefore make coherent claims about both their selves and 'what happened'. As forms of providing 'accounts', grievance hearings have, therefore, increasingly become a critical base for both union activity and collective resistance.

The paradox of grievance hearings is that they necessarily individualize the employee. Further, in so far as unions are able to deploy such hearings to mediate resistance to the technologies of individualization described, they become integrated into the modern work process as therapeutic agencies which articulate the grievances of individuals. In this 'confessional' world, a union comes to be another agency which provides a position from which to speak and listen. In recognizing and acting upon this development, the finance union moved towards establishing seminars and workshops, in the hearing and answering of questions of the person. This training of their members in new practices of speaking/ communication techniques involved hiring skilled therapeutic workers to assist in the process. In this shift towards a more interpretive role, the seminar, a teaching format, comes to replace the centrality of the committee meeting.

These developments were also associated with other moves towards personal marketing practices. The union under review here, for example, took it upon itself to assist people to represent themselves in their appraisal interviews. Having legal access to all workers, it also engaged in a strategy which involved talking with every member at least once a year in her or his place of work. In times of dispute or contract negotiations it established union telephone 'hot lines' which any member could use free of charge to enquire about the 'state of play'. The union as a provider of services was therefore increasingly engaged in catering to its individual members.

To further this form of 'new unionism', the finance union incorporated the practices of 'confession' and counselling as techniques for organizing. These techniques became the basis of its service- or market-based sensitivity. As a form of unionism it was not, however, engaged in creating identity but rather in providing subjects with positions from which they could resist through telling and acting upon their grievances. What the union heard and acted upon were narratives of the self. These narratives were the means by which grievances, or departures from routine work, were both managed and inscribed in members' biographies. In addition, the union journal was organized around members' biographies together with their photographs. This presentation of accounts of the lives of ordinary members lifted them out of the anonymity of membership and at the same time established the union's concern to speak the discourse of the individual.

Resistance in the new individualized finance industry therefore involves employees becoming potential 'cases'. To operate in this context, union officers position themselves as case workers. Cases are constructed through the employee keeping records of self and all transactions undertaken. The possibility of constructing such cases involves recognition that, in the first instance, employees are juridical personalities. As 'personalities' they are able to act in specific ways prescribed by law. In New Zealand, the same is true of the union officer. The union officer's position provides her with the authority to enforce legal codes governing work. Her position therefore provides for legal action but her position practices only make sense in so far as she is dealing with legally constituted personalities with specific rights.

If it is true that the workplace is increasingly being reconstituted as an examining technology, then the union's combination of an interpretive strategy grounded in participation, programmes of training and the marketing of services such as job counselling, makes sense. The new individualized work practices of the finance industry can be seen, therefore, to have opened up new ways for unions to resist and organize. These centre on the way in which unions are required to discursively represent the individual. This condition is the meeting point of unions and the practices of human resource management. In this new arrangement, the new accommodation that unions make with management is required to pass through the individual. At the extreme, unions act as bargaining agents for individuals on personal contracts. In this version, the union moves towards a model of professional expert and constitutes its members as clients. This line of development flows from everything that has been noted about the finance industry. It is also the case that this is not inevitable and that what I have termed a politics of appraisal and grievance can follow a different route. This route requires novel forms of participation in order to continually construct new positions from which to address the way in which work is organized.

In this struggle for position, personal grievance cases are viewed as a particularly important weapon by both unions and management. For unions they become organizing tools to strengthen bargaining power and advance membership through the establishment of precedent. For the human resource managers who have to pursue them, and sometimes lose them, they constitute lessons in how to fire employees. For employees they are a condition for resistance; for if it is possible to reply to cases made against the self it is possible to resist.

CONCLUSION

I have suggested that what I have termed the 'turn to Foucault' operated to produce an analysis of work in the finance industry which closed down rather than opened up the ambiguities inherent in human resource management. I have argued that it is not the case that individuals in new types of work arrangements typically found in the finance industry, have become more obedient or self-disciplined but rather, to continue Foucault's (1982) line of argument, that only an increasingly better invigilated process of adjustment has been pursued by management. I have not, therefore, accepted the argument for the production of a self-disciplined worker and in its place have attempted to develop further the analysis of the nature of the problems of collective resistance in individualized workplaces.

I have referred to two examples of resistance. These were termed a politics of appraisal and a politics of grievance. The politics of both are grounded in the recognition of the strategic positions from which workers speak. The complexity of this process of speaking was illustrated, first, with examples of the different appraisal systems used by management and the union. In the case of management it was not suggested that the use of appraisals was a new form of power. On the contrary, the managerial control of work has long involved the orchestration of encounters, such as appraisals, as forms of talk or speech exchange (Dingwall, 1980). Similarly, in the case of unions, resistance has also always been, in part, discursive and, therefore, always constituted through techniques which we might want to term appraisal. I argued, however, that, in the context of contemporary human resource management, in order to survive unions will be required to take up the issues of appraisals and grievances in a much more reflexive and interpretive manner.

To emphasize this point I argued that grievance procedures which bestow rights on the individual remain central to resistance. Where employer and employee are party to contracts which do not agree to honour the identity claims of the other, subordinates in the relationship have no choice other than to attempt to enforce dispute mechanisms which will allow them the opportunity to answer the important and necessarily ambiguous questions of both who they are and what happened.

Historically, this choice has involved employees introducing a union as a third party. In the context of modern human resource management, union representation itself is contested. In the case under review, the union survived by deploying the same human resource techniques as management. In this example the techniques were utilized by the union to be enabling rather than constraining (Giddens, 1984).

The concern with both appraisal and grievance procedures in the argument was part of a more general concern with what Goffman (1981) refers to as talk and Hirschman (1970) as voice. I argued that this concern shifts our analysis from a commitment to understanding the generalized social relations which sustain broad distinctions of occupational structure and identity, to specific local practices. This argument requires that, rather than focus directly on disembodied selves and problems of identity and meaning, we place these existential concerns in the context of the political machinery of talk that is characteristic of, and required in, work situations. I argued that only through an analysis of the positions from which this 'talk' is produced will we be able to understand both the new forms of management regulation and the resistance practices that arise in the labour process.

In this respect, I argued that the development of the labour process in the finance industry was the site for the production of a new range of positions and discourses from which subjects can construct themselves. Recognition of this process, with its emphasis on the specific and detailed configurations of questioning and talk, as both management and union practices, provides a new starting point for understanding resistance in the labour process. This resistance is grounded in the recognition of the dilemma that to speak is to be both positioned and judged. This dilemma has always been at the core of the experience of work. In the context of human resource management it is made explicit.

REFERENCES

Armstrong, D. (1983) *Political Anatomy of the Body*, Cambridge: Cambridge University Press.

Atkinson, J. M. and Heritage, J. (1984) *Structures of Social Action: Studies in Conversation Analysis*, Cambridge: Cambridge University Press.

Austrin, T. (1991) 'Flexibility, Surveillance and Hype in New Zealand Financial Retailing', *Work, Employment and Society* 5(2): 201–21.

Austrin, T. (1992) 'Electronic Texts and Retailing: The Transformation of work in the Finance Sector', in J. Deeks and N. Perry, (eds) *Controlling Interests: Business, Government and Society in New Zealand*, Auckland: Auckland University Press.

Badham, R. and J. Mathews (1989) 'The New Production Systems Debate', *Labour and Industry* 2(2): 194–246.

Ball, S. J. (1990) *Foucault and Education: Disciplines and Knowledge*, London: Routledge.

Bauman, Z. (1991) *Modernity and Ambivalence*. Cambridge: Polity Press.

Beynon, H. (1973) *Working for Ford*, Harmondsworth: Penguin.

Braverman, H. (1974) *Labour and Monopoly Capital*, New York: Monthly Review Press.

Brown, B. (1991) 'Litigating Feminisms', *Economy and Society* 20(4): 423–44.

Burawoy, M. (1979) *Manufacturing Consent*, Chicago: Chicago University Press,

Clegg, S. R. (1990) *Modern Organisations: Organisation Studies in the Postmodern Period*, London: Sage.

Cockburn, C. (1983) *Brothers: Male Dominance and Technological Change*, London: Pluto Press.

Collinson, D. and Knights, D. (1986) '"Men Only" Theories and Practices of Job Segregation in Insurance' in D. Knights and H. Willmott (eds) *Gender and the Labour Process*, Aldershot: Gower.

Davies, B. and Harre, R. (1991) 'Positioning: The Discursive Production of Selves', *Journal for the Theory of Social Behaviour* 20(1): 43–64.

Dingwall, R. (1980) 'Orchestrated Encounters: An Essay in the Comparative Analysis of Speech Exchange Systems', *Sociology of Health and Illness* 2: 151–73.

Foucault, M. (1979) *Discipline and Punish*, Harmondsworth: Penguin.

Foucault, M. (1980) *The History of Sexuality*, Vol. 1, New York: Vintage.

Foucault, M. (1982) 'The Subject and Power.' Afterword in H. Dreyfus and P. Rabinow (eds) *Michel Foucault: Beyond Structuralism and Hermeneutics*, Chicago: University of Chicago Press.

216

Giddens, A. (1984) *The Constitution of Society*, Cambridge: Polity.

Giddens, A. (1991) *Modernity and Identity: Self and Society in the Late Modern Age*, Cambridge: Polity Press.

Goffman, E. (1981) *Forms of Talk*, Philadelphia: University of Pennsylvania Press.

Hirschman, A. O. (1970) *Exit, Voice and Loyalty*, Cambridge, MA: Harvard University Press.

Horst, K and Sabel, C., (1991) 'Trade Unions and Decentralized Production: A Sketch of Strategic Problems in the West German Labour Movement', *Politics and Society* 19(4): 373–402.

Jones, D. (1990) 'The Genealogy of the Urban Schoolteacher', in S.J. Ball (ed.) *Foucault and Education: Disciplines and Knowledge*, London: Routledge.

Kochan, T. A. (ed.) (1985) *Challenges and Choices Facing American Labour*, Cambridge, MA: MIT Press.

Kochan, T. A., Katz and McKersie (1986) *The Transformation of American Industrial Relations*, New York: Basic Books.

Knights, D. and Collinson, D. (1985) 'Redesigning Work on the Shopfloor: A Question of Control or Consent?' in D. Knights, H. Willmott and D. Collinson (eds) *Job Redesign*, Aldershot: Gower.

Knights, D. and Morgan, G (1990) 'Management Control in Sales Forces: A Case Study from the Labour Process of Life Insurance', *Work, Employment and Society* 4(3): 369–90.

Knights, D. and Morgan, G. (1991) 'Selling Oneself: Subjectivity and The Labour Process in Selling Life Insurance', in C. Smith, D. Knights and H. Willmott (eds) *White-Collar Work: The Non-Manual Labour Process*, London: Macmillan,

Knights, D. and Sturdy, A. (1989) 'New Technology and the Self-disciplined Worker in Insurance', in M. Mcneill, J. Varcoe, and S. Yearly (eds) *Deciphering Science and Technology*, London: Macmillan.

Knights, D. and Willmott, H. (1985) 'Power and Identity in Theory and Practice', *Sociological Review* 33(1): 22–46.

Knights, D. and Willmott, H. (1989) 'Power and Subjectivity at Work: From Degradation to Subjugation in Social Relations', *Sociology* 23(4): 535–58.

Knights, D. and Willmott, H. (1990) *Labour Process Theory*, London: Macmillan.

Knights, D., Willmott, H. and Collinson, D. (eds) (1985) *Job Redesign*, Aldershot: Gower.

Lewin, D. and Mitchell, J.B. (1992) 'Systems of Employee Voice: Theoretical and Empirical Perspectives', *California Management Review* 34(3): 95–111.

McHoul, A. (1987a) 'Why There are No Guarantees for Interrogators', *Journal of Pragmatics* 11: 455–71.

McHoul, A. (1987b) 'Language and Institutional Reality: Reply and Response', *Organization Studies* 8(4): 363–74.

Nichols, T. and Beynon, H. (1977) *Living with Capitalism: Class Relations and the Modern Factory*, London: Routledge.

Pollert, A. (1981) *Girls, Wives and Factory Lives*, London: Macmillan.

Poster, M. (1990) *The Mode of Information: Poststructuralism and Social Context*, Chicago: University of Chicago Press.

Shotter, J. and Gergen, K.J. (1989) *Texts of Identity*, London: Sage.

Silverman, D. (1989) 'The Impossible Dreams of Reformism and Romanticism', in J. Gubrium and D. Silverman (eds) *The Politics of Field Research: Sociology Beyond Enlightenment*, London: Sage.

Willmott, H. (1990) 'Subjectivity and the Dialectics of Praxis: Opening up the Core of Labour Process Analysis', in D. Knights and H. Willmott (eds) *Labour Process Theory*, London: Macmillan.

7

SABOTAGE BY MANAGERS AND TECHNOCRATS

Neglected patterns of resistance at work

Danny LaNuez and John M. Jermier

The central thesis of this chapter is that some managers and techno-crats have sufficient motive to sabotage the production of goods and services. We begin by citing illustrative examples of episodes of managerial and technocratic sabotage. In reviewing the existing sabotage literature we find that low or reduced personal control and the experience of negative affect at the workplace underlie many acts of sabotage. We examine major societal and organizational forces that have eroded and redefined the power and privileges of managerial and technocratic positions and find that managers and technocrats have experienced increasing powerlessness and insecurity. We draw on neoclassical economics, managerialist literature and modern social-class analyses to establish the plausibility of the central thesis. As the interests, values and motives of managers and technocrats drift further from alignment with those of capital elites who desire to maximize profits, a willingness to engage in forms of deep opposition is more probable. Although it may seem counter-intuitive, we argue that for reasons similar to those of workers, some managers and technocrats resist capitalist domination by selecting sabotage responses. In the closing sections, a typology of managerial/technocratic sabotage is presented.

INTRODUCTION

Conflict and power struggles pervade contemporary corporations and profoundly shape the work experiences of all their members. Labour process theorists and other academic writers have given much attention to the antagonistic relationship between capital elites (i.e. owners of the means of production and their agents whose primary interests lie in capital accumulation) and workers who must sell their labour power for a wage. Most have focused on the dominating effects of managerial control (e.g. Braverman, 1974; Burawoy, 1979); some have emphasized the interplay between managerial control and worker resistance (e.g. Friedman, 1977; Edwards, 1979; Montgomery, 1979; Salaman, 1979; Edwards and Scullion, 1982; Gordon, Edwards and Reich, 1982). However, very few writers have called attention to the idea that managers and technocrats (e.g. accountants, engineers, technicians and other non-managerial experts) may also resist the imposition of capitalist control strategies.

In this chapter, we argue that a more realistic portrayal of corporate life may depend on the realization that all employees (managers and technocrats as well as workers) have the ability and motivation to resist administrative, structural and technical controls instituted by capital elites when these controls are perceived as excessive or undesirable. But, what forms of resistance are chosen by managers and technocrats? We argue that some managers and technocrats, in certain situations, resist controls by selecting sabotage responses. While this may not be the most frequent resistance tactic engaged in by managers and technocrats, it will add a unique perspective to resistance studies.

Before developing this argument, it is necessary to clarify the meaning of 'sabotage', a concept with a long history in industry, business and commerce, but also one that has received scant theoretical attention by academic researchers. This section is followed by selected episodes of managerial/technocratic sabotage described in popular press accounts which underscore the concrete reality of these acts and the need to develop a theoretical framework for their study. A brief review of existing sabotage literature is presented to examine likely motives that underlie many acts of sabotage. We assess the impacts of numerous societal and organizational forces that have served to reduce the power and privileges of these actors, thereby making sabotage responses more attractive. By drawing from neoclassical economics, managerialist literature and modern social-class analyses, we argue that the values and motives of managers and technocrats are often incompatible (or even in direct opposition) to capital accumulation imperatives, creating a space where deep opposition is both plausible and probable. In the closing sections, a typology of managerial/technocratic sabotage is presented.

THE CONCEPT OF SABOTAGE

Occasionally, organizational conflict is manifested overtly and dramatically in strikes, picketing and political protests. More often, conflict is expressed in less dramatic forms, such as grievances or informal conversations with one's superiors. Other forms of conflict may emerge that are more subtle and subterranean in nature, such as work slowdowns, rule violations, working-to-rule, unauthorized break-taking, theft and sabotage. Of all the surreptitious resistance tactics, sabotage is one of the least understood from a theoretical and empirical perspective (Jermier, 1988). While there are numerous popular and journalistic accounts of workplace sabotage, few serious academic studies have been undertaken.

Furthermore, academic writers have used the concept of sabotage to represent a wide variety of employee behaviours. For example, Brown (1977) used the label to refer to any employee actions that restrict output. Similarly, Dubois (1979) viewed activities such as strikes, go-slows, absenteeism, working without enthusiasm, or destruction that results in any reduction in the quality or quantity of goods produced, as forms of sabotage. Building upon Taylor and Walton's (1971) definition, we conceptualize sabotage more narrowly as *deliberate action or inaction that is intended to damage, destroy or disrupt some aspect of the workplace environment, including the organization's property, product, processes or reputation, with the net effect of undermining goals of capital elites.*[1]

At least two mythical images have been associated with workplace sabotage. First, sabotage has been characterized as the isolated and irrational acts of organizational misfits, that is, 'mad saboteurs'. Saboteurs are portrayed as malcontents who explode into destructive fits because they are unwilling or unable to cope with everyday organizational realities. But, a careful reading of labour history and empirical studies challenges this notion. Sabotage by workers is a complex behavioural process that is usually social, conspiratorial, restrained and highly symbolic in nature (Jermier, 1988). An underlying premise of this chapter is that workplace sabotage often is a rational and calculative act. Our position is that employees knowingly weigh potential risks (e.g. exposure, expulsion, criminal liability) and positive consequences of the act (e.g. changes to the system that benefit themselves, co-workers and/or society).

A second widely-held image of sabotage is the view that it is exclusively a blue-collar phenomenon. While no systematic re-search has been done in this area, a reading of popular press accounts provides growing evidence that this phenomenon is becoming more commonplace among managers and technocrats and its practice more creative.

ILLUSTRATIONS OF SABOTAGE BY MANAGERS AND TECHNOCRATS

In a recent article (*The New Times*, 26 January 1992), a large corporate investigative firm reported that its caseload involving corporate sabotage had increased threefold in just one year. Consider some cases that it has recently investigated:

- An energy company's internal report of quarterly earnings was doctored to reflect an apparent problem and then sent to Wall Street analysts.
- A chemical company's most valuable new formula was offered to a competitor.
- A multinational company's departed chief financial officer spent months visiting one foreign tax official after another, offering to blow the whistle on alleged tax evasions.
- A consulting firm's former officer sent bogus letters – on company letterhead – to clients, suppliers, bankers and competitors to reflect subtle changes in the relationships. By the time the victimized company figured out what happened, it was nearly out of business.

Similar instances in both the public and private sector appear in other press accounts:

- All computerized financial records of Prescott Valley, Arizona, are erased, leaving officials with no idea how much money has been spent this year or how much cash the town has left; sabotage suspected (*New York Times*, 15 February 1987).
- In Los Angeles, a computer in the water department was down for 10 days because an insider planted a computer logic bomb – a program timed to begin working at a given time . . . (*Tampa Tribune*, 17 December 1990).
- International Business Machine's Corp.'s regional office in Tampa was infiltrated with a so-called computer virus that spread throughout the company's computer, slowing performance to a

222

crawl. The program, which multiplied itself countless times was eradicated, but computer systems had to be shutdown (*Tampa Tribune*, 8 April 1989).

These incidents begin to illustrate the reality of sabotage by managers and other professionals. Even sabotage with catastrophic potential is becoming an increasing concern as future saboteurs 'may be able to do more damage with a keyboard than with a bomb, [and] without aggressive action, national exposure to safety and security catastrophes will increase rapidly (National Research Council findings reported in the *Tampa Tribune*, 16 December 1990).

Clearly, the full extent of this phenomenon is not known since reported incidents may represent only the tip of the iceberg. Failure of organizations to recognize or acknowledge acts of sabotage (often acts of sabotage are labelled under less emotionally charged terms such as pranks, carelessness or accident), use of creative sabotage techniques (e.g. 'logic bombs'), difficulty in identifying the specific saboteur, legal issues and costs, unwanted publicity and other reasons explain why many acts of sabotage go unreported. The above press accounts serve to illustrate that sabotage by managers and technocrats is not only plausible and probable but is rooted in the actual and everyday experiences of these organizational actors. While previous research has largely overlooked this form of organizational resistance, this chapter begins to develop the theoretical underpinnings and a framework required systematically to study managerial and technocratic sabotage.

SABOTAGE MOTIVES: DIMINISHED CONTROL AND NEGATIVE AFFECT

This section presents a brief review of the workplace sabotage literature.[2] Research findings indicate that the primary antecedents to workplace sabotage may be classified under two major categories: diminished/low control and negative affect. In the following two subsections, evidence is also presented from several psychological studies that strongly supports linkages between aggressive inclinations and personal control and negative affect. Hostility, aggression and destruction as a result of experiencing diminished control and negative affect seem to be basic human tendencies. The combination of evidence from workplace studies and the more extensive psychological research on aggression leads us to suggest that managers and technocrats experiencing diminished/low control and negative affect may engage in sabotage-related behaviours.

Diminished/low control

Numerous psychological studies have shown that reductions in perceived personal control to low or less than desired levels may result in a variety of unfavourable consequences (Greenberger *et al.*, 1989; Langer, 1975). These consequences include withdrawal (Thompson, 1981), decline in performance (Bazerman, 1982), learned helplessness (Martinko and Gardner, 1982), depression (Seligman, 1975) and sabotage/destructive behaviour (Allen and Greenberger, 1980). In fact, Greenberger and Strasser (1986) suggest that most individuals in organizations possess a generalized need for control and will actively pursue activities to increase their perceived control. Furthermore, Allen and Greenberger (1980: 107) noted in their study that 'destruction may be used as a technique for increasing control when other avenues of action are either not available or have been tried and found to be unsuccessful'. Although the desire for personal control varies based on an individual's experiences (de Charms, 1968), it appears to be a generalized human tendency that cuts across socio-economic boundaries.

Sabotage studies have typically involved blue-collar workers in factory settings. Some of these studies have found that sabotage episodes occur when the nature of the work is routine, monotonous, tedious or physically dangerous. Under such conditions, workers engage in sabotage to assert their individuality and self-worth and to make a creative symbolic gesture against the brutality of factory life. This is evident in the observations of slaughterhouse workers (Thompson, 1983), brewery workers (Molstad, 1986) and auto workers (Watson, 1971, King, 1978; Zabala, 1985).

Several studies reported that workers resorted to sabotage as a way to increase control over work-related issues. These included control over a wide spectrum of job-related issues, such as process or product planning (Watson, 1971, Elderidge, 1968); job bidding practices (Fennell, 1976); compensation systems (Edwards and Scullion, 1982); discipline and grievance procedures (Edwards and Scullion, 1982; Zabala, 1985).

Another factor frequently mentioned as an antecedent of sabotage is the desire to reassert control over time at the workplace.

Control of time emerged in two forms: control over the work pace (Watson, 1971; Fennell, 1976; Zabala, 1985); and control over break-times and rest periods (Watson, 1971; Ditton, 1979; Edwards and Scullion, 1982; Zabala, 1985).

Negative affect

The frustration–aggression hypothesis was first proposed by researchers over half a century ago (Dollard *et al.*, 1939). Although some social scientists have been critical of the original formulation (e.g. Bandura, 1973; Zillmann, 1979) and others have conducted studies that failed to support the core proposition (e.g. Pastore, 1952; Cohen, 1955), there is substantial psychological evidence that supports the proposition that frustration can produce hostility and aggression (see Berkowitz, 1989, for an extensive review of these studies). Some studies report that hostility and aggression are direct results of negative affect (e.g. Baron, 1984). A more sophisticated cognitive neo-associative model has been advanced by some researchers that posits the interplay of an aversive event, negative affect, emotional experiences and behaviours, and flight or fight tendencies (Berkowitz, 1983, 1988; Berkowitz and Heimer, 1989). In a proposed revision to the original formulation, Berkowitz (1989) suggested that frustrations create aggressive tendencies to the extent they produce negative affect.

Using self-report data, Spector (1975) examined the behavioural reactions of 82 mental-health facility workers to organizational frustration. Factors of interpersonal hostility and complaining (i.e. 'complaining to appropriate or inappropriate persons, saying derogatory things about your boss or organization') were strongly related to frustration. This behaviour may be characterized as 'open-mouth' sabotage. Frustration was also related to destructive sabotage (i.e. physical acts designed to destroy or deface property or equipment).

In their study of 1,327 wage and salaried workers, Mangione and Quinn (1975) found that sabotage was significantly related to job dissatisfaction, but in only a limited segment of workers – males, 30 years of age or older. Hollinger and Clark (1982) examined self-report data from 5,000 respondents employed by 35 mid-western corporations. They concluded that general and specific dimensions of job dissatisfaction were significantly related to reported involvement in acts of deviance against the organization's property and production by employees of all age groups.

Generalizability of findings

Generalizing these findings to a broader population that includes managers and other professionals is speculative. But the tendency for human beings to exhibit aggressive behaviours, including destruction of the physical environment, when their sense of control is severely threatened or perceived to be significantly diminished appears to be widely accepted. And, negative affect appears to cut across occupational boundaries as an explanatory factor in resistance behaviours. Again, a rich history of psychological research supports the propositions that negative affect/frustration may create aggressive inclinations. Both Spector's (1975) study on frustration and Hollinger and Clark's study on job dissatisfaction included professional subjects (e.g. nurses, mental-health aides, administrative/managers, engineers, technicians).

In the following section, we examine some macro-level forces that have changed the nature of managerial/technocratic work and contributed to creating an increased sense of powerlessness, insecurity and negative effect.

THE CHANGING LANDSCAPE OF MANAGERIAL AND TECHNOCRATIC WORK

Many employees holding managerial and technocratic positions have experienced decreases in power and privilege that traditionally have earmarked their corporate roles. Our review shows that many middle/low-level managers and technocrats increasingly experience powerlessness and insecurity in the sale of their labour power (cf. Carter, 1985). In this section, five major macro-level forces that have significantly altered the landscape of managerial and technocratic work are discussed. They are integral to the theoretical basis for proposing that sabotage by these organizational actors is not only feasible, but probable.

Major restructuring of organizations

Over the past three decades, American businesses have experienced a substantial increase in corporate mergers, takeovers, acquisitions and divestitures (Chandler, 1990). In response to increased international competition, shrinking domestic markets and deregulation, corporations have pursued restructuring strategies to increase profits (Smith, 1990). The result has been an increased concentration of power in relatively fewer corporate hands (Carter, 1985). In parallel with accelerated restructuring activities, the incidence of failure among well-established companies has also escalated. These economic realities have intensified fears and stress in the managerial and professional ranks (Scase and Goffee, 1989).

In light of these events, managers and technocrats have faced heightened vulnerability. First, an environment of uncertainty has emerged breeding job insecurity and a fear of being declared 'redundant' or being demoted (Carter, 1985). Apprehension of potential organizational changes in benefits, structures, procedures, work methods and the ultimate realization of accommodating these changes looms in this background of uncertainty. Second, restructuring is often characterized by the creation of even larger bureaucracies, further increasing impersonalization and standardization (Lumley, 1973). Third, as firms merge, duplicate or parallel managerial and technocratic positions are often subordinated to other positions, becoming more distant from the decision-making centres (Carter, 1985). As Jenkins and Sherman (1979) noted, takeovers and mergers reinforce the beliefs of affected managers and technocrats that control and authority have been transferred to corporate positions that are both physically and politically remote.

Increased measurement

The increased use of elaborate and sophisticated monitoring and other control techniques have made tasks performed by managers and technocrats more susceptible to surveillance and measurement. Environmental conditions, such as a depressed economy and intense global competition, often spurs the implementation of new control systems and techniques since organizational success (and survival) is highly problematic.

Bjorn-Andersen and Kjaergaard (1987, p. 245) commented that automated systems are frequently implemented because of their capability for 'keeping track of every activity, every break, and every mistake'. Current control systems make it relatively easy to monitor managerial performance *vis-à-vis* budgets, output rates and quality. Scase and Goffee (1989) found that these controls led to increased tensions among managers, since expectations were often unrealistic and conflicting. Control systems have altered the role of managers and their support staffs as they often undergo as much (or more) surveillance as lower-level workers.

Technological advances

Technological advances have provided a means to supplant mental and manual labour. The thrust of technological innovation and automation has been to replace labour with capital, and highly skilled workers with less-skilled labour (Cooley, 1977). Managerial and technocratic positions have not been immune to the rapid technological changes. Chamot (1987) found that many managerial tasks are now being performed via computerized networks requiring fewer people. This translates into the professional-level employee facing fewer job prospects. Other flexible manufacturing technologies, such as CAD/CAM, have also resulted in elimination of significant numbers of managerial and technocratic positions (Helfgott, 1988). The impact of rapid technological advancements and increased organizational control on managerial and technocratic work has been likened to the effects that assembly-line technology had on hourly workers (cf. Cooley, 1977, Oppenheimer, 1985).

Computers have also changed communication processes, interaction patterns, and the basic nature of managerial and technical work. As person-to-machine interfaces increase, the frequency and quality of people-to-people interfaces may degrade. Computer-mediated communications distance people emotionally making the exchange more impersonal (Kiesler, 1984). Zuboff (1982) proposed that computer technologies impersonalize the texture of the work itself by converting one's job into a string of electronic pulses.

Deskilling and deprofessionalization

Haug (1973) was among the earliest to predict the phenomenon of deprofessionalization. Most commentators concede that control over certain aspects of professional jobs has declined. Derber (1982) proposed a useful distinction related to this process. Professional work may be proletarianized, leading to the experience of a loss of control in two forms: (1) over the use of the work ('ideological proletarianization'), or (2) over decisions concerning how to do the work ('technical proletarianization'). According to Oppenheimer:

most professionals have suffered loss of control only over the first of these, although there are signs that the second is also deteriorating . . . some professions are undergoing ideological proletarianization, sometimes as a first step, with technical proletarianization following soon after . . . in either case, the whole notion of what professional life is supposedly about is being undermined.

(Oppenheimer 1985: 147)

Braverman's (1974) thesis that there has been segmentation and general deskilling of these types of jobs has generated much controversy. Application of this thesis to white-collar elites is even more controversial. Yet managers, professionals and other technocrats do find themselves in situations where they perform jobs that are more like those of other employees. Many have experienced diminished responsibility and autonomy. In their study of 384 managers from six major British firms, Scase and Goffee (1989) reported that the majority of respondents believed that new technology would severely deskill some parts of their jobs or eliminate the need for them entirely. Some professional groups, such as accountants, who participated in the study felt particularly vulnerable to this technological threat. Scase and Goffee concluded that as intrinsic rewards in these types of positions are reduced through deskilling, many activities may be 'performed by technicians whose primary function is to service computer-based information systems' (1989: 38).

Rewards, promotions and tenure

Technological obsolescence has displaced many managerial and technocratic employees or forced them to work at lower skill levels than commensurate with their credentials, experience and expectations. While during the 1950s and 1960s, career progress of managers and professionals was rapid and predictable (Scase and Goffee, 1989), recent technological and organizational changes have altered this pattern. Reward systems have been revamped to attract and keep younger, more technologically advanced employees. In order to improve promotional opportunities of the younger managers and professionals, it is not unusual for companies to offer early retirement or voluntary severance programmes to their longer-tenured employees or even more drastic measures, such as outright firing. Senior managers or professionals at the higher end of the salary scale have become the favourite targets in corporate downsizing programmes (Carter, 1985). Many longer-tenured, middle-aged employees face the dismal prospect of finding new careers or learning to adjust to forced early retirement. Career plateaus at about 45 years of age are becoming increasingly prevalent (Scase and Goffee, 1989). Smith observed:

> Reflecting a relatively new and noteworthy attempt to force white-collar managerial workers to pay for corporate hard times, firms faced with inescapable competitive pressures have extracted concessions in job regularity, security, and status from these employees. Corporations targeted the management employment contract: reports of wage freezes, salary cuts, newly instituted pay-for-merit systems, suspension of bonuses, and forced early retirement packages for staff and line managerial and professional employees.
>
> (Smith 1990: 10)

Changes in compensation and promotional strategies coupled with job displacement and underutilized skills are continuing sources of concern and anxiety among white-collar employees.

Summary

While sweeping generalizations concerning the effects of these forces on managers and professionals are not appropriate, some observations may be proposed. We contend the conditions discussed above have transformed the social relations and degraded the employment experiences of many managers and technocrats. Further, we posit that these macro-forces intensify feelings of lower perceived personal control and heightened negative affect thereby providing ample justification to reject the view that these actors act in concert with capitalists. Often, they may participate in activities and behaviours that run counter to capitalist corporate interests. We argue in the following section that the interests of managers and technocrats may significantly diverge or be in direct opposition to capitalist imperatives, creating a space where intense conflict and resistance behaviours may be enacted.

INTERESTS OF MANAGERS AND TECHNOCRATS AND SABOTAGE POTENTIAL

Neoclassical school of economics

To assess the potential of sabotage by managers and technocrats, it is helpful to begin with the traditional view of managerial interests advanced by neoclassical economists. According to neoclassicists, corporate managers are assumed to act in accordance with the objective of maximizing financial return on stockholders' investments (e.g. Marshall, 1920; Clark, 1923), fulfilling their fiduciary responsibility or they are replaced by other trustees. It is axiomatic that if managers and technocrats faithfully fulfil their trusteeship roles to protect capitalist dictates, they will not subvert the production process. In theory, owners can control corporate conduct by selecting and monitoring loyal trustees.

The pursuit of profit maximization by corporate managers on behalf of the firm as the sole or overriding consideration has not gone unchallenged. Reservations and scepticism about the reality of the profit maximization principle were expressed by many prominent economists over the past five decades (e.g. Hicks, 1935; Hall and Hitch, 1939; Boulding, 1950; Baumol, 1959; Nordquist, 1965; Alchian, 1965; Hirshleifer, 1984). At a minimum, the break with neoclassical views of trusteeship management established the possibility of managerial and technocratic interests and actions that may undermine capitalist imperatives for accumulation.

Managerialism: the issue of ownership and control

Debate among social scientists about ownership and control of the modern corporation has been far-reaching but inconclusive. At least since Berle and Means (1932) developed their 'new concept of the corporation', theorists have been aware of the possibility that managerial motivation and conduct may not coincide with preferences of owners. Berle and Means argued that diffusion of stock ownership resulted in a redistribution of control from owners to corporate administrators and concluded from their study that:

> it is therefore evident that we are dealing not only with distinct but often with opposing groups, ownership on one side, control on the other – a control that tends to move further and

231

further away from the ownership and ultimately to be in the hands of management itself, a management capable of perpetuating its own position.

(Berle and Means 1932: 124)

Extreme reformulations of the relationship between owners and managers were produced that emphasized the increased power and autonomy of managers in corporate affairs (e.g. Burnham, 1941).

The 'managerial revolution' thesis proposed that managers were replacing capitalists as society's ruling class. An extensive literature developed based on the idea that a complete separation between ownership and control in the firm led to domination of corporations (and society) by unrestrained managerial elites (e.g. Parsons, 1954; Bell, 1957; Lenski, 1966).

Scott (1985) categorized 'managerialism' into two distinct types. In 'sectional managerialism', managers act to serve their own interests. They seek power through 'empire-building', management perks or other amenities, inflated salaries, and so on. In 'non-sectional managerialism', managers are motivated by a greater sense of social responsibility and commitment to public welfare. Central to either variant of 'managerialism' is the notion that capital and management interests diverge, allowing management to establish and revise (within certain limits) the corporate agenda. Zeitlin (1974) and other political sociologists developed a sophisticated counterpoint to the managerialist position. They contended that owners in dispersed as well as closely held corporations exercise high levels of control over managers, but left ambiguous the effects of such control.

Although discussion about managerial autonomy continues, it seems reasonable to assume some degree of voluntarism on the part of these actors. Owners' interests are rarely monolithic. They usually exert pressure towards expansion and accumulation of capital, but their dictates are rarely unequivocal. The motives and conduct of managers and technocrats are constrained, not determined by their employers. Managers and technocrats can resist short-run capital accumulation exigencies in favour of long-term survival, growth or even socially responsible causes (Mulligan, 1986; Nunan, 1988). Furthermore, organizations accommodate numerous stakeholders with wide-ranging interests that results in even greater equivocality in managerial allegiances and subsequent behaviours.

Class location of managers and technocrats

In light of the sharp attacks against the neoclassical theory of the firm and the controversy raised in 'managerialist' literature, it is not surprising that the class position of managers and technocrats in capitalist society has been vigorously debated. Their class location has alternately been identified in four different strata: (1) part of the ruling class (or as a 'new ruling class'); (2) a 'new middle class'; (3) part of the working class (or a 'new working class'); or (4) an ambivalent and shifting group within the class structure. Which most accurately depicts the activities and interests of managers and technocrats in advanced capitalist societies?

New ruling class

Poulantzas (1975: 180) argued that managers, though non-owners of the means of production, direct the 'functions of capital' and participate in the decision-making process which directly leads to capital accumulation, making them 'an integral section of the bourgeoisie class'. Becker (1973–4) lumped the unproductive labour of managers with that of the ruling class, relegating managers to the lower rungs of the ruling class. Bell (1973) concluded that in the 'post-industrial society' technical and professional workers will become a 'new ruling class' based on their ability to accumulate and control specialized knowledge (intellectual capital). Viewed as either a subgroup of the ruling class or as their surrogates, the interests and motives of managers and technocrats parallel those of capital, minimizing the potential for sabotage.

New middle class

Another predominant perspective situates managers and technocrats within a loosely coupled group labelled the 'new middle class' (Carter, 1985; Burris; 1981; Carchedi, 1977). In the main, this class is distinct from capital and labour. Its members do not own or control the means of production, yet perform some activities that are objectively antagonistic to the working class. They are separate from and subordinate to capitalists, but are not in solidarity with labour. According to Carter:

> The organic unity of management and capital has been rup-
> tured. This is not to argue that a layer of management has

achieved proletarian status, but rather that management has polarized . . . to identify a clearer coalescence of the new middle class. This polarization means that even while carrying out the functions of capital, the new middle class has increasing need to defend itself against corporate capital.

(Carter 1985: 123)

In a further extension of the separate class theme, Ehrenreich and Ehrenreich (1979) proposed a new, distinct and emergent professional-managerial class (PMC) as a product of modern monopoly capitalism. They conceptually modelled a three-way polarization between capital, labour and the PMC – each antagonistic towards the others and each with its own interests. The potential for sabotage by these 'new middle class' actors is heightened as they seek ways to prevent encroachment by capital of their vested interests.

New working class

In a third perspective, managers and technocrats are identified with working-class interests. Movement away from theories of a unified elite class consisting of owners, managers and professionals towards a unified class consisting of workers, managers and technocrats is evident in the writings of some labour process theorists (Braverman, 1974; Thompson, 1988). The theme of the proletarianization of white-collar employees in capitalist societies has been extended to managers and technocrats. Systematic deskilling of white-collar work has narrowed the gap between managers, technocrats and workers. Thus, the interests and patterns of behaviour of labourers and white-collar employees converge as their employment is 'rationalized' and as the value of their labour product is 'cheapened'.

Consistent with this view is Freedman's (1975) two-class society where middle- and lower-level managers were grouped with the working class. In contrast, Becker (1973–4) postulated a cleavage between managers and administrative labour (i.e. technicians and professionals). While managers are located in the lower strata of the ruling class, administrative labour is 'not a part of managerial labor with which it is so often confused' but rather 'a part of the working class' (Becker, 1973–4: 276). According to Mallet (1975), increasing division of labour and automation have blurred the distinction between mental (unproductive) labour and manual (productive) labour, creating a new working class. Despite the fact that education and job autonomy place engineers, technicians and professionals in the vanguard of the new working class, in this perspective, their primary identification is with the interests of labour. This radical theoretical revision of the nature of managerial and technocratic work provides a strong rationale for anticipating sabotage as the ownership class stands in antagonistic opposition to the common interests of the non-owning classes. Even if the form of sabotage differs, exploitative practices by owners may be met with the same force of resistance by managers, technocrats and workers.

Ambivalent, shifting locations

In a fourth perspective, managers and technocrats are situated in a middle class, but their affiliations are complicated. Wright (1985) defined the class locations of managers and professionals as contradictory. There are positions in the middle class that are not simple to categorize as either capitalist or working class. Managers are exploiters (of labour) and exploited (by capital), dominators (of workers) and dominated (by capitalists), controllers (of organizational assets) and controlled (dispossessed of the means of production requiring the sale of their labour power to capital). This dual class character marks managerial positions as 'contradictory class locations'. This contradictory character is also evidenced by professionals since they enjoy substantial control over their work and exert power through their credentialled skills, but non-ownership of the means of production makes them able to be partially exploited and dominated (Wright, Costello, Hachen and Sprague, 1982).

Managerial identities and orientations

It has been argued that the contradictory and ambivalent class location of managerial and technocratic actors in modern capitalist societies has changed over time as their social stratum has evolved (Ehrenreich and Ehrenreich, 1979). Associated with this development, several forms of social orientation with ideological and political linkages have been identified (Peschanski, 1985). The social identities or orientations that may be assumed by members of the middle strata may be broadly classified as (1) corporate, (2) public good, (3) collegial/professional, (4) individual (self-centred) and (5) 'worker's' identity. It is recognized that groups or individuals with conflicting ideologies may be able to establish cooperative arrangements (e.g. political coalitions) or unify around some superordinate goal or ideology without resorting to aggressive or destructive behaviour. But, it is also reasonable to assume that these social orientations or identities may influence the work attitudes and behaviours of managerial and technocratic workers which may inspire varying degrees and forms of opposition and resistance. Sabotage potential may be conceptualized as a possible derivative of such orientations. This linkage is further discussed below and is depicted in Figure 7.1.

Low sabotage potential

A *corporate identity* is one where the manager or technocrat identifies closely with capital elites and is highly committed to the firm and its profitability. Implicit in this orientation is a deep sense of loyalty to corporate values and to the employer. High-level managers or corporate executives would be prototypes of this social orientation. Since, typically, the interests of this employee fully or very nearly coincide with capital, sabotage potential is hypothesized to be minimal.

Moderate sabotage potential

A *public good orientation* involves a broader view of the social responsibilities of the firm. Corporate commitments may conflict

Social identities	Alignment of interests	Sabotage potential
Corporate	Capital	Less likely
Public Good	Special interests	Moderate
Collegial/Professional		
Personal interests		
Workers	Labour	More likely

Figure 7.1 Relationships of managerial/technocratic orientations to class interests and sabotage potential

with the social consciousness and sense of loyalty to higher ideals held by these employees. Sometimes this results in a 'renunciation of commitment to the institution for the sake of the interests of society' (Peschanski, 1985: 252). Perrucci et al.'s (1980) case study of whistleblowing exemplifies this particular orientation as professionals jeopardized their careers and risked other reprisals to go 'outside their organizations to expose what they [felt were] illegal, inefficient, immoral or unethical practices of their employing organizations' (p. 149). Sabotage, like whistleblowing, may serve as a plausible and practical strategy for dealing with an intransigent organization which violates its members' ideals. It may serve as a symbolic form of protest and as an impetus for organizational change.

A *collegial or professional orientation* involves partial identification with the company and its interests, but closer identification with external colleagues or other professional/occupational referent groups. There is a shared system of values between the manager or professional and their external counterparts that transcends corporate values. A spirit of occupational collectivism undermines solidarity with capitalists' interests. This may lead to the formation of special interest groups, such as professional associations or white-collar unions. Managers and professionals with this orientation are not aligned with their employers or with workers. They emphasize independence and pursuit of their own collective agenda (Peschanski, 1985). The potential for sabotage is hypothesized to be moderate among managers and technocrats with this orientation.

Individual (self-centred) identities may be cultivated that are separate and distinct from work-centred values. One's job may be viewed in purely instrumental terms, as a means to achieve non-work goals. The manager or technocrat with this orientation may be psychologically distant from the work role and demonstrate reduced commitment to the employing organization. This attitude of managers was described in the study by Scase and Goffee:

> [they are] more inclined to define their jobs in almost instrumental, non-affective terms; as sources of income for achieving self-fulfillment outside employment. It ceases to offer psychological rewards and no longer acts as the pivot around which non-work activities and personal relationships are organized.
>
> (Scase and Goffee, 1989: 14)

Organizational conditions that threaten these personally vested

237

interests coupled with reduced loyalty to the firm and loss of work purpose may lead individuals with this type of orientation to participate in some forms of sabotage.

High sabotage potential

A '*workers*' *orientation* is typical of lower-level supervisors or certain semi-professional groups, such as technicians and foremen. Their interests are closely aligned with the working class. Peschanski (1985: 251) defines this orientation as 'a more or less complete departure of managers from their identification with the company and, conversely, by the identification of their interests with those of the mass of employees'. Individuals with this orientation would be more inclined to utilize resistance tactics (including sabotage) similar to those historically used by the working class.

Traditional strong managerial ties with capital have been loosened in favour of advancing their own interests or adopting one of the other alternative identities discussed above. As indicated by Peschanski:

> The confrontation between managers and managed, rank-and-file workers, cannot disappear under capitalism, though it may attenuate considerably and is already attenuating. At the same time, changes occurring in the attitudes of managerial cadres create opportunities for an alliance with them or, at least, for a drift of a significant part of them from pro-capitalist to 'neutral' positions. . . . Their orientation to their own social group is progressing, while identification with the boss, the employing organization, is weakening.
>
> (Peschanski, 1985: 253)

Summary and conclusion

We have drawn on neoclassical, managerialist, and modern social-class analyses to describe the nature of managerial and technocratic interests. Many of the issues discussed remain unresolved and subject to further debate and analysis. We do not propose a resolution of these controversial views. We have argued that the interests of managers and technocrats often may not intersect with those of capitalists and could even be diametrically opposed to them. This possibility has been evident in the critiques of neoclassical thought, in the 'managerialist' literature (i.e. separation of ownership and control) and in much of the modern social-class analysis reviewed.

Managers and professionals can form alliances with capital or labour (Wright, 1985). Alternatively, they can remain aloof and either act to serve their own interests in the spirit of 'sectional managerialism' or act to promote and advance the public interest in a variant of 'non-sectional managerialism' (Scott, 1985: 19). Even if a firm allegiance to the interests of capital is demonstrated, members that occupy these middle-class positions may be subjected to dramatic transformations in the nature of their work from forces within as well as external to the firm that may result in conduct contrary to capitalists' interests.

Divergent and often opposing interests coupled with their ambiguous class locations suggest that representations of managers and technocrats as highly tractable and controlled may be misleading. Characterizing managers and technocrats as actors engaged in workplace struggles and conflicts, sometimes in harmony with shifting capital accumulation exigencies, sometimes resisting control and domination by capital elites, may provide a more realistic image of organizational life.

In fact, sabotage potential may vary widely across localized settings and historical contexts because of the multiplicity of patterns of interests and identities that can emerge among these actors. Even though we propose, in the abstract, that the interests of managers and technocrats may align with capital or labour but not both, in local situations and varied historical contexts, interests of all participants are best understood as tendencies that can shift rapidly and that are riddled with contradiction. Thus, in general, managers and technocrats aligned with labour interests are more likely to have reason to use sabotage than are those aligned with capital or special interests. Still, this leads us to conclude only that allegiance to local, situated interests determines sabotage potential, not that it is possible to know in any objective, *a priori* sense what the interests of all labourers or capital owners might be. Nor can we conclude that their interests are always totally irreconcilable. Our framework advances a semi-voluntaristic actor whose 'true' interests are unknowable, and whose practical interests may shift as the result of struggles and accommodations among class-based coalitions.

TYPOLOGY OF SABOTAGE BY MANAGERS AND TECHNOCRATS

Earlier sections proposed the theme that managerial and technocratic actors may have sufficient motive to engage in workplace sabotage. Further, several work and job characteristics of these 'gold-collar' [knowledge] workers (Kelley, 1985) may facilitate various forms of resistance, including sabotage (1) detailed understanding of organizational systems, processes and procedures, (2) specialized knowledge bases, (3) macro perspective on interdependencies between sub-systems that reveal points of vulnerability, (4) considerable degree of behavioural latitude and (5) ease of access to records and other data, machinery, raw materials, finished products, confidential information and other organizational assets. This combination of motive, know-how, availability of resources and accessibility makes organizations (and society) particularly susceptible to potential acts of managerial or technocratic sabotage.

At this juncture, this chapter has not addressed several key questions. Are all acts of sabotage the same? If not, what types exist? What are the characteristics of each type? While sabotage has been extensively used as a catch-all term, it is important for researchers to define clearly its conceptual boundaries. We propose a typology that depicts two major forms of managerial/technocratic sabotage: (1) sabotage by circumvention and (2) sabotage by direct action (Figure 7.2).

Sabotage by circumvention (SC) describes a range of behaviours (from deliberate inaction/inattention to verbal/written actions) that serve as catalysts, setting into motion events or situations that may be potentially harmful to the organization's reputation, efficiency, effectiveness or competitiveness. Consequences of these events triggered by the SC behaviours are not entirely predictable. SC is initiated in a more roundabout fashion either through failure to act (letting events take their course) or through reliance on other internal or external parties' actions. There are three variations of SC behaviours: (a) non-cooperation, (b) open-mouth, and (c) falsification of data.

(a) Non-cooperative behaviours. There are at least five major manifestations of non-cooperative activities that may be identified: (1) deliberate failure to adhere to established policies, procedures and rules leading to organizational harm (e.g. increased machine-breaking by irregular observance of safety or maintenance checks or

TYPES OF SABOTAGE

Differentiating characteristics	SABOTAGE BY CIRCUMVENTION	SABOTAGE BY DIRECT ACTION
	Examples:	*Examples:*
	• Non-cooperation • Open-mouth • Falsification of data	Physical damage to property, data or product
Risk of detection	Low risk	Moderate/high risk
Frequency of occurrence	High	Low
Potential consequences in terms of:		
• Damage	More localized; intra-organizational	Greater potential for extra-organizational effects
• Timing	Delayed	Immediate
• Predictability	Less certain	Greater certainty
Perceived justifiability	Reasonable	Unreasonable

Figure 7.2 Typology of managerial/technocratic sabotage

degradation of product through poor quality control); (2) knowingly withholding relevant or critical information, such as competitive or technological data, from the organization; (3) intentionally allowing or condoning other employees to engage in destructive or damaging behaviours; (4) 'malicious obedience' or over-conforming to superiors' orders or organizational rules with the intent of impeding organizational efficiency; and (5) deliberate inattention to areas of responsibility leading to damage or destruction of property. Given the responsibility entrusted to these actors by the organization and their relative positional and professional status, these behaviours are particularly significant.

(b) Open-mouth sabotage behaviours. In this form of SC, the saboteur participates in verbal sabotage. It may be directed at three diverse target audiences:

1 Competitors: the deliberate revelation of sensitive or proprietary company information to competitor(s).
2 Customers/Clients: intentional denigration of the organization or its product and services to current or prospective customers/clients.
3 Employees: purposeful promulgation of negative, derogatory or malicious remarks about the organization to employees with the intent to decrease productivity through low morale or increased absenteeism and turnover.

Open-mouth sabotage becomes highly significant when members of the target audiences use the information provided in ways that will damage the organization's competitive posture or its productivity.

(c) Data falsification behaviours. Another form of SC is the wilful fabrication or provision of erroneous data for financial, operational and other key reports. Analogous to the impact of sabotage by the 'blue-collar' worker in disrupting the smooth flow of the assembly line, the managerial or technocratic saboteur can deliberately attempt to impede the decision-making process. Again, the effectiveness of these behaviours depends on others in key decision-making capacities accepting and acting upon the falsified data.

Sabotage by direct action (SDA) describes technocratic or managerial behaviours that physically damage, mutilate or destroy organizational property or product. The consequences of SDA may range from relatively minor physical destruction to catastrophic damage. Most often the damage is usually restrained or limited such that the symbolic impact usually exceeds the economic loss. But certain technologies have been characterized as non-linear and tightly coupled (Perrow, 1984). Sabotage of these complex technologies contain the potential for catastrophic destruction and damage. SDA in high-risk technological systems can result in organizational and societal crises since some technologies have become so interrelated and complex that even relatively minor destruction or damage in much lower subsystems can produce total system malfunctions that threaten society at large.

Physical destruction or damage in three distinct areas of the organization may be identified:

1 Property: this area includes all the physical assets or resources of an organization such as machinery, office equipment or physical plant.
2 Data: this includes all the records (manual or computerized), generated or maintained by the organization.
3 Product or service: the organization's product or service may be damaged, destroyed or undermined. Deliberately developing inferior designs or intentionally allowing defective goods to pass inspection serve as examples in this area.

Distinguishing characteristics of SC and SDA

What are some of the main characteristics that distinguish the various types of workplace sabotage? One key dimension is risk of detection. In most SC behaviours, the risk of detection is virtually non-existent. These behaviours, even if detected, are usually attributed to discipline problems or poor work performance. But normally there is little to fear in terms or sanctions or reprisals. As actors engage in SDA, there is an increased probability the saboteur may be exposed and legal or organizational sanctions imposed. However, dismissal of workers suspected of sabotage is usually a remote possibility (Jermier, 1988).

Another distinguishing characteristic between types of managerial/ technocratic sabotage is frequency of use. Many SC behaviours are rather routine occurrences in organizations. In a recent survey of more than 400 professionals and managers, it was reported that one out of every three managers is sabotaged on the job by engineers and other 'gold-collar' workers through work slowdowns, circumventing the manager in the decision-making process or deliberately filtering or withholding information needed by higher management (*Machine Design*, 10 May 1990). SDA tends to occur less frequently and usually under selective conditions.

A third differentiating feature between SC and SDA behaviour is the potential consequences resulting from these behaviours. Three aspects may be considered in this area: extent of damage; timing of outcomes; and predictability. The potential effects of SC behaviours tend to be more localized with the resulting impacts bounded within intra-organizational limits. While SDA may also have significant intra-organizational effects, the potential for catastrophic disaster (such as in high-risk technologies) reaches well beyond organizational boundaries and may have significant social implications in terms of environmental, human and technological costs. The timing for anticipated organizational damage for SC is delayed as intervening events are required for the damage to occur. The intervening actions of others (such as for clients, competitors or co-workers to act in prescribed ways) or by allowing events to occur due to deliberate inattention or rule-breaking create uncertainty in the final expected outcomes stemming from SC. In contrast, the consequences stemming from SDA are more immediate. As more direct control for damage is in the hands of the saboteur, the probability that the expected damage occurs as intended is enhanced.

Finally, the perceived justifiability (reasonableness or unreasonableness) of the actions needs to be considered.[3] Certain sabotage behaviours, such as those exemplified under SC, may be more readily accepted as justifiable by employees and outsiders. SDA will more likely be viewed as socially undesirable irrespective of the saboteur's motives or circumstances surrounding the particular incident. This may be because SC is perceived in a qualitatively different light than SDA. Analogous to the distinction made between 'white-collar' crime and violent criminal activity, SC episodes may be more readily accepted as 'soft' types of sabotage versus the 'hard-core' types where the individual resorts to physically destructive acts. Also, activities that have the potential to endanger the lives, quality of life or the livelihood of others (as in SDA behaviours) will generally be seen as socially undesirable and unacceptable by most observers. Behaviours that are limited to some moderate form of retaliation against one's boss or the company will be more easily justified as 'fair game'. If the actual physical damage is extensive or overwhelming, it is likely to be perceived as unjustified since the symbolism of the act is overshadowed by the act itself.

Reasons for sabotage

To differentiate sabotage behaviours, it is also necessary to reflect on the intent of the saboteur's actions. This intent may take two forms: (1) attempts to change the system or (2) attempts to cope with the existing system.

Sabotage may be used as a mechanism of change to equalize power imbalances, reassert greater control in the workplace, rectify perceived injustices, and so on. Some acts of sabotage are demonstrative in nature, making a symbolic statement of protest against certain values or system conditions (Dubois, 1979; Jermier, 1988). Sabotage aimed at change may range from seeking incremental improvements at the workplace to more radical changes in organizational or societal conditions. Incremental sabotage is not directed at an immediate result but rather serves as a subtle reminder of injustices, contestable organizational values or the existence of possible alternative work systems (cf. Dubois, 1979). The scope of radical sabotage is more ambitious and extreme as the saboteur seeks to destroy the system and begin anew.

Sabotage may also be intended to cope with immediate workplace problems. Reasons for employee sabotage, such as self-defence, revenge, release of frustrations, prankish antics (Giacalone and Rosenfeld, 1987), facilitation of work processes (Taylor and Walton, 1971), or the thrill of 'beating the system' are indicative of these coping mechanisms. These types of coping behaviours serve to satisfy the more specific, immediate and limited concerns or needs of the employee. In reaching a sociological understanding of managerial/technocratic sabotage, both the behaviours and the underlying motives must be examined.

CONCLUSION

Existing research on workplace sabotage has been largely descriptive and impressionistic in nature, somewhat lacking in methodological rigour, and focused on a narrow slice of employees and organizational settings (Jermier, 1988). Throughout this chapter, argument and some evidence have been presented to suggest that sabotage is not practised exclusively by working-class employees but is also practised by managers and technocrats. Managers and technocrats have sufficient motive to resist corporate demands and undermine the productive process. Alliances among managers, technocrats and capital elites have deteriorated. It is feasible that as 'new middle class' interests are articulated, further departure from the interests of capital may result, leading to more organized opposition by some managers and technocrats. While Jermier (1988) advanced workplace sabotage as a core component of working-class culture, it may also be an increasingly relevant facet of 'gold-collar' culture especially in light of the changes to managerial and technocratic work discussed earlier. Based on historical precedence and positional status, professionals have been instilled with relatively high job and personal expectations. As these expectations are left unfulfilled and unsatisfied, resistance behaviours may become more evident among these actors. While workers have historically had other means to resolve work issues and disputes (e.g. labour contracts, grievance procedures, threat of strikes), professionals have traditionally had fewer channels available to them to address their interests. When there are few legitimate means available to handle issues and concerns, affected individuals or groups may resort to the use of other tactics to advance their interests, such as resistance, aggression or sabotage.

If conceptualized appropriately, sabotage may be seen as a strategic weapon that can be used by any organizational actor to revise power imbalances or seek to re-establish control of their work and workplace. Often, it symbolically tells a story of exploitation and alienation, opposition and resistance.

Generally, workplace sabotage has been neglected as a research topic. This chapter raises another closely related and pertinent line of enquiry for inclusion on future research agendas. Understanding the methods, underlying motives and symbolic meanings of workplace sabotage by managerial and technocratic elites (and how they converge or diverge with lower level employees) suggests new and potentially exciting research avenues for advancing studies of resistance in organizations. The struggles and patterns of resistance of these more privileged workers in contemporary organizations suggest new meanings to the 'contested terrain' imagery (Edwards, 1979).

How should research in this area proceed? Some researchers (e.g. Giacalone and Rosenfeld, 1987) suggest that sabotage is a management problem and that future research should proceed to help management identify and deter the potential saboteur. In our view, this approach would lead researchers to treat symptoms rather than the disease itself, since it does not consider root causes of sabotage and exonerates management from any blame for these deeds. In contrast, we propose research in specific contexts that examines closely the interests and allegiances of managerial and technocratic actors and assesses their sabotage potential. Given the vast heterogeneity of managers and technocrats, the contradictory and shifting interests of class actors in organizational settings, and the rapidly changing nature of capitalist corporations, we think a strong argument can be developed to extend theoretical models of control and resistance beyond the interfaces between labourers and capital elites. In some circumstances, some managers and technocrats in the contemporary corporation develop and hold orientations, however temporarily, that separate them from the goals and interests of profit-maximizing capital elites. These orientations are the well-springs of open dissent and protest, but also of sabotage, a phenomenon not yet well-represented in resistance studies.

NOTES

1 The private sector is the focus of the arguments developed in this chapter, but the writers recognize that managerial/technocratic sabotage may also occur in the public sector. While sabotage behaviours between both sectors may be similar, the underlying motivations of each may have quite different origins. Space limitations preclude addressing public-sector organizations in this chapter.

2 For a comprehensive review of sabotage literature, see Jermier (1988).

3 As noted by Jermier (1988), the theoretical distinction between reasonable (principled) sabotage and unreasonable (stigmatized) sabotage may appear to be clear but the distinction is often blurred as events unfold. As individuals (groups) with vested interests (e.g. labour or management) attempt to impose their version of reality on others and turn events to their advantage, other processes (political, social and media) often intervene to force a negotiated reality. In this process, issues of morality, legality, rationality and social costs (though essential to piece together a comprehensive perspective on the justification of the destructive act) are publicly suppressed or compromised.

REFERENCES

Alchian, A. A. (1965) 'The Basis of Some Recent Advances in the Theory of Management of the Firm', *Journal of Industrial Economics* 14: 30–41.

Allen, V. L. and Greenberger, D. B. (1980) 'Destruction and Perceived Control', A. Baum and J. E. Singer (eds) *Advances in Environmental Psychology*, Hillsdale, NJ: Erlbaum, vol. 2, pp. 85–109.

Bandura, A. (1973) *Aggression: A Social Analysis*, Englewood Cliffs, NJ: Prentice-Hall.

Baron, R. (1984) *Human Aggression*, New York: Plenum Press.

Baumol, W. (1959) *Business Behavior, Value and Growth*, New York: Macmillan.

Bazerman, M. (1982) 'Impact of Personal Control on Performance: Is Added Control Always Beneficial?' *Journal of Applied Psychology* 67: 472–9.

Becker, J.F. (1973–4) 'Class Structure and Conflict in the Managerial Phase', *Science and Society*, Part I, 37 (Fall): 250–77; Part II, 38 (Winter): 437–53.

Bell, D. (1957) 'The Breakup of Family Capitalism', in D. Bell (ed.) *The End of Ideology*, New York: Collier-Macmillan.

Bell, D. (1973) *The Coming of Postindustrial Society*, New York: Basic Books.

Benquai, A. (1978) *Computer Crime*, Lexington, MA: Lexington Books.

Berkowitz, L. (1983) 'Aversely Stimulated Aggression: Some Parallels in Research with Animals and Humans', *American Psychologist* 38: 1135–44.

Berkowitz, L. (1988) 'Frustrations, Appraisals, and Adversely Stimulated Aggression', *Aggressive Behaviour* 14: 3–11.

Berkowitz, L. (1989) 'Frustration–Aggression Hypothesis: Examination and Reformulation', *Psychological Bulletin* 106 (1): 59–73.

Berkowitz, L. and Heimer, K. (1989) 'On the Construction of the Anger Experience: Aversive Events and Negative Priming in the Formation of Feelings', in L. Berkowitz (ed.) *Advances in Experimental Social Psychology*, New York: Academic Press, vol. 22, pp. 1–37.

Berle, A. A. and Means, G. C. (1932) *The Modern Corporation and Private Property*, New York: Macmillan.

Bjorn-Andersen, N. and Kjaergaard, D. (1987) 'Choices en Route to the Office of Tomorrow', in R. E. Kraut (ed.) *Technology and the Transformation of White-Collar Work*, Hillsdale, NJ: Lawrence Erlbaum.

Boulding, K. (1950) *A Reconstruction of Economics*, New York: Wiley.

Braverman, H. (1974) *Labour and Monopoly Capital: The Degradation of Work in the Twentieth Century*, New York: Monthly Review Press.

Brown, G. (1977) *Sabotage: A Study of Industrial Conflict*. Nottingham: Spokesman Books.

Burawoy, M. (1979) *Manufacturing Consent: Changes in the Labour Process under Monopoly Capitalism*, Chicago: University of Chicago Press.

Burnham, J. (1941) *The Managerial Revolution*, Harmondsworth: Penguin.

Burris, V. (1981) 'Capital Accumulation and the Rise of the New Middle Class', *Review of Radical Political Economics* 12: 17–34.

Carchedi, G. (1977) *On the Economic Identification of Social Classes*, London: Routledge & Kegan Paul.

Carter, B. (1985) *Capitalism, Class Conflict and the New Middle Class*, London: Routledge & Kegan Paul.

Chamot, D. (1987) 'Electronic Work and the White-Collar Employee', in Robert E. Kraut (ed.) *Technology and the Transformation of White-Collar Work*, Hillsdale, NJ: Lawrence Erlbaum, pp. 23–33.

Chandler, A. D. (1990) *Scale and Scope: The Dynamics of Industrial Capitalism*, Cambridge, MA: Harvard University Press.

Clark, J. M. (1923) *The Economics of Overhead Costs*, Chicago: University of Chicago Press.

Cohen, A. (1955) 'Social Norms, Arbitrariness of Frustration, and Status of the Agent of Frustration in the Frustration-Aggression Hypothesis', *Journal of Abnormal and Social Psychology*, 51: 222–6.

Cooley, M. J. E. (1977) 'Taylor in the Office', in R. N. Ottaway (ed.) *Humanizing Work*, London: Croom Helm, pp. 50–85.

de Charms, R. (1968) *Personal Causation*, New York: Academic Press.

Derber, C. (1982) *Professionals as Workers: Mental Labour in Advanced Capitalism*, Boston: G. K. Hall.

Ditton, J. (1979) 'Baking Time', *Sociological Review* 27: 157–67.

Dollard, K., Doob, L., Miller, N. Mowrer, O., and Sears, R. (1939) *Frustration and Aggression*, New Haven, CT: Yale University Press.

Dubois, P. (1979) *Sabotage in Industry*, Harmondsworth: Penguin.

Edwards, P. K. and Scullion, H. (1982) *The Social Organization of Industrial Conflict: Control and Resistance in the Workplace*, Oxford: Blackwell.

Edwards, R. (1979) *Contested Terrain: The Transformation of the Workplace in the Twentieth Century*, New York: Basic Books.

Ehrenreich, B. and Ehrenreich, J. (1979) 'The Professional Managerial Class', in P. Walker (ed.) *Between Labor and Capital*, Boston: South End Press, pp. 5–45.

Elderidge, J. E. T. (1968) *Industrial Disputes*, London Routledge & Kegan Paul.

Fennell, D. (1976) 'Beneath the Surface: The Life of a Factory', *Radical America* 10(5): 15–29.

Freedman, F. (1975) 'The Internal Structure of the Proletariat: A Marxist Analysis', *Socialist Revolution* 5(26): 41–8

Friedman, A.L. (1977) *Industry and Labour*, London: Macmillan Press.

Giacalone, R. A. and Rosenfeld, P. (1987) 'Reasons for Employee Sabotage in the Workplace', *Journal of Business and Psychology* 1(4): 367–78.

Greenberger, D. and Strasser, S. (1986) 'The Development and Application of a Model of Personal Control in Organizations', *Academy of Management Review*, 2: 164–77.

Greenberger, D., Strasser, S., Cummings, L. and Dunham, R. (1989) 'The Impact of Personal Control on Performance and Satisfaction', *Organizational Behavior and Human Decision Processes*, 43: 29–51.

Hall, R.L. and Hitch, C.J. (1939) 'Price Theory and Business Behaviour', *Oxford Economic Papers* 2: 12–45.

Haug, M. (1973) 'Deprofessionalization: An Alternative Hypothesis for the Future', in P. Halmos (ed.) *Professionalization and Social Change*, Social Monograph 20, University of Keele.

Helfgott, R. (1988) *Computerized Manufacturing and Human Resources*. Lexington, MA: D.C. Heath, Lexington Books.

Hirshleifer, J. (1984) *Price Theory and Applications*, Englewood Cliffs, N. J.: Prentice-Hall.

Hicks, J. R. (1935) 'Annual Survey of Economic Theory: The Theory of Monopoly', *Econometrica* 3: 1–10.

Hollinger, R. and Clark, J. (1982) 'Employee Deviance: A Response to the Perceived Quality of the Work Experience', *Work and Occupations* 9: 97–114.

Jenkins, C. and Sherman, B. (1979) *White-Collar Unionism: The Rebellious Salariat*, London: Routledge & Kegan Paul.

Jermier, J. M. (1988) 'Sabotage at Work: The Rational View', *Research in the Sociology of Organizations* 6: 101–34.

Kiesler, S. (1984) 'Computer Mediation of Communication', *American Psychologist* 39: 1123–34.

Kelley, R. E. (1985) *The Gold Collar Worker: Harnessing the Brainpower of the New Workforce*, Reading, MA: Addison-Wesley.

King, R. (1978) 'In the Sanding Booth at Ford', J. Perry and E. Perry (eds) *Social Problems in Today's World*, Boston: Little, Brown, & Company, pp. 199–205.

Langer, E. J. (1975) 'The Illusion of Control', *Journal of Personality and Social Psychology* 32(2): 311–28.

Lenski, G. (1966) *Power and Privilege* New York: McGraw-Hill.

Lumley, R. (1973) *White-Collar Unionism in Britain*, London: Methuen.

Machine Design (1990) 'Managing the New Workforce', 10 May, pp. 109–13.

Mallet, S. (1975) *Essays on the New Working Class*, St Louis: Telos Press.

Mangione, T. W. and Quinn, R. P. (1975) 'Job Satisfaction, Conterproductive Behavior and Drug Use at Work', *Journal of Applied Psychology* 60(1): 114–16.

Marshall, Alfred (1920) *Principles of Economics*, London: Macmillan.

Martinko, M. and Gardner, W. (1982) 'Learned Helplessness: An Alternative Explanation for Performance Deficits', *Academy of Management Review* 7: 195–204.

Molstad, C. (1986) 'Choosing and Coping with Boring Work', *Urban Life* 15(2): 215–36.

Montgomery, D. (1979) *Workers' Control in America*, Cambridge: Cambridge University Press.

Mulligan, T. (1986) 'A Critique of Milton Friedman's Essay "The social responsibility of business is to increase its profits" ', *Journal of Business Ethics* 5: 265–9.

Nordquist, G. L. (1965) 'The Breakup of the Maximization Principle', *Quarterly Review of Economics and Business* 5: 33–46.

Nunan, R. (1988) 'The Libertarian Conception of Corporate Property: A Critique of Milton Friedman's Views on the Social Responsibility of Business', *Journal of Business Ethics* 7: 891–906.

Oppenheimer, M. (1985) *White Collar Politics*, New York: Monthly Review Press.

Parsons, T. (1954) *Essays in Sociological Theory*, Glencoe, IL: Free Press.

Pastore, N. (1952) 'The Role of Arbitrariness in the Frustration–Aggression Hypothesis', *Journal of Abnormal and Social Psychology* 47: 728–31.

Perrow, C. (1984) *Normal Accidents: Living with High Risk Technologies*, New York: Basic Books.

Perrucci, R., Anderson, R., Schendel, D., and Trachtman, L. (1980) 'Whistleblowing: Professionals' Resistance to Organizational Authority', *Social Problems* 28: 149–64.

Peschanski, V. V. (1985) 'Middle Managers in Contemporary Capitalism', *Acta Sociologica* 28: 243–5.

Poulantzas, N. (1975) *Class in Contemporary Capitalism*, London: New Left Books.

Salaman, G. (1979) *Work Organizations: Resistance and Control*, London: Longman.

Scase, R. and Goffee, R. (1989) *Reluctant Managers: Their Work and Lifestyles*, London: Unwin Hyman

Scott, J. (1985) *Corporations, Classes and Capitalism*, London: Hutchinson.

Scott, J. C. (1985) *Weapons of the Weak: Everyday Forms of Peasant Resistance*, New Haven: Yale University Press.

250

Seligman, M. (1975) *Helplessness: On Depression, Development and Death*, San Francisco: Freeman.

Smith, V. (1990) *Managing in the Corporate Interest: Control and Resistance in an American Bank*, Berkeley: University of California Press.

Spector, P. E. (1975) Relationships of Organizational Frustration with Reported Behavior Reactions of Employees', *Journal of Applied Psychology* 60(5): 635–7.

Taylor, L. and Walton, P. (1971) 'Industrial Sabotage: Motives and Meanings', in S. Cohen (ed.) *Images of Deviance*, Harmondsworth: Penguin, pp. 219–45.

Thompson, E. P. (1978) 'Eighteenth-century English Society: Class Struggle without Class?' *Social History* 3: 133–65.

Thompson, P. (1988) *The Nature of Work: An Introduction to Debates on the Labour Process*, Atlantic Highlands, NJ: Humanities Press International.

Thompson, S. (1981) 'Will It Hurt Less if I Can Control It? A Complex Answer to a Simple Question', *Psychological Bulletin* 90: 89–101.

Thompson, W. E. (1983) 'Hanging Tongues: A Sociological Encounter with the Assembly Line', *Qualitative Sociology* 6(3): 215–37.

Watson, B. (1971) 'Counter-Planning on the Shop Floor', *Radical America* 5(3): 77–85.

Wright, E. O. (1985) *Classes*, London: Verso.

Wright, E. O., Costello, C., Hachen, D. and Sprague, J. (1982) 'The American Class Structure', *American Sociological Review* 47: 709–26.

Zabala, C. A. (1985) 'Sabotage in an Automotive Assembly Plant', in N. Lichtenstein and S. Meyer (eds) *The American Automobile Industry: A Social History* Urbana-Champaign: University of Illinois Press (preprinted mimeo, 41 pp.)

Zeitlin, M. (1974) 'Corporate Ownership and Control: The Large Corporation and Capitalist Class', *American Journal of Sociology*, 79: 1073–119.

Zillmann, D. (1979) *Hostility and Aggression*. Hillsdale, NJ: Erlbaum.

Zuboff, S. (1982) 'Problems of Symbolic Toil', *Dissent* 29: 51–61.

8

WHISTLEBLOWING AS RESISTANCE IN MODERN WORK ORGANIZATIONS

The politics of revealing organizational deception and abuse

Joyce Rothschild and Terance D. Miethe

This chapter brings to the literature on worker resistance the important and increasingly prevalent example of whistleblowing. We show that whistleblowing is a bottom-up method by which subordinates are challenging, and sometimes changing, organizational abuses that are directed or neglected by their superiors. In this way, we also bring to the literature on whistleblowing the insight that it can be viewed as political behaviour. Our analysis is dialetical. In brief, we argue that manager reprisals, intended to quiet the potential whistleblower, may actually serve to transform and politicize the individual. In the final analysis, it is in the process of opposing misconduct and fighting unjust reprisals that individual whistle-blowers come to distance themselves from what they see as elites' corrupt practices and to assert their own dignity and integrity.

INTRODUCTION

For the better part of a century, sociologists have concentrated their attention on the question of how systems of domination are established and sustained. Grounded in the seminal work of Max Weber, organizational studies have repeatedly shown how the hierarchical relations and the formal rules and procedures of bureaucracy can be harnessed to effect managerial control. Similarly, beginning with the work of Karl Marx, political and economic sociologists have demonstrated how the process of capital accumulation over time results in ever greater control over both ideological and material resources in fewer hands. Drawing from both traditions, some of the most influential contemporary works on industrial relations have depicted how comprehensive and impenetrable is managerial control in the

252

twentieth-century capitalist workplace (Braverman, 1974; Burawoy, 1979; Edwards, 1979).

As important as these works have been in emphasizing the structural basis of top-down control in modern work organizations, they have made their point at the cost of overlooking those crevices in the system, at the very point of production, where workers can and do resist, and seek to change, the way that work will be carried out. Bottom–up resistance can take many forms such as outright sabotage (Jermier, 1988), work avoidance strategies (Molsted, 1988) or whistleblowing. While whistleblowing has heretofore been overlooked in the literature on worker control, we argue in this article that modern economic organizations have created conditions in which whistleblowing is rapidly becoming a more prominent strategy by which non-supervisory employees assert influence in the workplace and actually halt specific abuses to themselves and the public. In so arguing, this study lends support to the growing focus in the sociology of work and organizations on 'worker agency' – the capacity of workers to influence the process and terms of production (Hodson, 1992; Wardell, 1992).

The perspectives and conclusions developed in this chapter are based on ongoing research we are conducting on whistleblowing in a variety of organizational settings. To date, we have collected data from three sources. First, the National Association of Social Work allowed us to examine their archival records on grievance cases for violations of codes of ethics in social work agencies. After reviewing all grievance cases, we identified and made detailed field notes on twelve cases of whistleblowing among these social workers. Second, semi-structured interviews were conducted with six persons who attended a retreat on whistleblowing. These interviews lasted anywhere between one hour and eight hours. We feature especially the insights of two key informants at this retreat, who were interviewed at length about their whistleblowing experiences. These two were chosen, one a professional employee and the other a blue-collar employee, as prototypical whistleblowers. Third, 36 persons have completed a ten-page survey about exposing misconduct in their workplaces. By comparing our results with those obtained from other studies, we can identify the impact of sampling limitations on our substantive conclusions. However, we must acknowledge that the individuals we have so far interviewed or surveyed are whistleblowers whose criticisms escalated into grievances. No doubt there are employees in organizations who bring internal criticisms and who meet with a more constructive response, and they never become labelled as 'whistleblowers'.

The current study begins with an examination of whistleblowing as a form of political resistance in the workplace. We then identify reasons why some workers 'speak up' in the face of strong pressures to remain silent. One reason for speaking up has to do with changes in the occupational structure of a modern economy that, we argue, unwittingly stimulate whistleblowing. The essence of our argument is that it is the ordeal of reporting misconduct and the experience of suffering reprisals that transforms and politicizes the individual. The chapter concludes with a discussion of the potential efficacy of whistleblowing as a bottom-up method of resistance in work organizations.

WHISTLEBLOWING AS POLITICAL RESISTANCE

It is important we believe to take a definition of whistleblowing that is inclusive of both internal and external disclosures, for either can be a form of worker efforts to change the practices of the employing organization. Therefore, we have chosen to define whistleblowing as the disclosure of illegal, unethical or harmful practices in the workplace to parties who might take action. Note that the disclosure can be to superordinates within the employing organization or to authorities outside the organization who are in a position to help such as a journalist, an attorney-general, or a regulatory agency that has oversight responsibility.

Unlike other forms of worker protest discussed in this volume which may be horizonal (e.g. where workers go to their peers), whistleblowers, by definition, must go either up the system or outside the organization. When workers see some practice in their organization that concerns them, they have a number of options. First, they can do nothing. Alternatively, they make take 'private' action such as going to co-workers, spouses or friends to grouse about the situation. However, their concerns never become a public issue and they cannot lead to social change unless they go up the organizational hierarchy, outside the company, or both. As revealed in our interviews and previous research (see Glazer and Glazer, 1989), employees generally begin by reporting their observations up the line in the belief that if senior managers knew of the abusive or illegal practice, they would surely intervene to end it. Only when they see that management is inert, complacent or themselves implicated in the wrongdoing, do they consider going outside the organization with their information.

While there may be many personal motives for reporting illegal activity, whistleblowing needs to be viewed as a political act. Indeed, the most glaringly obvious and perhaps significant finding that emerges from our research is that *whistleblowing is political behaviour.* From the start, it is intended to change the way that the work gets done in the organization, often in ways that restrain management's ability to garner profits or to control workers' behaviour. *Management's response to the whistleblowing act is also often political.* It is intended to discredit the whistleblower and any others who may be harbouring similar inclinations. Also, it is intended to neutralize the power of any information they may release. Missing from the extensive academic and popular discussion of whistleblowing, however, has been a political perspective: viewing it as a strategy by which subordinates of public and private organizations try to turn the tables on the power holders.

As Thompson (1968) has emphasized in his study of the working class, class identities do not develop in a vacuum and they cannot be assumed. It is only in the process of struggle that working people develop a class identity or consciousness. Our argument is parallel to Thompson's in two respects. First, it is the ordeal and struggle for vindication that generally follows the whistleblowing event that transforms the consciousness of whistleblowers. Insofar as they come to see that their original observation of misconduct was only a piece of more chronic or system-wide corruption, they become more politicized in their perspective. As their critical observations of 'something wrong' go from a sub-unit of an organization to the full organization and finally to the nation-state as a whole, they sometimes join a social movement, connecting their own discovered criticism to collective protest. Second, in the process of struggle to overcome reprisals, whistleblowers often come to morally repudiate managers, a class of people with whom they may have previously identified, and to identify instead with other workers in their own class whose actual work they may come to more greatly value and dignify. In these two ways we will be drawing a dialectical analysis of whistleblowing.

Rather than highlighting its political nature, academic works tend to focus on whistleblowing as an example of ethical expression in organizations (Westin, 1981; Brabeck, 1984; Elliston, 1982), as an assertion of professional responsibility (Greenberger, *et al.*, 1987;

Glazer and Glazer, 1989), as arising out of deeply held religious or humanistic values (Glazer and Glazer, 1989), or as a miscalculation of the costs (Miceli and Near, 1985). Meanwhile, managers tend to view whistleblowers as troublemakers or as crazy. Glazer and Glazer (1989) and Graham (1986) see in whistleblowing an act of conscience, but no one has seen in these burgeoning whistleblower grievances the stuff of which social movements are built. As in all social movements, whistleblowing has an expressive side *and* an instrumental side. While the previous authors are correct to see in this phenomenon the expressive side of dissent, we should not be blind to the instrumental (political) side as well. Whistleblowers are trying in their disclosures to change specific organizational practices that they find harmful or illegal, and sometimes, after considerable organizational learning, they may be trying to change 'the system'. For example, whistleblowing employees may begin by trying to end workers' exposure to toxic conditions on the shopfloor or toxic dumping in their communities; later, they may join the wider environmental movement.

Virtually all political behaviour and social movements are rooted in values, in people's sense of right and wrong. Political opposition develops when there is a values-based challenge to elites' ways of running things. Whistleblowers are no different than other types of political protestors in that they are opposing existing practices, and at the base of their opposition are alternative values or ethics. The only difference is that whistleblowers begin their opposition at the organizational level and only gradually (and sometimes) work their way up to the national level. However, many social movements (e.g. the civil rights movement) follow a similar historical progression: they frequently begin by attacking local conditions and only later connect these local injustices to a national pattern that they seek to change. So it is with whistleblowers.

Our main point here is that an ethical or professional understanding of whistleblowing alone misses the fundamental political aspect of this behaviour. Political action is aimed towards concrete change, and whistleblowing is a means, increasingly used, by which subordinates are trying to change their workplaces and their society. Indeed, whistleblowing has become a powerful tool by which ordinary employees, be they white-collar or blue-collar, can reveal the gap between the organization's purported 'mission' and its actual practices. By revealing organizational corruption, abuses and deceptions of the public, whistleblowers can succeed on occasion in bringing down their superiors, in impeding the capital accumulation process in their organization, and in extreme cases, in challenging the continued right and legitimacy of their organization to provide the product or service they claim to offer.

WHY WOULD ANYONE BLOW THE WHISTLE?

Given that the act of whistleblowing carries significant perils for the individual, what attractions does it hold as a strategy of dissent or protest? What are the organizational, economic and cultural factors that both impede and enhance the likelihood of whistleblowing in modern work organizations?

Compliance in organizations

Managers in organizations have at their disposal many ways of gaining cooperation and compliance from workers. Primary among these mechanisms of control is the ability to regulate the reward structure. Formal job evaluations, promotions, raises, firing, re-assignment or demotions are some of the more direct ways of gaining organizational compliance. The bureaucratic authority that managers have to allocate these rewards and punishments (usually without review or external scrutiny) gives them enormous power to control dissent within their organization.

Effective managers may also use less direct influence strategies to gain compliance from subordinates. These types of persuasion or social influence tactics (see Forsyth, 1990: 187–8) include: (1) 'promising' (e.g. pledging to do or give something in the future), (2) 'bullying' (e.g. using strong threats, insults or violence), (3) 'discussion' (e.g. using rational arguments or explanations for decisions), (4) 'negotiation' (e.g. making compromises, trading favours), (5) 'manipulation' (e.g. lying, deceiving), (6) 'demand' (e.g. forcefully asserting oneself, insisting on compliance), (7) 'claiming expertise' (e.g. claiming superior knowledge or skill), (8) 'ingratiation' (e.g. deliberately flattering or seducing the subordinate) and (9) 'evasion' (e.g. avoiding the issue, keeping the person in the dark). By using these influence strategies in conversations with subordinates, managers are able to elicit compliance without necessarily exercising their ultimate power to fire dissenters. For workers with unequal access to resources and power, it is easy to see why these social influence and persuasion tactics are so effective in maintaining organizational conformity.

Some work organizations claim that they want internal disclosure so that they can correct problems before they grow, and they have set up formal codes of ethics, open channels of communication with management, formal grievance procedures and anonymous 'hot lines' for reporting misconduct. However, even within these environments which claim to encourage whistleblowing or to at least make it normative, many workers remain sceptical about speaking out. Their fear may be well founded. As it turns out, many people who use the 'hot lines' in their organizations find themselves being investigated rather than the illegal acts that they reported (*Wall Street Journal*, 28 August 1992). It is our impression that it is rare to find an organization that honestly rewards critical information even when it remains internal.

Since pressures towards compliance, we believe, are ubiquitous in organizations, how do we explain the emergence of whistleblowing and other types of political dissent in these settings? What are the characteristics of individuals who resist these pressures to 'go along' with prevailing practices?

The characterization generally adopted by management that whistleblowers are disgruntled and embittered employees is generally not the case. On the contrary, the research literature (see Jos *et al.*, 1989; Greenberger *et al.*, 1987; Glazer and Glazer, 1989) and our interviews suggest that whistleblowers are highly competent and respected employees and among the core professionals within an organization. This may be due to the fact that such persons have a strong vested interest in the reputation of the organization (something that is severely tarnished by prolonged and systemic misconduct) and they are in more strategic positions than other workers to observe misconduct. These core employees may be insulated from the pressures to remain silent because they honestly believe that disclosure of wrongdoing is in the long-term, best interest of their company. Whistleblowers are often devoted to the organization's true mission, as they see it, and believe that the observed misconduct is undermining that mission (see also, Glazer and Glazer, 1989). Furthermore, as agents of social change, they may have more confidence that their information will produce the desired changes because they believe others will view them as credible members of the organization.

Another factor that separates the whistleblower from other employees is that they may hold a greater allegiance to extra-organizational principles than to strictly organizational norms. For example, whistleblowers in our sample were drawing from principles of behaviour or ethical standards they learnt in church, in their professional training, or in their families. These are people with a code of behaviour that often derives from extra-organizational sources and transcends organizational norms. Their adherence to their own principles is what insulates them from organizational pressures to 'go along' and gives them the independence and sense of larger duty it takes to buck the tide. Other researchers have also concluded that whistleblowing is more common among persons who subscribe to higher moral, religious or professional standards (see Brabeck, 1984; Fritche and Becker, 1984; Jos et al., 1989; Glazer and Glazer, 1989; Miceli and Near, 1990).

Finally, based on our personal interviews with whistleblowers in a variety of industries, we would also have to include naivety as a factor in explaining this type of organizational resistance. Most of the whistleblowers in our research, as in the Glazers' study (1989), tended at first to be naive or innocent in their initial beliefs that (1) the organization is actually devoted to what it says is its mission, (2) the organization wants to know about abuses in power, fraud and mismanagement in the work setting, and (3) reporting wrongdoing or illegal activity will be rewarded or at least appreciated. For individuals who held these initial beliefs, their experience with whistleblowing became a hard and painful lesson.

The growth of whistleblowing in an information economy

Another reason why individuals appear to be increasingly stepping forward to blow the whistle has to do with important shifts that are taking place in the occupational structure. Specifically, it is our view that the broad transformation in US society from a manufacturing-based, industrial economy to a service-based, information-processing economy has changed the job structure in such a way as to make whistleblowing both more important and more prevalent. Specifically, as jobs become more professionalized, specialized and expertise-based, employees are more likely to develop professional norms, ethics and bases for judgement that may differ from and run into conflict with organizational norms and practices.

The specialization of tasks in modern industry also provides more opportunities to observe misconduct by other work units.

As organizations grow larger and more complex, their activities become more hidden from public view and require greater levels of internal monitoring. The growing complexity of many products and services provided by modern organizations, and the greater legal liabilities that can result, has brought an important alteration in the occupational structure. For our purposes, the most important change has been the growth in self-monitoring within organizations.

Over the last few decades, the necessity of self-monitoring, itself the product of trying to avoid outside control and regulation, has led to the creation of a new tier of occcupations (or redefinitions of old occupations) that have responsibility for quality control of very complex products and services. For example, reliability engineers now determine whether the technical design of a weapons system, if built in accordance with the specifications drawn up by others, would actually work as intended. It is the responsibility of the internal auditor to determine whether there is any fraud in the financial operations of an organization. Social workers today are required by law in many states, and by their professional code of ethics, to report all suspected cases of abuse of clients. Architects and engineers must sign off as to whether a given set of building plans are structurally sound. In other words, quality control, we argue, has become more decentralized as complexity has increased. These examples illustrate that we have an increasing number of people employed in occupations where they have explicit responsibilities, by law, by formal job description or by way of their professional codes of ethics, to catch and report specific kinds of wrongdoing. Failure to act is not doing one's job properly. But to do so – to blow the whistle on the weapons system, building design or pharmaceutical product that would not perform as required – puts them in direct conflict with the line officers of their employing organizations. In the past, quality control may have been more centralized up the line, with supervisors deciding whether to ignore the problem or send things back as bad quality.

With the growth in these types of occupations, it is hardly surprising that we would see a growth in the incidence of whistleblowing. While other employees may diffuse the responsibility (e.g. 'someone else will report it, so I don't have to'), persons in quality control or internal monitoring positions have little choice but to report illegal activity. Whistleblowers in our study were sometimes in these types of positions and, as a result, they viewed their actions as 'doing my job' rather than 'blowing the whistle'. However, they came to see that their jobs put them in inherent conflict with their superiors. As one reliability engineer put it:

> Most of these guys [other reliability engineers] will sign on to anything. They know what management wants to build and wants them to sign. They don't care if it works or not. But if you have pride in your work, if you take it seriously and tell the truth, if you just don't want the taxpayers to waste their money on systems that don't work, then you're in natural conflict with management. Suddenly, you're the 'whistle-blower' because you did your job. . . . If I had it to do again, I would never have chosen this job.'

Put simply, we would argue that another important reason why whistleblowing is spreading is that over the last two decades the occupational structure in the US has been altered in such a way as to add more positions that involve monitoring the actions of others.

THE ORDEAL THAT TRANSFORMS AND POLITICIZES THE INDIVIDUAL

While whistleblowers are gaining in numbers, they still remain statistically unusual, indeed 'deviant', in their willingness to oppose normative organizational practices and to speak out against organizational wrongdoing. For example, two large-scale studies of federal workers found that only about 30 per cent of those who observed fraud, waste or management reported it (US Merit Board, 1981, 1984). In our earlier study of 158 workers in a high-security manufacturing industry (see Rothschild and Miethe, 1992), we found that only 32 per cent who observed illegal and unethical conduct reported it to their employer, and *none* of these workers reported this conduct to authorities outside the company. Whenever whistleblowers are isolated in criticism of the organization, however, they become easy targets for management retaliation. As we show below, management often feels justified in going to extraordinary lengths to destroy these people.

The ordeal of whistleblowing

Consider the case of Anne, a typical whistleblower. Anne is a

37-year-old woman, hired in late 1990 as a casting operator for a company that makes rubber belts. Her job was to mix the chemical compounds for production. She told us how 'happy and grateful she was to have found this $11 an hour job'. After just a few days, however, she began to notice some unusual physical reactions. Nevertheless, she continued at the job and worked hard. Within two months on the job, her supervisor gave her a special commendation. He said no one had ever learnt the job so quickly and asked if she would assist in the training of others. Anne responded to the praise and believed she was a valued employee. However, a few weeks later, her symptoms developed into significant physical problems, including a burning sensation inside her nose and mouth, headaches and some bone pain. At this point, Anne told her boss that she wanted to learn more about the chemicals in use and their exact nature and possible side effects. Specifically, she noticed that the 'pinksheets' giving the scientific names of each chemical were missing from some of the drums, and she proposed to send for them. Her supervisor told her that was a good idea. The next day she was fired.

After her dismissal, Anne talked to other employees and learnt that previous workers who had held her position had also left or been fired when they began to show medical problems. However, quite unlike other employees whose health had suffered from the position, Anne did not accept this plight. When she discovered, with the help of a university-based industrial hygienist and a toxicologist, that the company was (1) exposing its workers, without warning or protective clothing, to more than 100 times the levels allowed by law for certain chemical compounds and (2) dumping the toxic waste illegally as well, she became a political agent whose mission was to expose the company's practices to the media and to the community.

As a result of the chemical exposure, Anne within a short time had tumors growing in her mouth, permanent liver damage and her skull began to soften. The company had referred her to local doctors who soft pedalled the problem. Once she consulted with independent doctors and experts on chemical exposure, Anne was shocked to learn the full extent of her injuries.

Our interviews with Anne and other whistleblowers indicate that the reactions from management are crucial in the development of whistleblowers as active political agents. Indeed, the escalation of events as they unfold and especially the company's attempts to cover up their own abuses and discredit their detractors has a profound impact on the whistleblower's political and social consciousness. Anne became an active agent of political change in her company as soon as they fired her. Her change in political consciousness is strikingly indicated in the following quote:

> I felt so completely victimized by the company. I had been such a trusting person. When they hired me, I thought they had picked me because they could see that I was an intelligent and responsible person. Now I know that when they picked me they were picking out a person to murder.

Justifiably, Anne saw herself as trying to protect the public from the cancers and birth defects that independent scientists taught her are the sure outcome of the corporation's abuses. Perhaps the most bewildering and in the end embittering response that she encountered was from coworkers and community members who 'turned their back' on her and told her to be quiet because 'jobs were at stake'. The case is still unfolding. Anne is seeking medical treatment. She has just learnt that she has irreversible lung damage. Her civil suit against the company is in preparation. Her testimony and the testimony of the NIOSH and other independent scientists and doctors who have helped her, she hopes, will put the conspiring members of management in prison. The television programme *60 Minutes* has interviewed her for a possible story. Anne hopes that her case and the publicity that may follow it will reveal laxity at OSHA and thereby bring OSHA to take a more vigilant role in monitoring and enforcing legal standards that would protect workers from similar chemical hazards. She has moved from the local level to the national level in her concern.

This example illustrates well why a lone individual with significant information might want to take action alone rather than waiting for collective protest to develop. Specifically, those waiting for collective resistance may be waiting for a long time. Furthermore, it is in the nature of collective action that it requires democratic approval. At least a majority of the affected group must agree on the nature of the problem and its appropriate response. This will tend to water down the acts of resistance that are chosen. In contrast, the individual can act on his or her own conscience or sense of responsibility to other workers or to the public without awaiting the judgement of the group. As a result, the individual's actions can be quicker, more nimble, more surprising. They can surely be gutsier.

In Anne's case, she broke into the factory one night to get the paperwork on the chemicals being used. The downside, of course, is that the individual, if identifiable, makes an easier target for employer retaliation.

To those authors who have acknowledged only the prospect of collective resistance, we would direct attention to what whistle-blowers are accomplishing as individual agents of change. If it is true that employees are increasingly willing to see their duty as public citizens transcending their loyalty to their employer (Blumberg, 1971; Graham, 1986; Perrucci *et al.*, 1980), then we should witness the proliferation of whistleblowing.

If whistleblowing ultimately becomes, as we have argued, an effort by subordinates to turn the tables on their superiors – to have them removed for their corrupt or abusive behaviour or funda-mentally to change abusive organizational practices which their superiors have ordered – then we should expect whistleblowing to engender fierce management retaliation. The more effectively challenging of management's control, legitimacy or prerogatives, the more intense we should expect management reprisals to be. Similarly, we would posit that the more the whistleblower's infor-mation points to *systemic* abuses in the organization's way of doing business, as opposed to a one-time 'bad apple' claim, the stronger will be efforts to discredit and destroy the whistleblower.

Virtually all of the qualitative case material of our study supports these conclusions. In fact, like Glazer and Glazer (1989: 133–4), we find that whistleblowers start out expecting a constructive or at least modest organizational response to their disclosures. In our inter-views, whistleblowers told us time and again that they started out believing that because they were respected and valued employees, their information presented to 'higher-ups' would be taken seriously and would be the catalyst for the constructive organizational change they sought. As a result, few were prepared for what was about to happen to them. Few realized, in advance, that a 25-year record of 'excellence' in management's evaluation of their job performance could be turned overnight into management claims of 'incompe-tence', which is exactly what happened to the reliability engineer cited earlier who worked for the Department of Navy once he turned in his report showing that a new multi-billion dollar weapons system they were developing would not work. Few realized that a special commendation even one month earlier would provide no protection against being summarily fired, but this is what happened to Anne, our worker who asked to check on the contents of some chemical drums.

Often, what we find is that once employees reveal that they possess and might use information that challenges management's judgement, the full resources of the organization will be brought to bear against them, no matter how out of proportion it may appear to the observer. In cases we studied, upon learning that an individual had a concern and information that could be used against them, management *immediately* fired the individual, or if that was not possible, then they set up the process by which they could be later fired, by abruptly downgrading their job performance.

If their claims of 'incompetence' could not be sustained, then we found that management sometimes resorted to a tactic that we had not anticipated: they would endeavour to get the whistleblower labelled 'crazy'. Towards this end, management would direct the whistleblower to see an agency or company psychologist and would inform the psychologist that the person was being sent because they appeared to be 'out of their mind' or a 'paranoid schizophrenic'. We were first alerted to this form of reprisal by a psychologist in the Washington, DC area who has set up a nation-wide support and referral centre for whistleblowers. His job within the federal government was to counsel federal workers who were too stressed or dysfunctional to perform their jobs. Soon he discovered that many of the patients sent to him (by management) were actually whistleblowers, not crazy people, and they were chiefly distressed not by alcohol or drugs, but by their supervisor's daily harassment of them. These experiences led this person to set up a support system for whistleblowers. We were surprised by how often this ploy was used on the whistleblowers in our study. Elaine Draper (1994) also finds in her ongoing study of company doctors that they sometimes report being sent personnel problems, persons who are 'a thorn in the side' of management. How they evaluate these people presents them with a professional dilemma, especially if they know how management wants them to evaluate them. In some cases, these doctors have themselves become whistleblowers in response to such dilemmas.

The dialectics of reprisal: the struggle for dignity out of repression

The irony of all of these harsh measures – what we would consider to be excessive repression – is that it sets into motion a dialectical process. Management chooses harsh measures no doubt to quieten the potential whistleblower and anyone else who may be harbouring similar inclinations. But instead, the reprisals only serve to confirm to the whistleblower just how morally bankrupt and lacking in integrity their superiors are. If, in their naïveté, any of those studied here thought there was an unimpeachable or fair-minded individual several steps up the ladder who would intervene and correct the offensive organizational practice once he or she received the necessary information, they were quickly stripped of this belief.

Once the full resources of the organization are brought to bear against them, they cannot turn back. It becomes a contest as to which side can discredit the other more decisively. It is important to understand that as soon as management first hears of the concerns and information of the whistleblower, they often act immediately to downgrade the individual's job performance and begin explicitly to build a case for firing the individual. In other words, management reprisals begin as soon as management becomes aware that the individual *might* become a whistleblower. We are aware of one case of whistleblowing in which the person reported on their immediate supervisor for misappropriation of funds. By the time the whistleblower had come down the elevator to his work station, his immediate supervisor had already been told of his allegations and was waiting for him with his 'walking papers'!

Thus, even the individual who would have hesitated to go to external agencies with critical information is left with no choice. If they want to reclaim their good name, they must escalate; they must show their evidence of organizational wrongdoing. It becomes a matter of vindication. While at an earlier stage, management might have been able to coopt or intimidate some of these people into dropping their claims, once the organizational hierarchy chooses the harsh avenue of repression, potential whistleblowers have little choice but to defend themselves by publicizing the very information that management so wanted to suppress.

Psychologically, it becomes very important to whistleblowers to show that they were not involved in the organizational wrongdoing and that they were punished for their moral superiority. In Anne's words, a year and a half after her tragic chemical exposure and after learning that the effects of this chemical exposure have been in the company's knowledge for over a decade:

I ask myself all the time, how can they [her previous bosses] live with themselves? How can they do something like this, knowing they are destroying people's bodies, literally killing them, and causing mutations three generations out? Then I realize that I could never understand them unless I was like them, and I will never be like them.

Scott (1990) challenges us to consider how workers create their own sense of dignity out of their acts of resistance. The clearest way in which workers can sharply define and assert what they value, separate themselves from immoral practices they had no hand in creating, and dignify the value of the real work they want to perform is by exposing the gap between what the bureaucracy says its mission is and what are its actual practices. The experience of whistleblowers teaches that while resistance in the workplace challenges the practices, the ideology and the authority of those in power, it is also about the struggle for dignity and integrity in work organizations.

In the intermediate term, there can be no question (based on our interviews) that the severe retaliation suffered by these people is devastating. Marriages break under the stress. Between the unemployment and the need to pay attorney fees, the financial condition of the family is sometimes ruined. Female whistleblowers especially speak with tremendous pain of how they 'could not be there for their children' through the long months or years in which they were consumed by their (often legal) battle for vindication. The extent of the distress is so extreme that we found that our interviews on this point could go on almost indefinitely. It is a telling anecdote that the psychologist mentioned earlier, having established a support service for whistleblowers and having had the opportunity to hear the stories of numerous whistleblowers, now advises would-be whistleblowers who seek his advice *not to do it*, unless they can find a way to leak the information in an anonymous fashion. In this person's view, the likely suffering by the whistleblower is too great to justify the disclosure, no matter what fraud, waste or danger to the public may be involved.

The Glazers paint a similar picture of the personal devastation that results when people lose their careers for telling the truth: 'The anger that drove them forward threatened to overwhelm their lives, leaving them permanently scarred' (Glazer and Glazer, 1989: 155). In some cases, their distress can become so protracted that it becomes chronic and debilitating. However, others seem better equipped to accept their loss and to go about the business of rebuilding their lives. Often they are transformed and politicized by the ordeal.

Most of these people have had their identity shaped in a profound way by this experience. To a person they come to see themselves as strong and moral. They have developed an understanding of how greed and self-aggrandizement can result in deceptive practices, harmful products and fraudulent services being built into the fabric of many organizations. They feel free of the abuse and above it. Some have managed to establish themselves in a new work setting where they can do the kind of work they can feel good about. They feel a new dignity in their work. They express appreciation that at least it is 'clean, honest work', free of the abuses they originally observed. For instance, a medical technician in our sample who reported various types of fraud and overcharging in a vocational rehabilitation facility shows this personal growth:

> As a consequence of being a whistleblower, I have become more proactive with a stronger purpose in life. I am becoming active both at the state and national level as an advocate for licensing for people in my profession. I am helping to organize a support group for whistleblowers in my state.

Another former whistleblower spoke to us of forming a 'Toxic Action Committee' to fight toxic dumping in her community. A social worker who had blown the whistle on her former employer, a corrupt agency that actually tampered with the court records of clients, now speaks of the dignity and satisfaction she gets from helping clients in her current private practice.

The Glazers too found that years down the road many of the whistleblowers in their study *were* able successfully to rebuild their lives. Work was the key. Once they were able to find alternative jobs or careers, their emotional healing could begin. In the Glazers' study, 43 resisters were able ultimately to keep their original jobs or to build successful careers elsewhere, while 17 remained unemployed or underemployed (Glazer and Glazer, 1989: 230–1).

To reiterate our argument, then, many employees are uncomfortable with abusive or fraudulent practices in their workplaces. However, the pressure and the norms to 'go along' are strong enough, and the example made of those who do speak out is chilling enough, that most employees grouse about the prevailing pattern of abuse, but do not explicitly resist. For those who do resist, the more systemic are their observations, the swifter and more severe will be management's response. But rather than quieting the resister, the retaliation only serves to strengthen their convictions about the rightness of their cause and to escalate the conflict to a level and duration they may never have anticipated or intended.

Over time, many whistleblowers come to see that these reprisals constitute a premeditated strategy by management to discredit the whistleblower and neutralize the power of any incriminating information they may have that would indicate system-wide abuse or illegality. In this sense, it is management's response that serves in dialectical fashion to enhance the awareness of whistleblowers that what they have observed is not one 'bad apple', but rather the way the organization or the system regularly operates. The escalation of reprisals also brings, paradoxically, an escalation in individuals' commitment to clearing themselves by exposing and proving the organizational corruption. Thus, dialectically, it is in the process of resisting – of opposing organizational practices and fighting unjust reprisals – that individual whistleblowers express what they value, distance themselves from organizational practices they had no hand in creating, and assert their own dignity and integrity.

THE EFFECTIVENESS OF WHISTLEBLOWING AS POLITICAL RESISTANCE

While whistleblowing has enormous potential for eliminating fraud, abuse and unethical conduct in the modern workplace, it is only sometimes effective in achieving the desired changes in organizational practices. What are the conditions under which this type of political resistance is most successful in achieving its objectives?

A major situational determinant of the effectiveness of whistleblowing is the nature of the wrongful conduct. When the act that precipitated the disclosure is sporadic conduct done by a 'bad apple', organizations are likely to take heed and remove the offending party. Such action is in many cases beneficial to the organization because it enables the company to 'clean house' and shows external critics that they are self-monitoring and self-corrective. Only when the perpetrator is a member of the upper echelon of management is this plan of action problematic. However, as indicated by the recent resignation of the head of the United Way, having an elite position is no guarantee of immunity.

The situation is quite different for cases involving *systemic* and *chronic* abuse and corruption in the organization. For these types of cases, our interviews revealed that successful whistleblowing was contingent upon several additional factors. First, the whistleblower must be a credible source. Long-time members of the organization have more credibility than newcomers, but extensive document- ation of the abuse and support from staff and co-workers are needed in nearly all cases. Second, whistleblowers who are most effective in changing organizational practices have recruited others as allies. All cases of successful whistleblowing in our study and previous work (e.g. Glazer and Glazer, 1989) come to involve the extensive assistance of any or all of the following groups: co- workers, lawyers, newspaper or television reporters, elected officials, regulatory officials, professional societies and public advocacy groups. Corroborating testimony from co-workers and expert witnesses strengthens the credibility of the allegations. Outside interest from the media, Congress or other elected officials often provides the necessary power base to enact change. Having a strong support network (both emotionally and financially) is essential for the long and arduous task of bottom-up organizational change.

The type of organizational structure and culture (see Trice and Beyer, 1993) is also important for understanding when whistle- blowing is more likely to be successful. Organizations with a long history of open communication between staff and management, worker solidarity and a commitment to treating employees with dignity and self-respect seem more likely to encourage internal disclosure of wrongdoing. Similarly, more participatory or democratic organizations tend to be more open and self-correcting, thereby responding more constructively to internal criticism and minimizing the need for external whistleblowing as a mechanism of organizational change. However, in many hierarchical organiz- ations, efforts to enhance employee voice may be a façade or merely symbolic attempts at workplace democracy, used primarily to appease external monitors of company practices rather than being a fundamental aspect of the organization's culture. Under these con- ditions, whistleblowers may be confronted with the cold reality that even their 'progressive' company is vindictive to employees who 'rock the boat' and attempt to change organizational norms and practices.

On the other side of the coin, it is only fair to note that whistle- blowers are not saints and that whistleblowing can be grossly misused.

Specifically, whistleblowing can be used as a strictly political tool, not to report genuine wrongdoing that might harm the public, but as misinformation. It can be used as an aggressive attempt to disarm power-holders with whom one does not agree. However, in the cases we examined in this study, whistleblowers had observations of serious wrongdoing by organizational officials.

In the final analysis, then, we conclude that individual employees with strategic information about organizational wrongdoing can wield enormous power. But the threat of their disclosures will unleash only management retaliation and it will most likely *not* effect the desired organizational change unless the whistleblower is joined by others. In the end, whistleblowing and other forms of individual resistance must expand and evolve into collective resistance to be most effective at social change. The persons in our sample who were successful in achieving major changes did so by turning their individual resistance into collective action. This is not to diminish the role of the individual whistleblower who is at the heart of the conflict and most profoundly changed by the experience. Dialectically, the struggle against unjust reprisals solidifies in whistleblowers their beliefs about the moral validity of their actions and their awareness of the systemic or chronic nature of the organizational abuse. As we have stressed, the intense struggle that ensues may transform naïve and conscientious employees into activists with a new political consciousness and sense of purpose.

The ordeal of the whistleblowing experience affects people in different ways. In some cases, people may be so ruined by the process that they become permanently embittered and stuck in the battle. In other cases, however, the retaliation transforms former whistleblowers into persistent political resisters. Their critique evolves from the organizational level to the societal level, and they join with others in trying to change society. What begins for them as a spontaneous, individually taken act of internal whistleblowing may give rise to collectively supported exposure of the organizational abuse, turning the individual's original observations into a public issue and allowing for effective and fundamental social change.

REFERENCES

Blumberg, P. I. (1971) 'Corporate Responsibility and the Employee's Duty of Loyalty and Obedience', *Oklahoma Law Review* 24: 279–318.
Braverman, Harry (1974) *Labor and Monopoly Capital*, New York: Monthly Review Press.

Burawoy, Michael (1979) *Manufacturing Consent: Changes in the Labor Process under Monopoly Capitalism*, Chicago: University of Chicago Press.

Brabeck, Mary (1984) 'Ethical Characteristics of Whistleblowers', *Journal of Research in Personality* 18: 41–53.

Draper, Elaine (1994) *The Company Doctor: Risk, Responsibility, and Corporate Professionalism*, New York: Russell Sage Foundation.

Edwards, Richard (1979) *Contested Terrain*, New York: Basic Books.

Elliston, F. A. (1982) 'Anonymity and Whistle-Blowing', *Journal of Business Ethics* 1: 167–77.

Forsyth, Donelson (1990) *Group Dynamics*, 2nd edition, Belmont, CA: Brooks-Cole.

Fritzche, D. J. and Becker, H. (1984) 'Linking Management Behavior to Ethical Philosophy: An Empirical Investigation', *Academy of Management Journal* 27: 166–75.

Glazer, Myron and Glazer, Penina (1989) *The Whistleblowers: Exposing Corruption in Government and Industry*, New York: Basic Books.

Graham, Jill (1986) 'Principled Organizational Dissent', *Research in Organizational Behavior* 8: 1–52.

Greenberger, David B., Miceli, Marcia P. and Cohen, Debra J. (1987) 'Oppositionists and Group Norms: The Reciprocal Influence of Whistle-Blowers and Co-Workers', *Journal of Business Ethics* 6: 527–42.

Hodson, Randy (1992) 'Worker Agency: An Underdeveloped Concept in the Sociology of Work', paper presented at the annual meeting of American Sociological Association, Pittsburgh, PA.

Jermier, John (1988) 'Sabotage at Work: The Rational View', *Research in the Sociology of Organizations* 6: 101–34.

Jos, Philip, Tompkins, Mark E. and Hays, Steven W. (1989) 'In Praise of Difficult People: A Portrait of the Committed Whistleblower', *Public Administration Review*, November/December: 552–61.

Miceli, Marcia P. and Near, Janet P. (1985) 'Characteristics of Organizational Climate and Perceived Wrongdoing Associated with Whistle-Blowing Decisions', *Personnel Psychology* 38: 525–44.

Miceli, Marcia P. and Near, Janet P. (1990) 'Is There a Whistleblowing Personality? Personal Variables that May Be Associated with Whistle-blowing', *Working Paper Series 90-19*. College of Business, Ohio State University, Columbus, Ohio.

Miceli, Marcia P. and Near, Janet P. (1992) *Blowing the Whistle: The Organizational and Legal Implications for Companies and Employees*, New York, NY: Lexington Books.

Miceli, Marcia P., Near, Janet P. and Schwenk, Charles R. (1991) 'Who Blows the Whistle and Why?' *Industrial and Labor Relations Review* 45(1): 113–30.

Molsted, Clark (1988) 'Control Strategies Used by Industrial Brewery Workers: Work Avoidance, Impression Management and Solidarity', *Human Organization* 47: 354–60.

Perrucci, Robert M., Anderson, R. M., Schendel, D. E. and Tractman, L. E. (1980) 'Whistle-Blowing: Professionals' Resistance to Organization Authority', *Social Problems* 28: 149–64.

Rothschild, Joyce and Miethe, Terance D. (1992) 'Whistleblowing as Occupational Deviance and Dilemma', presented at the Annual Meetings of the American Sociological Association, Pittsburgh, PA, 20–4 August 1992.

Scott, James (1990) *Domination and Arts of Resistance: Hidden Transcripts*, New Haven, CT: Yale University Press.

Thompson, E.P (1968) *The Making of the English Working Class*, Harmondsworth: Penguin Books.

Trice, Harrison and Beyer, Janice (1993) *The Cultures of Work Organizations*, Englewood Cliffs, NJ: Prentice Hall.

US Merit Board (1981) *Whistleblowing and the Federal Employee: Blowing the Whistle on Fraud, Waste, and Management – Who Does It and What Happens*, US Merit Systems Protection Board, Office of Merit Systems Review and Studies, Washington, DC.

US Merit Board (1984) *Blowing the Whistle in the Federal Government: A Comparative Analysis of 1980 and 1983 Survey Findings*, US Merit Systems Protection Board, Office of Merit Systems Review and Studies, Washington, DC.

Wall Street Journal (1992) 'Tipsters telephoning ethics hotline can end up sabotaging their own jobs', 28 August 1992.

Westin, Alan F (1981) *Whistleblowing: Loyality and Dissent in the Corporation*, New York: McGraw-Hill.

Wardell, Mark (1992) 'Changing Organizational Forms: From the Bottom Up', in Michael Reed and Michael Hughes (eds) *Rethinking Organization*, London and Newbury Park: Sage, pp. 144–64.

9

POWER RELATIONS AND THE
CONSTITUTION OF THE
RESISTANT SUBJECT*

Stewart Clegg

The two principal ingredients of this chapter are the relation between the interconnection of power relationships and the constitution of subjectivity. One way of expressing this is through the construction of a continuum of 'the degree of intensiveness/extensiveness of the power relations constitutive of the subject'. Drawing on the chapters in this volume it is possible to identify at least three aspects of this dimension of power and subjectivity. There is, first, the question of individual organization. How coherently organized is the individual, in terms of their subjectivity, as a reflexive agent in power relations? How coherently organized is the individual as one who seeks to enrol, translate, interest or oppose others in their projects? Does the subject have sufficient self-cognizance to be able to exercise this agency? Second, at the mid-point, there is the question of social organization. To what extent is the subject able to draw upon resources of social organization greater than the self, such as familial networks or an ecology of local community networks? Third, the most extensive point is the question of solidaristic organization: to what extent can the subject draw upon the consciously organized resources of a social movement or collective organization in the pursuit of their agency? Or, to put the questions in another, equally appropriate way, to what extent does power constitute the resources of human agency in terms of self, significant and generalized others?

---

* I would like to thank Marcelo Falcao Vieira, David Collinson, Sandra Nutley, John Jermier, David Knights and Walter Nord for helpful comments on an earlier draft of this paper.

INTRODUCTION

Between Braverman's *Labour and Monopoly Capital* (1974) and Foucault's *Discipline and Punish* (1977) are three years, two divergent theoretical traditions and one problematic. The singular phenomenon is the troublesome problematic of the subject. Braverman (1974) neglected it; subsequent Labour Process Conferences did not. Foucault's (1977) import into 'labour process analysis' has been seen by Knights (e.g. Knights and Vurdubakis, 1993) as a necessary ingredient to ensure its long-term viability. Others regard it as no more than a 'fatal distraction' (Thompson, 1991) from the necessary task of returning one's intellectual posture back to the bedrock Braverman (1974) excavated from Marx (1976).

Yet, it is not so simple: perhaps it is only in the conventions of the early Hollywood western that the good guys and the bad guys are so easily distinguishable. Elsewhere, we might expect more transitory, fleeting, ambivalent and semiotically insecure subjectivities. A classic of the genre, Sergio Leone's *The Good, the Bad and the Ugly* (1967), is a case in point. In this movie the changing relations of power ceaselessy shape shifting subjectivities.[1] There is an absence of any routine fixing of the relation of interests between these eponymous figures in predictable and organized ways. Much of the narrative is structured around shifting dyads within the triad. Cease shifting subjectivities and relations between them and one has stable organization. Organization seeks to secure fixity. The absence of such fixity is an indication, through its absence, of what organization seeks to achieve with respect to power. Also, it shows what the likely sources of resistance will be by those subject to power. Organization achieves stability through routine channelling of the shifting subjectivities of its members. Power fixes these in predictable circuits. By 'shifting subjectivities' one means the propensity for aspects of the person's selfhood, their biographical and biological relevancies, to be the source of changes of self-definition with implications for organization membership. Such membership, usually fixed in terms of an occupational title, is often resistant to these shifts in subjectivity. These subjectivities are a key source of resistance to organization power.

Subjectivities might best be thought of as shifting and contingent on power relations, as becomes evident from the representations of selected movies, such as those of Leone. Yet, such views are not shared by many influential representations of power relations in organizations, for instance, that of Braverman (1974). We do not find a similar view of the complex, shifting significations of power relations and their contingent fixing by organization. For Braverman, the conduits fixing power relations were clear and one way. The flow is always from capital to labour. The subjectivities appropriate to each are fixed objectively, through class position; that is, by relation to the means of production.

Plotting and narrative structure become more complex after Foucault's (1977) theoretical revisionism implicitly challenges any notion of 'sovereign power'. The supreme sovereign status of capital as *the* conduit of power becomes much harder to justify after the realization of a cast of characters with a larger range of identities than those fixed by a model of class relations. The salience of identity is not an incidental or marginal part of the narrative that forms the lived experience of many people. Identities are not only occupational and disciplinary, and thus forged or fused in the organizational division of labour, but also derive from aspects of embodiment such as gender, ethnicity and sexuality. In creating a space within which this more complex idea of identity might be recognized, Foucault (1977) became a primary route for post-Marxist critical scholarship in general, and of power in organization studies and labour process debates in particular. Hence, this chapter will begin with Foucault.

FOUCAULT AND POWER AND RESISTANCE: IMPLICATIONS FOR THE LABOUR PROCESS DEBATE

In Foucault's *Discipline and Punish* (1977) power is conceived of as a technique that achieves its strategic effects through its disciplinary character. Foucault (1977) sees the methods of surveillance and assessment of individuals first developed in state institutions such as prisons, as effective tools developed for the orderly regimentation of others as docile bodies. This is so, he maintains, even when such methods provoke resistance. Resistance merely serves to demonstrate the necessity of that discipline that provokes it, according to Foucault. It becomes a target against which discipline may justify its necessity by virtue of its lack of omnipotence. These disciplinary practices become widely distributed through schools, the army and the asylum, and eventually enter into the capitalist factory. They become strategic to the extent that they are effective constitutions of powers. As a form of knowledge they work through their on-togenesis. Because they are knowledge constituted not just in texts but in definite institutional and organizational practices, they are 'discursive practices': knowledge reproduced through practices made possible by the framing assumptions of that knowledge. The knowledge is very practical: it disciplines the body, regulates the mind and orders the emotions in such a way that the ranking, hierarchy and stratification that follows is not just the blind reproduction of a transcendent traditional order, as in feudalism. It produces a new basis for order in the productive worth of individuals as they get defined by these new disciplinary practices of power.

To assume fixed interests on the one hand, and definite discourses representing them, on the other, would be mistaken, suggests Foucault:

> There is not, on the one side, a discourse of power, and opposite it another discourse that runs counter to it. Discourses are tactical elements or blocks operating in the field of force relations; there can run different and even contradictory discourses within the same strategy; they can on the contrary, circulate without changing their form from one strategy to another, opposing strategy.
>
> (Foucault, 1984: 101–2)

'Discourses have no fixed referent in particular values or systems of morality' as Weedon (1987: 123) has observed.[2] If there is no given elective affinity between discourse, practice and interests, then power cannot be understood as a 'single, all-encompassing strategy' (Foucault, 1984: 103). Power will be a more or less stable or shifting network of alliances extended over a shifting terrain of practice and discursively constituted interests. Points of resistance will open at many points in the network (Foucault, 1984: 95) whose effect will be to fracture alliances, constitute regroupings and reposit strategies (Foucault, 1984: 96). In such formulations power is to be seen in

> the multiplicity of force relations immanent in the sphere in which they operate and which constitute their own organization; as the process which, through ceaseless struggles and confrontations, transforms, strengthens or reverses them; as the support which these force relations find in one another, thus forming a chain or a system, or on the contrary, the disjunctions and contradictions which isolate them one from

another; and lastly, as the strategies in which they take effect, whose general design or institutional crystalization is embodied in the state apparatus, in the formulation of the law, in the various social hegemonies.

(Foucault, 1984: 92)

Central to Foucault's conception of power is its shifting, inherently unstable expression in networks and alliances. Rather than a monolithic view of power as invariably incorporating subjectivities, the focus is much closer to Machiavelli's (1958) strategic concerns or Gramsci's (1971) notion of hegemony as a 'war of manoeuvre', in which points of resistance and fissure are at the forefront.

Particular concepts of power should not be viewed simply as an effect of a particular discourse. Such discourses are a means by which a certain power (of theorizing: a theorizing power) is itself constituted. For Foucault the discursive field for formal academic theorizing about power is one primarily derived from notions of sovereignty. In this context sovereignty refers to an originating subject whose will is power. The allusion is obviously to Nietzsche. Against this originary subject, (which in Western history becomes transmuted from the ruling monarch into 'the state', in Marxism into the 'ruling class', and in labour process theory into 'capital'), Foucault argues for a reversal of terms. Instead of concentrating on the sovereignty of power he argues that, on the contrary, we should 'study the myriad of bodies which are constituted as peripheral subjects as a result of the effects of power'. That theorists might traditionally have conceptualized the subjects of power as 'individual(s) . . . a sort of elementary nucleus, a primitive atom, a multiple and inert material on which power comes to fashion or against which it happens to strike . . . is already one of the prime effects of power'.

Foucault's conception of power is one that attempts to break decisively with the 'mechanistic' and 'sovereign' view. New forms of social power crystallize in the seventeenth and eighteenth centuries, outside the terms that by now have become conventional for addressing and constituting a concept of 'power'. What emerges is a 'capillary form' of power, a power that 'reaches into the very grain of individuals', a 'synaptic regime of power, a regime of its exercise within the social body, rather than from above it' (Foucault, 1980: 39), a disciplinary power. The subjectification that is identified with disciplinary power is regarded as operating primarily through enhancing the 'calculability' of individuals (Foucault, 1977: 192–4).[3] Minson (1986: 113) renders it clearly: 'The human individual constructed in such discourses is calculable to the extent of being subject to comparative, scalar measures and related forms of training and correction'. The objective of disciplinary techniques is normalization,[4] the creation of routines, predictability, control.

Foucault's (1977) conception of disciplinary power, although compatible with the Marxian focus on control and resistance in the capitalist workplace, differs from it in two important respects. First, control via discipline does not first develop in the factory but in various state institutions. Capitalist masters adopt it from prison masters, from beadles, from the superintendents of asylums. Second, it is not a control functionally oriented to capitalist exploitation but to the creation of obedient bodies. Increasingly, it becomes structured into institutionalized bodies of knowledge: the disciplinary practices of modernity, with their distinct ways of fixing subjectivities within the professional 'gaze' of medicine, of psychiatry, of social administration, and so on. Each of these forms of discourse have regard for the body in distinct ways: as an object of therapy, management and so on. Foucault spends considerable detail on the 'embodiment' of power,[5] as do others who have developed analysis in a Foucauldian vein.[6]

Foucault does not focus *a priori* on 'capital' or the 'ruling class' as the embodiment of power. Instead, he focuses on the historical range of professional discourses that increasingly limit, define and normalize the 'vocabularies of motive' (Mills, 1940) that are available in specific sites ('situated contexts' in Mills's terms) for making sensible and accountable what it is that people should do, can do and thus do (Clegg, 1989). Power normalizes through discursive formations of knowledge. The terms of these ways of constituting the normal get institutionalized and incorporated into everyday life. Our reflexive gaze takes over the disciplining role as we take on the accounts and vocabularies of meaning and motive that are available to us as certain other forms of account get marginalized or simply eased out of currency.[7] Socially available accounts are not random. What gets said and done in and around organizations as 'management' and forms of resistance to it is thus a suitable case for treatment. Where there is something other than randomness there must be pattern. Pattern requires rules for its constitution, and unlike randomness, offers the possibility of its decoding through what is apparent.[8] The concept of rule has a central theoretical role to play in this account.

RULES AND RELATIONS OF MEANING

Conceptually, power is inscribed within contextual 'rules of the game' that both enable and constrain action (Clegg, 1975). Rules may be considered as implicit and contextual to the reasoning that subjects engage in. In this case they are inherent and articulatable aspects of the subjects' own reasoning. They may know and sometimes they can express what it is that they are doing when they are doing ruling and making discriminations of various kinds. Sometimes, however, as in the case of grammatical rules used to make coherent conversation, the person may be unable to formulate what the rules are even as they are aware that they are and others are employing rules. In addition, rules may be conceptualized as an analytically *post hoc* device. In this case the subjects are able to make sense, use discriminations adequately and intersubjectively yet be at a loss to be able to describe the rules that they use to do so. Such would be the case with native speakers of a language untrained in its grammatical deconstruction and thus unable to formulate the rules that enable them to make sense one to the other. The conception of social life held in this chapter is that it is peopled by practitioners accomplished in the arts of everyday reasoning and discrimination. Sometimes they will be able to articulate the rules that they are using. Sometimes they will not be aware of the rules. Where the latter is the case a role for the social analyst is to formulate as well as to interpret the rules and to observe the use that is made of them.

Rules provide the underlying rationale of those calculations which agencies, both individual and collective, routinely make in organizational contexts. Action can only ever be designated as such-and-such an action by reference to whatever rules identify it as such, a position that has significant implications for the conceptualization of subjectivity. It is important when making claims for having accessed 'subjectivity' (which, presumably would be achieved best when the accounts of those studied are duplicated perfectly by the researcher, where there is no room for elision, even if considerable opportunity for irony), that the access mechanisms to the mind of the other be made transparent. Methodological protocols need to be outlined. Where subjectivity is deemed vital it seems both important and advisable to explain the methodological protocols that enable one access to the subjectivity of others (see Collinson, 1992). There is a simple reason for this. As Dylan (1968) once put it, 'The moral of this tale is that one should not be where one does not belong'. One does not belong in the subjectivity of another. Instead, one might regard the subjectivities of resistance as a member's category available in a language community. Member's use these resources in the work of making sense of others and other things. To treat the matter of subjectivity sociologically is to regard it as a publicly observable element in the language games of specific settings, such as organizations. It also means that one can be precise in the collection of conversational data that, after transcription, allows for any researcher to access and judge the ways in which 'subjectivity' is constituted (see the discussion and supporting appendices for 'Al, the ideal typist', in Clegg, 1975). Second-order accounts tend to be better sociologically the more methodologically and theoretically self-conscious they are. Yet, they are always second-order accounts and should never claim a privileged access to another in any way other than through the forms of reasoning intersubjectively available. In this way categories like 'intention' make sense.

Intention does not refer to a category to which the subject has a unique or privileged access. It is not a mental state prior and interior to some action that is its expression. Outside language and other semiotic systems intentions remain inscrutable. There is no other access to the contents of the other's mind. All we have to guide us are the changing rules of social life as we fleetingly and creatively instantiate them.

Rules can never be free of surplus or ambiguous meaning: they are always indexical to the context of interpreters and interpretation. Where there are rules there must be indexicality, shown by texts as diverse as Wittgenstein (1968), Garfinkel (1967), Clegg (1975) and Barnes (1986). No rule can ever provide for its own interpretation. At its simplest, a 'No Standing' street sign does not mean what it literally seems to say. All rules mean more than they may seem to say because all rules require contexts of interpretation. Contexts of interpretation, however variable, can be stabilized across people, time and space as any translator of any language into any other language knows only too well. Yet, everyday life is not so much like a language as similar to a multiplicity of overlapping and incomplete language games with ambiguous, shifting and frequently undercoded rules. Where rules are instantiated and signified, where people say, do or otherwise act on them, interpretation occurs. 'Ruling' is an activity. Some agency, or more usually, a plurality of agencies must do the constitutive sense-making process which fixes meaning.

The metaphor of rules implies that of games, necessarily. The favoured metaphor for linking power and subjectivity through resistance is that of language games. Where rules tend to be the subject of contested interpretation, there will be resistance. However, power games are only similar in some respects, and not others, to board games or other sports. Some players have not only play-moves but also the refereeing of these as power resources. Consequently, the invocation of rules implies discretion.

DISCRETION, CONTRACTUAL RELATIONS AND CONTROL

The concept of discretion plays a key role in labour process theory. The central relation in this theory is that of the labour contract through which an employer hires labour power. Normally contracts secure the terms by which employers seek to incorporate the person hired as labour power into an effective and functioning member of the organization.[9] Labour power represents a capacity to labour embodied in a person who always retains discretion over the use to which their labour powers are put. From the employers' point of view, or that of their agents, an employee represents a capacity to labour that is hired from the market. Members of organizations are incorporated through the hiring contract, however informal it may be. The knack of successful management and supervision involves translating into actual labour power the hours of the day that the person hired rents to the employing agent. The discretion of the hirer has to shape and channel that of the hiree, if the realization of the capacity to labour is to be achieved in and through labour power subordinated to a strategic purpose. These are the conditions of effective management. Standing in the way of their realization is the fact that the potential labour power hired is always embodied as the capacities of people who may be more or less willing to work as subjects actually ruled by managerial discretion and control. Always, because of embodiment, the people hired as labour power will retain ultimate discretion over themselves, what they do, how they do it. After all, it is their bodily capacities which have been hired and that the hirer(s) seek to use. A potential source of resistance resides in this inescapable and irreducible embodiment of labour power.

The gap between the capacity to labour and its effective realization implies power and the organization of control. The depiction of this gap is the mainstay of some Marxian traditions of analysis, particularly of alienation (Schacht, 1971; Geyer and Schweitzer, 1981; Mézáros, 1970; Gamble and Walton, 1972). Yet, management are forever seeking new strategies or tactics through which that discretion can be deflected. The most effective and economical of these strategies are those that substitute self-discipline for the discipline of an external manager. Less effffective but historically more prolific, have been the attempts of organizations to close the discretionary gap through the use of rule-systems, the mainstay of Weberian influenced analyses of organizations as bureaucracies. Such rule systems seek to regulate meaning in order to control relations of production. Hence, relations of meaning and production are inexorably interlinked.

Organization means control. Control is never total, of course; indeed, in some formulations it is the contradictions inherent in the evolution of regimes of control that explain its development (Clegg and Dunkerley, 1980). Control can never be totally secured, in part because of agency. It will be open to erosion and undercutting by the active, embodied agency of those people who are its object: the labour power of the organization. To think of people as 'labour power' immediately invites reflection on them not only as Durkheimian dwellers and members of an idealized moral community but also as labourers toiling to preserve their 'species-being', resisting alienation, in Marx's metaphor. It is not only in Marx's view of the active embodied person resisting the wasting of their creative powers that we find the locus of agency against organization. It is also implicit in Durkheim's moral community. What one takes to be sacred and what one takes to be profane depends utterly on relations of meaning: the rules of meaning and membership. Such relations of meaning are as resistant to total control as are relations of production. This much has been clear ever since Saussure's (1974) project sowed the seeds for a decoupling of any necessary relationship between the signified and the sign. Resistance to any attempt that seeks to freeze meaning in any specific regulation of it will always be intrinsic to the nature of language as a moral community. In the terms of Durkheim's heirs to the study of the moral order, ethnomethodology, indexicality[10] may be shown to be present in even the most mundane utterance (Garfinkel, 1967).

The implications for the organization and control of the labour process of this double focus on the relations of meaning and the relations of production are evident. Organization encounters agency in at least two forms that have been prototypical for recent organization theory: the person as an agent of signification, in social action theory (Silverman, 1970) and the person as an agent of production, in radical theory (Clegg and Dunkerley, 1980). The separation of these concerns has been an unfortunate aspect of the majority of labour process theory. To separate them in this way is to focus one-sidedly on conditions of organization participation. It is to resist the cognition that the member of an organization is a speaking subject, a labouring subject and an embodied subject. One is so simultaneously and ineradicably. Both meaning and body, fused in the person, can resist the encroachment of organization control on the discursive play of individuals as well as on their capacities to work.

RESISTANCE AND A PARADOX OF POWER

A paradox of a central concept of power, one that stresses normative compliance and consent as the achievement of sucessful power, is that while the authority of an agency increases in principle by that agency delegating authority, this delegation may well undemine power; the delegation of authority can only proceed by rules; rules necessarily entail discretion and discretion potentially empowers delegates in ways that might not be organizationally authoritative. In this context not being organizationally authoritative means that the actions are not authorized by those who enjoy formal and de jure dominance within the organization. In the orthodox literature of organization theory, for example, Mintzberg (1983), these uses of power are referred to as both illegitimate and as resistance.

The tacit and taken-for-granted basis of organizationally negotiated order and resistance to it has been well observed by Strauss (1978). Events and others must be rendered routine and predictable if resistance is to remain an unusual and out of the ordinary state of affairs. Knowledgeable construction of states of affairs is achieved by routines so that subordinate agencies know what should be done. In this way sanctions can be minimized. Power is premised not only on exclusive control or privileged access to knowledge, and the disciplinary mechanisms securing these. It can also involve subordination: as Barnes puts it, agencies 'must recognize that the output of appropriate action that they produce is what minimizes the input of coercion and sanctioning that they receive' (1988: 103). For this reason, wherever questions of time–space extension become necessary for securing organization action, some form of rules of practice to which agents can be held become important. The freedom of discretion requires disciplining if it is to be a reliable relay. Whether done through what Foucault called 'disciplinary' or other modes of practice is unimportant. It may be direct surveillance, the interiorized normalizing gaze of professional self-regulation, a standardized reporting scheme, common economic interest or client reports that serve as the rules of practice.

Authority implies power and rule constitution. The interpretation of rules must be disciplined and regulated if new powers are not to be produced and existing powers transformed by resistance. Of course, they invariably will be, with the passage of time and meaning. It is not just that the meaning of rules is tied to the occasions of their use that leaves space for resistance. Rules can never be exhaustive because they can never anticipate the occasions of their use or non-use. Given the inherent indexicality of rule use, things will never be wholly stable; they will usually exhibit tolerances to stress, strain and strife in rule constitution whose limits can only ever be known for sure in their ill-disciplined breach of regulation. By definition, wholly effective discipline would admit no breach, no 'disobedience', total rule-boundedness.[11] Yet, as Wrong has put it 'Politics includes both a struggle *for* power and a struggle to limit, resist and escape *from* power' (1979: 13). Consequently, as power always involves power over another and thus at least two agencies, it will usually call forth resistance because of the power/knowledge nature of agency. Power and resistance stand in a relationship to each other (Knights and Vurdubakis, 1993). One rarely has one without the other.

It might be thought that without overt conflict there will be no resistance to power. This would be to confuse the notion of resistance *per se* with a particularly dramatic expression of it. Excessive formality and politeness in dealing with one to whom one is subject may well ironicize resistance. It can do this by drawing formal attention to rules that are normally presumed to guide interactions but are usually only tacit, rules ordinarily relaxed in less antagonistic settings. The point is that excessive politeness is only available as a member's category, according to whatever the contextual rules may be interpreted as being. Working to rule may not produce overt conflict with a superior if one can legitimate one's actions with reference to a rule book governing what one should be doing, but it may be an effective form of resistance, as many unionists will attest (also see the discussion in Clegg, 1987). Barbalet (1985: 531) has characterized that resistance that imposes limits on power as 'frictional' – an absence of interest in the realization of the goals of power – in contrast to intended or direct resistance.

Resistance should be regarded as a phenomenon in its own right: one that will be directly implicated in power relations. From this perspective resistance would be the 'efficacious influence of those subordinate to power' (Barbalet, 1985: 542). The criteria that constitute what is 'efficacious' are problematic. At the broadest and least problematic empirically one would be looking at the transformation of extant circuits of power and the replacement of institutionalized rules and relations of meaning. Less broad criteria of efficaciousness are more problematic empirically. Is it 'excessive politeness' that makes power relations more transparent because it draws attention to the institutionalized rules and relations of meaning efficacious? To some extent, because it makes more evident the rule basis of power relations than they would otherwise be, particularly where it is evident from the deference that is shown that the rules and the relations that they legitimate are being ironicized.

Some conceptions of resistance are over-extensions of a sweeping concept of power, a criticism justifiably made by Dews (1979: 165) when he notes Foucault's (1977) 'tendency to slide from the use of the term 'power' to designate one pole of the relation power–resistance, to its use to designate the relations as a whole'. More calibrated conceptions are important because they acknowledge that capacities can never be sure to determine outcomes. Social relations may constitute agencies that use means to control resources to secure consequential outcomes for these agencies. One cannot imply from this that power, as the realization of outcomes, can simply be read-off from the capacities of those exercising power (see Hindess, 1982; Knights and Vurdubakis, 1993). There is always a dialectic to power, always another agency, another set of standing conditions pertinent to the realization of that agency's causal powers against the resistance of another. Consequently, as Barbalet (1985: 539) has suggested, the power of an agent will always be less than the capacities that agent mobilized when attempting to achieve a specific outcome. Rarely will intentions be realized, if we mean by 'intention' reports of the outcome projected by an agency at the outset. Without resistance we would note either that there is a genuine consensus of wills and thus no antagonistic agency or that there is a capitulation by B and their strategic subordination to A.

Resistance to discipline will be irremediable, from a Foucauldian perspective, because of the power/rule constitution as a nexus of meaning and interpretation. Indexicality can always refix meaning and interpretation. It is this that couples power/knowledge in Foucault's (1977) formulation, because, at its most pervasive, power positions the subject, through the organization of disciplinary practices that constitute the potentialities, incapacities and correlates of specific forms of agency. Conceptualizing these power relations as constitutive of the subject, we can identify at least three 'subject positions' discussed in this book, that differ precisely in terms of the extensiveness of organization. First, there is the most intensive, self-organization, the acquisition of more or less disciplined and coherent self-capacities; second, social organization that implicates the self-organization of significant others, usually known in and through face-to-face relations, and third, solidaristic organization, involving the most extensive and generalized organization of others known only at a distance. For each of these degrees of extensiveness there are conditions by which one might anticipate the minimization of resistance. First, let us deal with the parameters of power relations and subjectivity. Second, we can deal with those objective organizational conditions that are more conducive to accommodation rather than to resistance. Generically the latter may be thought of as strategies of outflanking.

POWER RELATIONS AND SUBJECTIVITY

Organizations are constituted around power relations between people; people have differential subjectivities and identities. Different identities and the subjectivities that they make relevant can be postulated as offering differential resources for accommodating to or resisting organizational power relations. Further, it can be hypothesized that organization elites typically seek compliance through the accommodation of others to their will. The hypothesis seems reasonable, yet, as the empirical research represented in this volume shows, resistance can be a characteristic response to the organization of power. Power cannot be relied on to routinely produce consent, although the tendency to equate power and authority assumes that it does.

The purpose of this chapter is to bring some preliminary theoretical order to the specifics of the case studies that comprise this volume. Inductive reasoning, using the cases as the basis for induction, suggests that there are two axes for theory construction. One axis may be represented as a continuum constructed of 'the degree of intensiveness/extensiveness of the power relations constitutive of the subject'. The assumption is that subjectivity is not a pre-given attribute of identity. A given identity might suggest the likelihood of resistance; for instance, being incarcerated in an organization against one's will, as an inmate. Yet, without a subjectivity formed around a will to resist, organizational power relations will be accommodated. Many factors enter into the formation of subjectivities more or less likely to be resistant or accommodative. How do differential subjectivities get made in and out of organizational and other socially ascriptive identities?

Drawing on the chapters in this volume it is possible to identify at least three aspects of this dimension of power relations and subjectivity. There is, first, the question of individual organization. How coherently organized is the individual, in terms of their subjectivity, as a reflexive agent in power relations? How coherently organized is the individual as one who seeks to enrol, translate, interest or oppose others in their projects? Does the individual subject have sufficient self-cognizance to be able to exercise this agency? Second, at the mid-point, there is the question of social organization. To what extent is the subject able to draw upon resources of social organization greater than the self, such as familial networks or an ecology of local community networks? Third, the most extensive point is the question of solidaristic organization: to what extent can the subject draw upon the consciously organized resources of a social movement or collective organization in the pursuit of their agency? To what extent does power constitute the resources of human agency in terms of self, significant and generalized others (Fig. 9)?[12]

Questions contingent upon 'how power relations constitute the subject' pose one dimension of the concerns in this book. The other dimension may be theorized in terms of a set of questions that ask what are the specific types of consciousness through which resistance occurs in specific organizational settings? For the latter, there can be no exhaustive answer and none will be attempted. Any listing of consciousnesses of resistance can only be an inductive response to empirical specifics. This chapter will be no exception. Codifying the types of resistant consciousnesses testifies to a re-

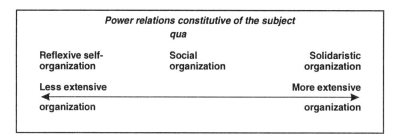

Figure 9.1 Power relations constitutive of the subject

markable ingenuity and creativity. Analysis of types of resistant consciousness in association with different types of power relations constitutive of the subject makes the sociological parameters of organizational power and resistance more apparent. We will move to this codification shortly. First, it is necessary to discuss those strategies of outflanking which can render resistance redundant. The reason for this is the analytical primacy attached to power in this chapter. Resistance as a form of power will first be explained in its absence, or at least its minimization, before considering its presence and those conditions conducive to its amplification.

STRATEGIES OF OUTFLANKING

In considering the conditions that might contribute to the minimization of resistance, the first to consider is 'ignorance'. At the individual level, one may simply not know or understand the power relations constitutive of one's own identity. Many 'coming out' accounts of the experience of sexual liberation from the assumptions of 'normal' heterosexuality often have this character. Subjects simply were ignorant of the possibilities of sexual identity other than the one dimension proffered as 'normal', in the confines of the family, the small town or whatever conditions had to be breeched so that other forms of identity could be seen and thus resistance to 'normalcy' organized. Simultaneously, however, ignorance contributes to resistance to change at the same time that it facilitates the acceptance of the established order. Ignorance is a factor which both can facilitate or restrict the imposition of a specific kind of power from one subject to others. It depends on the context.

Ignorance at the level of social organization might consist of those who are somewhat powerless remaining so because they are ignorant of the social organization of power – ignorant, that is, of informal conduits as well as formal protocols, the style and substance of power, its shared culture embedded in a distinct social organization. It is not that they do not know the rules of the game so much as that they might not recognize the game, let alone know the rules. Of course, this is a particular problem where an overwhelmingly technologically superior form of life meets one that is by contrast less developed in technical terms. Historically the vast majority of cross-cultural contact has occurred on this basis: consequently it has been the force of arms that has settled the outcomes. In this context resistance usually occurs through a clash of strongly held cultural systems.

In the context of solidaristic organization, ignorance often extends to a simple lack of knowledge of the organizational agencies with whom one might construct an alliance. Here resistance cannot be part of a concerted action. It remains unorganized defiance, easily surmounted and overcome even when its irruption is not infrequent across the whole scope of power. Since the outbreaks remain uncoordinated they can easily be dealt with by defeat, exile or incorporation.

An absence of knowledge may be premised on isolation. At the level of individual organization one might experience as a situational snub, slight or handicap a form of power whose systemic quality remains obscure because one lacks or has not yet developed the reflexive capacities to organize oneself coherently across the multiple scenes of one's individual life. What is being resisted is ones' self but one lacks a coherent account of oneself and sees as particular misfortunes what others might see as systematic oppression, varying only in its locales. Marxian accounts of the politics of criminology have this quality, when, for instance, Taylor *et al.* (1974: 278) conclude their analysis of the 'new criminology' with the statement that 'The conditions of our time are forcing a reappraisal of [the] compartmentalization of issues and problems' and go on to speak of the 'total interconnectedness' of extensive social deprivation and the crisis of the 'master institutions' of the state and the political economy. From this perspective, the private troubles of those unfortunates who are homeless, or stigmatized or dispossessed are the public biography of a system in crisis. It would remain the case even where the subjective experience of these troubles is wholly in terms of individual effort losing out to particularistic fate in the by-ways of the state, the market and the increasingly uncivil society. It is only with the development of frustration with the stacked deck of life chances that 'fate' seems to have dealt that this gets channelled into action in this world (rather than into a project concerning the next).

In terms of social and solidaristic organization, isolation may mean that one is simply without ready access to potential allies. Though one might easily outweigh one's protagonists if one could only connect with other kin or socially organized networks, one cannot because one cannot readily access them. Isolation often leads to resistance that is personalistic and easily subject to organizational treatment as individually deviant.

A step further from isolation is division. The individual's self-organization may be constructed in terms of divided life-worlds in which one manages the trials and tribulations of relative powerlessness in one sphere by hermetically sealing experience in situational specificity. Subject compartmentalization into segmented and thus psychically protected spheres is a form of resistance in itself, as witness the 'instrumental' worker (Goldthorpe *et al.*, 1969). In terms of social organization time and space may be ordered and arranged to minimize the possibilities for networks of kin or kith or other social organization emerging. Complex divisions of labour, anti-union prohibitions and the extreme experience of competition are examples. Other, more macro-historical examples include the use of armies from elsewhere for the business of intra-imperial subordination, a strategy that has a long history reaching to Tianamen Square in recent times. Where one might anticipate solidaristic organization time and space can be ordered and arranged to minimize the interaction and mutual awareness of subordinates, or even to render one group of subordinates invisible to another (Barnes, 1988: 101). Resistance usually tries to seize upon some common aspect of this seemingly divided humanity that opposes them. An example of the role that division can play in the outflanking of potential resistance occurs in the example that Collinson (1993) cites of the multinational corporation, where divisionalization reinforces 'insecurities and barriers to resistance'. Solidaristic organization in multinational corporations always suffers from the potential risk of isolation. (In fact, isolation and division are, as it were, two sides of the same coin.) One might achieve solidaristic organization and a successful strike in one country against an employing organization that is a multinational. Yet, one is relatively powerless where there is a propensity for the multinational to isolate and substitute for that national production with an increase from elsewhere outside the national basis of solidarism, where competing national solidarisms come into play. Coordination across the boundaries of division can provide a basis for resistance.

Organizational outflanking, based on the knowledge that those outflanked have, operates in a quite distinct manner to instances premised on ignorance. What is at issue is knowing not only what is to be done but, equally, knowing that the costs of doing so may be far more than the probability of achieving the desired outcome. Barnes (1988: 43–4) offered the unpleasant if apposite example of a 'concentration camp', one of this centuries more odious techniques of power, in collecting, categorizing, marking and exterminating whole bodies of people. At the individual level, as Collinson (1993) reminds us, existential resistance by individuals is always possible, such as that charted by Primo Levi (1987a; 1987b), where the sense of self that one has remains intact through techniques of 'mental distancing'. From Goffman (1971) on, there is a voluminous literature to consult. At the existential extreme, individual acts of resistance, including the defiance explicit in one's own suicide, are *always* possible. Yet, resistance through social and solidaristic organization is much more difficult in the circumstances of the camp where counter-organization is far more difficult. Existing in severe deprivation under a regime of brutality, terror and horror is not conducive to closely organized ranks of relatively undisciplined individuals. The aggregate impact of individual acts of resistance may be effective, but it is easy for the individual's will to power to be broken, by death, if necessary. Without organization resistance will not survive the individual's death. In addition, disparate acts of recalcitrance by people exposed to certain terror if the uncertain enterprise of resistance is exposed, make the achievement of collective organized resistance more fragile and precarious a probability. While there may be little or no chance of organizing for success, there is every chance that the attempt at organization will lead to certain failure and death. Even if it were successful, then the confines of the camp may be breached only for one to be picked out as part of the fleeing mob of inmates at the leisure of the authorities who command the environs of the camp. For these reasons opportunism will always be a problem. Few may be willing to sacrifice themselves for the altruistic good of the others by initiating a charge on the armed guards. Others may hope to save their skins by exposing others to the authorities. Within such a camp the thousands of inmates might succeed in concerted action against the relatively few armed guards. It would depend upon the vulnerability of the watchtowers, the security of the perimeter and the strength of arms.[13]

It could be objected that, with sufficient sacrifice, the inmates might resist and overcome the obstacles. Yet, there is the technical difficulty of getting concertation among the inmates when they are unable to organize explicitly. Implicit organization is possible, perhaps, based on contained sub-unit social organization such as dormitories, but exceedingly difficult with neither mechanisms nor arena of organization. In prisoner-of-war camps, by contrast to death camps, the existence of a recognized command structure, its disciplines and rules, make this organization that much easier. There is an extensive social organization around which resistance can function more effectively.

Finally, organizational outflanking may operate not so much on knowledge of what achievements can be anticipated so much as the conditions that exist that render any such knowledge useless. One knows that one is an exploited wage earner but the routines of everyday living and life or the identity of one as a 'man' (or some other category meaningful for existence) have greater salience than ones 'exploitation'. The necessity of dull compulsion to 'earn' one's living, the nature of that dull compulsion as busy work, as arduous exertion, as ceaseless activity, as routinely deadening, compulsory and invariable – such techniques of power may easily discipline the blithest of theoretically free spirits when the conditions of that freedom become evident. The most resistant of wills may bend when it realizes that it has no chance of increasing freedom to manoeuvre through recourse to some alternative. Time is double-edged here: both using the time of an agent on the routine performance of routine tasks as well as the habituation that this produces over time as personal and intersubjective routines take on a ritual nature as bulwarks against the encroaching meaninglessness of externally imposed routine. Such rituals may be both informal and formal, the former a kind of resistance to the meaning of the latter as Burawoy (1979) charts. Formal rituals, myth and ceremony serve to reinforce and make meaningful the routines of everyday subordination just as resistance may seek to ironicize, distance or undercut these routines. In this way the formal rituals of power may

Outflanking of resistance through:	Power relations constitutive of the subject qua		
	Reflexive self-organization	social organization	solidaristic organization
	Less extensive organization ←——————————————→ More extensive organization		
Ignorance	Ignorance through sense of self-isolation: 'coming out' as resistance.	Ignorance of the cultures of power: resistance through culture clashes.	Ignorance of potential organizational allies through isolation: resistance through defiance.
Isolation	Isolation of systematic events and actions due to a fatalistic acceptance of a non-strategic view of injustice: resistance through frustration.	Who and where are the allies that might share the common experience of oppression and rise with us in resistance? Isolation often leads to resistance that is personalistic and easily treated as individually deviant.	
Division	Divided life-worlds leading to situational specificity. Resistance through the creation of psychic compartments, e.g. the instrumental worker.	Divide-and-rule: the use of imperial strategies that a strategic apex of power allows. Resistance would have to occur through coordination and common cause and consciousness across the divisions: 'Workers of the world unite'.	
Knowledge	The likely costs of resistance weigh heavily on the consciousness of those who might resist. Resistance against percievedly overwhelming odds tends to be through existential and symbolic gestures. Issues of everday life may have greater salience than the struggle to resist.	Knowledge exists, but without both formal arenas for organization and the formal resources of that organization, there is a low probability that resistance will occur successfully. Often, the knowledge basis that exists for resistance becomes institutionalized and expressed through rituals that are embedded in social and solidaristic organization. Power and resistance require each other in a drama where neither threatens the reproduction of the other.	

Figure 9.2 Power relations constitutive of the subject and outflanking

sometimes be endured. The preceding discussion is summarized graphically in Figure 9.2.

Collinson suggests (in this volume) that a focus on 'organizational outflanking' should not enjoy analytical priority over that of a focus on resistance. Yet, given the way in which debates about power have tended to focus, after Lukes (1974), on the 'third dimension' of power as incorporation, hegemony and inaction, I think that it is appropriate to regard outflanking as *analytically* prior to resistance. That is not to say that, empirically, it will always precede resistance and that resistance will have to unfetter whatever the chains of outflanking are, but that resistance requires consciousness. Hence, the problematic of the third dimension of power, focused on 'unconsciousness', is analytically prior. Before resistance there must be consciousness. In terms of the Lukesian problematic we require an understanding of how a consciousness of power is possible before we are able to discuss resistance. Resistance is not a natural correlate of power, in other words, however characteristic its experience may be. The linking of concepts of outflanking and knowledge does not involve the deployment of a set of highly rationalistic assumptions regarding subjectivity in which subordinates are seen as totally rational, calculative and highly instrumental with extensive skills of prediction, as Collinson suggests. Realizing that the sociologically differential probabilities of resistance vary with conditions of self, social and solidaristic organization, should serve to counter this view. However, against this, one should acknowledge that nonetheless people can exercise power without knowing that they are doing so and this holds also for the practices that, *post hoc*, one might categorize under the rubric of 'outflanking'. A few points of additional clarification may also be of assistance.

First, one does not assume the possibility of knowledge of the content of other minds other than through conventionally encoded ways of interpretation. Second, the assumptions about outflanking serves sociologically to delimit and illuminate different conditions that might mobilize resistance to one's power. Third, the argument does not deny the possibility of resistance. On the contrary, it sought only to note that the concept of resistance requires some calibration if it is to be a sociologically useful category. If resistance is everywhere it is conceptually equivalent to saying that it is nowhere. All analysis requires some discrimination, theoretical assumptions and methodological accountability.[14]

EMPIRICAL CASES OF RESISTANCE

The chapters in this book will now be considered in terms of the parameters developed thus far, and used as occasions to develop some key points further. They present many detailed accounts of acts of resistance. Each case can be considered in terms of the horizontal axis already established in Figure 9.1. Any act of resistance requires some degree of organization. At the very minimal it requires reflexive self-organization of one's self as a 'resistant subject', as someone who chooses to make a stand, even if that stand is a wholly personal one, a seemingly idiosyncratic act of outrage, rebellion or an existential gesture. One thinks, for example, of the minor act of vandalism that landed *Cool Hand Luke* (directed by Stuart Rosenberg, 1967) in gaol. Yet, this kind of personal resistance, the first step against the defeat of any tyranny, hegemony or regime of normalcy, is the most vulnerable to defeat. At the very simplest, snuff out the person and the resistance might also be defeated. Courage, conviction and a consciousness that is reflexively self-organized is no guarantee of success. Where it is possible to marshal extensive organizational resources, such as are provided by a family or kin network or an informal social organization within one that is formal, the resistance is inter-subjective; it involves not only the self but also significant others whose support can nourish and sustain individually resistant self-consciousness. Resistance, like the experience of democracy (Pateman, 1970), can thrive on its experience. Yet, even where linked through family, kin or informal organization, such resistance suffers in contrast to power that is representationally organized. One thinks of the peak organization of the pillars of state and society, such as the church, the state, capital and labour. Here there is extensive formal organization that, if it is to be resisted beyond the scope of individual acts of indifference, evasion and gesture, requires some solidaristic organization capable of uniting disparate bodies across space and time in a formal organization against that power it seeks to oppose. Hence, one axis for analysis concerns the power relations that are con- stitutive of the resistant subject. What organizational capacities do they imply?

There is another axis, more inductive and variable. It concerns the actual forms that resistance takes in specific settings, the bases of that resistance, its triumphs, anxieties and failures. Such stories are infinite: they know no end and any collection of them will be but a small testament to the will of resistance.[15] In this volume are collected a number of disparate examples. With what is perhaps more inductive enthusiasm than wisdom might warrant one has attempted to arrange these cases into some theoretical order. The basis for doing so is to have read each case in terms of the type of resistant consciousness that it implies. Resistance does require consciousness, does require that those who are resisting have a consciousness of doing so. Consciousness may be more or less reflexive, more or less capable of recollecting its own auspices, of articulating what it is that it seeks to do or have done, but it requires a minimum of some such reflexivity. The conditions of resistance that are elaborated in the research collected here are many and variable. In an attempt to collect them within the frame of this chapter I have organized them into the following categories: distanciated consciousness; plural self-consciousness; occupational knowledge self-consciousness; whistleblower self-consciousness; saboteurs' self-consciousness; rule self-consciousness; gender self-consciousness and a natural rights self-consciousness. No privilege attaches to the pattern in which they are introduced, other than its contrivance for purposes of presentation in Figure 9.3.

Each of these types of consciousness will be used to introduce and arrange the cases presented earlier in this volume and will be elaborated in the context of these cases. Wherever it is relevant to do so, I will refer back to the earlier discussion in this chapter, particularly that of 'outflanking', because, as we shall see, it frequently makes little sense to consider resistance one-sidedly, without also considering opposing strategies that seek to accommodate or to outflank. Let us begin at the beginning.

PERSISTENCE, DISTANCE AND FORMS OF CONSCIOUSNESS

Collinson's paper focuses on social organization (see ch. 1). In one case this social organization is premised both on informal organization on the shopfloor and the way that claims to reflexive self-organization are made through this informal organization. In the other the focus is less on the identity of reflexive self-organization and more on the social organization of a formally concrete issue. Although the two case studies presented both focus on the social organization of the specific workplaces, the actual patterns of resistance differ between the two cases. Although both focus on the

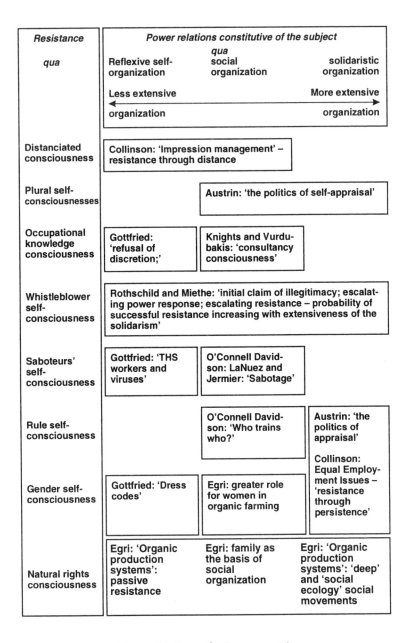

Resistance qua	Power relations constitutive of the subject qua		
	Reflexive self-organization	social organization	solidaristic organization
	Less extensive organization ←—————————————→		More extensive organization
Distanciated consciousness	Collinson: 'Impression management' – resistance through distance		
Plural self-consciousnesses		Austrin: 'the politics of self-appraisal'	
Occupational knowledge consciousness	Gottfried: 'refusal of discretion;'	Knights and Vurdu-bakis: 'consultancy consciousness'	
Whistleblower self-consciousness	Rothschild and Miethe: 'initial claim of illegitimacy; escalating power response; escalating resistance – probability of successful resistance increasing with extensiveness of the solidarism'		
Saboteurs' self-consciousness	Gottfried: 'THS workers and viruses'	O'Connell David-son: LaNuez and Jermier: 'Sabotage'	
Rule self-consciousness		O'Connell David-son: 'Who trains who?'	Austrin: 'the politics of appraisal' Collinson: Equal Employ-ment Issues – 'resistance through persistence'
Gender self-consciousness	Gottfried: 'Dress codes'	Egri: greater role for women in organic farming	
Natural rights consciousness	Egri: 'Organic production systems': passive resistance	Egri: family as the basis of social organization	Egri: 'Organic production systems': 'deep' and 'social ecology' social movements

Figure 9.3 Power/resistance matrix

deployment of knowledge as a strategy of resistance, in the one case, it is achieved through 'distance', in the other through 'persistence'.

Distanciated consciousness: resistance through distance

Distanciation through role distance is a well-known coping strategy (Goffman, 1971). As a strategy of resistance 'distance' involved social organization around the (masculine) identity of shopfloor work and its representation through impression management in the organization. A conscious impression of shopfloor work and culture was managed as more authentically English, working class and masculine in comparison to the workforce reception of the representations of American management. Workforce impression management of the nature of work allowed workers to reclaim time and redefine space, both metaphorically and physically, in terms of the locale of the toilets as 'private space'.

The management fixing of bonus rates in the organization was a particular zone of contention, as it so often is. Yet, this resistance was limited. It was not solidaristic. Resistance through distance, premised on informal social organization on the shopfloor, did not prove to be a basis for resistance to redundancies. Again, impression management was important, but this time by management. The strategy that they followed was one where shopfloor resistance was effectively 'outflanked' through managerial knowledge, as an unintended consequence of accounting practices. Workers became overwhelmed with technical justifications for the redundancy decision by management. The previous strategy of resistance by distance eased the acceptance of these justifications: a part of the discursive basis of the 'distance' strategy was that workers ought to keep their distance from managerial prerogative. Doing otherwise risked co-optation or incorporation. The social organization of resistance thus undercut possibilities for solidaristic resistance. Solidaristic knowledge foundered not only on a lack of knowledge-capacity by the shopfloor to counter managerial information. Informal social organization on the shopfloor in terms of impression management of effort combined with maximization of pay through the bonus. When the redundancies were threatened bonus maximization was sacrificed by the shop stewards for job security. Thus, this case study tends to confirm the analytic points made in the earlier section of this chapter. Social organization, through the shared networks of information and identity on the shopfloor, proved to be only a partial strategy of resistance and one easily outflanked by management deployment of knowledge in a context where the terms of the social organization of resistance served as a limit.

Rule consciousness: resistance through persistence

Collinson's case study of resistance through persistence is an instance of the utilization by a subordinate of the resource of formal organizational rules to overturn an earlier decision. It points again to the 'liberal' potential of bureaucracy as a system, something highlighted elsewhere (Perrow, 1986; Clegg, 1990). Rules allow for holding organization actions accountable in terms of the formal rhetoric governing organizational practice. Collinson offers a case study of resistance premised on the social organization of overlapping union and gender relations, using the formal resources of the organizations' commitment to, and governance by, the Equal Opportunities Commission. The 'rights' inscribed in this governance can function both as powers that subjugate and as points for the articulation of resistance. Collinson's case serves as an example of resistance overcoming the limits of 'ignorance' at the level of social organization. The relatively powerless clerk did not remain formally discriminated against because she was able to draw from the union network and her resources a knowledge of the social organization of power. Although the case focuses on dyadic and triadic interpersonal relations, the dynamics of the case seem to rest on the solidaristic relations of the complainant and her union representative. The solidarism is both one of women and the union. Therefore, this is an example of gender consciousness articulated through a consciousness of the legal rights contained in the Equal Employment Legislation requirements governing the organization. Knowledge of informal conduits as well as formal protocols, the style and substance of power, its shared culture embedded in a distinct social organization, that of formal organizational bureaucracy, allowed the grievance to be resisted. The rules of the game were understood.

Despite the conclusions that Collinson draws, it seems evident that the emphasis that he develops is not inconsistent with a more nuanced account of resistance. Outflanking and resistance can readily be related to each other, as this commentary demonstrates. Collinson's chapter only too clearly makes the point about outflanking. Collinson notes that when the experience of division 'combined with the additional pressures of domestic responsibilities and the need to provide for children and to finance a mortgage dissatisfied employees may well decide to just "grin and bear it" and to accommodate to the status quo in order to guarantee a wage or salary'. Further, we are advised that

> conformity or compliant practices can often have self-fulfilling effects. If the majority of work colleagues are unwilling to take action to oppose management, those who would resist are aware that their actions have even less chance of being effective. The conformity or compliance of the many thus frequently disciplines the oppositional practices of the few . . . whilst current systems and practices of control and discipline are deemed to be normal and legitimate, oppositional behaviour is thereby treated as aberrant, deviant and unjustifiable. In such discursive struggles, managers are in an advantaged position because they often have the material and symbolic resources and information to facilitate the widest dissemination of their definition of reality.
>
> (Collinson, this volume)

I think that at this stage one can rest one's point with respect to the need for concepts of *both* resistance *and* outflanking. Conceptualization of the one should not suggest the redundancy of the other. Surprisingly, both Clegg and Collinson seem in agreement on this.

Collinson suggests a hypothesis. The more closely related a case is to reflexive self-organization in terms of identity, the less likely it is that oppositional practices will be effective, compared with opposition premised on issues. In other words, when resistance is tied to a preoccupation with securing one's identity, it may be less effective than when issue focused. The hypothesis is really a form of the argument that collective resistance is generally more effective than individualistic forms of opposition.[16] The hypothesis is that 'strategies that seek to increase employee involvement in organizational processes and to render managerial practices more visible and accountable may be more effective forms of workplace resistance than those primarily concerned with distancing'. We shall return to this hypothesis.

In both of Collinson's cases the examples of resistance were reactive to managerial initiatives. For the male shopfloor workers the initiative was one directed towards the introduction of a new corporate culture influenced by the American ideas of the new owners; in the latter case it was a reaction by the woman involved to a specific internal personnel decision seen in the context of the commitment of the new owners, also from the United States, to equal employment opportunity.

SUBJECTIVITY IS NOT SOVEREIGN

In the chapter by O'Connell Davidson the initiation of change was contingent upon the privatization of a public utility, and the introduction of a new computer system and multi-functional team-working in the clerical work area, 'designed to deskill clerical work' (see ch. 2). It also had the objective, we are advised, of creating more flexible working arrangements from the more standardized work process that the computerization should have allowed. As should be evident, to intend an objective is not to secure it.

Rule consciousness and sabotage

A survey showed discontent with the changes by the female clerical workforce. In addition, the study demonstrated that the computerization had not achieved managerial objectives. The continuity of the work process was frequently assured only when the clerical workforce exerted a discretion which the change had been designed to minimize. While the computerization did deskill workers, its frequent software limitations, as well as hardware problems, also provided opportunity for workforce initiative and discretion, lodged in tacit knowledge, action frequently expressed in resistance to managerial fiat, in introducing the new work design and system. Moreover, the changes made the nature of management's relations with the clerical workforce less legitimate in the workforce perception.

The resistance that followed was not organized on a solidaristic basis through the union, although the union was involved in the early stages of the dispute. The reason for this was inadvertent organizational outflanking contingent upon the division within the union organization between the regional and national structure. The national structure, involved in a separate and overlapping timetable of industry-wide negotiations, did not want the officers at the regional level to settle on a basis that might prove detrimental to national negotiation. Also, the national union officers seemed less than fully informed of the organizational changes that had occurred at the regional level. Organizational division contributed to organizational ignorance. Finally, at the regional level, the gender division between predominantly female clerical workers and male branch union officers, meant that for many female workers they were ignorant of the social organization of union power – ignorant, that is, of informal conduits as well as formal protocols, the style and substance of power, its shared, masculinist culture, embedded in a distinct social organization. The quotation from the young woman who had recently joined the union is an excellent example of a person who feels outflanked through ignorance, not by her employer but by her union

> 'When I joined [the union] I just got this plastic wallet with all this information . . . I read through it, understood bits, didn't understand other bits . . . no one sort of said "we do this and that, and we can do this for you" . . . they just give you the pamphlet and I suppose they think you'll pick it up as you go along. But I still don't really understand. I know they fight for us and stuff, but whereas at these meetings there's a few that stand up and speak their minds, I wouldn't do that, because I don't know much about the unions. I stand in the back row and keep my mouth shut. I'm worried about this Beta structure, so I've been to all the meetings, but to be honest, I don't understand what they're on about.'
>
> (quoted in O'Connell Davidson, this volume, p. 90)

Nonetheless, resistance did occur, even if it not led by the national union. Based at first on the workplace social organization of the clerks, it used the 'rights' enshrined in the formal organizational rules (who could train who) as a resource, as well as brief 'walkouts'. It also took more individualistic forms related to reflexive issues of identity. Customer care was something that the workforce normally wanted to offer, but some, at risk to their identity, declined to do so in response to the management move towards profit maximization and away from the workforce view of customer service (being helpful, the state that they regarded as 'normal'), through 'sabotaging' the software system. Hence, they displayed not only a rule consciousness but also a saboteur's consciousness. In both cases the basis of resistance involved the subjectivity of the workers, their view of what their identity should be. As O'Connell Davidson points out, this subjective identity also gets constrained by objective conditions, such as the state of the labour market. Indeed, these enter the constitution of managerial subjectivities as well. Management is more likely not to back-peddle on changes that a workforce might resist where they guage that the objective conditions for the expression of that resistance are less than fully propitious. From this chapter, we can draw the important hypothesis that subjective identity and the propensity of resistance to occur will be contingent upon the objective conditions within which people constitute the sense of their subjectivity. Subjectivity is not sovereign.

REFLEXIVE SELF-ORGANIZATION AND FORMS OF CONSCIOUSNESS

Labour process theory has developed in the space that exists between the fact of employers contractually hiring labour and the actuality of employers achieving effective and designated deployment of the human labour employed. This space can be conceptualized in terms of 'indeterminacy', a concept derived from the sociology of the professions (e.g. Boreham, 1983) that has spread across the study of occupations more generally. Indeterminacy creates an imperative for control, a fact readily visible in the ordinary language of management as it emerged historically, with its emphasis on 'super-vision' and 'sub-ordinates', those *with* superordinate vision *and* supervisory roles, compared with those being ordered, arranged, ordinated.

Power relations are the core of organization and management. People are born free but everywhere they are in chains, metaphorical chains of organization and management. Such metaphorical chains are not necessarily ties that bind tightly, but can be impressions of management sustained by socially organized and cultural collusion between subordinates to create an impression of control for those above them. In such indeterminate impressionism small spaces of retrieval and recovery of symbolic signs of freedom may be constructed, however illusory or fleeting the impression may subsequently turn out to be (see Collinson, ch. 1 of this volume). It is because the collusion is constituted through cultural resources that resistance can be both open-ended and creative in content, yet also have predictable configurations. Aspects of identity such as gender, ethnicity, sexuality, religiosity and so on, will invariably enter the constitution of resistance, because of their pivotal role in providing cultural resources that enable one to identify who one is in relation not only to the reflexive sense of self-consciousness but

also the others with whom one colludes or conflicts in organizational locales. The notion of organizational locales suggests the
idea of spatially and temporally located conjunctures. Within these
routines of cultural creativity can be extemporized, rehearsed,
rejected, revised and embraced by bodies of labour. A recurrent
complex of face-to-face, at-a-distance and removed relations get
produced that offer opportunities for stable organization of the self,
the self in relation to significant others and the self in relation to
bases of solidarism.

Saboteurs' gender and rule self-consciousness

Typically, organizational characterizations imply routine spatio-
temporal conjuncture, a situation that has been typical of the vast
majority of labour process studies. Organizational settings where
these characteristics are not present represent fertile ground for
labour process research. The sample of female clerical workers who
contracted with Temporary-Help Service (THS) Agencies studied by
Gottfried (ch. 3, this volume) in a medium sized mid-western city in
the United States, suggest that 'Temps' (the vernacular term in
common usage in Britain and Australia), represent an increasingly
important type of contractual labour for many organizations. They
are employees of an external agency that sub-contracts their labour
in the market to whatever organization requires temporary help.
Therefore, the site of the labour process is not the site of contractual
employment – that remains the agency with whom they initially
contract – but the sub-contracting site: an alien culture, an unknown
locale. One consequence of this split is that agency and client
organizations may be said to have different interests in how the
contracted employee works. The agency is paid for time; the client
for effort. Maximization of the latter may foreshorten the former.

How do control and resistance get done in the potentially contradictory context of agency/client contracting of labour, where the
resources for both are situationally specific and, for the 'temp',
fleeting? First, there are tight entry and training controls on THS
labour. Second, there are strict recommendations on 'appropriate
feminine' impression management. Third, there are formal attempts
to situate subjects in a nexus of meaning simultaneously in work
and in womanhood, the latter at varying stages of the presumed
life-cycle. Yet, resistance still occurs, even where temporary status
does not allow for that 'substantial control over the labour process'

that Edwards and Scullion (1982: 271) anticipated as a prerequisite for resistance premised on the restriction of effort. What is immediately evident from Gottfried's participant observation account is that the examples of resistance that she discusses are of reflexive self-organization, consisting of a series of 'disinclinatory refusals' and forms of 'sabotage'.[17] These include a disinclination to assert occupational self-consciousness by not remedying errors in text instructions, a disinclination to dress just like a woman in the terms that the agency prefers, and thus a refusal of a pre-packaged gender identity and its appropriate gender self-consciousness. In addition, the saboteurs self-consciousness offers many further opportunities: from the unleashing of a computer virus that can wreck a system to minor disruptions of occupational routines, that are 'defensive, accommodative and intermittent'. There will be more on sabotage later.

CULTURES OF CULTIVATION

Historically the concept of culture implied cultivation, initially in terms of horticultural cultivation, only later in terms of social distinction. Egri's paper focuses attention on cultures of cultivation as an object of labour process analysis. Agriculture has been a relatively neglected area of application for labour process analysis, although Canadian researchers, in particular, such as Clement (1983), have applied labour process analysis to fishing and farming industries. Agricultural production has seen the subordination of an autonomous branch of petty bourgeois commodity production organized in the familial form to an agribusiness form. Agribusiness is dominated by oligopolistic production and distribution systems within which the farm labour process is contractually captive. From the early 1980s onwards, in North America (and elsewhere), these tendencies have produced a 'farm crisis'. The crisis is expressed in personal bankruptcies and increasing quit rates from the land, either wholly or partially, as family members seek other forms of employment.

Natural rights and gender self-consciousness

Resistance to the decline of petty commodity production as an autonomous sphere of classic values of petty bourgeois control and individualism has principally taken a solidaristic form within the subordinated petty commodity mode of agrarian production. In general it has not been successful: a petty bourgeois oppositional class consciousness, is, of necessity, a difficult ideological community to forge and sustain. Resistance to the capitalist class domination of agribusiness has come not from an explicitly class consciousness but from a strong consciousness of 'natural rights': one where certain 'rights' are attached to nature.

In what I have termed the 'natural rights' framework, the farmer is considered to have the right to cultivate the land, but only within the natural rights seen to attach to them. Farmers ought not violate these rights through technological, bio-chemical, or other 'unnatural' forms of intervention. The farmer cares for and cultivates nature on terms that do not violate nature's rights. It is a form of natural rights doctrine extended to the cultivation of the earth, of which Egri identifies four variants: organic farming; regenerative agriculture; ecological agriculture and bio-dynamic agriculture. These aid the re-invention of the farmer as a contemporary craftsperson, socially organized around the form of the family farm, complete with the emergence of contemporary guildlike structures of certification and support. The identity of organic farmers forms in many ways, yet one common feature is that organic farmers consistently report a more radical orientation towards the environment than do conventional farmers. That is, their values already mesh with organic farming. At the furthest extent there is a resonance through the philosophies of deep ecology (Devall and Sessions, 1985) and social ecology (Bookchin, 1990) with a transformational social movement ideology.

Between the 'passive resistance' of organic farming as one's chosen way of displaying one's values and the more militant social movement aspects lies the path of governmental recognition and collaboration with existing agribusiness organizations, an incremental strategy for innovation that does not threaten existing power relations, a strategy that some farmers' favour. Would institutionalized forms of the social movement that did not have radical potential still figure as examples of 'resistance'? Egri does not raise this issue, but it points to an underlying issue that this collection raises. If we are to think of resistance as the 'efficacious influence of those subordinate to power' (Barbalet, 1985: 542) does the institutionalized path of collaboration and recognition constitute an instance of the concept? Can the category of resistance be so extended to embrace at one extreme, an individual grievance, and at the other, the institutionalization of a social movement? If so, what is the value of the concept? Is it so elastic as to go anywhere?

DEFEATING DUALISM

The work of David Knights and his collaborators (represented in chapter 6 of this volume, by Knights and Vurdubakis in a contribution that is primarily theoretical), has been a major conduit for the introduction of Foucauldian themes into recent labour process analysis. In the chapter represented in this volume the focus is on correcting certain mechanistic conceptions of the relation of power and resistance. These conceptions flow from what they term a 'dualistic perspective', one that veers between an abstract structuralism (in this context, Braverman's 'objectivism' *vis-à-vis* class structure) and a subjectivist humanism (in this context, one might regard Collinson's privileging of 'subjectivity' as leaning towards this error). Against these tendencies Knights and Vurdubakis suggest that

> Rather than seeing power as something held by the powerful and mechanistically enforcing conformity among the powerless, we believe it is more productive to attend to the practices, techniques and methods through which 'power' becomes operable. By this we mean those contextually specific practices, techniques, procedures, forms of knowledge and modes of rationality routinely developed in attempts to shape the conducts of others.

The corollary of this view, as they point out (and with which the author of this piece concurs) is that if a global theory of power is impossible then so is a global theory of resistance. Instead there is a wholly contingent view of power and resistance, where the one may creatively produce the other.

Occupational self-consciousness

In the course of what is a philosophically grounded attempt to clarify certain issues and confusions raised for labour process analysis by the Foucauldian corpus, Knights and Vurdubakis discuss research that they have done on IT consultants. These consultants develop a socially organized 'consultancy consciousness'. It is one rooted in the claims of their occupational knowledge. With this knowledge they are able to offer a 'solution' that displays a counter-rationality that resists resistance. The resistance resisted belongs to those organizational members who remain rooted in their occupational knowledge self-consciousness. This becomes challenged by the changing power relations that the IT technology introduces. 'Resistance consequently plays the role of continuously provoking extensions, revisions and refinements of those same practices that it confronts', as they put it. As noted at the outset of this chapter, perhaps it is only in the conventions of the early Hollywood western that the good guys and the bad guys are so easily distinguishable. More recently we might expect such identities to be more transitory, fleeting, ambivalent and semiotically insecure. This is the case with this example. 'Power' and 'resistance' are not phenomena that, pre-scripted, belong to the bad guys and the good guys, respectively, whatever the criteria of identification: class, gender, ethnicity whatever. Analysis that presumes otherwise already needs no argument. It already knows who the subjects of history are; who are the oppressors and the oppressed, the good and the bad.

There are no *necessary* pre-scripted human agents with *a priori* subject positions – men/women; capital/labour; black/white, and so on. Human subjects bring qualitatively different forms of knowledge into power relations. These knowledges get to be deployed in the specific contexts of these power relations. Hence, different subjectivities may be embodied in the one person but because they are situationally specific need not be contradictory. What makes power relations so complex and so interesting is the plurality of people involved, each seeking to configure the relations and the arenas that they structure. In these ways identities and difference become configured and contested, often in terms of claims to universality expressed in terms of specific subject positions, such as men/women, capital/labour, nature/culture, and so on. With respect to the last couplet, from a Foucauldian perspective, it is evident that no grounds exist that allow one to privilege 'natural rights' over specific forms of (agri)culture. There may be many reasons why one might want to oppose certain forms of agricultural production but the extension of a doctrine of 'rights' to nature is not a necessary nor a sufficient ground for such opposition: it is, instead, best seen as a discursive strategy, a form of self-consciousness, much as any other. Seen from this perspective, much of the criticism of Foucault's 'fatal distraction' falls into place as an ungroundable nostalgia for a world in which the codes by which we understand old western movies remain secure in the intellectual firmament (Thompson, 1991).

RESISTANCE AND RATIONALITY

Saboteurs' self-consciousness

The classic accounts of sabotage as a form of resistance have tended to see it as a predominantly working-class phenomena, a vital and subversive act against managerial surveillance and attempted control. Sabotage can be celebrated as a sign of spontaneous human creativity surviving extreme forms of surveillance that seek to bend it into a shape externally designed and imposed by management and capital on labour (e.g. Brown, 1977). Yet, as LaNuez and Jermier argue in this volume, 'workplace sabotage often is a rational, calculative action by which employees knowingly weigh the exercise of this extreme form of protest and resistance against its associated risks . . . and consequences'. Besides, it is also a form of social action that is not exclusively working class or blue collar: it is also the provenance of line mangers and technocrats, particularly in certain contexts. From O'Connell Davidson's chapter we have already drawn the important hypothesis that subjective identity and the propensity of resistance to occur will be contingent upon the objective conditions within which people constitute the sense of their subjectivity. Subjectivity is not sovereign. One also might add that objective conditions not only restrain but they also enable human subjectivity (see Clegg, 1975, for this use of enabling and constraining conditions). An achievement of the paper by LaNuez and Jermier (ch. 8) is the way that it attends systematically to the objective conditions that enable sabotage to occur amongst middle- and lower-level managerial and technocratic workers. Amongst these are changes to individuals' consciousness of organizational and occupational realities contingent upon: major restructuring of organizations, tighter measurement in surveillance, changes in technology, tendencies towards deskilling and deprofessionalization, and diminution of perceived rewards, promotions and tenure. Despite the argument constructed in the paper (see Fig. 8.1) that sabotage potential diminishes as one ascends the corporate hierarchy of social identities, in the light of revelations about insider trading on Wall Street, share-rigging in Guinness and most evidently the systematic looting of employee pension funds by Robert Maxwell (Clarke, 1992), it is hard to sustain the view that, using the authors' definition of sabotage, 'deliberate action or inaction intended to undermine the goals of capital elites or protest against the capitalist system by damaging, destroying or disrupting some aspect of the workplace environment, including the organization's property, product, processes or reputation' is less likely to be exhibited by 'capital elites'. A further and related issue is the definition of sabotage offered – why tie it so tightly only to the organizational conditions of capitalist enterprises? Don't public servants or university academics ever engage in sabotage? It seems most unlikely that they do not. The conditions that LaNuez and Jermier specify as job characteristics that facilitate sabotage are a checklist for 'strategic contingency' (Hickson *et al.*, 1971). We will find the potential for 'strategic contingency' wherever we find organizational relations, not just capitalistic relations.

Sabotage is conceptualized in terms of a continuum that stretches from sabotage by circumvention to sabotage by direct action. Sabotage by circumvention is characteristic of the type of sabotage as resistance already encountered in O'Connell Davidson's chapter. In fact, her examples were cases of the non-cooperative behaviour and data falsification types of this sabotage. Such sabotage is hard to detect and relatively safe for the perpetrator. So, it is a routine organizational behaviour, albeit one with effects typically limited to organizational and non-catastrophic effects. The saboteurs' self-consciousness associated with this type of action will often be regarded as legitimate by peers, to a far greater extent than the second type of sabotage. Sabotage by direct action, where property, services, products or data get damaged would be exemplified by the example that she provided of unleashing a computer virus into software. Where organization systems are tightly coupled and non-linear the damage probability of this type of sabotage will increase.

LaNuez and Jermier attempt to build 'intentionality' into their typology. One is sceptical about this, as anything other than a vocabulary of motive type statement of the typically available members accounts in specific organizational settings. It is doubtful that these can be constructed decontextually, but are part of the research task that the authors outline of attempting to restore rationality to those whom organizations so often deem irrational.

Whistleblowers' self-consciousness

To treat someone as irrational when they resist is a favourite ploy of power, one shown to brilliant effect in Jack Nicholson's characterization of McMurphy in *One Flew Over the Cuckoo's Nest*. McMurphy was a whistleblower in the Mental Hospital as well as a case study in resistance for which existing circuits of power proved too strong. Seeking to disclose 'illegal, unethical or harmful practices' he got treated as a deviant case in terms of the organizational norms and became subject to what those norms defined as appropriate treatment.[18] Whistleblowing involves the complainant going either up or outside the organization with a grievance about a perceived illegitimate practice in the organization. In this volume the chapter by Rothschild and Miethe is a treatment of whistleblowing as resistance in modern organizations, drawing on data collected by a variety of methods that mix documentary analysis, semi-structured interviews and survey data (see ch. 4). The essence of their argument is that many whistleblowers only enter resistance because of the

> ordeal of reporting misconduct and the experience of suffering reprisals that transforms and politicizes the individual ... Only when they see that management is inert, complacent, or themselves implicated in the wrongdoing, do they consider going outside the organization with their information.
>
> (Rothschild and Miethe, this volume)

Whistleblowing is a political act; resistance to it by management is also a political act. Each party, the whistleblower and the management, is seeking to define reality in terms of competing representations that lead to different courses of action that are mutually exclusive. At the outset the 'whistleblower' consciousness is not already formed as an identity. It emerges in and through a struggle for vindication. Such a struggle can often lead to the whistleblower accepting a new self-consciousness forged in the struggle, with new alliances as a result. A solidaristic consciousness can emerge where none previously existed.

To blow the whistle on some behaviours or action is not easy. Management can all too easily outflank those who resist their definitions of reality. At their disposal they have many sources of coercion and inducement for securing organizational compliance, without exerting the ultimate discipline of unemployment on the worker. Organizations rarely welcome the airing of what their senior management perceive as negative representations, even, it seems, when formal rhetoric claims otherwise. Yet, people still blow the whistle on perceived illegitimacies. How are they able to do this in the face of so much potential power to outflank them? There are a number of reasons. First, they can set themselves up to be outflanked by their own ignorance – or naïvety as it is termed in the study. They take the formal rhetoric of the organization for granted. It can come as a painful learning experience to realize that the organization elite does not welcome the shortcomings of their management being publicized and that their co-workers do not welcome the exposure or offer solidaristic support. Second, whistleblowers are usually core members of the organization, respected and valued, whose values have been genuinely affronted by some aspect of the organization. Often these values have a firm extra-organizational anchorage in some transcendent value system. Third, the increase in organizations and jobs in the information economy has led to the development of more jobs that represent opportunities for a conflict between professional values, legally mandated responsibilities and organizational practices. In particular this is true of people employed in some kind of monitoring or quality control function.

How does management resist the whistle being blown? Usually they will victimize the complainant, with greater pressure where the exposure seems more threatening. Few whistleblowers expect the ferocity and pressure of the counter-power unleashed, such as dismissal, or their labelling as a crazy person, someone insane. Such ferocity is much as we might expect from the Foucauldian perspective outlined earlier in this chapter. Superior power not only does not achieve its effects but also it develops, dialectically, resistance to its own exercise. Power revealed in such stark terms often strips away any illusions and reservations about the actions chosen that those who become subject to such power might still have harboured. 'Once the full resources of the organization are brought to bear against them, *they* cannot turn back'. To retrieve their sense of self as the person of integrity who raised the issue in the first place they have no option other than to fight the management representation of them as illegitimate, as wrongdoers. Not to do so is to accept the definition of themselves which management action presents to the world. The exercise of management power escalates employee resistance in this situation and further strengthens and dignifies the sense of injustice that the whistleblower feels. Moral outrage is no guarantee of victory. Indeed, the personal costs of whistleblowing rarely justify taking the action in such a way that one can be victimized. Yet, where people are able to get alternative work, where they have not been so publicly rubbished by management that no one will employ them, they can rebuild their identities.

Sometimes whistleblowing works. Issues get raised and resolved, most usually when the issue is less organizationally systemic and more a case of individual malfeasance. Where this is not so, then if the whistleblower is regarded as a credible source, one able to forge alliances with significant authorities or institutions, able to access a support network, then there is more chance of success. Further, the organization culture is important. Democratic, participative organiz-ations, organizations that treat their members with respect, tend to function better in response to criticism than do those that are hierarchical, authoritarian systems, even where, perhaps, they have a veneer of concern, commitment and care for employees. Unfortunately, a concern for participation is all too often a stage in the evolution of cycles of control (Ramsay, 1977, 1983), an in-authentic mode of rationality as thin as a cheap veneer.

Rule, gender and plural self-consciousness

Rationality is not something that characterizes particular models of what it is that actors and organizations ought to do but instead should be thought of as something emergent from the action scenes and sense-making of the actors themselves. Much of this sense-making, particularly in managerial labour, consists of talk (see Clegg, 1975). Austrin, in an account of the politics of appraisal and grievance hearings taken from the New Zealand finance industry, distinguishes a particular sub-set of this talk as 'identity talk' – talk that 'involves constant negotiations of contexts and questions in which subjects are provoked or required to articulate accounts of their self', referred to as 'positioning practices' (see this volume, ch. 7). At issue is a conception of workers in this industry that has been developed by Knights and Sturdy (1989) in the British finance industry as 'self-disciplined subjects'. In brief, these are supposed to be people whose reflexive self-organization becomes more oriented towards intra-organizational forms of productive power, rather than power that is negative and resistant. Voice declines as an option; loyalty increases and dissent, signalled by exit, increases, in Hirschman's (1977) terms. Opportunities for acting as a 'practical experimentalist' diminish (Clegg, 1990).

314

Austrin is sceptical about the emergence of these self-disciplined workers. Again, we are pointed towards objective conditions within which subjectivity is constituted, in this case the importance of decentralized means of budgetary control, a new form of managerial discipline. It is premised on 'identity talk' – structured occasions in which employees have to talk about themselves in terms that the human resources management appraisal inventory dictates, in a form of simultaneous interrogation and therapy. Yet, rather than self-disciplining workers, Austrin suggests that this occasion for talk has become the centre of new strategies of both managerial discipline and union resistance. At the centre of this new politics is the way in which the occasion for talk becomes a locale in which a plurality of subject self-consciousness can be developed and displayed. These pluralities are given through the rule consciousness of union officials and employees in terms of

> issues which impact upon the worker such as health and safety, race, and gender discrimination (which) have now been codified and legitimated as resources in law. This new form of the politics of work has made the fine detail of the subject of work both a part of everyday discourse and, at the same time, a sphere in which expert knowledge is required for purposes of its representation. The result of these developments is that if it occurs, resistance must take on a discursive form which deploys as resources the very texts that have codified work. In this context, a politics of appraisal can become a resistance strategy.
>
> (Austrin, this volume)

Of particular interest in this case is the way in which a therapeutic mode, which Rose's (1989) research has characterized as one of the dominant themes of management intervention in the twentieth century, has become a basis not just for creating accommodative and co-opted subjects but also ones who are resistant. The therapeutic mode, as a way of relating gender to the rules constituting the formal rationality governing the organization, opens up the possibilities of entirely new and plural possibilities for self-consciousness. The rhetorical form of the appraisal process allows for a more ideal speech conversation (Habermas, 1979) than would otherwise be the case.

CONCLUSION

While there may be reasons for thinking that the horizontal dimension of the axis in Figure 9.3 is generalizable as a coordinate for further work on power and resistance in the labour process, the vertical axis is more context dependent. Some categories, such as gender, one would anticipate having a general salience for future research (although gender does not have a universal salience for the chapters under review here). It would be unwise to use the figure too mechanistically; that is not the point of having produced it. Its initial function was as a piece of scaffolding for writing this chapter, scaffolding that, as a means of intellectual production, I decided to leave in because of its summary purpose for the chapters under review. It also shows the wide range of material covered in the book. Some general points, as well as those that were case or topic specific, emerge from the chapters. One is that, in general, Collinson's hypothesis that power 'strategies that seek to increase employee involvement in organizational processes and to render managerial practices more visible and accountable may enable more effective forms of workplace resistance than those primarily concerned with distancing', seems well borne out by the cases under review. It is the case in both Austrin's study of appraisal and grievance procedures in the New Zealand finance industry, in Rothschild and Miethe's study of whistleblowing in the United States as well as supported by Egri's analysis of British Columbian organic farming. The hypothesis that subjective identity and the propensity of resistance to occur will be contingent upon the objective conditions within which people constitute the sense of their subjectivity, is also strongly supported by several of the chapters. The importance of considering resistance in the context of the resources available for organizational outflanking is corroborated.

To agree with Knights and Vurdubakis's Foucauldian line in its insistence that a general theory of power and resistance is neither desirable nor possible places the labour process literature in double jeopardy. First, it began with such a theory and then progressively eroded it through detailed case studies that disconfirmed the general direction of Braverman's (1974) hypotheses about deskilling (e.g. Littler and Salaman, 1982). To return down that road is clearly to stay in an intellectual cul de sac, a road to nowhere. On the other hand, the infinite iteration of case studies of an extremely elastic concept of resistance is also somewhat aimless.[19] The initial thrust, to rectify

Braverman's (1974) underplaying of human agency and creativity, has been achieved. It has become akin to a ritual mantra. Repeat often enough and it should ward off some old fears. But what do we do with an endless number of case studies?

Let me propose a solution. If the dimension of degree of intensiveness/extensiveness of the power relations constitutive of the subject is a useful dimension to aid analysis, it may be possible to build up a case-based knowledge of the conditions most facilitative of resistance, much as Austrin's chapter recommends, using this dimension to order the material. The chapters seem to suggest that there is more probability of resistance affecting a transformation in established circuits of power as cases move further down this dimension of extensiveness.

There is a risk of romanticizing resistance, much as Braverman (1974) frequently was accused of romanticizing labour. Without an attempt at building inductive and grounded theorizations of power and resistance that are premised upon empirical investigations informed by analytically sophisticated conceptualization, the theoretical progression of the labour process literature in the past 20 years may be seen as somewhat limited. To move from one kind of romance to another, from a romance of labour to a romance of resistance, would be an inadequate response to the ethical and analytical imperatives that brought resistance to prominence against the fatalism of the 'dominant ideology thesis' (Abercrombie *et al.*, 1980). Ironically, the subjectivity whose name is attached to this chapter intends a small contribution designed to avoid that fate.

NOTES

1 Throughout the Dollar trilogy of films, of which the last, *The Good, the Bad, and the Ugly* is generally regarded to be the best, characters frequently change sides, unable to be *interested* in any one cause except their own. One might take this as symptomatic of one key aspect of power: it seeks to fix interests.

2 Weedon (1987: 123) demonstrates this with reference to eugenicist arguments, that 'have been used to support widely conflicting interests over the last eighty years, for women's individual rights to contraception in inter-war Britain, to Nazi sexual policy. Indeed, biological arguments are employed by widely contradictory interests, from radical feminism to the most conservative forms of sociobiology, with their strong investment in the reproduction of patriarchy'. Where signifiers float subjectivities can never be wholly secure and predictable.

3 Disciplinary power, particularly in its 'time-discipline' (Thompson, 1967) clearly emerged from the monasteries as Keiser (1987) argues.

However, it adapted rapidly in the competitive learning environment of early capitalist industrialization. A general transition may be said to have taken place from a domestic economy premised on the 'putting out' system to one that was factory based (Clegg and Dunkerley, 1980: 49–56; 59–70), though, as O'Neill (1987: 47) observes, it would be a myth to regard this family as a 'natural' economy. Yet, evidently the chronology of the world transformed, often in a generation, from one of holy days, local feasts and the unremitting but seasonably variable rhythms of agricultural production into one based on the rhythms of the industrial machine, overseer, and the clock of factory discipline applied to factory workers who were, literally, interchangeable 'hands' recruited as such. In the competitive ecology of nineteenth-century production regimes, the possibilities for theft, casualness and ill-discipline of the putting-out system of domestic production compared unfavourably with factory control (Marglin, 1974; Landes, 1969). The keynote of this factory control was what Weber (1978) referred to as 'military discipline'. Such discipline had not only military but also had monastic roots, particularly in the subjugation of one's own time to an externally imposed discipline of the master's time (Keiser, 1987).

O'Neill (1987: 47–8) notes, after Smelser (1959), that certain technological changes such as steam power and mule spinning cemented the loss of worker's control and the ascendancy of the master's, in the spinning trades. These changes, gradually were emulated in the weaving trades, with women and children replacing previously craft-based male labour, labour whose resistance was stubborn, violent, political and drawn-out. Indeed, some writers who focus on class struggle at the point of production (Burawoy, 1979, 1985; Littler, 1982; Edwards, 1979; Clawson, 1980) see this as a battleground in which a dialectic of capitalist control and worker resistance occurs that is structurally irresolvable as long as capitalist relations of production get reproduced. Therefore the dialectic of power and resistance has a precise structural location in Marx's (1976) general theory of capitalism as relations of production. From this basis general theories of capitalist organization and control of the labour process have developed (Clegg and Dunkerley, 1980).

4 Foucault's (1977) conception of disciplinary power developing to re-place the older sovereign power of which Machiavelli's (1958) precepts in *The Prince* were a veritable, although sketchy, handbook, is not inconsistent with Weber's (1978) account.

5 This focus was not entirely novel, as Marx (1976) was only too well aware of the violence done to human bodies by the new capitalist discipline, as many of his more descriptive passages indicate. Gramsci (1971) was also aware of the impact of the 'Fordist' system on workers bodies. Weber (1948: 261–2) too was aware of the 'tuning' of the 'psycho-physical' apparatus produced by the 'ever-widening grasp of discipline', although his focus was more on the role that Protestantism could play in producing a morally tuned and willing apparatus, (Weber, 1976; see the commentaries by Poggi (1983) and Marshall (1982); also the studies by Thompson (1968), Hobsbawm (1969), Wearmouth (1939),

Eldridge (1972), Anthony (1977) and Guttman (1977) all of whom stress the role religion played in disciplining the workforce.) Religion undoubtedly had a role to play, although as Eldridge (1972) notes, it is not always clear on the evidence of religious conviction that it was quite as dramatic as is sometimes assumed.

6 Writing of the forced labour of the workhouses that followed the breakdown of the Elizabethan Poor Laws under the supply of increasingly surplus quantities of labour, driven off the land by enclosure, O'Neill noted that 'When labour became increasingly plentiful, unemployed and driven to crime and rebellion, the houses of correction became even more punitive, while labour in the houses of correction was limited to intimidating and useless tasks so that no one would ever enter them voluntarily. The overall effect was to teach free labour the discipline of the factory outside and inside the factory. . . . Thus, the employed and the unemployed learn their respective disciplines. Thereafter, we might say that in the bourgeois social order the prison, the factory and the school, like the army, are places where the system can project its conception of the disciplinary society in the reformed criminal, the good worker, student, loyal soldier, and committed citizen. In every case, it is a question of reproducing among the propertyless a sense of commitment to the property system in which they have nothing to sell but their labour and loyalty' (O'Neill, 1987: 51–2). It is in this panoply of disciplinary organizations, in Foucault's account, that the new complex of bio-power emerges. It is this aspect of power relations, tied up with new discourses of medicine, administration and so on, which is additional to either Marx or Weber's accounts, which provides a framework for the carrying capacity of new forms of disciplinary power to spread like a contagion from their initial institutional sites.

7 With DiMaggio and Powell (1983) one would see the carriers of institutional isomorphism in this respect as primarily the state and the professions. Moreover, as certain 'radical' organization theorists have argued, it is these knowledges and the practices which they license which produce what O'Neill (1987: 55) refers to as the *natural discipline* of the workplace and the wage system (see, for example: Clegg and Dunkerley, 1980). The Foucauldian twist is a useful corrective in making the process far less instrumental than these accounts presume.

8 In this respect it differs from randomness. That which is random may have been produced according to a rule but the rule will not be visible in that which is produced. One cannot, for instance, retrieve the random pattern of dice from a number sequence generated by 'letting the dice decide' (Rhinehart, 1972).

9 Such contracts are rarely the reciprocal, conflict free and equal exchanges axiomized in organizational contract theory in terms of 'transaction costs' (Williamson, 1981; also see, 1985). The axioms of these approaches are profoundly unrealistic and, indeed, ill-conceived. One aspect of contracts, the resources that empower employees (e.g. the acquisition of firm specific skills and knowledge; collective organization; ownership of physical assets) are stressed as against the resources that empower employers, notably, ownership of the means

and product of production, the support of the state and the legal system, and managerial prerogative within organizations.

10 Indexicality may be defined as the way in which meaning is always tied to the occasions of its use.

11 None of this is far from Weber (1978) or for that matter Foucault (1977), despite protestations to the contrary; see Foucault (1980).

12 It should be acknowledged at the outset that the figure referred to, and those that appear subsequently, are an effect of the theorizing power that I have been able to bring to the collected works that appear in this book. That I was able to do this was only because I had the privileged position of being able to see all the completed papers and then use them as the basis for my own. While I was a participant at the conference at which most of these papers were first presented in earlier versions, I did not present a paper there myself. This paper is a response to the other chapters collected here. In other words, to read the text as a whole in terms of the figures and reading that are provided in this chapter is to be enrolled to one way in which one subjectivity would exercise power in constituting the theoretical subjectivities of the other authors collected here. Theorizing necessarily involves power: hence theorizing power. Nonetheless, one should point out that as an heuristic device classification may be permissible, but that any claim to the representations used here being more than such heuristic devices is not to be entertained. This is not a definitive 'scientific' representation of 'power, resistance and subjectivity', but a grounded empirico-theoretical enquiry into the text in question.

13 David Knights has suggested to me, in a personal communication, that the case of the concentration camp is not one where power operates, because of the absence of 'rights' that exists in its logic of exterminism. I find this an unacceptable argument. First, it is the operation of power through the creation of discursive categories of classification, such as 'Jew', 'Slav', 'Homosexual' or 'Gypsy', that the rights are eliminated. Second, power marks and organizes the body of those categorized, through uniforms, badges, the stripping of identity, the degradation of the body and of norms of privacy, the inscription of a non-identity, a number, on the bodies of the inmates, and finally, the annihilation of life – not just individually and recklessly but methodically, with a bureaucratically perfect logic, based upon the ascription of identity that those numbered have been classified and categorized as displaying, due to various discursive practices: of forms of eugenics, genetics, phrenology and so on.

14 One is aware that such an argument may leave one open to charges of 'essentialism'. So be it: perhaps sociological thought requires it.

15 This relates to one reason for the frequent use of literary and cinematic references in this chapter. Our popular cultures allow a point of commonality in the experience of resistance that might otherwise be difficult to achieve. Given the open-endedness of human imagination and creativity, resistance is infinite. Yet, cultural texts provide one with reference points for its expression. Who, having read Amado (1983), could forget the significance of the 'closed bread-basket' in the annals

of urban planning? That this relates to Pelhourino, in Salvador, Bahia, an area that is now a United Nations World Heritage site, makes it even more significant.

16 Against this there is the counter-argument, suggested to me by David Knights in a personal communication, that individual resistance may be more disruptive since it is more difficult to co-opt. I would have thought, along with Marx (Marx and Engels, 1970; Marx, 1976) that it is easier to overcome an individual consciousness than the conscious organization of a collective consciousness.

17 The methodological procedures reported in this study are excellent in that they make quite clear the nature of the research process and methods used, although the bulk of the rather sparse data on 'resistance' seems to have been drawn from the two cases of 'participant observation' that the author briefly reports, rather than from the more extended survey research.

18 There was the added irony that the norms were such that they defined him as abnormal. In this context any claims as to the normative character of the organizational regime however 'reasonable' their content might be, were necessarily further signs of madness (A *Catch-22*: Heller, 1962). From what legitimate grounds can the inmates of an institution critique it? Experience suggests that this problem is not confined to inmates of asylums; in at least one university of my acquaintance a similar regime functions, where the primary way that resistance gets to be heard is as disloyalty and deviance. Where conformance to executive fiat is the preferred role for non-executives, on the part of an executive, there is little in the way of an alternative and legitimate option with respect to any who seek to challenge the strategies of power through independent judgement.

19 Which is not to presume that one thinks that there may be some 'telos' that is worth getting to. The idea of 'aim' or 'direction' here is less one of politics and more one of epistemology. How does one define the point of doing labour process analysis when the belief in anything like a 'labour process theory' has evaporated, at least for those practitioners who have been monitoring the self-destructive tendencies of that 'theory' in its development from the initial Bravermanian and Marxian premises? Of course, one can always defend the old faith (e.g. Thompson, 1991).

REFERENCES

Abercrombie, A., Hill, S. and Turner, B. S. (1980) *The Dominant Ideology Thesis*, London: Allen & Unwin.

Amado, J. (1983) *Tereza Batista: Home from the Wars*, London: Sphere.

Anthony, P. D. (1977), *The Ideology of Work*, London: Tavistock.

Austrin, T. (1993) 'Positioning Resistance and Resisting Position: Human Resource Management and the Politics of Appraisal and Grievance Hearings', in J. M. Jermier, D. Knights and W. Nord (eds) *Resistance and Power in Organizations: Agency, Subjectivity and the Labor Process*, London: Routledge.

Barbalet, J. M. (1985) 'Power and Resistance', *British Journal of Sociology* 36(1): 521–48.

Barnes, B. (1986) 'On Authority and Its Relationship to Power', in J. Law (ed.) *Power, Action and Belief: A New Sociology of Knowledge?* Sociological Review Monograph 32, London: Routledge & Kegan Paul, pp. 190–5.

Bookchin, M. (1990) *Remaking Society: Pathways to a Green Future*, Boston, MA: South End Press.

Boreham, P. (1983) 'Indetermination: Professional Knowledge, Organization and Control', *Sociological Review* 31(4): 693–718.

Braverman, H. (1974) *Labour and Monopoly Capital: The Degradation of Work in the Twentieth Century*, New York: Monthly Review Press.

Brown, G. (1977) *Sabotage*, Nottingham: Spokesman Books.

Burawoy, M. (1979) *Manufacturing Consent: Changes in the Labour Process under Capitalism*, Chicago: University of Chicago Press.

Burawoy, M. (1985) *The Politics of Production*, London: Verso.

Clarke, T. (1992) 'The Business Descent of Robert Maxwell', *Media, Culture and Society* 14: 463–73.

Clawson, D. (1980) *Bureaucracy and the Labor Process: The Transformation of US Industry 1860–1920*, New York: Monthly Review Press.

Clegg, S. R. (1975) *Power, Rule and Domination: A Critical and Empirical Understanding of Power in Sociological Theory and Organizational Life*, London: Routledge & Kegan Paul.

Clegg, S. R. (1989) *Frameworks of Power*, London: Sage.

Clegg, S. R. (1990) *Modern Organizations: Organization Studies in the Postmodern Era*, London: Sage.

Clegg, S. R. and Dunkerley, D. (1980) *Organization, Class and Control*, London: Routledge & Kegan Paul.

Clement, W. (1983) 'Property and Proletarianization: Transformation of Simple Commodity Producers in Canadian Farming and Fishing', in W. Clement *(ed.) Class, Power and Property: Essays on Canadian Society*, Toronto: Methuen pp. 225–43.

Collinson, D. (1992) 'Researching Recruitment: Qualitative Methods and Sex Discrimination', in R. Burgess (ed.) *Studies in Qualitative Methodology*, Greenwich, CT: JAI Publications, vol. 3, pp. 89–122.

Collinson, D. (1993) 'Strategies of Resistance: Power, Knowledge and Subjectivity in the Workplace', in J. M. Jermier, D. Knights and W. Nord (eds) *Resistance and Power in Organizations: Agency, Subjectivity and the Labour Process*, London: Routledge.

Devall, B. and Sessions, G. (1985) *Deep Ecology: Living as if Nature Mattered*, Salt Lake City, UT: Peregrine Smith Books.

Dews, P. (1979) 'The Nouvelle Philosophie and Foucault', *Economy and Society*, 8(2): 127–71.

DiMaggio, P. and Powell, W. (1983) 'The Iron Cage Revisited: Institutional Isomorphism and Collective Rationality in Organizational fields', *American Sociological Review* 48(2): 127–71.

Dylan. B. (1968) 'Drifters Escape', *John Wesley Harding*, New York: CBS, lyric copyright of Big Ben Music Ltd.

Edwards, P. K. and Scullion, H. (1982) *The Social Organization of Industrial Conflict*, Oxford: Blackwell.

Edwards, R. (1979) *Contested Terrain: The Transformation of the Workplace in the Twentieth Century*, London: Heinemann.

Egri, C. P. (1993) 'Working with Nature: Organic Farming and Other Forms of Resistance in Industrialized Agriculture', in J. M. Jermier, D. Knights and W. Nord (eds) *Resistance and Power in Organizations: Agency, Subjectivity and the Labour Process*, London: Routledge.

Eldridge, J. E. T. (1972) *Max Weber: The Interpretation of Social Reality*, London: Nelson.

Foucault, M. (1984)*The History of Sexuality: An Introduction*, Harmondsworth: Peregrine.

Foucault, M. (1977) *Discipline and Punish: The Birth of the Prison*, Harmondsworth: Penguin.

Foucault, M. (1980) *Power/Knowledge: Selected Interviews and Other Writings 1972–1977*, edited by C. Gordon, Brighton: Harvester Press.

Gamble, P. and Walton, A. (1972) *From Alienation to Surplus Value*, London: Sheed & Ward Stagbooks

Garfinkel, H. (1967) *Studies in Ethnomethodology*, Englewood Cliffs, NJ: Prentice Hall.

Geyer, R. F. and Schweitzer, D. (eds) (1981) *Alienation: Problems of Meaning, Theory and Method*, London: Routledge & Kegan Paul.

Goffman, E. (1971) *The Presentation of Self in Everyday Life*, Harmondsworth: Penguin.

Goldthorpe, J. H., Lockwood, D., Bechofer, F. and Platt, J. (1969) *The Affluent Worker in the Class Structure*, Cambridge: Cambridge University Press.

Gottfried, H. (1993) 'Learning the Score: The Duality of Control and Everyday Resistance in the Temporary-Help Service Industry', in J. M. Jermier, D. Knights and W. Nord (eds) *Resistance and Power in Organizations: Agency, Subjectivity and the Labour Process*, London: Routledge.

Gramsci, A. (1971) *Selections from the Prison Notebooks*, London: Lawrence & Wishart.

Guttman, H. G. (1977) *Work, Culture and Society in Industrializing America*, Oxford: Blackwell.

Habermas, J. (1979) *Communication and the Evolution of Society*, London: Heinemann.

Heller, J. (1962) *Catch-22*, London: Corgi.

Hickson, D. J., Hinings, C.R., Lee, C.A., Schneck, R.E. and Pennings, J.M. (1971) 'A Strategic Contingencies Theory of Intra-Organizational Power, *Administrative Science Quarterly* 16: 216–29.

Hindess, B. (1982) 'Power, Interests and the Outcomes of Struggles', *Sociology* 16: 498–511.

Hirschman, A. O. (1970) *Exit, Voice and Loyalty*, Princeton: Princeton University Press

Hobsbawm, E, J. (1969) *Industry and Empire*, Harmondsworth: Penguin.

Keiser, (1987) 'From Asceticism to Administration of Wealth: Medieval Monasteries and the Pitfalls of Rationalization', *Organization Studies* 8(2): 103–24.

Knights, D. and Sturdy, A. (1989) 'New Technology and the Self-disciplined Worker in Insurance', in M. McNeil, J. Varcoe and S. Yearly (eds) *Deciphering Science and Technology*, London: Macmillan.

Knights, D. and Vurdubakis, T. (1993) 'Foucault, Power, Resistance and All That', in J. M. Jermier, D. Knights and W. Nord (eds) *Resistance and Power in Organizations: Agency, Subjectivity and the Labour Process*, London: Routledge.

LaNuez, D. and Jermier, J. M. (1993) 'Sabotage by Managers and Technocrats: Neglected Patterns of Resistance at Work', in J. M. Jermier, W. Nord and D. Knights (eds) *Resistance and Power in Organizations: Agency, Subjectivity and the Labour Process*, London: Routledge.

Landes, S. (1969) *The Unbound Prometheus: Technological Change and Industrial Development in Western Europe from 1750 to the Present*. Cambridge: Cambridge University Press.

Leone, S. (1967) *The Good, the Bad and the Ugly*, Milan: Cinecitta.

Levi, P. (1987a) *If This Is a Man*, London: Abacus

Levi, P. (1987b) *If Not Now, When?*, London: Abacus.

Littler, C. R. (1982) *The Development of the Labour Process in Capitalist Societies*, London: Heinemann.

Littler, C. R. and Salaman, G. (1982) 'Bravermania and Beyond: Recent Theories of the Labour Process', *Sociology* 16: 251–69.

Lukes, S. (1974) *Power: A Radical View*, London: Macmillan.

Machiavelli, N. (1958) *The Prince*, London: Everyman.

Marglin, S. M. (1974) 'What Do Bosses Do? The Origins and Functions of Hierarchy in Capitalist Production', *Review of Radical Political Economics* 6: 60–112.

Marshall, G. (1982) *In Search of the Spirit of Capitalism: An Essay on Max Weber's Protestant Ethic Thesis*, London: Hutchinson.

Marx, K. (1976) Capital, Vol. 1, Harmondsworth: Penguin.

Marx, K. and F. Engels (1970) *The German Ideology*, Moscow: International Publishing Company.

Mézáros, I. (1970) *Marx's Theory of Alienation*, London: Merlin.

Mills, C. W. (1940) 'Situated Actions and Vocabularies of Motive', *American Sociological Review* 5: 904–13.

Minson, J. (1986) 'Strategies for Socialists? Foucault's Conception of Power', pp. 106–48 in M. Gane (ed.) *Towards a Critique of Foucault*, London: Routledge & Kegan Paul.

Mintzberg, H. (1983) *Power in and around Organizations*, Englewood Cliffs, NJ: Prentice Hall.

O'Connell Davidson, J. (1993) 'The Sources and Limits of Resistance in a Privatized Public Utility', in J. M. Jermier, D. Knights and W. Nord (eds) *Resistance and Power in Organizations: Agency, Subjectivity and the Labour Process*, London: Routledge.

O'Neill, J. (1987) 'The Disciplinary Society: from Weber to Foucault', *The British Journal of Sociology* 37(1): 42–60.

Pateman, C. (1970) *Participation and Democratic Theory*, Cambridge: Cambridge University Press.

Perrow, C. (1986) *Complex Organizations: A Critical Essay*, New York: Random House.

Poggi, (1983) *Calvinism and the Capitalist Spirit*, London: Macmillan.

Ramsay, H. (1977) 'Cycles of Control: Worker Participation in Sociological and Historical Perspective', *Sociology* 11(3): 481–506.

Ramsay, H. (1983) 'An International Participation Cycle: Variations on a Recurring Theme', in S. R. Clegg, G. Dow and P. Boreham (eds) *The State, Class and the Recession*, London: Croom Helm, pp. 257–317.

Rhinehart, L. (1972) *The Dice Man*, London: Panther.

Rosenberg, S. (1967) *Cool Hand Luke*, Los Angeles.

Rothschild, J. and Miethe, T. D. (1993) 'Whistleblowing as Resistance in Modern Work Organizations: The Politics of Revealing Organizational Deception and Abuse', in J. M. Jermier, D. Knights and W. Nord (eds) *Resistance and Power in Organizations: Agency, Subjectivity and the Labour Process*, London: Routledge.

Saussure, F. de (1974) *Course in General Linguistics*, London: Fontana.

Schacht, R. (1971) *Alienation*, London: George Allen & Unwin.

Silverman, D. (1970) *The Theory of Organizations*, London: Heinemann.

Smelser, N. (1959) *Social Change in the Industrial Revolution*, Chicago: University of Chicago Press.

Strauss, A. (1978) *Negotiations: Varieties, Contexts, Processes and Social Order*, London: Jossey-Bass.

Taylor, I, Walton, P. and Young, J. (1974) *The New Criminology*, London: Routledge & Kegan Paul.

Thompson, E. P. (1967) 'Time, Work, Discipline and Industrial Capitalism', *Past and Present* 38: 56–97.

Thompson, E. P. (1968) *The Making of the English Working Class*, Harmondsworth: Penguin.

Thompson, P. (1991) 'The Fatal Distraction: Postmodernism and Organizational Analysis', paper presented to the Conference on New Theories of Organization, Keele University, May.

Wearmouth, R. F. (1939) *Methodism and the Working Class Movements of England 1800-1950*, London: Epworth.

Weber, M. (1978) *Economy and Society: An Outline of Interpretive Sociology*, 2 vols, edited by G. Roth and C. Wittich, Berkeley: University of California Press.

Weedon, C. (1987) *Feminist Practice and Poststructuralist Theory*, Oxford: Blackwell.

Williamson, O. F. (1981) 'The Economics of Organization', *American Journal of Sociology* 87 (548): 77.

Williamson, O. F. (1985) *The Economic Institutions of Capitalism*, New York: Free Press.

Wittgenstein, L. (1968) *Philosophical Investigations*, translated by G.E.M. Anscombe, Oxford: Blackwell.

Wrong, D. (1979) *Power: Its Forms, Bases and Uses*, Oxford: Blackwell.

INDEX

absenteeism 92, 221
accommodation 108, 118, 119, 120
Ackers, P. 37
Adams, S. 63
Adas, M. 132
affective production 114
affirmation 192, 193
agency 182–6, 191, 286; individual 182–4, 309; and organization 283–4
aggression 223, 225, 226
agrichemicals 145, 146, 159, 160
agricultural labourers, 131, 138
agricultural reform organizations 135
agricultural technologies, 129
agriculture: crisis in 130, 306; government intervention in 157; *see also* industrial agriculture
Alchian, A.A. 231
alienation 3
allegiance, of whistleblowers 259, 313
Allen, V.L. 224
Alliance of British Columbian Organic Producers Associations (ABCOPA) 149, 151, 153
Anthony, P.D. 319
appraisal systems *see* performance appraisals
Armstrong, P. 168, 173
Aronowitz, S. 6, 168
Austrin, T. 17, 314, 315

authority 285, 287; delegation of 284

Bachelard, G. 170
Badham, R. 201
Bakhtin, M. 170
Bakunin, N. 149, 150
Balfour, Lady Eve 139
Banaji, J. 129, 132
Bandura, A. 225
Bannon, E. 26
Baran, B. 69
Barbalet, J.M. 286
Barker, J. 116
Barnes, B. 281, 284, 292
Baron, R. 225
Barras, R. 69
Batstone, E. 69, 98
Baumol, W. 231
Bazerman, M. 224
Becker, H. 259
Becker, J.F. 233, 234
Bell, D. 233
Bentham, J. 193n
Berkowitz, L. 225
Berle, A.A. 231
Berry, W. 139
Beta structure 73, 85, 88; opposition to 79–81, 86, 90–1
Beyer, J. 270
Beynon, H. 6, 26
bio-dynamic agriculture 140–1
Bjorn-Andersen, N. 227
Black, J. 37

326